Analytical Hypnotherapy

Volume 1
Theoretical Principles

Jacquelyne Morison

With contributions from Georges Philips

Crown House Publishing
www.crownhouse.co.uk

First published by
Crown House Publishing Ltd
Crown Buildings, Bancyfelin, Carmarthen, Wales, SA33 5ND, UK
www.crownhouse.co.uk

and

Crown House Publishing Ltd
6 Trowbridge Drive, Suite 5, Bethel, CT 06801-2858, uSA
www.crownhousepublishing.com

© Jacquelyne Morison 2001, 2011

First published 2001. Reprinted 2004.

First published in hardback (ISBN: 9781899836772).
Published in paperback 2011.
Transferred to digital printing 2011.

British Library Cataloguing-in-Publication Data
A catalogue entry for this book is available
from the British Library.

ISBN 978-184590682-5
LCCN 2011925579

Praise for *Analytical Hypnotherapy Volume 1*:

"*Analytical Hypnotherapy Volume 1* is a remarkable book that I would unhesitatingly recommend to both students and seasoned practitioners alike, and regardless of their particular psychotherapeutic approach. It is a pleasing synthesis of style and content – ingredients all too seldom found in the correct ratio.

"For the student, the work affords a balance of the theoretical with the practical, by presenting an overview of all the major methodologies together with actual case-study examples and clinical applications. It provides succinct explanations of all the seminal therapeutic models from Psychoanalysis to Cognitive Therapy, pausing along the way to explain precisely how common psychotherapeutic terminology and concepts fit within each.

"For the experienced practitioner, this book will remind you (should you need reminding) why you were attracted to the field of therapy in the first place. It will re-inspire you with the desire to assist your fellow man (and woman) towards both self-empowerment and the achievement of their full potential. It will also greatly contribute to your ability to do so.

"*Analytical Hypnotherapy Volume 1* is, in short, a modern classic that should feature among the essential libraries of all who are interested in the field of psychotherapeutic intervention."

– William Broom, Chief Executive and Registrar,
The General Hypnotherapy Standards Council.

"I consider this book ESSENTIAL for anyone involved in hypnotherapy, be they a student or a seasoned practitioner. The eclectic approach the book takes will be of great benefit to practitioners and will help widen the horizon of anyone who wants to further their knowledge about the subject. *Analytical Hypnotherapy Volume 1* will become the new bible for hypnotherapists. It should be on the reading list of every hypnotherapy training course in the country!"

– Vera Peiffer, hypnotherapist and author.

Table of Contents

How to Gain Maximum Benefit From Reading This Book

Analytical Hypnotherapy – Theoretical Principles is essentially a reference book for the practitioner who wishes to gain a comprehensive understanding of the practice of analytical hypnotherapy. A reference book, by its very nature, encourages a dip-and-dive usage. The therapist may, for example, elect to extract from these pages the information and guidance that will be appropriate to his/her work and then to put the rest on ice for future study. In order to gain maximum benefit from this book, therefore, the practitioner should use it as a servant rather than a master.

The purpose and design of *Analytical Hypnotherapy* will be to enlighten and to inspire the therapist within an eclectic discipline. The message behind the text will be to invite the therapist to partake of the wisdom that is relevant to his/her practice, to expand his/her mind in order to embrace a more effective approach and to develop a unique and individual style when working with the client. The practitioner is neither being asked to swallow the doctrines contained within these pages as if they were the gospel truth, nor being urged to apply techniques that are not in keeping with his/her individual style or personal belief structure. The therapist may, therefore, read and digest material that is new and exciting for him/her, or may wish to review matter that has previously been studied in order to refresh learning and, perhaps, gain a deeper understanding.

Analytical Hypnotherapy aims to be an invitation and an encouragement for the therapist rather than a prescriptive tenet based on unshakeable principles. When reading through the various therapeutic passages, questioning techniques, client profiling and general methodology liberally sprinkled throughout the book and its companion volume, *Analytical Hypnotherapy Volume 2 – Practical Applications*, the practitioner will be advised to add his/her own brand of magic to that which is portrayed here. The therapist will be hereby besought to translate material into his/her own words rather than use the matter provided in a verbatim and, perhaps, lifeless fashion. Therapy is a creative art and not a rigid set of rules for methodology. The more creative and flexible the practitioner can be at work, the greater the number of cases that he/she will be able to handle with ease and facility. The secret is to enhance whatever natural style the therapist currently adopts – whether it be highly permissive or somewhat authoritarian. With this premise in view, the hypnoanalytic practitioner – whether a raw fledgling or a seasoned master – can now simply sit back and enjoy *Analytical Hypnotherapy!*

Introduction

To every man who struggles with his own soul in mystery, a
book that is a book flowers once, and seeds, and is gone.

– DH Lawrence

The Foundation Stone of Analytical Hypnotherapy

Analytical hypnotherapy is that branch of psychotherapy that
investigates the client's innermost conflict, trauma and distress at
the deepest psychic levels in order to bring about resolution and
beneficial change. Essentially, this form of therapy is an insight-
oriented method akin to psychodynamic methodology in that it
draws out from the client that which is debilitating and unfruitful
and that which hinders his/her personal development. Analytical
hypnotherapy will allow the client, therefore, to grow emotionally,
to mature psychically and to fulfil his/her own true potential in
life. The practice of analytical hypnotherapy, moreover, will also
embrace the field of humanistic psychology in that it seeks to assist
the client to realise his/her own potential once intransigence and
barriers to change have been lifted. Aspects of cognitive philosophy are also incorporated into analytical practice, because during
the therapeutic process the client can begin to understand what
governs his/her thinking processes.

Although the modern equivalent of classical psychodynamic treatment is analytical hypnotherapy, this book seeks to open up the
field of hypnoanalysis in order to give it a more eclectic and, thus,
more flexible appeal. This farsighted orientation will be of the
greatest assistance to the working practitioner who may need a
broader base from which to approach the client. Every facet of psychological doctrine will play a vital function in the unravelling of
the client's distress, trauma and psychic conflict and, therefore,
each will exercise its essential role as an integral part of the

holographic picture. In the following chapters, we shall, therefore, not only examine the orthodox analytical approach but also incorporate aspects of humanistic thinking and cognitive strategies that concentrate on activating the client's inner resources in order to bring about self-development and self-actualisation.

Analytical hypnotherapy differs from traditional forms of psychotherapy in that treatment is combined with hypnosis as the medium through which therapeutic intervention can be facilitated. This method of hypnotherapy also departs from the standard clinical practice of hypnotic intervention in that the client takes the more active part in his/her therapeutic journey by being invited to speak about his/her personal life experiences as opposed to those instances in which the therapist is principally active in applying techniques or in orchestrating proceedings.

In the companion volume to this work, *Analytical Hypnotherapy Volume 2 – Practical Applications*, the practitioner will be introduced to the symptomology and methodology that can apply the learning and insight gained from this text.

What Is Psychodynamic Therapy?

> The term "psychodynamic" denotes the active forces within the personality that motivate behaviour and the inner causes of behaviour (in particular the unconscious conflict between the different structures that compose the whole personality). Whilst Freud's was the original psychodynamic theory, the approach includes all those theories based on his ideas, such as those of Jung, Adler and Erikson.
> – *Richard Gross & Rob McIlveen*

Psychodynamic therapy is a means of investigating the client's recollections and perceptions of life experiences in order to identify where the nuggets of psychological trauma and distress have been lodged. It is assumed that the root cause of any presenting problem has been buried deeply in the client's unconscious mind and that this inertia will need to be uprooted and resolved before he/she can gain any lasting relief from symptoms. The psychodynamic approach, therefore, has been based on the theory of cause and effect and the practitioner will advocate a means of resolving the originating cause of the client's disorder in order to alleviate the effect or to eliminate the symptoms. This method of therapeutic intervention, therefore, is in contradistinction to any therapeutic methods that are aimed solely at the alleviation, amelioration or removal of symptoms.

The aim of psychodynamic therapy will be to empower the client to undergo a process of maturation in which his/her unconscious mind will come into touch with his/her conscious mind in order to achieve a harmonious enlightenment and a balancing effect. This process will then bring the client nearer to reality by highlighting his/her strengths and weaknesses and by smoothing out any dissociation between the conscious mind and the unconscious mind, that has occurred usually as a result of traumatic experiences in formative years. The client can be awakened to the realisation of impediments to psychological health, can find his/her own true nature and can gain an understanding of his/her own unconscious motivations, internal conflicts and compensatory behaviour that have hitherto dominated his/her existence. The psychodynamic school believes that human behaviour is predetermined and is motivated by unconscious desires, drives and influences that were set up in early life. Such phenomena may lead the client not only to manifest irrational behaviours, inappropriate reactions, psychological ill health and psychosomatic illness but also may cause him/her to form dysfunctional relationships with others.

The prime strength of psychoanalytic practice lies in its attempt to unearth suppressed or repressed material using a variety of methods, that will be outlined in detail in forthcoming chapters. Analytical techniques provide an in-depth psychic examination of precisely what drives the client by comparing the past with the present. In employing such skills, the practitioner can provide the client with the maximum chance of resolving intrapsychic conflicts by relieving crippling guilt complexes, by discharging devastating emotive responses and by accessing those areas of his/her subjective experience that have caused the greatest distress and psychological damage.

Freud's novel work initially set the stage for clinicians to explore the unconscious mind and Jung, in being one of the major protagonists to break free of the fold and to develop his own ideas, also made a major contribution to this body of knowledge that has been of inestimable value to clinical practice ever since. Freud's strengths were his conviction about the need for therapeutic investigation into childhood conflicts while Jung contributed to a profound understanding of the workings of the psyche. Even though Freud's exaggerated claims about sexuality and instinctual processes and Jung's religious and mystical preoccupation have been heavily criticised and repudiated by latter-day practising therapists, it is still thought that virtually all other therapies were, in some way, born out of Freudian and Jungian thinking. The work of these theorists forms not only the backbone of psychodynamic practice but also has influenced disciplines such as humanistic psychology, transactional analysis, transpersonal therapy, art therapy, Gestalt therapy and, even, the concept of role models in cognitive psychology.

Initially, we shall consider the Freudian basis of analytical hypnotherapy as well as the breakaway sectors that have impacted greatly on the original theory. Those disciplines that form the bedrock of psychodynamic therapy – and, hence, analytical hypnotherapy – comprise those elements listed below.

Psychoanalysis (see Chapter 1 – "Psychoanalysis") which is based on the work of Sigmund Freud (1856–1939).

Analytical psychology (see Chapter 2 – "Analytical Psychology") which is based on the work of Carl Jung (1875–1961).

Individual psychology (see Chapter 3 – "Individual Psychology") which is based on the work of Alfred Adler (1870–1937).

Ego-state psychology (see Chapter 4 – "Ego-State Therapy") which is based on the work of Anna Freud (1895–1982).

Object-relations psychology (see Chapter 5 – "Object-Relations Psychology") which is based on the work of Melanie Klein (1882–1960), Margaret Mahler (1897–1985) and John Bowlby (1907–1990).

Insight, it seems to be believed, will transmute symptoms into health,
understanding into personal change, and developmental arrest into
personal growth.
– *Helmut Karle & Jennifer Boys*

What Is Humanistic Psychology?

The 1950s also saw the emergence of the humanistic school in
psychology, in large part as a reaction to the mechanistic approach of the
behaviourists, but also partly as a reaction to what was perceived as the
negative picture presented by psychoanalysis.
– *Nicky Hayes*

Humanistic psychology supports the theory that the individual
has an inherent growth potential for self-actualisation and a
propensity for self-realisation. Humanistic therapy is based on the
principle that the client's nature is essentially positive and
resourceful, that his/her attitudes and behaviours can be self-
directed and that the responsibility for his/her welfare will be in
his/her own hands. The humanistic therapist, therefore, will have
an essential trust in his/her client's ability to make progress in
therapy and will believe that every individual has a potential for
self-understanding. The humanistic approach, furthermore, maintains a fundamental respect for the dignity of the client and, thus,
the therapist will regard the client as a subject and not an object.

Humanistic psychology – like psychodynamic therapy – adheres
to the phenomenological approach whereby the client, in therapy,
can delve into his/her own subjective experience. The humanistic
therapist will acknowledge that such delving can be expansive but
that it is a painful process and that there will be a constant struggle between staying with the security of what is known and undergoing the pain of growth, self-knowledge and personal insight.
Therapeutic intervention, therefore, will tap into the client's own
internal resources in order to activate and to further the self-
actualisation process.

The humanistic approach puts forward a perspective based on the
client's free will and self-determination. The client will be deemed
to have a freedom of choice and should be encouraged to take
personal responsibility for his/her own self-improvement. This
can then lead the client towards autonomy, personal choice,

purposeful development and meaningful self-growth. The humanistic therapist ultimately and steadfastly believes that the client is capable of improving his/her lot and, indeed, that he/she has been genetically programmed to do so in the interests of his/her own survival. The humanistic view – the so-called third force in psychology – promotes the belief that the client is neither the unwilling victim of his/her unconscious processes, as with psychodynamic doctrines, nor a machine-like animal whose behaviour is determined by his/her reactions to external stimuli, as with behavioural psychology. The humanistic persuasion, therefore, was a significant departure from the more rigid, deterministic stance of the classic psychodynamic school of thought but, by the same token, retains many of the original themes. The subtle combination of both these themes within analytical hypnotherapy brings colour and life into the practice.

> Both the psychoanalytic and behaviourist approaches are *deterministic*. People are driven by forces beyond their control, either unconscious forces from within (Freud) or reinforcements from without (Skinner). Humanistic psychologists believe in *free will* and people's ability to choose how they act.
> – *Richard Gross & Rob McIlveen*

The humanistic therapist will also note the particular relevance of observing and respecting the client's subjective experience in the therapeutic context. The therapist will be of assistance to the client by creating a relationship in which he/she can mature and can develop according to his/her own dictates. This developmental process is described as the self-actualisation process because the client makes real or actualises his/her own personal and social transformation. Humanistic psychology also regards the client from a holistic viewpoint: the client is both mind and body inextricably interrelated. This stance emphasises the completeness of the client as having within him/her all the resources that he/she requires for that essential self-growth. The client, thus, has within him/her the knowledge, the understanding, the determination, the insights, the power and the courage that can ensure and further his/her self-development and progress throughout life.

> The humanistic psychologists also emphasised the holistic nature of the
> personality, rejecting the fragmented picture of the mind in perpetual
> conflict with itself which was presented by psychoanalysis, and also
> rejecting the atomistic picture of human behaviour presented by the
> behaviourists. While various factors may have combined to influence
> someone, that someone was nonetheless a person, complete in
> him/herself, with his/her own ideas and plans.
> – *Nicky Hayes*

In our study of humanistic psychology, we shall consider the disciplines below.

Client-centred therapy (see Chapter 6 – "Client-Centred Therapy") which is based on the work of Carl Rogers (1902–1987) and Abraham Maslow (1908–1970).

Existential therapy (see Chapter 7 – "Existential Therapy") which is based on the work of Viktor Frankl (1905–1997), Rollo May (1909–1994) and Ronald Laing (1927–1989).

Gestalt therapy (see Chapter 8 – "Gestalt Therapy") which is based on the work of Fritz Perls (1893–1970).

> Humanistic psychology was largely based on insights gained through
> psychotherapy, where patients – particularly ones who were getting
> better – persisted in referring to themselves as whole people with
> intentions, plans and ambitions, instead of seeing themselves as battling
> ids and superego, or as collections of stimulus–response links and
> behavioural contingencies. Perhaps, suggested the humanists, this
> implied that looking at the person as a whole might be a good idea.
> – *Nicky Hayes*

What Is Cognitive Therapy?

> Third is the cognitive trend in behaviour therapy. The behaviourists of
> both the classical-conditioning and operant-conditioning models
> excluded any reference to meditational concepts (such as the role of
> thinking processes, attitudes, and values), perhaps as a reaction against
> the insight-oriented psychodynamic approaches.
> – *Gerald Corey*

Cognitive therapy stands between psychodynamic disciplines, that focus on underlying unconscious processes, and behavioural therapy, that is solely interested in understanding conscious motivation and related behaviour. The cognitive approach seeks to understand and to alter the client's motivational activities together with his/her irrational-emotive responses. The client in therapy will be considered to be acting in a disturbing manner that will have upset his/her equilibrium and caused him/her psychological distress. Although not, strictly speaking, the province of analytical therapy, it is true to say that some appreciation of this important discipline will be of service to the analytical therapist who should appreciate that psychic conflict will have an effect on every aspect of the client's mind, including his/her thinking, reactions and behaviour.

In our study of cognitive therapy, we shall briefly consider a number of persuasions as set out below.

Cognitive therapy (see Chapter 9 – "Cognitive Therapy") which is based on the work of Aaron Beck (1921–).

Reality therapy (see Chapter 9 – "Cognitive Therapy") which is based on the work of William Glasser (1925–).

Rational-emotive behaviour therapy (see Chapter 9 – "Cognitive Therapy") which is based on the work of Albert Ellis (1913–).

Why Does the Client Seek Analytical Hypnotherapy?

> Fortunately, in her kindness and patience, Nature has never put the fatal question as to the meaning of their lives into the mouths of most people. And where no one asks, no one needs to answer.
> – Carl Jung

Let us spend some time now considering the reasons why the client may be initially prompted to seek therapy. We shall examine how and why the client's symptoms, emotive reactions and anxiety-provoking distresses can arise and how these can strongly influence his/her personal development and his/her social interaction. Once these factors have been outlined, the way in which therapeutic intervention can facilitate the client's therapeutic journey can be clearly identified by the practitioner (see Figure 1: "The Hypnoanalytic Process").

Figure 1: The Hypnoanalytic Process

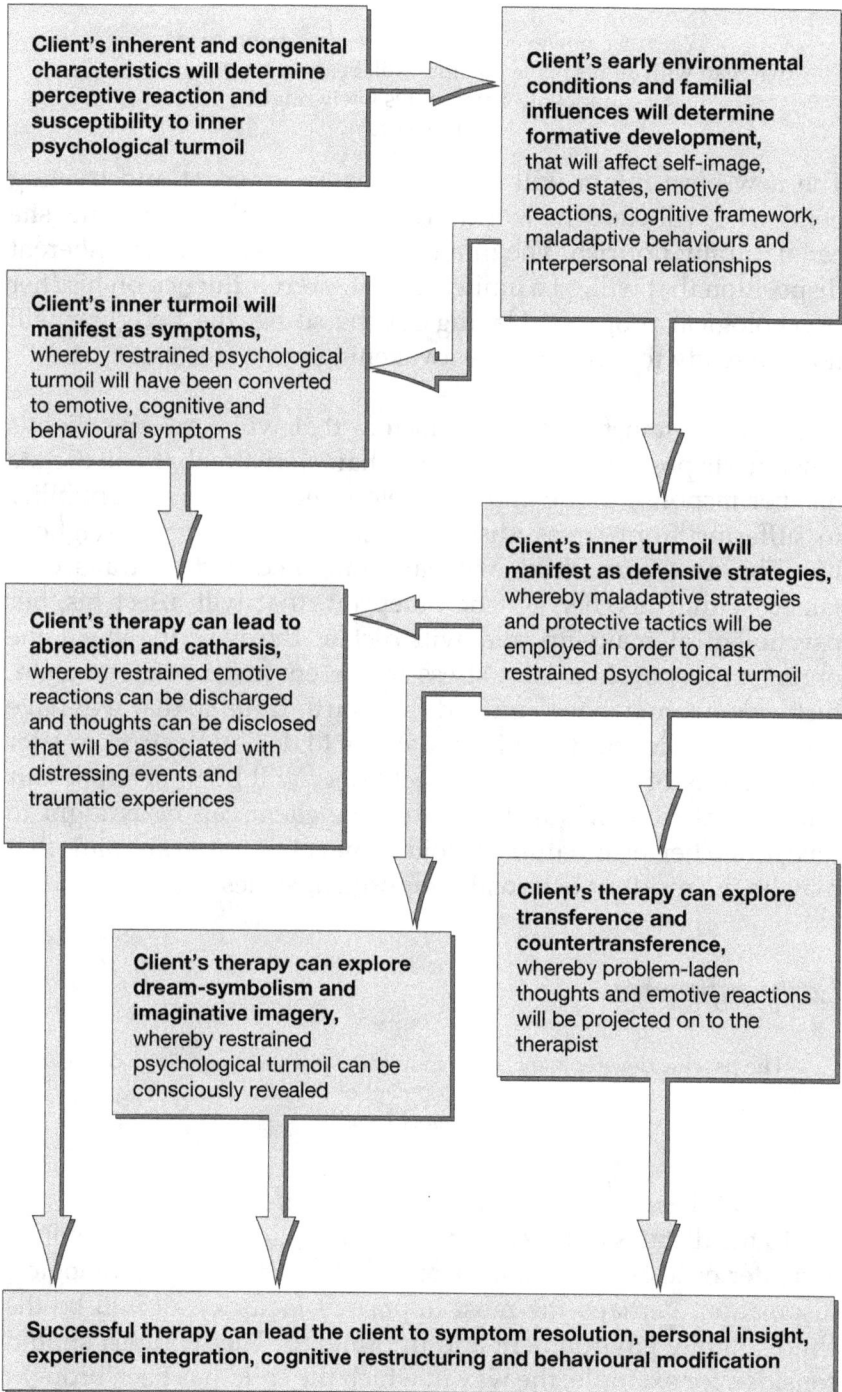

Client's inherent and congenital characteristics will determine perceptive reaction and susceptibility to inner psychological turmoil

Client's early environmental conditions and familial influences will determine formative development, that will affect self-image, mood states, emotive reactions, cognitive framework, maladaptive behaviours and interpersonal relationships

Client's inner turmoil will manifest as symptoms, whereby restrained psychological turmoil will have been converted to emotive, cognitive and behavioural symptoms

Client's inner turmoil will manifest as defensive strategies, whereby maladaptive strategies and protective tactics will be employed in order to mask restrained psychological turmoil

Client's therapy can lead to abreaction and catharsis, whereby restrained emotive reactions can be discharged and thoughts can be disclosed that will be associated with distressing events and traumatic experiences

Client's therapy can explore transference and countertransference, whereby problem-laden thoughts and emotive reactions will be projected on to the therapist

Client's therapy can explore dream-symbolism and imaginative imagery, whereby restrained psychological turmoil can be consciously revealed

Successful therapy can lead the client to symptom resolution, personal insight, experience integration, cognitive restructuring and behavioural modification

Inherent Disposition

> We must, however, acknowledge, as it seems to me,
> that man with all his noble qualities, still bears in his bodily frame the
> indelible stamp of his lowly origin.
> – *Charles Darwin*

The new-born infant will begin life as an innocent and trusting being who will view the world as a fascinating place where he/she can naturally flourish. The infant will be possessed of an inherent disposition that will, to a limited extent, exert influence on his/her psychological progress. Having set the scene, the fledgling will now be ready to face the rude awakening known as reality itself.

There are certain fundamental factors that will form the client's inherent disposition and congenital characteristics that will dictate his/her response to life and will determine his/her susceptibility to suffering from stress, distress, conflict or trauma throughout life. The new-born child will have inherited certain traits contained within his/her genetic blueprint, that will affect his/her psychological make-up and will dictate the way in which the organism responds to any stress in the environment. The child, furthermore, may have suffered from birth trauma, that will have had an intrinsic effect on his/her ability to deal with stress in later life. The role of the analytical practitioner will be to facilitate this unfoldment from within the client. The client can be brought to reveal his/her true nature devoid of negative programming that may be the result of externally imposed agencies.

Early Influences

> The psychic development of the individual is a short repetition of the
> course of development of the race.
> – *Sigmund Freud*

As the child grows and learns to deal with life, he/she will be subject to the dictates of his/her immediate environment, that will, to a greater or lesser extent, have an effect on his/her psychological disposition. Perhaps the most important factor of all will be the child's family environment and upbringing. The therapist should consider, for example, the way in which the child has been brought up. Were the client's primary carers loving and caring, protective and nurturing? Alternatively, did the client's family suffer from financial hardship, or were his/her parents overstrict, neglectful, self-absorbed, preoccupied or fundamentally absent during his/her developmental years? These factors will inevitably exert an undeniable influence on the client's psychic development and adjustment within the social world. The child's response to significant others and negative life factors, moreover, will affect his/her self-image, emotional states and reactions, cognitive framework and adaptive and maladaptive behaviours, as well as affecting the way in which he/she will form interpersonal relationships and can communicate with others. When interacting with others, the young child, moreover, may be affected by his/her own physical appearance, level of intelligence, talents and natural gifts. Perhaps a good-looking or talented child, for example, will be admired for his/her beauty or accomplishments. Conversely, perhaps the child who does not have a pleasing appearance or is lacking in intelligence may be shunned by others and become branded at an early age merely for his/her physical countenance or dearth of attractive attributes. Perhaps the baby who smiles frequently and seldom cries will be more acceptable to his/her parents. A number of such issues can be carefully considered by the analytical hypnotherapist, who may wish to study the client from all angles.

Symptoms

> To be alone is the fate of all great minds – a fate deplored at times, but still always chosen as the less grievous of two evils.
> – *Arthur Schopenhauer*

The client who has been subjected to negative influences during formative development will, in adulthood, manifest symptoms that are in direct relationship to his/her perception and reaction to psychological pain. The client may, for example, develop a negative self-image or a pessimistic outlook on life, may become hypersensitive to criticism, may adopt unsociable habits, may suffer from anxiety states or psychosomatic disorders. Such symptoms may or may not bother the client but, if and when these disadvantages do, he/she may be prompted to elicit outside assistance. When the client's symptoms, moreover, begin seriously to stifle his/her growth or to impinge upon his/her happiness or simply to trip him/her up far too frequently, then he/she may earnestly endeavour to seek therapeutic assistance in order to resolve such problems with concerted effort.

The client's unconscious mind will inevitably find a way of bringing distressing matters to his/her attention. The mind uses this primitive – and usually unsuccessful – means of endeavouring to rectify past wrongs. The distressed client, for example, will often strive to get past needs met by demanding attention or by searching for the elusive commodity of love, will replay past tapes by reconstructing dramas with unhappy endings and will re-enact strategies that have previously failed. Often such patterns are built into the client's problems and difficulties and, thus, may become uppermost on his/her list of symptoms.

Defensive Strategies

> Men are rewarded and punished not for what they do, but rather for how their acts are defined. This is why men are more interested in better justifying themselves than in better behaving themselves.
> – *Thomas Szasz*

In a vain attempt at resolving psychic distress, the client will unconsciously adopt defensive strategies that endeavour to maintain the status quo within his/her inner mind (see Chapter 11 – "Defensive Strategies"). A defensive strategy is a survivalist psychological means of ensuring that distress or trauma within the organism is compressed, contained and reduced to an absolute minimum. The prospective client may or may not be aware of his/her defensive strategies and avoidance mechanisms and, therefore, may find his/her own behaviour confusing and illogical. The client's defensive tactics, furthermore, will be a means of keeping unpleasant emotive reactions out of his/her conscious awareness, although the result will often be that his/her symptoms will be exacerbated, his/her emotive responses will escalate owing to the nature of this self-deception, and the quality of his/her life will be impaired.

> He who does not need to lie is proud of not being a liar.
> – *Friedrich Nietzsche*

Transference and Projections

> First, we can observe and describe the experiences of the patient and of
> the analyst; some of these may be more or less typical of the analytic
> encounter. Many statements about psychoanalytic treatment refer to this
> aspect of the problem.
> – *Thomas Szasz*

Manifestations of transference in the client's life and, especially, within the therapeutic relationship are an indicator that personal interaction is a medium of exchange that can affect both parties profoundly (see Chapter 13 – "Transference and Counter-transference"). The client will react in prescribed ways to those about him/her and, when interacting with another, will be bringing the ghosts of all previous relationships into the encounter.

Analytical hypnotherapy will seek to highlight the importance of the therapeutic relationship between the client and the practitioner in an endeavour to assist him/her to unearth traumatic material from the past. The therapeutic relationship, of course, is an artificial relationship in that, in the main, the client will tell all but the therapist will endeavour to remain obscure and faceless. It will, in fact, be this artificial quality that can be capitalised upon by both parties in order to maximise the client's chances of unveiling restrained psychic conflict. In forming this unique type of relationship, the client can be encouraged to project all his/her neurotically-driven thoughts and feelings on to the therapist as a means of bringing such realisations out into the open. This projection or transference of thoughts and feelings will then allow the client to gain insight into his/her unique problems and the work of resolving them can then begin.

The therapeutic encounter will also utilise any transference from the therapist on to the client – known as *countertransference*. Countertransference is a valuable indicator to the practitioner that the client may need to open up in a given area or that the practitioner himself/herself may require personal therapeutic assistance or relief from working pressures.

What Is the Premise of Hypnoanalytic Practice?

> Freudian therapists do not strive to turn "disturbed" people into "normal" people. "Normal" people are simply those who have been able to suppress their inner conflicts to such an extent that they are quite unaware of them. "Disturbed" people are less psychologically complacent. They are unable to manage their inner turmoil and therefore cannot ignore its existence, but the real nature of these inner concerns remains unconscious. Disturbed people know that they are disturbed but do not know what, at bottom, is disturbing them. The normal person is not conscious of any disturbance. The Freudian psychotherapist seeks to help a person become more self-aware than those who are normal, and better able to cope with this awareness than those who are disturbed.
> – *David Smith*

Analytical hypnotherapy is founded on the premise that distressing and traumatic material that has been repressed, suppressed or denied from the client's conscious awareness can be gradually unearthed as the originating cause of his/her neurotically based symptomology. Simultaneously, the accompanying negative emotion can then be cathartically discharged by the client and some much-needed insight may be gained when he/she works through exposed material. It is the winning combination of root-cause analysis, emotive release and therapeutic resolution – each one of which will be essential in order to achieve the client's psychological homeostasis – that puts analytical hypnotherapy in a class of its own.

Anxiety-laden material can usually be teased out of the client's unconscious mind by employing a number of techniques such as free association, pinpointing, bridging, guided imagery, journal writing and dissociative methodology (see Chapter 2, Volume 2 – "Therapeutic Investigation"). This form of enquiry may also be supported by investigative methods such as dream interpretation (see Chapter 14 – "Dreams and Symbolic Imagery"), resistance utilisation (see Chapter 12 – "Resistance") and the analysis of transference and countertransference (see Chapter 13 – "Transference and Countertransference"). Life-enhancing resolution can usually be undertaken using a number of techniques such as inner-child work, self-empowerment and cognitive restructuring in order to initiate and to maintain the client's self-growth as an ongoing process (see Chapter 5, Volume 2 – "Therapeutic Resolution").

This first volume of *Analytical Hypnotherapy* will deal essentially with setting the scene and outlining the practice in detail. The companion volume, *Analytical Hypnotherapy – Practical Applications*, will endeavour to equip the practitioner with the relevant tools in order to allow him/her to put a sound knowledge of the groundwork into living practice.

Part I

Therapeutic Foundations

In Part I we shall explore those therapeutic concepts that comprise the practice of analytical hypnotherapy in order to identify the origins of the discipline. Essentially, this section will cover the work of Freud and his collaborators and the theories put forward by the humanistic school and the cognitive persuasions. The aim of this field of study will be to empower the practitioner to put analytical hypnotherapy in context and to view it from all angles as a holographic and eclectic therapeutic discipline.

Chapter 1

Psychoanalysis

Things are seldom what they seem,
Skim milk masquerades as cream;
Highlows pass as patent leathers;
Jackdaws strut in peacock's feathers.
Very true, so they do.
Black sheep dwell in every fold;
All that glitters is not gold;
Storks turn out to be but logs;
Bulls are but inflated frogs.
So they be, Frequentlee.

– William S Gilbert

What Is Psychoanalysis?

The Freudian approach understands psychological illness as an inability
to rationally manage inner states of intense anguish, dread and longing.
Psychological health is therefore equated with the ability to handle such
intense inner states adaptively and creatively.
– David Smith

The foundations of psychodynamic therapy began notoriously
with Sigmund Freud (1856–1939) who created psychoanalysis. It is
from Freud's teachings that all insight-orientated theories and
therapies have evolved. Freud was also responsible for introducing
certain psychological concepts and bringing specific terminology
into common usage. He has been much maligned for certain far-
fetched theories but many of the principles of his theoretical concepts are still acknowledged as being invaluable assets for the
therapeutic practitioner in the understanding of the mind and the
way in which it works. Freud and his collaborators have provided
the preparatory groundwork that, over the years, has been
expanded, developed, modified and incorporated into many other

psychotherapeutic persuasions. The so-called neo-Freudians, for example, took Freud's work and added a new dimension to it by looking at the social and cultural influences with which the client has to contend.

Psychoanalysis was, of course, the first therapeutic discipline to place emphasis on the client's subjective perception of his/her experience – known as the *phenomenological approach* – in that he/she will be encouraged to discover his/her own truth rather than that which could be proven by strictly scientific or empirical means. The emergence of the phenomenological approach opened up the way for later schools of thought – particularly the humanistic doctrines.

Psychoanalysis will identify elements contained within the client's unconscious mind and will examine the intrapsychic conflicts that can result from his/her early experiences. The basic concept of trauma, distress and conflict and its resolution, in essence, will hinge on the fact that the client's personality development will have been the product of his/her life experiences that are perceived according to the dictates of his/her inherent temperament and psychological disposition and have, to a greater or lesser extent, had a psychological impact on him/her. Early-established maladaptive emotional or behavioural patterns tend then to become reinforced and to set up inaccessible symptoms in the client. Therapeutic intervention, however, can enable the client to access these inaccessible areas of psychological damage in order to effect a resolution at the root-cause level.

Traditionally such therapeutic intervention has taken years to bring about beneficial change within the distressed client, but hypnoanalytical therapy can often accelerate this process and can ensure a more effective access into the client's unconscious processes. Hypnosis can have the effect of quietening the client's mind and temporarily ridding him/her of the thoughts that would normally permeate his/her thinking. In hypnosis, the client can achieve a state whereby a parasympathetic stillness can be attained, that can separate conscious logical mental activity from illogical and irrational thought processes. It will be as if the oil of the conscious mind were to separate from the waters of the client's mysterious and untapped unconscious functioning in hypnosis.

With hypnosis, the client, therefore, will have the benefit of not having to spend years in therapy and will also gain the maximum opportunity for success into the bargain. Hypnoanalysis as a therapeutic practice is grossly and scandalously underused and possibly underestimated by the bulk of the therapeutic community.

> It hardly needs re-iterating, but emphasis must always be placed on the fact that recovery of a repressed memory or of repressed affect is not enough to effect relief of the problem in any but a few cases. Psychotherapy is much more than "uncovering", and the latter is only the first step in a process of re-working the uncovered material in such a way as to reduce traumatic impact, resolve conflicting feelings and attitudes, and above all to work through the manifold and complex ways in which such traumata have become woven into the life of the patient and, indeed, the very structure of his personality.
> *– Helmut Karle & Jennifer Boys*

The Philosophy of Psychoanalysis

> The more complicated and profound process of gaining "insight", which involves affective as well as cognitive recognition of intrapsychic associations, was sought by Freud as a more potent and far-reaching procedure effecting more profound and therefore long-lived changes in intrapsychic organisation.
> *– Helmut Karle & Jennifer Boys*

With regard to psychoanalytic intervention, Freud advocated that a procedure should be followed when conducting therapy in order to ensure that the client is fully apprised of his/her role in the unfolding of his/her psychic conflict and distress. Let us, therefore, examine some of Freud's stipulations as they apply to the therapeutic encounter in order to get a flavour for the analytical process. We should also be mindful of the fact that Freud's revelations were groundbreaking at the time and that such notions had never before been collated and presented to practitioners of psychological medicine. The birth of psychoanalysis might be likened to the discovery of DNA: it profoundly changed working practices within the scientific, medical, law-enforcement and criminal communities.

Unconscious Motivation

> Freud believed that we repress those thoughts that are simultaneously
> highly exciting and riddled with guilt or shame. Chief among these are
> sexual and aggressive impulses. Freud believed that pressures of
> socialisation cause us to hide aspects of our sexuality that contravene
> social mores and to suppress our tendency to obtain pleasure through
> harming and exploiting others. We all, therefore, possess a store of
> highly charged unconscious sexual and aggressive fantasies.
> *– David Smith*

The client will be principally driven by his/her unconscious processes but usually will have not yet learned to appreciate this fact until he/she engages in therapy. Emotive responses, thoughts and willpower will emanate from the client's unconscious mind and not from conscious awareness. Logical reasoning, conscious effort and determination, therefore, are not the transport medium though which the client can rectify or resolve his/her symptomology. If this were so, no-one would ever need therapy – merely supportive reassurance and comfort-zone encouragement!

Freud gave emphasis to instinctual impulses that can have a destructive effect on the psyche and, of course, he is renowned in the eyes of the populace for attaching overriding importance to sexual desires and aggressive impulses. This assertion, however, has been tempered by modern-day psychological thinking so that sexual desire and aggressive inclinations become only part of a number of destructive psychological motivations. In therapy, the client will be faced with having to deal with many destructive impulses on which his/her symptoms will hinge in order to bring to fruition his/her creative aspirations so that he/she can then pursue cultural, artistic and spiritual interests that can manifest personal contentment and harmony. The social world will, of course, dictate that the client must suppress or sublimate his/her unsociable desires or motivational forces in order to take his/her place in society in the name of civilisation. In this climate, the client may deny a part of himself/herself in the interests of social survival. In the therapeutic context, however, the client can be invited to cast aside social pressures in order to find that rudimentary missing link.

The Therapeutic Medium

> We instruct the patient to put himself into a state of quiet, unreflecting
> self-observation, and to report to us whatever internal perceptions he is
> able to make – feelings, thoughts, memories – in the order in which they
> occur to him. At the same time we warn him expressly against giving
> way to any motive which would lead him to make a selection among
> these associations or to exclude any of them, whether on the ground that
> it is too *disagreeable* or too *indiscreet* to say, or that it is too *unimportant* or
> *irrelevant*, or that it is *nonsensical* and need not be said. We urge him
> always to follow only the surface of his consciousness and to leave aside
> any criticism of what he finds, whatever shape that criticism may take;
> and we assure him that the success of the treatment, and above all its
> duration, depends on the conscientiousness with which he obeys this
> fundamental technical rule of analysis.
> – *Sigmund Freud*

Freud advocated that the therapist should point out the difficulties
and drawbacks of analytical therapy, its possible protracted duration and the efforts and sacrifices for which it calls (see Chapter 1,
Volume 2 – "The Hypnoanalytic Approach"). The therapist should
then state that no promise of success can be guaranteed with any
degree of certainty and that ultimate victory depends on the
client's own willingness, conduct, personal understanding, adapt-
ability and perseverance. Success, furthermore, cannot normally
be objectively measured, verified or quantified. This advice may
well still hold true today for every client who engages in any form
of therapeutic unfoldment. Freud also reminded his lecture audi-
ences that nothing takes place in a psychoanalytic treatment but an
interchange of words between the patient and the analyst behind
closed doors. It will, of course, be the quality and nature of these
verbalisations that will dictate the outcome of the client's therapy
– producing either unparalleled magic or hopelessness, despair
and ultimate failure.

The Therapist's Role

> The soul – or psyche – is that which constitutes our powers of sensing,
> feeling, and thought, the entirety of our experiences and all
> our memories.
> – *Konrad Stettbacher*

Although it is relatively easy to learn how to apply analytical techniques, it is, of course, a highly demanding practice because its
application will depend on the personality, disposition and evolu-
tionary psychic development of the therapist (see Chapter 1,
Volume 2 – "The Hypnoanalytic Approach"). The therapist's willingness, therefore, to undergo self-investigation in the form of a
training analysis will, of course, be an essential component when
working in this field. It will be this initial training analysis and the
ongoing process of continuing self-analysis and therapeutic supervision that will lay the foundation for becoming a competent hypnoanalytic therapist.

Psychoanalytic Concepts

> The techniques of psychoanalytic therapy are aimed at increasing
> awareness, fostering insights into the client's behaviour and
> understanding the meanings of symptoms. The therapy proceeds from
> the client's talk to catharsis to insight to working through unconscious
> material. This work is done to attain the goals of intellectual and
> emotional understanding and re-education, which, it is hoped, lead to
> personality change. The six basic techniques of psychoanalytic therapy
> are (1) maintaining the analytic framework, (2) free association,
> (3) interpretation, (4) dream analysis, (5) analysis of resistance, and
> (6) analysis of transference.
> – *Gerald Corey*

Freud reasoned that there was evidence for the existence of the
unconscious mind by identifying a number of psychic phenomena, that we shall now discuss. His theories about the functioning
and workings of the mind have been widely acknowledged by the
layman and serious professional alike. The message conveyed by
Freud's discoveries is that the human organism is impressionable
and susceptible to stress, and can retain it in many forms but can

resolve it successfully given the opportunity and a conducive environment.

The Structure of the Mind

Freudian theory upholds that the human organism has both a conscious mind and an unconscious mind. Freud, as a medical practitioner, highlighted many aspects of the power and the scope of the unconscious mind, although earlier philosophers had documented a number of theories on this topic. Freud and his collaborators, who were neither purely scientific nor wholly philosophical, were all influenced by earlier philosophers such as Arthur Schopenhauer (1788–1860), who expounded theories about the repression of human instincts and emotions; Friedrich Nietzsche (1844–1900), who advocated the sublimation of guilt; and Immanuel Kant (1724–1804), who investigated human perception. Freud, however, tabulated the notion – that is now widely accepted, particularly in the therapeutic community – that the human unconscious mind is powerfully programmed by instinct and is capable of being intuitive, creative, imaginative and inspirational. The client's unconscious mind, moreover, has the ability to learn modes of behaviour, to acquire skills, to adopt habits and to create obsessions.

Consciousness itself is merely an intermittent phenomenon and only between one fifth and one half of an individual's life is actually spent in a conscious state of mind. It is believed that the first three to five years of childhood are spent in the unconscious state – rendering the child fully open to the maximum impact of suggestion, influence and lasting impression. The client's awareness of the external world will be obtained through a succession of conscious impressions. Consciousness is the product of perception and orientation in the external world and is probably localised in the human cerebellum. The conscious mind, moreover, is characterised by a certain degree of narrowness and can hold only a few simultaneous contents at any given moment. The human organism cannot hold a total image of anything because of this narrowness and can actually see only flashes of existence.

Freud also documented the idea of a preconscious mind – a state in which material is neither fully in conscious awareness nor totally consigned to unconscious processes. Such material may break the surface in therapy when the client begins to recall memories that have been temporarily forgotten and/or are not readily recalled because they lie immediately below the upper perimeter of his/her mind.

External Influence

Freud, among many others, revealed the fact that the unconscious mind is susceptible to external suggestion and outside influence (see Chapter 10 – "Memory"). The client can be influenced in both direct and subtle ways by others, by social pressures, by the media and, indeed, by the inner voice of reason. It will be as if the client is continually shaped by his/her environment and his/her social orbit. A knowledge of this factor can assist the therapist, who may seek to free the client from being the supplicant victim of his/her personal circumstances on the one hand, and to utilise his/her suggestibility in order to encourage beneficial change, on the other.

Memory

Memory can invariably be faithfully relied upon to be unreliable (see Chapter 10 – "Memory"). The client's memory of events will usually be vague and inaccurate and can be seriously misleading. Freud realised that the memory is susceptible to the unconscious processes of disavowal, repression and amnesia – particularly when the organism is overwhelmed by stress or trauma (see Chapter 11 – "Defensive Strategies"). The client, however, will hold the key to his/her psychological and psychosomatic distress within his/her own memory banks both psychologically and physiologically. Often the enigma with which the therapist will need to wrestle is the fact that the client's so-called memory of the past will actually be retained in the present.

Imagery and Symbolism

The client's thoughts can reveal the stresses and trauma contained within his/her psyche. The psychodynamic theorists advocate that both dream symbolism and imaginative imagery can identify the client's unconscious needs, conflicts and wishes (see Chapter 14 – "Dreams and Symbolic Imagery"). A thorough examination of the client's fantasy life, therefore, will be of enormous assistance to the therapist when helping him/her to uncover his/her unconscious disturbances.

Language and Communication

Freud identified the fact that thoughts and psychic distress can be revealed in the client's innermost thoughts that, in turn, can surface unconsciously within his/her language patterns and modes of speech. The famous Freudian slips – known as *parapraxes* – can reveal the client's unconscious disturbance through forgetfulness and mistakes (see Chapter 3, Volume 2 – "Unconscious Communication"). The therapist, therefore, will need to be acutely observant of that which the client is presenting behind the façade of social niceties. The competent therapist will need to be continually looking beneath the surface of the client's words, phrasing, inflexion and bodily expression. Hear at the front door but listen always at the back entrance.

Symptoms and Effects

Essentially, Freud gave us the notion that the client's unconscious mind has the ability to sweep aside or bury unpleasant, conflicting or traumatic material that may then surface as a distressing and unwanted symptom known as a *conversion symptom* (see Chapter 11 – "Defensive Strategies"). If matter has been buried in the client's psyche, it will still require an outlet that may take a psychological or a physiological form. Matter is said to be suppressed or repressed by the client's mind because he/she fears to acknowledge his/her own personal truth. Freud defined suppression and disavowal as the mind's necessary withdrawal of attention from a given occurrence or thought process in order to allow the human organism to attend to other things. Alternatively, he regarded repression as a continued withdrawal of attention – a practice that will supposedly occur without the client's conscious awareness or deliberate intervention.

Freud also posited that the human mind is capable of the symbolic representation of symptoms within the body. Freud, therefore, was one of the first writers to identify the presence of the mind–body relationship whereby emotional distress and/or pressure can manifest not only as psychological trauma but also as physiological pain and discomfiture (see Chapter 11, Volume 2 – "Psychosomatic Disorders").

Freud maintained that evidence for the existence of unconscious distress can also manifest itself through unhealthy relationship attachments and outbursts of anxiety and aggression towards others (see Chapter 12, Volume 2 – "Dysfunctional Relationships").

Defensive Strategies

Freud attributed the emergence of defensive strategies to intrapsychic conflicts between various aspects of the personality that can control the client's behaviour (see Chapter 11 – "Defensive Strategies"). A defensive strategy will be the primitive means by which the client will cope in times of distress. The defence mechanism can also be a survival strategy that will be employed by the human mind, whereby the client will contain the knowledge of psychic disturbance caused by his/her reaction to threatening experiences.

Transference and Countertransference

Freud advocated that the unconscious mind is capable of projection and transference phenomena (see Chapter 13 – "Transference and Countertransference"). By this means, the client will internally hold memories of past personal contacts with significant others and, in given circumstances, will re-create these dilemmas in order to project such feelings on to persons entering his/her current life. In the therapeutic context, the client will often seize on

the therapist as a neutral being and unconsciously attribute qualities to him/her or imbue him/her with emotions and behaviours
that are, in fact, indicative of the behaviours of significant others
from his/her formative years. The therapist's role, then, will be to
help the client to understand that the source of his/her convictions
about the therapist lie with the problem people in his/her life. By
this means, the phenomenon of transference can be utilised in
order to assist the client's therapeutic enlightenment.

Free Association

Freud's philosophy behind the talking cure gave birth to the technique of free association, that has become widely employed as a
viable means of investigation and has been used almost universally in a myriad therapeutic disciplines now for many decades
(see Chapter 2, Volume 2 – "Therapeutic Investigation"). With free
association, the therapist will urge the client to verbalise his/her
thoughts in a random fashion. Free-association methodology can
access unconscious distress, conflict and trauma and, in doing so,
can move the client towards the unleashing of his/her innermost
disturbances. This technique demands that the client keep nothing
back from the therapist when reporting his/her train of thought
because, in doing so, he/she would deprive himself/herself of a
prime opportunity for discharging some of his/her psychic conflict or trauma. Freud described this as the *fundamental technical
rule* of analysis.

> Difficulty with the selective and organising functions of consciousness is
> a common symptom of neurosis. Sometimes emotionally disturbing
> ideas are stubbornly rejected; at other times they break through and
> interrupt every effort at concentration. Thus the neurotic unconscious
> seems to block the normal flow of preconscious processes. Unconscious
> processes typically have their own dynamism, independent of the
> situation in which the person finds himself; they are wounds that never
> healed, losses never mitigated, remnants of the ancient battles of
> childhood. These are realms explored by psychoanalysis.
> – *George Miller*

13

Client Profiling

The analytical hypnotherapy practitioner may wish to ponder the following points when formulating a profile for the client.

- In what way does the client view his/her problems subjectively?
- What types of conflict are evident within the client?
- What drives the client at an unconscious level?
- What does the client perceive as the root of his/her problems or difficulties in life?
- What appears to have made a lasting impression on the client?
- What factors have had the most emotional impact on the client during his/her childhood?
- Does the client habitually adopt any obvious language patterns or phrases?
- How much of the client's past can he/she readily remember?
- What defensive strategies does the client employ with regard to therapy?
- How does the client react to being in therapy?

Chapter 2

Analytical Psychology

There is nothing worse than self-deception where the
deceiver is always with us.

– Plato

What Is Analytical Psychology?

Jung uses the term Analytical Psychology to describe his own approach,
which is not only a way of healing, but also of developing the personality
through the individuation process. Since, however, individuation is not
the goal of all who seek psychological help, and in many cases more
limited aims are indicated, he varies his treatment according to the age,
state of development, and temperament of his patients, and does not
neglect either the sexual urge or the will to power, if these are
operative factors in the neurosis.
– Frieda Fordham

Carl Gustav Jung (1875–1961) sought to continue the spadework
undertaken by Freud in order to devise his own theory of the
treatment of unconscious conflicts and neurotic behaviours and
this branch of psychodynamic therapy he termed *analytical psychology*. Jungian psychotherapy, essentially, incorporates Freud's
investigative and elucidative approach (see Chapter 1 –
"Psychoanalysis"), supplemented by Adler's educational stance
(see Chapter 3 – "Individual Psychology"), but then adds a self-
education and transformational stage while maintaining an eclectic viewpoint. Jung's main thrust was to give the client an insight
into himself/herself and the way in which he/she lives in the
world. Jung believed that it was the way in which the client
utilised the information that he/she discovered about himself/her-
self in therapy that was important, rather than the information
itself. The strength of analytical psychology, therefore, lies in the

fact that it takes an all-embracing view of the client's life both past and present by tracking and facilitating his/her maturation process and, in doing so, this angle can resolve the trauma of yesterday yet lay plans for the future.

Jung maintained that the aim of every human being is that of *individuation* or mature self-realisation. Individuation can begin for the client when the energy that is liberated from psychic conflicts and disturbance is resolved and channelled into fruitful and productive development. The client may previously have been alienated from himself/herself by too much identification with his/her personal and social image, but the recognition and rectification of this survivalist shortcoming will help him/her on the path towards individuation.

Jungian philosophy supports a more spiritual approach to psychotherapy in encouraging the client to search for meaning and insight, as compared with Freudian theories, which adhere to the belief that the individual is determined by psychological and biological forces. Analytical psychology embraces many classical Freudian concepts but makes a departure from this approach by studying character types (see Chapter 15 – "Personality Structure"), by interpreting the meaning of the transference relationship between client and therapist (see Chapter 13 – "Transference and Countertransference"), by studying and interpreting dreams and by considering the effects of archetypal imagery (see Chapter 14 – "Dreams and Symbolic Imagery"). The concept of archetypes in imagery, fantasy and dreams is a fundamental way of understanding the workings of the client's mind and a means of providing a starting point for the exploration of his/her thoughts and beliefs. An understanding of Jung's theories of personality structure and development in terms of psychological types and functions can also be of enormous benefit in helping the therapist to understand the client from a holistic viewpoint (see Chapter 16 – "Personality Development").

Both Freudian psychoanalysis and Jungian analytical psychology involve an in-depth examination of the client's intrapsychic and interpersonal conflicts, but Freud was concerned principally with reintegrating the conflicting elements of the personality torn apart by trauma, while Jung favoured movement towards psychic wholeness and unification via a dialogue between the conscious and the unconscious aspects of the client's mind. Freud regarded the elimination of neurosis as the freeing agent that will lead the client to prosper and to find a suitable mate, whereas Jung saw the attainment of a spiritual goal as the ultimate aim of analytical psychology and regarded neurosis as the organism's futile attempt at a self-cure. The association between Freud and Jung lasted about six years and resembled a dynamic father–son relationship in which Jung became Freud's favourite, echoing his own mother's treatment of him, and Jung acquired a powerful father figure – a commodity evidently lacking in his own childhood. Their relationship was, moreover, a mixture of affection, tolerance and political necessity. The estrangement occurred principally because Jung could not accept the prominence of sexuality in Freud's theory – possibly because sex was a commonplace aspect of his rural upbringing rather than a clandestine experience. Freud's rational, deterministic approach, furthermore, was insufficient for the aesthetic Jung, who sought solace in religion, the occult and mysticism in order to provide a wider meaning to his existence. Jung was also influenced by Richard Wilhelm (1873–1930), who stimulated his interest in Eastern principles.

> Andrew Samuels has constructed a tripartite classification of analytical psychology into schools: the developmental school which incorporates psychoanalytic theory and practice; the classical school, seeking to extend Jung's own ways of thinking and working; and the archetypal school, concentrating on the play of images in the psyche.
> – *Ann Casement*

The Philosophy of Analytical Psychology

> The individuation process is sometimes described as a psychological journey; it can be a tortuous and slippery path, and can at times simply seem to lead round in circles; experience has shown, however, that a truer description would be that of a spiral. In this journey the traveller must first meet with his shadow, and learn to live with this formidable and often terrifying aspect of himself: there is no wholeness without a recognition of opposites. He will meet, too, with the archetypes of the collective unconscious, and face the danger of succumbing to their peculiar fascination.
> – *Frieda Fordham*

Analytical psychology will endeavour to lead the client towards advancing his/her own individuation process, that will allow him/her to continually strive towards psychological maturity and self-fulfilment both during and after therapy. The direction of Jungian philosophy is, therefore, that of allowing the client to mature or become more individual while undertaking therapy. Let us now consider the factors that underlie this premise and the way in which individuation can be activated by the client in therapy.

The Individuation Process

> Part of the nature of humans is to be constantly developing, growing, and moving toward a balanced and complete level of development. For Jung, our present personality is determined both by who and what we have been and also by the person we hope to become. The process of self-actualisation is oriented toward the future. His theory is based on the assumption that humans tend to move toward the fulfilment or realisation of all their capabilities. Achieving individuation, or the harmonious integration of the conscious and unconscious aspects of personality, is viewed as being an innate and primary goal.
> – *Gerald Corey*

The individuation process can assist the client to attain a state of psychologically balanced development by acknowledging himself/herself as an individual in his/her own right. The therapeutic process will provide a means of allowing the client to grow and to develop towards recognising and accepting his/her true adult self. This can be achieved by integrating the opposing elements of the client's personality by balancing the acceptable or the constructive elements with those that are deemed to be dark and destructive forces. The theory of individuation can, thus, be regarded as the client's continual process of assimilating variance within his/her own psyche by harmoniously integrating the conscious and the unconscious aspects of his/her personality and by working towards a spiritual, meaningful enlightenment. The individuation process will work towards the client's psychic wholeness, integration and unity – usually undertaken in mature years – by suspending both objective, rational thinking and irrational, subjective inclinations in favour of achieving insight. When attaining this inner equipoise, the client can then interact autonomously both with the environment and with his/her own internal world. Jung himself was acutely aware of the duality of the mind, having leanings towards both the terrestrial and the spiritual, that led him to make some advantageous discoveries about personality types and structures. Jung's whole life, of course, may be regarded as a personal struggle in order to reconcile the disunity of his own inner and outer world in such a way.

Jung advocated that the client can investigate the ways in which he/she has been compelled to distort his/her personality. The client can then unseat repression, can resolve psychic conflict or trauma and can learn to rely on the messages from his/her own unconscious mind. The emphasis in analytical psychology will be on a developmental approach in which the client is future-oriented in an endeavour to grow towards becoming the person he/she hopes to be and, in doing so, to embrace the learnings of what he/she has been in the past. Jung asserted that the principal aim of psychotherapy is not to take the patient to an impossible state of happiness but rather to help him/her to acquire the steadfastness and the philosophical patience to withstand suffering. He claimed that behind every neurotic condition there is often the suffering and the conflict that the client has been unable or unwilling to bear and, because of this burden, he/she seeks therapeutic assistance.

Analytical Psychology Concepts

As far as we can discern, the sole purpose of human existence is to
kindle a light in the darkness of mere being.
– *Carl Jung*

Jung expounded his theories on the ways in which the psyche
functions and the ways in which the child develops into the adult
state. Let us examine some of his theories and philosophies, therefore,
that are of particular importance to the hypnoanalytical therapist.

The Nature of the Psyche

In speaking of mind and mental activity Jung has chosen the terms
psyche and psychic, rather than mind and mental, since the latter are
associated primarily with consciousness, whereas the psyche and
psychic are used to cover both consciousness and the unconscious.
– *Frieda Fordham*

Jung gave us the concept of the inner mind as the psyche – a
dynamic, ever-moving, constantly changing and self-regulating
mechanism. The self-regulating psyche will be fuelled by an
energy that Jung termed the *libido*. In Jung's parlance, the meaning
of the word "libido" became synonymous with psychic energy
rather than being restricted to Freud's use of the word to mean
sexual or erotic energy. Jung maintained that it is the amount and
the direction of libido in the client's psyche that will dictate
his/her psychological health or ill health.

The natural flow of libidinal energy may be either a *progression*
towards conscious awareness or a *regression* away from reality in
the form of suppression, repression or denial. Progression will satisfy the demands of the client's conscious mind as an active adaptation to the environment while regression will placate his/her
unconscious mind in the guise of an accommodation of inner
needs. If the client tries to force his/her libido into a rigid channel
or to create a barrier with a repression or a conscious adjustment,
then his/her attempts will inevitably fail and natural forward
movement will become impossible. Libido will, therefore, flow
back into the client's unconscious mind, that will eventually
become overcharged, and this excess of energy will then seek an

outlet. This excessive libido may, for example, leak through into the client's conscious mind involuntarily as a fantasy or as a neurotic symptom or, alternatively, it may overwhelm the conscious mind with a violent outburst. Jung believed that, if the client perceived trauma, then such an experience would drive psychic energy back towards becoming either consciously suppressed or unconsciously repressed. Once this had occurred, the repressed material would then surface as a symptom, in dreams, in fantasies, as infantile behaviour, as an outburst or as a spontaneous regression. Excessive libido may even develop into a psychosis, as if a dam were bursting and flooding the land. The more the client endeavours to suppress his/her involuntary expression, of course, the more it will be determined to manifest itself, usually as a disturbing symptom. In extreme cases, where libido fails to find an outlet, the client will, in some way, withdraw from a participation in life. Suppression of one symptom, furthermore, without root-cause resolution will undoubtedly result in the development of an alternative symptom – known as a *symptom-substitution*.

Jung was one of the first writers to emphasise the fact that the client will have his/her own unique brand of reality by which he/she can perceive the external world – known as the *solipsistic principle*. Jung stated that everything, including physical and emotional pain, will be a psychic image that the client will perceive and, therefore, experience. The client's psyche will transform and falsify reality to such an extent that he/she must resort to artificial means in order to determine what constitutes his/her internal perception of external reality. Everything manmade, therefore, will emanate from the client's psyche in the form of ideas, visions, dreams and imagery. One client's reality may be different from that of another but he/she will be the product of what he/she experiences as real, as valid and as equal to – even if different from – what is experienced by others. Jung's conviction in this area of mind study has added weight to the phenomenological tenet in psychotherapy that has been echoed loudly in humanistic disciplines.

> The natural movement of the libido is forwards and backwards – one
> could almost think of it as the movement of the tides. Jung calls the
> forward movement which satisfies the demands of the conscious,
> *progression*, the backward movement, satisfying the demands of the
> unconscious, *regression*.
> – *Frieda Fordham*

The Polarity Principle

> Jung's conception of the psyche is of a system which is dynamic, in
> constant movement, and at the same time self-regulating; he calls the
> general psychic energy libido.
> – *Frieda Fordham*

The analytical psychologist will adhere to the concept of opposing
factors – which are termed *polarity principles* – within the psyche
whereby the client will be drawn by the flow of psychic libido in
one of two directions. The greater the tension between the two
polarities, the greater will be the client's psychic energy. Lack of
tension between the two opposites will, however, fail to generate
libido. Examples of the polarity principle within the client's personality may be cited as extrovert or introvert characteristics,
active or passive reactions, aggressive or submissive qualities and
self-preservative or self-destructive tendencies. Other manifestations of the polarity principle will include the client's internalisation or externalisation of psychic conflict, his/her objective or
subjective viewpoints and his/her reality or fantasy manifestations. The polarity principle can also be observed in the physiological fight-or-flight response and in male or female elements of
an individual, a nation and a culture.

Jung postulated the theory that the client's libido has a vital regu-
latory function in that a pull too far in one direction will result in
a shift towards the opposite direction. Striving for psychic balance
will, thus, be the client's prime purpose in life. Jung saw the psyche as a self-regulating, dynamic system in constant motion with
libido acting like an electric current that flows between the two
opposing poles. The opposites, however, have an important regu-
latory function. When one extreme has been reached, libido will
pass to its opposite. The client, for example, may switch rapidly
from rage to calm and from hate to liking or love. Jung described

this phenomenon as being like a tidal flow and called this the law of *enantiodromia*.

The therapist who observes a given polarity principle that manifests within the client may need to appreciate the other side of the coin. The client may, for instance, veer in one direction as a form of avoidance or resistance (see Chapter 12 – "Resistance"). Has the client, for instance, been inclined towards intellectual argument at the expense of emotional experience as a result of having been hurt in the past? Has the client become fantasy-prone in order to avoid stark reality? Has the client adopted a damage-limitation policy, whereby his/her life has been stultified as a result?

The Psychic Complex

A fundamental concept of all analytically-based therapeutic models is that some especially potent experiences, whether brief and traumatic, repetitive, or continuous and painful, are repressed, blocked from consciousness, and that the repressed "complexes" (the complex constellations of cognition and affect) exert a determining influence on mood, behaviour, apperception and relationships into and through adult life.
– *Helmut Karle & Jennifer Boys*

Jung regarded a complex as a conglomeration of psychic contents characterised by a peculiar or painful-feeling tone, that will usually be hidden from the client's conscious awareness. A complex, therefore, will be the tendency for the client's ideas to become associated around a certain basic nucleus. This nucleus will contain energy and will act like a psychic magnet and will then attract ideas in proportion to the degree of energy that the complex contains. A complex may be a conscious manifestation, an unconscious phenomenon or a partially conscious or subliminal factor – whereby the client may be partially aware of the existence of the complex but will not be fully aware of its nature. The nucleus of a complex may result from the client's life experience, perception of reality and reactions when a disturbing event occurs.

The nuclear complex will have two components: a *dispositional* component that will be determined by the client's way of reacting to an experience, and an *environmental* component that will constitute the experience itself. Some complexes belong to the personal unconscious and others to the collective unconscious, while some belong to both. The mother complex, for example, will be personal to the client but will be collective in relation to the maternal archetype (see Chapter 14 – "Dreams and Symbolic Imagery"). Jung also declared that the existence of one or more complexes within the client does not, in itself, signify a neurotic disorder because a complex can be the normal focus of psychic happenings. The fact that a complex may be painful for the client is, therefore, not proof of pathological disturbance. A complex will become pathological only when the client believes that he/she does not have one and, thus, a part of him/her will deny or disavow the psychic evidence.

Jung defined the conscious mind as that set of ideational complexes that are directly associated with the client's ego and with psychic factors of only slight intensity. Those thoughts that have lost their intensity by being under the threshold subliminally, therefore, belong to the sphere of the client's unconscious mind. The balance between the client's conscious mind and his/her unconscious mind will be continually shifting. Ideas that have lost their intensity, for instance, will become forgotten by the client and will be consigned to the unconscious mind, whereas new ideas and tendencies will rise to conscious awareness from the unconscious mind – generally as fantasies or impulses. The aim of analytical psychology, however, will be to balance these elements within the client.

The Personal Unconscious

> The personal unconscious belongs to the individual; it is formed from his repressed infantile impulses and wishes, subliminal perceptions, and countless forgotten experiences; it belongs to him alone.
> – *Frieda Fordham*

While Freud believed that the unconscious mind was derived from the conscious brain, Jung believed the reverse was true. Jung saw the unconscious mind as more than merely a repository for repression: he considered that it also contained the seeds of the possibilities for new life. Jung made a distinction, therefore, between the personal unconscious of the client and the collective unconscious of humanity.

The contents of the client's personal unconscious mind will comprise all the material that can be recognised as having a personal origin. The personal unconscious, therefore, is that part of the client's psyche that contains the catalogue of his/her life experiences. The client's personal unconscious mind will contain deep-seated and subliminal memories, thoughts, emotions, attitudes, opinions, convictions, values and beliefs. The personal unconscious mind will, therefore, contain the product of the client's instinctive processes that will make up his/her personality as a whole. The personal unconscious will be utterly unique to the client because every individual will experience and react to life in different ways. Jung also regarded the personal unconscious mind as a shadow land made up of repressions and subliminal perceptions. He believed that these partially comprehended experiences exist within the personal unconscious as a halfway house between sub-zero unconsciousness and the ego as the centre of consciousness. Jung believed that the client can experience clear consciousness in only those phases between waking and sleeping – and even the clarity of this is questionable.

The client will develop psychically in a manner that will be the easiest for him/her by enhancing his/her best functions while, at the same time, having a tendency to conform to social and educational pressures. The client will, therefore, suppress or repress much of what rightly belongs to his/her personality in order to conform. Significant adults in the child's life – such as parents, teachers and other surrogate relatives – may believe that they have changed the client in childhood in order to develop his/her personality because he/she will have a tendency to adopt parental teachings in adulthood. Suppressive and repressive tactics, therefore, can often be so effective that the client will actually believe that he/she is exactly what he/she may appear to be but often this belief will manifest disastrous results in the form of character distortion. Jung maintained that these repressive tendencies will belong to the client's personal unconscious mind and that this process will lead to a compromise between the self and society that can, then, bring about the formation of the social mask – known as the *persona*.

The Collective Unconscious

> The collective unconscious is a deeper stratum of the unconscious than
> the personal unconscious; it is the unknown material from which our
> consciousness emerges. We can deduce its existence in part from
> observation of instinctive behaviour – instincts being defined as
> impulses to action without conscious motivation, or more precisely –
> since there are many unconsciously motivated actions which are entirely
> personal and scarcely merit the term instinctive – an instinctive action is
> inherited and unconscious and occurs "uniformly and regularly".
> *– Frieda Fordham*

Jung distinguished between the personal unconscious history of
the client and those aspects of human existence that are shared in
terms of history, culture, social interactions and traditions. He
termed this phenomenon the collective unconscious.

> The collective unconscious, however, as the ancestral heritage of
> possibilities of representation, is not individual but common to all men,
> and perhaps even to all animals, and is the true basis of
> the individual psyche.
> *– Carl Jung*

The collective unconscious will be a representation of everything
that has gone before the client's earthly existence and that has had
an effect on his/her life. The client, for example, will be deemed to
be an interdependent part of his/her childhood upbringing, particular family circle, social community, social culture and nation.
The client, furthermore, will be an inextricable part of a universal
humanity that has a history of heredity. These aspects of the
client's past cannot be denied or negated when considering
him/her as an individual and such influences will have an
aggregate effect on him/her as an inextricable part of a whole
system.

The contents of the collective unconscious mind will have a
mythological characteristic and cannot be ascribed to individual
acquisition. The collective unconscious presence, thus, will belong
to mankind in general and not to any particular person. Jung often
referred to mystic participation (or *participation mystique*), as
devised by the French philosopher Lucien Lévy-Bruhl
(1857–1939), that describes the lack of distinctiveness between

individuals and the lack of boundaries between one person and another during social interaction. Mystic participation will, of course, be influenced strongly by the collective unconscious force. Blurred boundaries within relationships, therefore, that can cause either harmony or strife for the client, are but products of the collective unconscious mind (see Chapter 12, Volume 2 – "Dysfunctional Relationships").

> Jung attached relatively little importance to childhood experiences (and the associated personal unconscious) but considerable importance to the collective (or racial) unconscious, which stems from the evolutionary history of human beings as a whole.
> – *Richard Gross & Rob McIlveen*

Archetypal Imagery

> Archetypes are felt to possess emotional significance. They are, if one likes to put it that way, typical human experience; but experience raised to what is felt to be of superhuman, or even cosmic significance. All human beings, at least in Jung's view, experience life archetypically, at least at times.
> – *Anthony Storr*

Central to Jungian philosophy is the concept of archetypal imagery. Archetypes are those universally accepted motifs, symbols, images and representations that have significance with regard to the client's psychic conflict or trauma. Archetypal imagery is borne out of the collective unconscious and is seen in the form of myths, legends, folklore, visions and dream symbolism.

Jung posited that the brain has been moulded and influenced by the remote experiences of mankind. Jung described this tendency of the individual to apprehend and to experience life in a manner conditioned by the past history of mankind as archetypal. Archetypes, both conscious and unconscious, are the intuitive images that can be found in mythology and psychic experiences. Jung believed that the client could connect with the collective unconscious via archetypal imagery in order to perceive harmony and balance within his/her life and that this connection could have an enriching effect. Jung also had firm convictions about the validity of unusual coincidences – a principle known as *synchronicity*. Amazingly, synchronous coincidences are those that are separated in space and/or in time with no causal connection but yet have an undeniable connecting principle. Jung's tenet of synchronicity, thus, carried Einstein's view on relativity into the world of the psyche and therapeutic investigation. How often does the practitioner think of one of his/her clients and – guess what – that client's voice will soon be heard on the telephone answering system?

Jung introduced and delineated in his writings a number of commonly recognised archetypes (see Chapter 14 – "Dreams and Symbolic Imagery"). Jung spoke of the *self*, that represents the wholeness and the central balancing agent within the client's psyche. He wrote of the *persona*, that represents the protective social mask that the client adopts in society, and the *shadow*, that represents the unacceptable traits within his/her character that he/she fears to acknowledge. Jung, moreover, emphasised the role of the *anima*, that represents the feminine aspects of the male personality, and the *animus*, that represents the masculine aspects of the female personality. Archetypal images are considered to be at the root of every psychic complex but defensive strategies can sweep away such imagery and, thus, can render representative material inaccessible to the client's conscious mind, that, in turn, will cause him/her psychological distress.

> It is necessary to point out once more that archetypes are not determined as regards their content, but only as regards their form and then only to a very limited degree. A primordial image is determined as to its content only when it has become conscious and is therefore filled out with the material of conscious experience.
> – *Carl Jung*

Transference and Countertransference

In analytical psychology, Jung was interested in investigating the meaning of the transference relationship and the countertransference relationship in therapy (see Chapter 13 – "Transference and Countertransference"). He believed that the client has a tendency to project archetypal images on to the therapist, that can influence the therapeutic relationship and will highlight areas where further analytical work might be needed. An appreciation of such symbolism, therefore, can be of great assistance to the analytical hypnotherapist.

Client Profiling

The analytical hypnotherapy practitioner may wish to ponder the following points when formulating a profile for the client.

- Does the client have any spiritual leanings that should be considered in therapy?
- How can the client be helped with the individuation process?
- Does the client take a mature approach to therapy?
- In what directions is the client's psychic energy being channelled?
- How does the client perceive his/her external world?
- What polarity principles does the client exhibit?
- In what ways is the client's psyche attempting to regulate itself?
- What are the dispositional and environmental components of any complexes that the client may exhibit?
- What are the client's unique talents, attributes and capabilities that serve him/her best in the social world?
- What needs to be considered in terms of the client's social and cultural background?
- In what ways does the client relate to archetypal imagery?

Chapter 3

Individual Psychology

The unreflecting man can know no peace and lacking peace
how can there be bliss?

– Bhagavadgita

What Is Individual Psychology?

Like Jung, Adler rejected Freud's emphasis on sexuality, stressing instead
the will to power or striving for superiority, which he saw as an attempt
to overcome feelings of inferiority by all children as they grow up. He
also shared Jung's view of the person as an indivisible unity or whole,
and Erikson's emphasis on the social nature of human beings.
– Richard Gross & Rob McIlveen

Individual psychology is based on the work of Alfred Adler
(1870–1937) who was, for about a decade, a collaborator with
Freud. Individual psychology is a branch of psychodynamic therapy that was a significant departure from Freud's biological,
instinctive and deterministic theories, in that Adler, like Jung, subscribed to the doctrine that upholds that every individual has
unique perceptions and evaluations of his/her own experiences –
the so-called solipsistic principle (see Chapter 2 – "Analytical
Psychology"). The Adlerian approach views the client holistically
as an indivisible whole, yet an integral part of a number of
external systems. The nature of the Adlerian approach regards the
client as being a self-contained unit as opposed to having many
conflicting elements within his/her personality. Adler was one of
the first writers to acknowledge openly that the client must be
considered as a social animal and a creative being with a specific
purpose in life.

31

Individual psychology expounds the theory that the client can work towards the attainment of personal goals in a purposeful manner. By realising suitable goals, the client can achieve recognition and value in society and can interact successfully with others in the social context. If the client has been unable to become an acceptable part of his/her social world, then his/her happiness and peace of mind will be impaired accordingly. Adlerian therapy, therefore, empowers the client to realise his/her potential and to set realistic goals for self-improvement that will engender satisfaction and self-acceptance.

Adlerian psychology fills a number of gaps left by classical psychodynamic theories in that it views the client as a holistic entity with both a past and a present and, simultaneously, as a product of his/her environment and society. Individual psychology has, in addition, made a valuable contribution to psychological knowledge by looking at family dynamics in terms of inadequate parenting and the position the child holds within the family unit. Where Freud investigates and interprets, Adler educates. Adler decided that the pleasure instinct was insufficient to explain all neurotic disturbance and maintained that, in fact, the power instinct accounted for many more neuroses. The Adlerian therapist will believe that the client has unconsciously arranged his/her symptoms and exploited his/her neuroses in order to achieve a fictitious personal importance. Adler also believed that transference and other fixations subserved the client's will to power and represented a protest against imaginative suppression. The client, for instance, may continually feel hard done by and may unconsciously put his/her life goals out of reach.

> The holistic socio-teleological approach of Adlerian therapy based on Adler's Individual Psychology, maintains that people should be viewed in their social contexts in order that their goals can be identified. People choose their own goals based on their subjective perceptions of themselves and their world, their bodies, minds and feelings in harmony with their consistent movement towards these goals. Adlerians consider that people are creative, responsible, self-determined and unique.
> – *Jenny Clifford*

The Philosophy of Individual Psychology

The counselling process focuses on providing information, teaching,
guiding, and offering encouragement to discouraged clients.
Encouragement is the most powerful method available for changing a
person's beliefs. It helps clients build self-confidence and stimulates
courage. Courage is the willingness to act *even when fearful* in ways that
are consistent with social interest.
– *Gerald Corey*

With individual psychology, the therapist will act in an educative
capacity by becoming a mentor, a guide and a facilitator who can
show the client the appropriate path to self-discovery. The therapist's role will be to inspire, to empower and to imbue the client
with courage in order to allow him/her to accept himself/herself
as a unique being who is able to interact successfully with others
socially. The therapist's stance will be to feel truly equal to the
client and the therapeutic relationship will be built on cooperation,
on mutual respect and on an honest interchange of expression.

The individual psychologist will assist the client by helping
him/her to overcome inferiority and discouragement and to correct mistaken and faulty private logic. The client can be guided
towards identifying and exploring faulty assumptions that have
been formulated from his/her own perceptions of himself/herself
and from information gleaned about the world in which he/she
resides. This process will endeavour to correct the client's faulty
perceptions and erroneous social values and to foster social interest and social contribution. The client will be further encouraged
to attain productive life goals, to gain insight into unrealistic goals
and to modify illogical or unrealistic life plans. Any mistaken or
unrealistic goals can be reconstructed so that the client can achieve
his/her full potential and maximum satisfaction from the successful attainment of these aims. During this process, the client will
discover what has erroneously or unproductively motivated
him/her in the past. The therapeutic process, therefore, will motivate the client towards behavioural change, self-acceptance and
the acceptance of others. The client will be invited to accept
his/her own fallibility and to acknowledge his/her own choices
and responsibilities in life. The healthy individual, therefore, will
become involved in life activities and will adopt a lifestyle that
will be in harmony with his/her environment. Distressing symp-

toms may be exhibited by the client as social withdrawal, as a retreat from life tasks and as a psychological disorder that can alleviate his/her inability to face failure. Unwanted behaviours may be exhibited by the client as a malfunction in society, as an inability to fulfil obligations, as a lack of purpose and as an excessive striving for success and perfection.

Individual psychology will often encompass several therapeutic phases, that will entail establishing the therapeutic relationship, understanding the client's perspective, assessing his/her current lifestyle, allowing him/her to gain insight and reorienting him/her into society.

> *Psychological disturbance* occurs when an individual *feels inferior* and unworthy of an equal place amongst his or her fellows. Social interest, which is an innate potentiality in every human being, does not grow in the presence of strong feelings of inferiority. The inferiority feelings are substituted by *a compensatory striving for personal superiority.*
> *– Jenny Clifford*

Establishing a Relationship with the Client

> Adlerian psychotherapy can be described as a co-operative educational enterprise between equals – therapist and client. The first stage of therapy is to *establish a co-operative relationship*, one between equals that is recognised by the presence of mutual respect.
> *– Jenny Clifford*

The client and the therapist must develop and endeavour to maintain a sound, cooperative, therapeutic relationship as the foundation on which the therapeutic process can successfully progress. From this standpoint, the client's life goals can be honestly formulated. The client can, by this means, be encouraged to make his/her own decisions and to take responsibility for his/her own life. The encouraged individual will have a high social interest, will engage in social activity, will have a positive attitude, will be self-confident and will strive for social equality.

Understanding the Client's Lifestyle

The second stage of the therapy is to *gather information* and *understand
clients' lifestyles* and then to show clients how the presenting problem fits
into their overall characteristic pattern of movement.
– Jenny Clifford

The client will be invited to describe his/her presenting symptoms
and to state the way in which these problems have affected
his/her lifestyle. The client will be besought to relate his/her
thoughts and feelings about his/her problems in a subjective manner and should endeavour to identify the means by which unrealistic goals have been set. The client will also be asked to furnish the
therapist with details of his/her childhood, so that both client and
therapist can understand the client's position in the family and
how this role has influenced his/her personal development.

Enabling the Client to Gain Insight

The third phase of *interpretation* and *giving insight* is now entered. The
therapist's approach is to find enough points on a line to begin to make
a hypothesis. This informed guess is then put to the client, so that
it can be verified.
– Jenny Clifford

The client should be encouraged to gain insight into himself/her-
self and to take strength from this self-knowledge. The client may
be invited to uncover those dynamic influences that have formed
the basis of his/her motivation and have influenced the formation
of his/her life goals. The client's faulty private logic and mistaken
beliefs should naturally unfold during the therapeutic process
and, subsequently, neurotic tendencies can be uncovered and
reduced to insignificance and irrelevance. The client, for example,
may be unrealistically self-critical, may reject others and may have
low expectations if he/she feels himself/herself to be inferior in
his/her life position. The client, furthermore, may believe that no-
one cares for him/her or that he/she has let others down.

Reorienting the Client

> The *re-orientation phase* follows on from gaining insight. The Adlerian
> therapist will use a mirror technique to show clients familiar patterns of
> movement towards consistent goals in all their behaviour.
> – *Jenny Clifford*

Finally, with his/her new-found knowledge, the client can be guided towards setting more appropriate goals, can take his/her place in society and can make a more positive contribution, that, in itself, will allow him/her to acquire fulfilment. The client should be empowered by the therapeutic process so that he/she can assume personal courage and can act with a social interest. The encouraged client will have a positive self-attitude, self-confidence and self-respect. When the client is imbued with personal courage and strength, he/she will be in a position to accept himself/herself as an equal in society. Any justification for unwanted behaviour will also diminish because the client's irrational private logic will have been undermined by the therapeutic process. The client can now move in the direction of change by forming new and more appropriate behavioural patterns.

> Adlerian psychotherapy is a learning process where there is a re-
> education of clients' faulty perceptions and social values, and
> modification of their motivation. It is intended that clients should gain
> insight into their mistaken ideas and unrealistic goals, both of which are
> a source of discouragement. After insight there is a stage of reorientation
> of short- and long-term goals and readjustment of personal concepts and
> attitudes. They feel encouraged as they recognise their equality with
> their fellow human beings. They concentrate on making their contribution
> and co-operating instead of looking at their personal status within groups.
> – *Jenny Clifford*

Individual Psychology Concepts

Adler brought to the fore a number of therapeutic elements that underpin the therapeutic practice of most disciplines both within and outside the psychodynamic umbrella. Let us now examine these approaches to therapeutic intervention as documented by the Adlerian school, that have quietly set the pace for others to follow. A knowledge of these principles can greatly assist the analytical practitioner in understanding the personal development and motivations of the client.

The Phenomenological Approach

Adlerians attempt to view the world from the client's subjective frame of
reference, an orientation described as phenomenological. It is
phenomenological in that it pays attention to the individual way in
which people perceive their world. This "subjective reality" includes the
individual's perceptions, thoughts, feelings, values, beliefs, convictions,
and conclusions. Behaviour is understood from the vantage point of this
subjective perspective. How life is in reality is less important than how
the individual believes life to be.
– *Gerald Corey*

The phenomenological approach subscribes to the notion that the
individual will subjectively perceive his/her experiences in life
and the way in which such perceptions are interpreted will have a
profound effect on his/her personal development and psychological health. The client should, therefore, be regarded as being
unique in every respect. The interpretation, moreover, that the
client will put on his/her experiences will correspondingly be
unique and will constitute a biased perception of reality. In this
respect, Adler built on the theories set forth by both Freud and
Jung.

According to Adlerian theory, the client will draw from experiences mainly in the present because of their immediacy and relevance. Although past influences will, undoubtedly, have had an
effect on the client, such elements are not as significant as those
impressions that predominate in the present. Adler postulated that
the past will dictate the client's decision-making only in as much
as it sets a pattern for the direction in which he/she is moving. The
past will, thus, merely provide a theme of continuity rather than
have a direct influence. Childhood perception can only be a generalisation and an oversimplification of what really took place,
because of the child's naïveté. Here Adler made a significant
departure from Freud's deterministic thinking in that dwelling on
the past was not the main thrust of therapy but merely a spring-
board from which the client can propel himself/herself into a better life (see Chapter 1 – "Psychoanalysis"). The individual
psychologist will maintain, therefore, that the client is not simply
a victim of his/her unconscious processes but can be motivated by
choices and responsibilities. The client can endeavour to find the
meaning of life and can then strive for success and perfection as a

primary drive. Adler adumbrated that the client will be essentially interested in where he/she is going and not where he/she has come from. It will be as if the client had been dealt a random hand of cards, but it would be up to him/her as to the way in which he/she would play those cards in life. The client would then have a unique form of private logic that would determine his/her movement towards his/her life goals as these cards were laid upon the table.

> People can always choose how to respond to their inherited qualities and to the environment in which they grow up. People's basic concept of themselves and of life provides a guiding line, a fixed pattern; this is called the lifestyle. The ideas and beliefs according to which a person operates are called *private logic*. They are not common sense but
> *biased apperception.*
> – *Jenny Clifford*

The Teleological Approach

> Individual Psychology assumes that all human behaviour has a purpose. Humans set goals for themselves, and behaviour becomes unified in the context of these goals. Adler replaced deterministic explanations with teleological (purposive, goal-oriented) ones. A basic assumption of Individual Psychology is that what we are striving for is crucial.
> – *Gerald Corey*

The teleological approach considers the individual to be purposeful and goal-oriented in his/her life. The Adlerian psychologist will believe that the client's unconscious goals reveal his/her total personality and that he/she will set himself/herself the task of moving towards his/her goals, displaying elements of personal choice and exercising responsibility. In striving for a superior position in the hierarchy of life, the client will become goal-oriented and task-oriented and it is this directed purpose that will make life worthwhile for him/her – either as a leader or as one who elects to be led in the interests of his/her own survival. The client who has come to therapy may, however, have strayed off course or have formulated beliefs about his/her inability to achieve a given goal. The therapeutic process, therefore, will aim to unravel such faulty private logic in order to get the client back on target.

The Sociological Approach

Social interest, or *Gemeinschaftsgefühl*, is probably Adler's most
significant and distinctive concept. The term refers to an individual's
awareness of being a part of the human community and to the
individual's attitudes in dealing with the social world; it includes
striving for a better future for humanity. The socialisation process, which
begins in childhood, involves finding a place in one's society and
acquiring a sense of belonging and of contributing.
– Gerald Corey

Adler adhered to the doctrine that motivation will be derived from
social pressures rather than from the instinctive urges of the
client's unconscious mind. The sociological approach will consider
the client in terms of the way in which he/she behaves and reacts
during social interaction and human communication. The basic
Adlerian assumption is that the client will be driven by the concept of the *will to power* or the *drive to power*. The will to power was
first purported by Friedrich Nietzsche (1844–1900) in his philosophical works. This concept states that every individual has a
need to belong to a society and to take his/her place in that society. Whether the individual is the leader of the pack or merely the
lowest underling, he/she will have an innate potential to strive
from any perceived inferior position towards a superior position.
This concept is the basis of the notion of the inferiority complex
and the overcompensatory behaviour that can accompany it.

Adler stresses that striving for perfection and coping with inferiority by
seeking mastery are innate. To understand human behaviour it is
essential to grasp the ideas of basic inferiority and compensation.
According to Adler, the second we experience inferiority, we are pulled
by the striving for superiority.
– Gerald Corey

The individual psychologist will have a basic assumption that the
client will strive to better his/her perceived position within
his/her social group and, in doing so, will become of significance
within that group. If the client considers himself/herself to be
inferior to others, then he/she will intrinsically strive to overcome
this perceived personal disadvantage, usually by initiating ways
of bettering himself/herself in order to become part of the community and to make a useful contribution to society. As the client
will be a part of a given social structure, each group member will

strive for development within that structure in order to attain mastery of his/her immediate environment by overcoming obstacles and drawbacks as a means of ensuring survival. This can be achieved by the client when he/she recognises that he/she is in an inferior position – such as feeling helpless, weak or inadequate. Once this recognition has taken place, the client can then strive to overcome it. The helpless client, for instance, can strive for independence, the weak client for strength and the inadequate client for competence. The client's uniqueness of character will be derived from the fact that he/she can strive for mastery, competence and superiority as a personal and unique experience.

> Wherever an inferiority complex exists, there is a good reason for it.
> There is always something inferior there, although not just where we
> persuade ourselves that it is.
> – *Carl Jung*

The practitioner should appreciate that the client will be a part of a family system, a social structure and a cultural environment. It will be the client's purpose within each of these systems that will give meaning to his/her life and will put it into context. Striving within one social group will, in turn, have an effect on another in a wider context for the client. Family behaviours will influence community activities, community actions will influence a nation's thinking and, ultimately, this will escalate into having an influence on the entire human race. The client's interaction in society, therefore, can be regarded as being of monumental importance. In the family context, the child will have been subjected to parental values, family discord and sibling rivalry that, naturally, will have a profound knock-on effect on his/her behaviour and motivations in terms of interacting with others in adult life.

Symptoms of psychological disturbance will occur when the client finds that he/she cannot function adequately in society and that he/she is unable to fulfil his/her obligations in that society. The client will then be likely to withdraw from his/her responsibilities and to retreat from fulfilling his/her life tasks. Often the client will make excuses for his/her inaction and will discover that his/her symptoms are a crisis-management attempt to alleviate his/her inability to face such failures. The psychologically healthy individual, on the other hand, will have a social interest in the world and will exhibit a positive attitude to social interaction. This individual will also have a strong interest in gaining a place in society and will feel himself/herself to be socially equal to others around him/her.

> Neurosis will develop as soon as we feel unable to fulfil our obligations in one of the life tasks – at work, in friendships, in an intimate relationship. The symptoms and behaviour will be the excuse for not fulfilling the tasks adequately, not engaging in them at all, or retreating from them. Rather than facing failure and being found to be inadequate the symptom enables the discouraged individual to hesitate or evade and yet not lose face.
> – *Jenny Clifford*

Lifestyle-Creation

> The meaning we attribute to life will determine our behaviour so that we will behave as if our perceptions were true. Life will turn out as we expected and people will respond as we expected; this is a self-fulfilling prophecy.
> – *Jenny Clifford*

The creation of the client's lifestyle – known as his/her *strategy for living* – will be a product of his/her self-concept, that will become a fixed guiding line for decision-making and for problem-solving. In Adlerian philosophy, every individual will be deemed to be a self-determining personality who will react, who will behave and who will be motivated by his/her inner choices. This premise will give consistency and continuity to the client's behaviour because of the meaning he/she ascribes to it. The client, therefore, will create his/her own strategy for living from his/her own personality and from his/her own behaviour. The individual psychologist will speak of *fictional finalism*, whereby the client will have an imagined or fictional central life goal that will ultimately prescribe all his/her behaviour. The attainment and realisation of this decisive goal will then become the client's ultimate aim in life – the finalism of his/her aspirations and self-seeking path. Often a goal may be oriented towards being accepted by society, being admired by others and attaining perfection. The client, alternatively, may have abandoned his/her life goals or resigned himself/herself to defeat and to alienation from society.

The individual psychologist will, naturally, regard the client as being task-oriented. Adlerian philosophy considers that the client's accomplishment of goals and his/her attainment of satisfaction can be achieved by facing up to and mastering self-prescribed life tasks in different areas of his/her life. These life tasks relate to five discrete areas of the client's life, that can provide meaning to life and can allow for goal setting. The client's life tasks will embrace relationships with friends and acquaintances, relationships with intimate partners and family, self-acceptance and self-identity, professional or occupational employment and his/her spiritual dimensions. The achievement of life tasks in these areas will give the client his/her own sense of belonging so that he/she can regard himself/herself as the equal of others. The concept of belonging in the sociological context means contributing to society.

> Adler considered there were three major *life tasks* required of each member of the human race – work (or occupation), friendship and love. Dreikurs added two more – getting on with oneself and relationship to the cosmos.
> – *Jenny Clifford*

Family Dynamics

> An adult, spoilt as a child, may find partners, relatives, children, friends who are willing to give in to her demands. An adult, pampered as a child, may find sufficient rescuers, helpers and advisers to take over responsibility for his life. If these individuals should lose their slaves or supports a crisis would ensue and disturbing behaviour might emerge in order to attract more applicants for the vacant posts.
> – *Jenny Clifford*

The individual psychologist will be concerned with the way in which the child has been brought up within the family, and Adlerian therapy looks at family dynamics in terms of inadequate parenting and the child's position within the family. Inadequate parenting may take the form of spoiling, pampering, neglecting or excessively criticising the child. In adulthood, the spoiled child, for example, may become the client who solicits people to supply his/her demands. If the child has been unduly spoiled or overindulged, he/she may gain a false impression of his/her own importance and the parent figure will be seen as a superior being from whom bounty can be derived. Spoiling will often be the option taken by a parent who seeks an easy life by giving in to the child's demands. The pampered child, similarly, may become the client who seeks people to rescue him/her. The child who has been excessively pampered because the parental figure does too much for him/her will find life's struggle even more daunting than might normally be the case. The pampered child, therefore, may be hampered in his/her development because often he/she will lack self-confidence and will not want to risk venturing into the external world. Childhood neglect or excessive criticism, moreover, will be deemed to affect adversely the child's psychological development when inappropriate stances are taken by his/her parents. The child who has been heavily criticised will, for example, lack initiative and self-confidence. The client will often fear making mistakes and, thus, will be reluctant to take even slight risks. The neglected child, furthermore, will also be discouraged from generally participating in life tasks, owing to the hopelessness of his/her position in childhood.

Family Hierarchy

> The birth order and the interpretation of one's position in the family have a great deal to do with how adults interact in the world. The child acquired a certain style of relating to others in childhood, and they formed a definite picture of themselves that they carry into their adult interactions. In Adlerian therapy, working with family dynamics, especially relationships among siblings, assumes a key role.
> – *Gerald Corey*

The Adlerian approach places special emphasis on examining sibling relationships and the birth order of the child in the family hierarchy. The child may well have been affected by this birth order and his/her perception of his/her place in the family may have given rise to sibling rivalry. In a competitive family atmosphere, for instance, the client may have become emotionally distressed because unhealthy competition had been encouraged and, thus, has sapped his/her self-courage. The client may then desperately attempt to excel in other ways, may resent or even hate his/her siblings and may adversely interpret his/her place in the family hierarchy.

Adler identified five psychological positions by which the therapist can place the client in the context of the family. It should, of course, be stressed that the client's own perception and unconscious interpretation of his/her place in the family hierarchy would override any theories postulated by the practitioner.

The eldest child

The eldest child may delight in being the centre of attention and may be overindulged until a sibling arrives on the scene. This dethronement may then give rise to jealousy but it may motivate the child to be competitive by striving to maintain his/her top-dog position.

The second-eldest child

The second-eldest child may never command an exclusive position as the centre of attraction. This child may strive, in subtle ways, to keep afloat, therefore, and may endeavour to attract favour by manipulative or aggressive means in order to deflect the limelight from the eldest child. This second-eldest child may also develop a special talent or a worthy attribute with which to secure recognition and to obtain favour. The success of the second-eldest child, however, may discourage the eldest from developing.

The middle child

The middle child may feel out in the cold and unable to compete with older siblings. The middle child, in this position, may react by becoming either a victim or a peacemaker when older siblings are in conflict.

The youngest child

The youngest child will tend to be pampered and spoiled as the baby of the family. An older sibling, for example, may have a vested interest in keeping the youngest child as the baby of the family in order to enhance his/her own superiority. An older sibling may, alternatively, feel jealous of the pet of the family and may react accordingly. The youngest child may, however, become an independent thinker and may find original ways of asserting himself/herself.

The only child

The only child may learn to mix well with adults as these persons may be his/her only companions. This child may develop a high degree of independence or, alternatively, he/she may bask in the glory of being spoiled and pampered, and so may not make any effort to gain independence.

> People's perception of their position in their family constellation forms the basis of their lifestyle. The parents set family values and create a family atmosphere and the children decide their place in the family. A competitive family will produce discouragement, the children competing against each other and eventually channelling themselves into separate spheres of success. They each choose something they can be best at, even if that is being naughty. As each child strives for superiority this necessitates putting the other siblings down.
> – *Jenny Clifford*

Let us now consider a client who was deeply affected by his family hierarchy. In the case-study example given below, the client's self-esteem had been impaired because of the label that his family had given him as the middle child.

Case-study example – the black sheep of the family
This male client had a significantly impaired self-esteem because his family had labelled him as the black sheep of the family.

The client's father had remonstrated with him about the fact that he had not followed in the family tradition of becoming a medical practitioner, as his elder and younger brothers had done. This sentiment was also echoed by his mother and his two brothers. In adult life, however, the client had tackled his father about this black-sheep label and had pointed out that his elder brother had become a drug addict and his younger brother had become a dropout. Finally, the client's father agreed that, of all his sons, the client was the most responsible. This retraction of the black-sheep label, however, did not clean the slate for the client, who still considered himself to be a failure.

Therapeutic intervention focused on the client's relationship with his father. It transpired, on investigation, that, although his father had, in essence, taken back the black-sheep label, the fact remained that the client still keenly felt the loss of love and respect from his father. The client's mother, too, was unsupportive, simply by going along with the myth because of the client's lack of conformity to his father's wishes. The therapeutic encounter brought the client to the realisation that his father and mother were unfair in their judgment, that his brothers had been jealous of him and that no other person had the right to dictate his choice of career or life direction. Facing up to the fact that he felt unloved allowed the client to mourn this loss and to feel anger and resentment at the attitudes taken by his family. This act, in itself, served to raise the client's self-esteem and self-respect.

Client Profiling

The analytical hypnotherapy practitioner may wish to ponder the following points when formulating a profile for the client.

- In what ways does the client consider himself/herself to be inferior to others in his/her immediate social environment?
- In what ways does the client strive to overcome his/her perceived inferiority?
- What forms of illogical private reasoning does the client adopt?
- What mistaken values or perceptions has the client taken on board?
- In what ways has the client been discouraged by his/her early childhood experiences?
- In what ways have the client's early childhood experiences polluted his/her perceptions of life?
- What life goals, if any, has the client formulated for himself/herself?
- What kind of strategy for living has the client adopted?
- Where does the client fall in his/her family hierarchy?
- How does the client perceive himself/herself within the family structure?

Chapter 4

Ego-State Therapy

I have no idea what a poor opinion I have of myself and how little I deserve it.

– William S Gilbert

What Is Ego-State Therapy?

Ego psychology promoted by Freud's daughter, Anna, focused on the mechanisms used by the ego to deal with the world, especially the *ego defence mechanisms*. Freud, by contrast, stressed the influence of the id's innate drives (especially sexuality and aggression) and is often described as an instinct theorist.
– Richard Gross & Rob McIlveen

Ego-state therapy was first mooted by Anna Freud (1895–1982), who recognised the functions of the ego-defence mechanisms (see Chapter 11 – "Defensive Strategies") and the importance of ego-splitting in terms of the creation of subpersonalities (see Chapter 16 – "Personality Development"). An ego-state will be an alternative personality – known as an *alter* – which can be formed consciously or unconsciously. The client will often adopt conscious roles in order to take his/her place in society – to act in the role of parent, for example, or business executive – because such stances will be beneficial when interacting socially or when raising a family. The client will easily be able to differentiate between one life role and another when such patterns of behaviour are consciously-driven. The client, however, can also adopt an alternate ego-state that has a wholly or partially unconscious element. The client may, for instance, have integrated his/her alternate state so firmly into his/her mindset that he/she cannot differentiate between his/her true self and his/her assumed demeanour.

The ego-state therapist will adhere to the doctrine of compartmentalisation of the mind whereby certain aspects of awareness are hidden or, in some way, inaccessible to other parts. This theory is akin to the phenomenon of repression in that the human mind will be deemed to be capable of holding various pockets of repression that can afflict the client in a variety of ways. The therapist will often be able to utilise this concept of compartmentalisation and detachment from reality in his/her quest to understand the client's reactions and motivations. An understanding of the multifaceted nature of the mind can then equip the clinician with the capacity to deal with the client at different levels and to treat a given area of distress in a way appropriate to that level of psychological disorder. A number of dissociative techniques, furthermore, may then be employed in order to help the client to gain access to the originating cause of his/her distress (see Chapter 5, Volume 2 – "Therapeutic Resolution").

> Ego analysts are sometimes referred to as the *second generation* of
> psychoanalysts. They believe that Freud over-emphasised the influence of
> sexual and aggressive impulses and under-estimated the ego's importance.
> – *Richard Gross & Rob McIlveen*

The Philosophy of Ego-State Therapy

> An ego state may be defined as an organised system of behaviour and
> experience whose elements are bound together by some common
> principle, and which is separated from other such states by a boundary
> that is more or less permeable.
> – *John Watkins & Helen Watkins*

The ego is said to comprise collectively one *core ego-state* and several other *alternate ego-states*, that are formed from the original central core. The core ego-state will be a self-representation and will be the true element of the client. The offshoot ego-state may be an object representation that will be formed by the client in order to cope with the rigours and vagaries of social life (see Chapter 5 – "Object-Relations Psychology"). The alternate ego-state, therefore, may be formed when the demands placed on the client from significant others will have overwhelmed and invaded his/her personality and will have thus been created in the interests of his/her survival, particularly in childhood (see Chapter 6 – "Client-Centred Therapy").

Ego-State Characteristics

Ego state therapy is the use of individual, group, and family therapy
techniques for the resolution of conflicts between the various ego states
that constitute a family of self.
– John Watkins & Helen Watkins

An ego-state may solely comprise behaviours or attitudes at one
level, or a whole plethora of motivations, beliefs, attitudes, convictions, emotive responses, thought patterns and bodily postures
at the other end of the scale. The characteristics and components
of a given ego-state will differ according to the way in which the
client perceived the circumstances at the time when the ego-state
was formed. If the client perceived trauma with which he/she
would have been totally unable to cope, for example, then an ego-
state may have been formed with many facets as a result. The ego-
state, thus, will have become a coping-strategy, that will then be
incorporated into the client's psyche as a direct result of his/her
psychic distress. Consequently, the qualities of an alternate ego-
state will often be childlike in character and will be immune to
adult logic or mature reason.

An ego-state can assume an entirely separate subpersonality that,
as far as the client is concerned, will bear no relationship whatsoever to any of the other ego-states within his/her psyche. This factor will be dictated by the degree of dissociation that the client
experienced when the ego-state was developed (see Chapter 11 –
"Defensive Strategies"). The phenomenon of dissociation cuts off
one ego personality from all others. In extreme cases of trauma,
dissociative-identity disorder (DID) or *multiple-personal disorder*
(MPD) will develop whereby the client can become an entirely different personality in an instant and will have no conscious recollection of having been in any other state. The client may, for
instance, switch in and out of alternate ego-states when reacting to
circumstances with little or no conscious awareness of the personality changes that are taking place during the rapid transition from
one state to another. The therapist dealing with the client who
exhibits several ego-states will be beset by the difficulty of detecting the apparent states, discovering their protective purposes and
overcoming the client's understandable reluctance to relinquish
them.

Ego-State Boundaries

> The boundaries between the core ego, the various ego states, and the
> external world constitute the sense organs of the self, permitting one to
> discriminate between external and internal reality.
> – *John Watkins & Helen Watkins*

An ego-state will be surrounded by its own ego-state boundary, that will touch the client's external world and will permit him/her to distinguish between his/her internal reality and the external environment. When a conscious ego-state has been formed in the client's psyche, the ego-state boundary will be under conscious control. The client, for example, may consciously assume the role of parent when dealing with his/her children. Here the ego-state boundary will meet the external world of reality and the client will be aware of this healthy role assumption. When an ego-state has been unconsciously generated, however, the ego-state boundary will be likely to be fuzzy and unstable. The sufferer, for example, may develop an uncontrollably violent disposition. Here the ego-state boundary may not contact external reality and the client may well be only cursorily aware of his/her prevailing actions. The client, moreover, with weak or blurred ego-state boundaries may, consequently, enter into a series of unsatisfactory partnerships or destructive relationships with others (see Chapter 12, Volume 2 – "Dysfunctional Relationships"). The extent to which the client's ego-state boundaries come into contact with reality will often denote the extent of his/her psychic damage. Very strong influences on the client's personality may retain a degree of permanence when being incorporated into his/her psyche. Extremely penetrable ego-state boundaries, therefore, will inevitably result in severe psychological disorders because of the degree of dissociation that was experienced when the client's ego-state and the ego boundary were formed. The client's core self, in such a case, may be so heavily disguised that it can become virtually unrecognisable.

The practitioner should, of course, ensure that his/her own ego-state boundaries are, at least, intact if not impenetrable. For this reason, adequate personal therapy and case-load supervision should be an essential requisite for the practising analytical hypnotherapist (see Chapter 1, Volume 2 – "The Hypnoanalytic Approach").

Perhaps the most influential of those who have revised Freudian
therapeutic approaches are the *ego psychologists* or *ego analysts*. Rather
than emphasising the id's role, these therapists focus on the ego and the
way in which it acts as the *executive* of personality. As well as personality
being shaped by inner conflicts, contemporary analysts believe that it
may be shaped by the external environment.
– *Richard Gross & Rob McIlveen*

Ego-State Therapy Concepts

One of the by-products of forgetting is a feeling of being divided into
more than one person. There is the little girl having the good childhood
but underneath there is the child who's prone to nightmares and sees
people hiding in the corner of the room.
– *Ellen Bass & Laura Davis*

Let us now examine some of the principles of ego-state theory
with regard to the way in which an ego-state may be formed
within the client's psyche. An appreciation of these concepts will
further extend the practitioner's understanding of the client who
may exhibit unpredictable reactions, mood swings,
uncharacteristic behaviour and uncontrollable symptoms.

Ego-State Cathexis

The essential concept in whether any part of the body or mind is
experienced as "me" or "not-me" is determined by the nature or kind of
energy with which it is invested. If the activating energy is object
cathexis, then it is experienced as an object, not-me. If its activating
energy is ego cathexis, then it is experienced as subject, me, myself.
– *John Watkins & Helen Watkins*

An ego-state will need to be imbued with psychic energy in order
to be formed and, indeed, to enable it to survive. Ego-state philosophy has been based on the premise that psychic energy may be
invested or *cathected* in a given ego-state. When energy has been
invested in one ego-state, the client may then be totally consumed
by that state because of the amount of energy cathected in it. The
client may also become dissociated from all other states when
huge resources of psychic energy are ploughed into that one sin-

gle state. When an ego-state has been ego-cathected and, as a result, will assume control of the client's psyche, this ego-state will then become the leader of the orchestra and so diminish the power of all other ego-states. This executive quality will then dominate the client's mind at that time. Energy may, for example, be directed at the self – known as *ego-cathexis* – whereby the client will be consumed with self-interest. Energy may, conversely, be directed at a significant other – known as *object-cathexis* – whereby the client will become preoccupied with the significant other to the exclusion of his/her own needs and interests.

Ego-State Function

Psychic trauma will manifest in the client's mind when a distressing incident either occurs in reality or takes place as a perception of his/her personal reality. The advantage of adopting specific roles or ego-states will be that both the client's conscious mind and unconscious mind will be able to protect him/her from perceived harm.

An ego-defence strategy, furthermore, will endeavour to protect the client from his/her own psychic distress by means of self-deception in order to maintain the psychological status quo (see Chapter 11 – "Defensive Strategies"). A process of distortion, deletion and generalisation of incoming information will achieve this survivalist form of self-deception. The protective nature of the client's defensive strategy will result in a concealment, a disguise, a distraction and a withdrawal of attention from the perceived stress. Such a process will also bring about an escape from the client's harsh reality, a self-devaluation and an inclination to dump emotional problems on others. Self-deception will aim to make life simpler for the client, to avoid pain, to boost his/her ego and to provide a degree of self-criticism via the superego (see Chapter 16 – "Personality Development"). The ego-defence strategy will attempt to block the client's experience of real, neurotic or moral anxiety (see Chapter 7, Volume 2 – "Fear and Anxiety Disorders"). Ego-state defences, therefore, will have a protective function for the client in cases of overwhelming or unmanageable trauma or conflict. Such defences will endeavour to relieve the client's distress or to allay anxiety by a retreat from reality by giving the illusion of protecting him/her from himself/herself and from others.

When an ego-state has been set up, however, it will usually convert to an emotional, a behavioural or a psychosomatic symptom, that may, in fact, serve to reinforce past trauma rather than to relieve it (see Chapter 11, Volume 2 – "Psychosomatic Disorders"). Despite its protective role, the formation of a defensive ego-state, therefore, will not be of true service to the client, whose emotional life may be diminished as a result and whose psychological problems may well be aggravated.

Ego-State Formation

Ego-states will usually be formed in childhood by a number of means, all of which aim to assist the child to cope with life's circumstances and to make him/her feel acceptable in the social world. The child, for example, may be preoccupied with pleasing his/her parents in childhood but, in adulthood, may be determined to exhibit fear or intolerance of others. Once an ego-state has been formed, the client will then adopt a characteristic pattern of behaviours and reactions in keeping with that particular ego-state. Such patterns can also be reinforced by life's circumstances, in which case the client's ego-state will then become recathected with libido in order to keep it alive and active. Let us now consider the ways in which an ego-state can be formed within the client's psyche.

Ego-state formation through differentiation

> Differentiation is adaptive, and some separation of personality segments should make for better personality functioning. Otherwise, it would be like an office in which all papers are thrown together and not separated into classified files.
> – *John Watkins & Helen Watkins*

Ego-state formation may occur by a process of differentiation, whereby the child can distinguish between his/her own actions and those of significant others (see Chapter 5 – "Object-Relations Psychology"). Differentiation will be a semiconscious process in child development, whereby the infant will adapt to his/her social or family environment by assuming appropriate behaviour and, at the same time, suppressing his/her own essential character traits (see Chapter 6 – "Client-Centred Therapy"). The child, therefore, will learn to adopt different styles of behaviour and different life roles by distinguishing between what is and what is not acceptable to significant others.

Ego-state formation through introjection

> An introject is like a stone in the stomach, within the self but not part of
> it, ingested but not digested. For the individual to act and talk
> spontaneously like the other, the object cathexis must be withdrawn and
> the image ego cathected.
> – *John Watkins & Helen Watkins*

Ego-state formation may occur by a process of introjection, whereby the child will wholeheartedly incorporate the demands of significant others into his/her own psyche (see Chapter 11 – "Defensive Strategies"). Introjection will usually be an unconscious process that will occur in childhood when the child's ego deems it vitally necessary to embody the values of significant others into his/her own psyche. The child, by this means, will attempt to secure the love and affection that he/she so instinctively craves in order to ensure his/her own survival by complying vigorously with the wishes and expectations of his/her closest carers.

Ego-state formation through dissociation

> The therapist must realise that this need for a rigid, fixed belief, "I am
> bad and I am to blame for what happened when Daddy came to my
> room", is a kind of psychological glue that binds together the whole
> protective, dissociative structure.
> – *John Watkins & Helen Watkins*

Ego-state formation may occur by a process of dissociation, whereby the child divorces himself/herself completely from his/her own natural emotive responses and/or physical sensations (see Chapter 11 – "Defensive Strategies"). A traumatic experience, for example, can result in a dissociation that will lead to the formation of an ego-state in order to permit the child to distance himself/herself unconsciously from the pain inflicted. Traumatic manifestation may be caused by rejection, abuse or neglect, that cannot be tolerated by the child's concept of reality.

Let us now consider a case-study example that will serve to illustrate the way in which ego-state formation can upset the even tenor of the client's life. In the following case-study example, the client reported having unpredictable mood swings, that could result in his becoming aggressive towards his work colleagues. This example demonstrates the way in which the client's ego-state took over his personality and assumed an uncharacteristic demeanour that seriously troubled him and threatened his job.

Case-study example – uncontrollable aggression

This client found that in his profession he could not keep a secretary for any length of time. It transpired that he had a reputation in the office for being belligerent and unreasonable and had, on several occasions, been reprimanded for his rudeness by the chairman of the board. The client sought therapy, therefore, because he felt that his job was under threat.

The client reported that he often experienced an overwhelming feeling of confusion when he was faced with the prospect of giving instructions to his secretary and other junior staff. He stated that he had frequently lost his temper with his secretary and then afterwards experienced overwhelming feelings of guilt about his conduct. At this stage, the client then never knew whether to apologise profusely or to change the way in which he addressed his secretary. The situation became so intense that the client had even taken time off from work or feigned illness in order to avoid any form of confrontation with work colleagues for fear of losing control and saying something that he might later regret.

Analytical investigation revealed that the client had experienced communication problems with his younger sister – especially in childhood – and had often felt anger towards her subsequently. The client also confessed that his mother was cold and unfeeling and, therefore, had provided him with no blueprint for personal interaction. It was only when the client was able to express his anger openly towards his sister and his mother in the therapeutic context that he was then able to learn how to communicate successfully with others and to handle any form of social confrontation.

Client Profiling

The analytical hypnotherapy practitioner may wish to ponder the following points when formulating a profile for the client.

- What subpersonality traits does the client exhibit?
- Has the client been able to identify his/her core ego-state?
- What are the characteristics of the client's subpersonalities?
- In what ways has the client compartmentalised his/her thinking or behaviour?
- In what ways does the client act uncharacteristically in everyday situations?
- In what ways have the client's personal boundaries been blurred or corrupted?
- In what ways does the client deceive himself/herself or appear defensive?
- In what ways might the client have taken on parental thinking or action?
- In what ways might the client have dissociated himself/herself from past distresses or trauma?

Chapter 5

Object-Relations Psychology

Nor let the beetle nor the death-moth be your mournful
psyche.

– *John Keats*

What Is Object-Relations Psychology?

These newer approaches are often classified under the labels *self
psychology* or *object-relations theory*. Object relations are interpersonal
relationships as they are represented intra-psychically. The term of *object*
was used by Freud to refer to that which satisfies a need, or to the
significant person or thing that is the object, or target, of one's feelings or
drives. It is used inter-changeably with the term *other* to refer to an
important person to whom the child, and later the adult,
becomes attached.
– *Gerald Corey*

Object-relations psychology or *self psychology* was expounded
collectively by Melanie Klein (1882–1960), Margaret Mahler
(1897–1985) and John Bowlby (1907–1990). Object-relations theory
considers the effect that significant relationships with others will
have on the infant in the first months of life. The nature of the relationship that an infant will develop with his/her primary carers
will fundamentally affect his/her interpersonal relationships with
others in adult life. Childhood experiences will, naturally, affect the
way in which the client interacts with others in adulthood as a
result of established infantile patterns. These patterns of interacting with primary carers will, consequently, be repeated in later life
because the client will constantly search for a relationship that will
replicate his/her own personal childhood experiences.

The main thrust of object-relations theory will consider the way in which the client has viewed significant others in his/her childhood and will study the way in which such perceptions have influenced him/her as an adult. If the client views others consciously or unconsciously as objects for the satisfaction of his/her wants, then he/she will be indulging in an immature *subject–object* relationship. If, on the other hand, the client can acknowledge the other person as a separate individual, then he/she will have formed a mature *subject–subject* relationship, that will be indicative of mature separation and individuation (see Chapter 2 – "Analytical Psychology"). The therapist adhering to the object-relations school will endeavour to assist the client with his/her relationship problems and can encourage him/her to achieve individuation and to make a mature separation from significant others. The practitioner may use techniques in order to work through the feelings of loss that accompany personal growth and separation from primary carers, to increase the client's awareness of reality and to assist him/her in coming to terms with the conflicting elements of love and hatred. Object-relations theories will stress the importance of the role of the primitive id in psychodynamic conflicts and, for this reason, it is often regarded as an *id psychology* in order to distinguish it from other psychodynamic doctrines that concentrate on balancing the ego (see Chapter 16 – "Personality Development"). Id psychology will place emphasis on the fact that the infant will have been the helpless victim of his/her instinctive drives.

An understanding of object-relations philosophy will be of importance to the analytical therapist in comprehending the way in which the client's relationships with others have been formed and the way in which the effects of transference and countertransference can manifest in the therapeutic encounter (see Chapter 13 – "Transference and Countertransference"). Armed with such knowledge, the therapist can then gain valuable insight into the reasons why the client may suffer from distresses and anxieties when discord arises in intimate relationships (see Chapter 12, Volume 2 – "Dysfunctional Relationships").

The Philosophy of Object-Relations Psychology

> The I–It attitude would mean that the world and one's fellow men are
> seen only as objects. This can of course take place on many different
> levels. People can be objects of my reflections and my criticisms, but I
> can also turn them into objects of my own needs or my own fears, which
> means that other people get used for one's own conscious and very often
> unconscious purposes.
> – *Mario Jacoby*

Object-relations theory was influenced by the work of the philosopher Martin Buber (1878–1965) who theorised the *I–It* and the *I–Thou* concepts in order to illustrate the way in which the client views his/her relationship with another person. Let us now examine the ways in which relationships are viewed by the client and the ways in which relationships with others can be formed.

Object and Subject Relationships

> The I–Thou attitude would involve a relation to the genuine *otherness* of
> the other person. It would mean that I in my own totality am relating to
> Thou in his or her own totality. *Consciously* I may have the attitude of
> letting the other person live in his own right and not making an object of
> him for my own purposes. But how do I know this does not happen
> unconsciously all the same?
> – *Mario Jacoby*

The client may form a relationship with another according to whether he/she views the other person unhealthily as an object or more maturely as a subject. Subject–object relationships adopt the I–It stance. The I–It attitude will be taken when the client, as the subject, views the other person as an object for the satisfaction of his/her personal needs when the relationship is developed. The client, in this case, will regard the other person as if he/she were an inanimate or impersonal being. Subject–subject relationships, on the other hand, adopt the I–Thou stance. The I–Thou attitude will be taken when the client, as the subject, views the other person in a relationship as an independent being whose personality will be worthy of respect. The client, in this instance, will view the other person as an independent and fully functioning person.

If the therapist can note whether the client regards him/her as an object for the satisfaction of his/her needs or as a separate entity in his/her own right, it will then be clear to the therapist what state of individuation the client has achieved. From this vantage point, therapeutic work can commence and progress can be gauged. Often the client may initially regard the practitioner as an object and, later, when the results of therapeutic intervention have become evident, he/she may then take a more mature stance in the presence of the clinician.

Love-Objects and Hate-Objects

> Melanie Klein's view was that in the early years of life the objects that surrounded the infant were not seen and understood in *visual terms*. This included a wide range of "objects" – parents, siblings, blankets, food, bathing, cots, prams, toys, etc. These would be construed only as they were *experienced* as good or bad.
> – Cassie Cooper

Conventional object-relations theory postulates the view that an infant who tries desperately to make sense of his/her experiences and surroundings will fantasise about the elements or the objects in his/her environment. The infant will then automatically classify these objects into either good objects or bad objects according to his/her experience of them. A good object – known as a *love-object* – for the infant may be mother's breast or a warm and comfortable blanket. A bad object – known as a *hate-object* – may be an absence of mother or a soiled nappy. The infant will, then, form relation-ships with each of these objects and will, naturally, seek out love objects.

When the baby's primary love object – usually his/her mother – is attentive to his/her needs, then all will be well. Inevitably, how-ever, the baby's primary love object will fail him/her, albeit occa-sionally, and he/she will feel the pangs of anxiety as a direct result of this perceived neglect. At this point, the baby will feel anger towards his/her primary love object but will, simultaneously, despise himself/herself for so maligning his/her essential means of survival. These unacceptable feelings of anger and the guilt that having them can engender will then be repressed by the baby's ego in order to ensure his/her survival. Similarly, other unacceptable emotions will be repressed by the child's ego in order to avoid any alienation of himself/herself from love objects. In making the ultimate separation from mother, the child will need a period of adjustment and acclimatisation. This process can often be aided by the adoption of *transitional objects* – such as a toy or a comfort blanket – that can act as a temporary substitute for an absent love object of primary importance.

Ego-Splitting

> In the earliest months, before the infant has clearly recognised the difference between fantasy and reality, between what is inside and outside itself, the death instinct, according to Klein, leads to feelings of destructive rage even without experiences of frustration, and images of a bad mother are split off and projected outside.
> – *Dennis Brown & Jonathan Pedder*

When unacceptable emotions are repressed in the infant's psyche, the ego may become divided or split into a number of aspects. This can sometimes lead to severe ego fragmentation within the client (see Chapter 4 – "Ego-State Therapy"). Klein cited greed and envy as the primary elements that can cause severe ego-splitting. We shall now consider those theories that relate to early psychic functioning, because this viewpoint may be of use to the analytical therapist who will meet the client riddled with feelings of greed and envy. An appreciation of such theories can also help the practitioner to understand childish logic, that, after all, will be mainly what the client will exhibit in abundant quantities.

Klein maintained that greed or acquisitiveness will result from the anxiety that the infant will feel at being deprived of his/her primary love object. An infant who perceives deprivation will become more demanding in his/her desire for love and attention to such an extent that his/her appetite cannot be satiated. If the mother has been unable or unwilling to satisfy the baby's demands, then anger towards her may turn to murderous rage. A vicious cycle will then be set up whereby the baby desires to exterminate his/her mother on the one hand, but, as an alternative, contemplates his/her own suicide on the other. This may be because life has been rendered so unbearable for the infant by his/her situation and he/she will, therefore, take personal blame for his/her mother's failure. Unsatisfied greed, moreover, can lead the adult to develop depressive disorders and to harbour suicidal tendencies.

Envy, similarly, can be said to develop when the baby perceives that love and attention from his/her primary love object has been withheld or has been diverted elsewhere. The infant will deduce that his/her mother has been keeping for herself or giving to others the love that was meant for him/her. The child will then become suspicious and envious of his/her primary love object and this, in turn, may generate more uncontrollable anxiety.

If the client as an infant has been beset by feelings of greed and envy, this will inevitably have a knock-on effect during both childhood and adulthood. The child, for example, may form an abnormal relationship with objects such as toys or pets in childhood. The child may view a toy or a pet as being human and may form an intense relationship with that object in order to compensate for earlier disappointments. These factors may, furthermore, set the scene for poor object relationships to manifest in the future. Klein also argued that these feelings of greed and envy gave a plausible explanation for the rivalry inherent in Freud's oedipus complex (see Chapter 16 – "Personality Development").

> Klein and Mahler have stressed the child's separation from the mother and interpersonal relationships as being important in psychological growth. *Object relations theorists* believe that some people have difficulty in telling where the influences of significant others end and their "real selves" begin. Mahler's approach to therapy is to help people separate their own ideas and feelings from those of others so they can develop as true individuals.
> – *Richard Gross & Rob McIlveen*

The Paranoid-Schizoid Position

> The good feelings and images are introjected and kept inside, but threatened by the return of the projected "persecutory" mother (the so-called paranoid-schizoid position). As the child learns that it is the same mother who both gratifies and frustrates, it has to cope with ambivalence, i.e., loving and hating the same person.
> – *Dennis Brown & Jonathan Pedder*

The paranoid-schizoid position describes the infant's state of mind when he/she discovers that the same mother who furnishes him/her with comfort and love is also the source of his/her anxiety and frustration. The infant will then unconsciously adopt a persecution complex towards himself/herself as a helpless and vulnerable being who is totally dependent on the maternal love object. Klein believed that the child had a death instinct, that was activated when he/she made this fundamental realisation about the nature of his/her love-hate relationship with his/her primary love object. It will then be as if the infant will become paranoid about his/her own vulnerability. If detrimental ego splitting occurs at this stage of development, the adult may then be likely to exhibit tendencies towards paranoia or schizophrenia.

> The infant lives in a constricted world peopled by individuals who are experienced as good or bad. These are the early distortions which Klein described as the paranoid position.
> – *Cassie Cooper*

The Depressive Position

> This more mature *depressive position* allows for the coexistence of love and hate, and thus promotes concern for the other, and a wish to make amends and repair any damage the child imagines it has caused. Inadequately worked through, the depressive position can lead to unreasonable fears in later life that any hatred will damage or destroy a loved person.
> – *Dennis Brown & Jonathan Pedder*

The depressive position describes the child's state of mind when he/she acknowledges the differentiation between himself/herself and his/her mother (see Chapter 4 – "Ego-State Therapy"). The child will learn to acknowledge mother as an independent being and to accept the fact that he/she can both love her and hate her almost simultaneously. The infant, however, will feel some degree of responsibility for this separation because of his/her unconscious hatred of the mother-figure. This state of mind may set up a depressive state within the child because of the perceived loss of his/her mother and his/her own feelings of guilt at having supposedly caused this deprivation to occur. It will be as if the infant will become depressed at the loss of his/her mother as an integral part of himself/herself and then take on the self-blame for this separation. If detrimental ego splitting occurs at this stage of development, the adult will then be likely to exhibit tendencies towards states of depression or guilt complexes.

> Its previous fears of being the frail object of destruction extend subtly to an inner knowledge that it too can destroy the one person it loves and needs for survival. The anxiety has changed from a paranoid to a depressive one. In acknowledging the very existence of a separate being, the baby becomes exposed to the fear that it has made the cut. Aggression has destroyed the cord which linked the baby to the mother, leaving the child with feelings of unutterable guilt, sadness and deprivation, a hurt that can never be healed, a pain that can never be assuaged.
> – *Cassie Cooper*

Object-Relations Psychology Concepts

It may be of particular importance for the hypnoanalytical therapist to understand the nature of relationship formation because the client will have formed a relationship both with himself/herself and with others that may be causing a great deal of distress. Such distress, moreover, may also appear as a wearisome adjunct to any symptoms the client may present. Let us now further examine some of the concepts within object-relations theory whereby the client's interpersonal relationships in adult life will have been affected by his/her negative childhood experiences with significant others.

Relationship Formation

> Melanie Klein is often seen as a key transitional figure between Freud's instinct theory and the object relations school. Like Anna Freud, she

adapted Freud's techniques (such as pioneering *play therapy*) in order to
tap a young child's unconscious, and maintained that the superego and
Oedipus complex appear as early as the first and second years of life.
– *Richard Gross & Rob McIlveen*

Klein focused on and expanded the theories behind the Freudian defence mechanisms of projection and introjection as being of fundamental importance in relationship formation and development (see Chapter 11 – "Defensive Strategies"). She also explained why these defensive strategies are employed by the client and why psychic conflict can have an impact on his/her subsequent relationships.

Relationship formation through introjection

When the mother removes her presence from the baby, two things
happen. One is that the loss or removal of the means to satisfy its needs
(the breast or its substitute) produces an anxiety in the baby. Anxiety is
an affectual state that warns the baby of danger. In order to cope with
this anxiety, the baby has to re-create a mother for itself. This satisfaction
she represented has to be fantasised so that the baby can conjure up in
its mind the imagery and feeling of a good feed. This in turn becomes
the ego: a separate area within oneself.
– *Cassie Cooper*

Introjection as a defensive strategy will occur when the client incorporates the values of a significant other into his/her own psyche. Object-relations theorists contend that the infant will become so obsessed with the need to please his/her parents that he/she will totally subsume parental thinking and values into his/her own psyche. Introjection will, therefore, be a form of overidentification with another whereby the client wholeheartedly embodies that person's traits into his/her own personality. This unavoidable process of introjection will be undertaken unconsciously, because the child's carer will be of such paramount importance to his/her existence and survival.

The child may begin the introjection process merely by emulating his/her carers. When the child realises that such behaviour meets with external approval, his/her tendency will then be resiliently to assume a new personality. The trouble, of course, will arise when the child continues to assume this new personality and when external values, beliefs, attitudes and motivations are embodied into his/her personality in childhood. Psychological damage may occur, particularly when such traits are destructive both to the client and to others. The act of introjection will frequently mean that the client will not take responsibility for his/her own life and that he/she will shun any attempt at self-determination.

> For every human being the outer world and its impact, and the kind of experiences they live through, the objects they come into contact with, are not only dealt with externally but are taken into the self to become part of their inner world, an entity inside the body. As we *introject* these new experiences into our personalities, we take on the concept that we can truly *rely on ourselves*. An enduring self-image and increased self-esteem can be facilitated by this form of introjection.
> – *Cassie Cooper*

Relationship formation through projection

> *Projection* goes on simultaneously. It is a manifestation of a person's ability to project on to other people those aggressive and envious feelings (predominantly those of aggression) which by the very nature of their "badness" must be passed on either by projection or, alternatively, carefully repressed.
> – *Cassie Cooper*

Projection as a defensive strategy will occur when the client endows others with characteristics that are, in effect, a reflection of his/her own personality. Often the projected characteristics will be those that the client will find it impossible to tolerate in himself/herself and, therefore, the act of blaming others will be perceived as being a better option than self-blame. The client, moreover, may often admire qualities in others that he/she will not have the self-confidence to recognise in himself/herself.

Relationship formation through projective identification

> Projective identification illustrates most clearly the links between human instinct, fantasy, and the mechanisms of defence. Sexual desires, aggressive impulses, can be satiated by fantasy.
> – *Cassie Cooper*

Projective identification as a defensive strategy will occur when the client projects on to others in a manipulative manner in order to elicit a response from the other person. The classic example of this mechanism will, of course, be the love-hate relationship in which both love and hate are simultaneously projected by the client on to an intimate partner. The client's partner – receiving mixed messages of both love and hate – will, consequently, react with confusion and may then overrespond by trying harder to capture the illusive love or may retaliate by becoming aggressive. Here, the recipient of the projective identification will, in reality, be enacting the projected fantasies of his/her intimate partner.

Attachment Theory

Happiness is an imaginary condition, formerly often attributed by the living to the dead, now usually attributed by adults to children, and by children to adults.
– *Thomas Szasz*

Within the object-relations school, Bowlby first expounded the notion of relationship attachments. Attachment theory looks at the infant's secure and insecure attachments to love objects based on the degree of separation anxiety to which he/she has been exposed (see Chapter 7, Volume 2 – "Fear and Anxiety Disorders").

The secure attachment
A secure attachment to a love object will develop when the child becomes the subject of caring and considerate parenting. A secure attachment to a significant other will develop when the child feels wanted and loved by his/her carers. Responsible parenting will allow the child to develop trusting relationships naturally because he/she will be able to tolerate some degree of anxiety or frustration knowing that sooner or later his/her survival needs will be met by significant others. When the child develops a secure attachment, he/she will then have the confidence to explore, to learn and to develop naturally without any undue degree of anxiety. The child will soon come to realise that life does not simply consist of the instant gratification of his/her needs but that a slightly bumpy ride can be sustained for a limited time period in the confident expectation of a return to the status quo.

The insecure attachment

An insecure attachment to a love object will occur when the child has been regularly neglected, abused or maltreated. The child will, consequently, become anxiety-prone but will have a need to repress his/her anger and frustration. The client will almost certainly experience psychological problems in later life as a result of delayed-grief reactions due to the perceived loss of his/her parent or carer. An insecure attachment will almost inevitably result in relationship problems for the client in that the appropriate separation from primary carers will not have been achieved. An insecure attachment manifested in childhood can also lead to extremes of anxiety, compulsive disorders, dependency states, commitment issues, avoidance behaviour and confusional states for the client.

In the following case-study example, the client was beset by fears of maturity, that stemmed from a perceived maternal abandonment when she was a baby.

Case-study example – fear of relationship commitment

This client had lived with her mother until well into her adulthood. The client's mother was financially secure but was something of a hypochondriac. The client, therefore, pandered to her mother's every whim.

The client reported that she had, however, met a suitable male partner but was fearful of leaving her mother in order to start a life of her own with him. The client protested that her mother might take offence and cut her out of her will. She also claimed that her mother was not physically well enough to be left to fend for herself. Conversely, the client also felt resentment at being confined to her mother's home for life and intrepid at the prospect of fully committing herself to an adult relationship. The client confessed that she was reluctant to be sexually intimate with her new partner because this would signify such a commitment.

When the client was able to explore the fact that her mother had been selfish and possessive towards her for most of her life, the client was able to come to terms with these conflicting issues. The client also examined the early years of her life when her mother had been taken into hospital when she was a baby and had left her in the care of her aunt. The client felt, therefore, that she had been abandoned at a young age and realised how desperate she had been ever since to cling to her mother's apron strings. This realisation freed the client to release herself from her mother's clutches and to start a life of her own.

Client Profiling

The analytical hypnotherapy practitioner may wish to ponder the following points when formulating a profile for the client.

- Does the client tend to regard others as objects or as subjects?
- Has the client formed a subject–object relationship or a subject–subject relationship with the practitioner?
- Has the client moved from regarding the practitioner as an object to considering him/her as a subject during the therapeutic process?
- Has the client identified any love objects or hate objects?
- What distresses has the client experienced that may have resulted in ego splitting?
- Does the client exhibit a tendency towards the paranoid-schizoid position or the depressive position?
- Does the client suffer from states of extreme anxiety with regard to human interaction?
- Does the client tend to withdraw from social interaction?
- Does the client project his/her thoughts and feelings on to others?
- Does the client display manipulative traits or devious tactics when dealing with intimate associates?
- Did the client form a secure attachment or an insecure attachment to his/her primary carers in childhood?

Chapter 6

Client-Centred Therapy

That blessed mood
In which the burden of the mystery,
In which the heavy and the weary weight
Of all this unintelligible world,
Is lightened.

– William Wordsworth

What Is Client-Centred Therapy?

The question of free will has been the subject of human enquiry for
thousands of years. Are we entirely free agents, making all our own
choices, or is what we do somehow determined by factors that are out of
our control? Most of us experience the subjective impression that our
own decisions will determine our behaviour; but at the same time
we recognise that we are influenced by more than just our own
intentions and ideas.
– Nicky Hayes

The main thrust of humanistic psychology is the client-centred
therapeutic approach advocated primarily by Carl Rogers
(1902–1987). Essentially, Rogers contended that the human organism has a fundamental need for personal growth and development
in order to realise its potential, to gain autonomy and to achieve
independence. This doctrine maintains that every individual has
within him/her an intrinsic tendency for *self-actualisation*. Rogers,
therefore, posited that the client will be essentially positive and
resourceful by nature rather than being the innocent victim of what
life has had to offer. This stance was, in fact, a fundamental reaction against the deterministic view of the psychoanalytic body of
thought (see Chapter 1 – "Psychoanalysis").

> The actualising tendency is the single basic motivating drive. It is an
> active process representing the inherent tendency of the organism to
> develop its capabilities in the direction of maintaining, enhancing
> and reproducing itself.
> – *Richard Nelson-Jones*

The humanistic approach recognises that the survivalist instincts
of the client render him/her hungry for a need for approval from
his/her parents, from surrogate parents and from other carers in
order to be able to satisfy his/her basic needs. When the child
recognises that he/she is loved and cherished by his/her parents,
then all will be well. If, however, the child is valued only for
his/her achievements or good behaviour, then a poor sense of self
will manifest. The infant will, therefore, continually evaluate the
effect of his/her actions on significant others and, when he/she
perceives that approval has not been forthcoming, this will, consequently, affect his/her personal self-concept and self-image. If the
child fails to attain his/her basic needs, moreover, he/she may
then interpret this as a reflection of his/her own inability to please
others. The developing child may then become a universal people-
pleaser, may engage only in approval-seeking tactics and may set
for himself/herself unrealistically high self-expectations. This
false existence may, in turn, cause the child to suffer from inner
distress and may bring about a distorted sense of self because
he/she will endeavour to alter his/her personality in a fruitless
attempt to comply with the wishes of those in charge of his/her
upbringing. These tendencies, of course, will automatically be
transported into adulthood.

> If life or therapy gives us favourable conditions of continuing our
> psychological growth, we move on in something of a spiral developing
> an approach to values which partakes of the infant's directness and
> fluidity but goes far beyond him in its richness.
> – *Carl Rogers*

The Philosophy of Client-Centred Therapy

These attitudes are (1) congruence (genuineness, or realness),
(2) unconditional positive regard (acceptance and caring), and
(3) accurate empathetic understanding (an ability to deeply grasp the
subjective world of another person). According to Rogers, if these
attitudes are communicated by the helper, those being helped will
become less defensive and more open to themselves and their world,
and they will behave in social and constructive ways.
– Gerald Corey

The fundamental principle of client-centred therapy will be to enable the client to begin or to continue his/her journey towards person-centred growth and self-actualisation. The therapeutic journey will require that the client make a sound commitment to therapy and take his/her share of the responsibility for his/her own change by facing up to painful recollections and emotions. The activation of self-actualisation will mean that the client can move away from the façade of keeping up appearances, can resist the temptation to uphold a valiant sense of duty and can eschew any self-destructive obligations. The client, furthermore, can then change his/her outlook and not feel obliged to live up to the un-realistic expectations of others. Personal growth for the client will also entail growing towards honesty, integrity and reality with the self, moving towards choice and self-control and attaining self-worth and personal value. The client can engage in valuing the present by acknowledging continued growth, by respecting and understanding others and by achieving intimate and lasting relationships. As the client develops, he/she can become open to new experiences, can indulge in risk taking, can become level-headed, can take personal responsibility and can adhere to an ethical code of living.

The client-centred therapist will have an essential trust in the client's ability to progress in therapy, a belief in his/her inherent potential for growth and self-understanding and a conviction that his/her attitudes and behaviour can be self-directed. The responsibility for the client's therapeutic recovery will fundamentally be in his/her own hands and throughout this process the therapist will merely be a facilitator rather than a leader or a dictator.

Let us now examine the factors that underpin the practice of client-centred therapy. These fundamental principles will be of relevance to the analytical hypnotherapist who may be consulted by the client for a vast spectrum of psychological symptoms and disorders.

> It is this acceptance of both the mature and the immature impulses, of the aggressive and the social attitudes, of the guilt feelings and the positive expressions, which gives the individual an opportunity for the first time in his life to understand himself as he is.
> – *Carl Rogers*

Fostering Empathy

> Empathy is a continuing process whereby the counsellor lays aside her own way of experiencing and perceiving reality, preferring to sense and respond to the experiences and perceptions of her client. This sensing may be intense and enduring with the counsellor actually experiencing her client's thoughts and feelings as powerfully as if they had originated in herself.
> – *Dave Means & Brian Thorne*

The therapist can maximise the success of the therapeutic process by endeavouring to become attuned to the client. When fostering empathy, the practitioner, therefore, should be able to show a natural feeling of warmth towards the client together with an accurate understanding of his/her situation or predicament. The therapist should strive to enter the subjective world of the client in order to be able to understand where he/she is coming from. When such empathy can be fostered, the therapist will then be able to view things from the client's unique perspective. The effect of this approach on the client will be that he/she can become less defensive and more open and, as such, can then be free for meaningful self-exploration. A genuine empathetic resonance may spell success for the therapeutic process, while a weak or nonexistent rapport may result in an impasse for the client.

> Counsellors need to 'get into the shoes of' and 'get under the skin' of their clients to understand their private subjective worlds. They need to be sensitive to the moment by moment flow of experiencing that goes on both in clients and in themselves. They need the capacity to pick up nuances and sense meanings of which clients are scarcely aware.
> – *Richard Nelson-Jones*

Providing Unconditional Positive Regard

> Unconditional positive regard is the label given to the fundamental
> attitude of the person-centred counsellor towards her client. The
> counsellor who holds this attitude deeply values the humanity of her
> client and is not deflected in that valuing by any particular client
> behaviours. The attitude manifests itself in the counsellor's consistent
> acceptance of and enduring warmth towards her client.
> – *Dave Means & Brian Thorne*

In client-centred therapy, the therapist should be instrumental in consistently providing the client with unconditional positive regard in order to enable him/her to release his/her inner self. Rogerian theory holds that the therapist should have absolute respect for the dignity and the integrity of the client. The client should be regarded as a human subject and not as merely an object for treatment. The practitioner should, thus, be able to show a caring nature and a full acceptance of the client. In this setting, the client can then be encouraged to begin the process of self-acceptance. This approach can provide the client with a secure environment in which he/she can learn to be himself/herself without any fear of disapproval. The client should, by this means, be able to maximise his/her chances of finding his/her true self and be empowered to muster the internal resources to do so.

> Given the right facilitative climate, clients will feel less need to be
> defensive and to look for external regard. Though painful at times, they
> may progressively take more risks in disclosing themselves to their
> counsellors. Counsellors who accept clients and prize their rights to be
> their true selves allow them to share parts of themselves that they may
> find embarrassing, abnormal or frightening.
> – *Richard Nelson-Jones*

When the therapist gives value to the client, he/she, in turn, will learn to value himself/herself. Once the client has been shown that it is possible for another person to show him/her a healthy respect, he/she can then begin to ascribe less value to the worthless opinions of others. The client may also begin to realise how presumptuous it will be of one person to attempt to rule the personality of another by judgmental pronouncements or unwarranted criticism. The therapeutic process will, therefore, be designed to shift the client's locus of evaluation away from the ephemeral approbation of others in the external world and turn it inwardly towards a steadfast self-evaluation. The client may, henceforth, begin to engage in constructive interaction with others. The client may gradually learn how to handle departures from the norm, to take up the challenge of initiating change and to make the profound and paradoxical realisation that life may be a continuing struggle in order to gain further personal insight and self-enlightenment.

First, having the hidden and unacceptable parts of themselves understood and accepted dissolves clients' alienation and helps connect them to the human race. Second, being cared for and valued for their true selves allows clients to think "this other individual trusts me, thinks I'm worthwhile. Perhaps I *am* worth something. Perhaps *I* could value *myself*. Perhaps I could care for myself". Third, not being judged by their counsellors may lead clients to judge themselves less harshly, thus gradually increasing the possibility of self-acceptance. Also, as clients gain in self-esteem, they are likely to shift their focus-of-evaluation from other people's standards and beliefs to their own. Thus, they become less vulnerable to the damaging effects of conditions of worth.
– *Richard Nelson-Jones*

Attaining Self-congruence

The more the therapist is himself or herself in a relationship, putting up no professional front or personal façade, the greater is the likelihood that the client will change and grow in a constructive manner.
– *Carl Rogers*

The therapist who achieves psychological self-congruence within his/her own personality will be genuine and free of any façade or pretence in his/her relationship with the client. The therapist should endeavour to show his/her real and genuine self to the client and be devoid of any self-deception and affectation in his/her dealings with him/her. The practitioner's own personal self-congruence will foster an environment in which the client can feel safe and free to explore psychological self-expression. If both the client and the practitioner can be themselves in the therapeutic relationship, then this will set the scene for maximising the client's chances of success in terms of an accurate self-evaluation.

Congruence is the state of being of the counsellor when her outward responses to her client consistently match the inner feelings and sensations which she has in relation to the client.
– *Dave Means & Brian Thorne*

Providing a Nondirective Approach

> When the therapist is experiencing a positive, non-judgmental, accepting
> attitude toward whatever the client is at that moment, therapeutic
> movement or change is more likely.
> – *Carl Rogers*

The aim of a nondirective therapeutic approach will be to enable the client to grow towards becoming a fully functioning and independent individual. This state of being can be achieved by fostering a therapeutic relationship in which the client can be allowed to be himself/herself without the need for pretence or adaptation as a people-pleasing personality. A nondirective and noninterventionist approach can allow the client to discover himself/herself unprompted by the therapist's view. Nondirective therapy will mean that the therapist should endeavour to give no advice, no suggestion, no direction, no persuasion, no teaching, no diagnosis and no interpretation. This therapeutic approach will be based on the principle of putting the client in a position whereby he/she can allow his/her true nature to emerge.

Client-centred therapy will emphasise the role of the client in the therapeutic encounter rather than the position of the therapist. The client's actualising process should not be prompted by or interfered with by the views of the practitioner. The therapist must, therefore, remain neutral in his/her dealings with the client in order to prevent any imposition of his/her personal wishes. The therapeutic setting should be a permissive climate in which the practitioner merely reflects or clarifies the client's own views and, in doing so, permits him/her to express himself/herself freely. The practitioner's beliefs and thoughts will be of no consequence and no advantage to the client, who is, in fact, the only person who can make the appropriate personal choices.

Providing Nonjudgmental Therapy

> The therapist senses accurately the feelings and personal meanings that
> the client is experiencing and communicates this acceptant
> understanding to the client.
> – *Carl Rogers*

The practitioner should be totally nonjudgmental in all his/her dealings with the client. The therapist should, therefore, aim to be devoid of all personal criticism of the client. Whatever the client voices should be received with equanimity and merely acknowledged in order to ensure that the therapeutic climate will be conducive for the client to reveal all (see Chapter 17 – "The Case for Therapy").

It has been widely acknowledged, of course, that it is arrogant for one person to judge another, because a pronouncement cannot possibly be made on the basis of hearsay or intuition. The person making the judgment, consequently, can never be certain of being in possession of all the relevant facts. In therapy, moreover, where the client may reveal much in the way of personal guilt-provoking information, the same premise obtains but, in fact, even more so. In analytical therapy, particularly, the practitioner should withhold judgment when the client reveals some form of obvious misdemeanour and should wait in order to identify what prompted his/her action. If the client discloses violence or abuse against another person, for example, it would be the practitioner's place to help that client to appreciate why such action was taken. In such circumstances, the therapist could, if anything, appear to condone the client's behaviour in the interests of giving him/her permission to reveal more information in an unhampered manner. This would be a consciously taken decision on the therapist's part, therefore, as a guilt-relieving strategy for the client (see Chapter 8, Volume 2 – "Guilt and Shame Disorders"). What can be said is that the therapist will be acting purposefully in the interests of the client while he/she cathartically confesses to his/her unconsciously-motivated behaviour.

Any judgment will, in all respects, be misplaced because the therapist cannot possibly pinpoint the depth of severity of the client's actions precisely. An angry client, for example, may express unconsciously-driven behaviour by, at one end of the spectrum, hitting a wall or kicking the cat or, at the other, by committing gratuitous violence (see Chapter 10, Volume 2 – "Anger and Rage Disorders"). This expression of anger could, therefore, be on a continuum and it might be purely chance that dictates how such uncontrollable rage may manifest itself from the client's perspective. Society tends to criticise overt violence but its root may emanate from the same source as a childish temper tantrum. If the therapist reserves judgment, he/she may be assisting the client to alleviate the underlying guilt, fears and emotional suppression that uphold his/her violent tendencies. In handling the client in this way, the practitioner, therefore, may be indirectly serving society as well as furthering the wellbeing of the client. External judgment and criticism from significant others may, in fact, be the very reason why the client has sought therapy. Often the client may have been the victim of harsh criticism during childhood and will have suffered from this misuse of parental authority. If the clinician criticises or judges the client, therefore, he/she may be inadvertently taking on the parental role. However tempting the prospect of being the judge and the jury may be, the therapist should steadfastly endeavour neither to approve nor to disapprove of the client's behaviours, but merely become a witness to life in general. The therapist who may experience difficulties in this area might be advised to seek supervisory guidance without delay.

> Today I will judge nothing that occurs.
> *– Gerald Jampolsky*

Client-Centred Therapy Concepts

> A central part of the humanistic approach is the human capacity for positive personal growth and change. Human beings are not just passive victims of circumstances, or of early experiences: instead, the humanists argued, human beings strive to develop themselves, and to fulfil their potential. The problems occur when that striving is frustrated, because human beings have a deep-seated need to learn new things, to make their own choices, and to be in control of their own behaviour.
> *– Nicky Hayes*

Many of the concepts within the humanistic approach of client-centred therapy are concerned with the needs of the client and what can be the result when such needs remain unsatisfied. The process of self-actualisation may be hindered when the child puts priority on the needs of others in an attempt to ensure that his/her own basic needs in life will be met. Let us now consider, in general, the needs of the human organism as a way of understanding the client's inner functioning.

The Hierarchy of Needs

> The goal of identity (self-actualisation, autonomy, individuation, Horney's real self, authenticity, etc.) seems to be simultaneously an end-goal in itself, and also a transitional goal, a rite of passage, a step along the path to the transcendence of identity.
> – *Abraham Maslow*

Abraham Maslow (1908–1970), who contributed much to the debate on humanistic doctrines, spoke of a hierarchy of human needs, that culminates in self-actualisation in the psychologically healthy person. Maslow emphasised that self-actualisation is a continuing goal towards which the human organism will strive. Once the goal of self-actualisation comes within reach, the client will then be able fully to enjoy pleasurable peak experiences in life.

Maslow also regarded the therapeutic process as one in which the client will change from having to fulfil *deficiency needs* (D-needs) to being able to achieve existential growth needs or *being needs*

Figure 2: The Humanistic Hierarchy of Needs

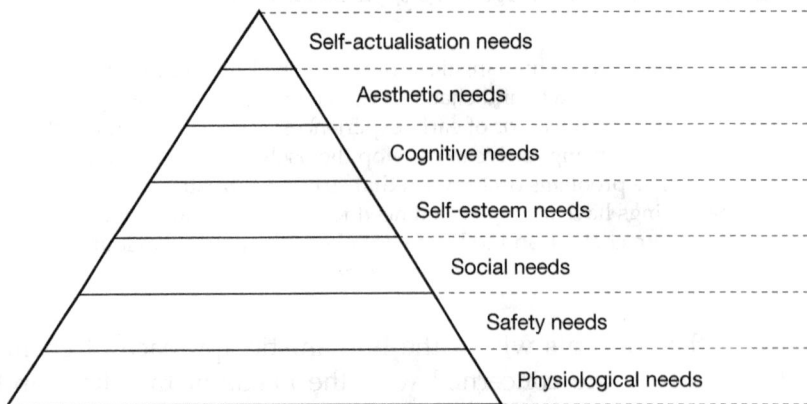

Self-actualisation needs
Aesthetic needs
Cognitive needs
Self-esteem needs
Social needs
Safety needs
Physiological needs

(B-needs). Deficiency needs will aim to replenish those commodities that the client may lack such as safety, love, respect, self-esteem and the need to belong. Once these needs have been satisfied, then the client can turn towards pursuing being needs, that will motivate him/her to strive for self-actualisation. Maslow devised a pyramidal or hierarchical structure of human needs in order to illustrate that, once the client's survivalist requirements have been met, he/she can then progress towards striving for his/her higher needs (see Figure 2: "The humanistic hierarchy of needs").

> These basic cognitive happenings in the B-love experience, parental experience, the mystic, or oceanic, or nature experience, the aesthetic perception, the creative moment, the therapeutic or intellectual insight, the orgasmic experience, certain forms of athletic fulfilment, etc., these and other moments of highest happiness and fulfilment I shall call the peak-experiences.
> *– Abraham Maslow*

Physiological needs

> Ongoing actualisation of potentials, capacities and talents, as fulfilment of mission (or call, fate, destiny, or vocation), as a fuller knowledge of, and acceptance of, the person's own intrinsic nature, is an unceasing trend toward unity, integration or synergy within the person.
> *– Abraham Maslow*

First in the hierarchy comes man's basic instinctual and physiological needs, that are to satisfy hunger, to quench thirst, to breathe, to find shelter and to reproduce. The caveman first needed to obtain food and water in order to fuel his body, to maintain a body temperature that would sustain life and then to ensure the survival of the species by reproduction. A dying person, for example, will be preoccupied with satisfying his/her basic physiological needs in his/her fight for survival rather than worrying about whether the gas bill has been paid or the goldfish has been fed.

Safety needs

> Safety is a more proponent, or stronger, more pressing, more vital need
> than love, for instance, and the need for food is usually stronger than
> either. Furthermore, all these needs may be considered to be simply
> steps along the path to general self-actualisation, under which all basic
> needs can be subsumed.
> – *Abraham Maslow*

Next, the client will have a need for safety, security and protection from harm in the form of stability and freedom from fear and anxiety. The client, furthermore, may have an earnest desire for an acceptable life structure and freedom from chaos, and a need for the imposition of law and order, that can be enforced in a civilised society. The caveman needed to ensure that he and his family were safe from attacks by wild beasts or unwelcome predators. In times of natural disaster, the need for safety from malicious or fatal attack will often outweigh man's need for other forms of comfort. When the office building is on fire, for example, the fleeing staff do not worry too much about turning the computers off or drawing lots to decide who is next to make the tea.

Social needs

> General illness of the personality is seen as any falling short of growth,
> or of self-actualisation, or of full-humanness. And the main source of
> illness (although not the only one) is seen as frustrations (of the basic
> needs, of the B-values, of idiosyncratic potentials, of expression of the
> self, and of the tendency of the person to grow in his own style and at
> his own pace) especially in the early years of life.
> – *Abraham Maslow*

The client's social needs appear next in line, once his/her physiological and safety needs have been established. The client will have a need for love, for affection, for a feeling of belonging, for acceptance and for friendship in his/her social settings. Once the caveman had attained his food and shelter, he then sought the additional security and comfort of the social group. This afforded him additional protection and peace of mind, owing to the safety-in-numbers factor. Both the caveman and modern man are intrinsically social animals for this reason.

Self-esteem needs

> Self-actualisation is defined in various ways but a solid core of
> agreement is perceptible. All definitions accept or imply, (a) acceptance
> and expression of the inner core or self, i.e. actualisation of these latent
> capacities, and potentialities, "full functioning", availability of the
> human and personal essence, (b) they all imply minimal presence of ill
> health, neurosis, psychosis, of loss or diminution of the basic human and
> personal capacities.
> – *Abraham Maslow*

Next, the client will have a need for self-esteem and for ego
strength. These needs will encompass the desire for self-respect
and autonomy and the ability to attain life goals. Such achievements also bring the client much-sought-after personal status,
recognition, dignity and attention from others. Once social group-
ing has become the norm, man's role within the group may then
take on a new dimension. A competitive or a submissive attitude,
for example, may be called for according to the client's allotted
place within the group (see Chapter 3 – "Individual Psychology").

Cognitive needs

> Control, will, caution, self-criticism, measure, deliberateness are the
> brakes upon this expression made intrinsically necessary by the laws of
> the social and natural worlds outside the psychic world, and secondly
> made necessary by fear of the psyche itself.
> – *Abraham Maslow*

The client will also have a need for intellectual stimulation. The
client will have a desire for curiosity and for exploration and this
will often be manifested in terms of a quest for learning in order to
extend his/her intellectual powers. Sometimes the client will
search for the meaning of life and may endeavour to understand
his/her purpose in the great scheme of things. The client may,
moreover, have a need to reduce tedium to a minimum in order to
be fully stimulated both at work and at play. Man, as a survivor,
will often need to be naturally curious in order to be able to
explore the unknown, to carry out research in order to conquer ill
health or to control his/her environment. A desire for intellectual
understanding, of course, will aid the survival process in that man
can learn to appreciate his environment and can discover ways of
conquering any difficulties and any obstacles that may arise.

Aesthetic needs

> A musician must make music, an artist must paint, a poet must write, if
> he is to be ultimately at peace with himself. What a man can be,
> he must be.
> – *Abraham Maslow*

The client will also have a need for pleasurable and aesthetic stimulation. People frequently desire to behold the beauty and the majesty of art, culture and nature and will have a requirement for order and symmetry in order to counteract chaos. Man is essentially an unremitting, fun-loving and hedonistic sybarite who looks for luxury and comfort in his environment.

Self-actualisation needs

> Maslow saw "self-actualisation" at the peak of a hierarchy of needs,
> whilst Rogers talked about the actualising tendency, an intrinsic
> property of life, reflecting the desire to grow, develop and enhance our
> capacities. A fully functioning person is the ideal of growth. Personality
> development naturally moves towards healthy growth, unless it is
> blocked by external factors, and should be considered the norm.
> – *Richard Gross & Rob McIlveen*

Finally, the client will have an inherent need for self-actualisation so that he/she may be able to be what he/she wants to be. Success and the accumulation of wealth, for example, will not bring happiness in its wake if the client is not fulfilled in other ways. The client will have to fulfil his/her own aspirations and to attain his/her own destiny in order to be able to satisfy the greatest need of all – the intrinsic need for self-actualisation. Self-actualisation will empower the client to move towards autonomy and individuation, to restore his/her true self, to have a positive self-regard, to relieve tension and conflict, to be creative and resourceful, to attain life goals, to fulfil his/her potential, to exert free will, to exercise choice and to aspire to peak experiences. Self-actualisation has been variously described as a working towards unity, a striving for individuality and a quest for freedom and spontaneous expression. This will mean that the client can free himself/herself from the fetters of the past and, in doing so, can find his/her own natural self. This restoration process can be accomplished by the client who takes a self-directional and constructive growth path towards change and wholeness. The client may constantly feel that he/she needs to strive in order to achieve a purpose, to realise potential, to attain ambitions, to expand horizons and to improve his/her life circumstances in order to become a complete and satisfied person. Before this maturation can occur, of course, all other basic needs must be fully met. When all other needs have been satiated – as in those modern societies that are free from hunger, deprivation, war and anarchy – the client will naturally seek self-realisation, insight and self-fulfilment. It may be at this juncture that the sophisticated individual will seek to better his/her lot by a process of self-searching, often initiated in therapy.

The client-centred philosophy upholds the view that the self-actualising inclination will be inherent within the client because his/her primary need will be to seek experiences that are consistent with his/her self-concept. This will mean that, if the client believes something about himself/herself or about his/her capabilities, then he/she will live life within that framework. If the client believes himself/herself to be successful and capable, for instance, then he/she will realise that lifestyle. If the client believes that he/she cannot succeed or that he/she is inadequate or ill-equipped, on the other hand, then this disposition will prevail. The client, in addition, may then have a secondary need for a positive regard from others and for positive self-evaluation based on the opinions of others.

Supporters of the humanistic doctrine subscribe to the notion that the client has free will and personal choice, that can manifest itself in a number of ways when he/she seeks to satisfy human needs. Sometimes the client may be motivated by anxiety and tension or by survival needs and drives. Sometimes the client will be creative and display pleasure-seeking tendencies. Sometimes the client may believe that he/she has a mandate to fulfil an inherent potential. The point at issue here will be that the client can be subjected to a constantly reinventive process whereby movement can be continually accompanied by struggle as the essence of life. Client-centred therapy, therefore, will encourage the client to take full responsibility for his/her own self-determination. The client will start the process of self-discovery and self-awareness by encountering aspects of his/her own reality and by discovering ways in which to realise his/her own potential. The client can then identify ways of modifying his/her behaviour in order to utilise his/her capabilities and to maximise his/her own potential.

> Rogers describes people who are becoming increasingly actualised as having (1) an openness to experience, (2) a trust in themselves, (3) an internal source of evaluation, and (4) a willingness to continue growing. Encouraging these characteristics is the basic goal of person-centred therapy.
> *– Gerald Corey*

The Organismic Self

> A poor self concept and countless internalised conditions of worth are typical attributes of clients coming for counselling. Such people are cut off from their essential resources as human beings and divorced from the real self or their *organismic self* as it is generally referred to in the person-centred tradition.
> *– Dave Means & Brian Thorne*

The child, who cannot fend for himself/herself, will sacrifice his/her own needs in order to keep favour with significant others who, in turn, will, hopefully, ensure that his/her basic needs are met. In making these instinctive adjustments, the child will be forced to sacrifice that true natural part of the human organism known as the organismic self. The child's true self will be the unconscious underlying part of his/her personality, that will be unique and trustworthy and will have growth potential. The client's organismic self in childhood will have become distorted, corrupted or, even, temporarily obliterated in order to acquire value in the eyes of significant others. The child, by this primitive means, will endeavour to avoid the penalty of rejection and abandonment. Parental regard will, therefore, inevitably be conditional and, for this reason, the child will adopt the values desired by his/her parents and other carers in order to acquire acceptable conditions of self-worth.

The human organism will be instinctively able to detect what it needs. The body will know when the organism is hungry, thirsty, needs rest or requires exercise. The mind, too, can tell a person when to venture forth or when to withdraw, when to acquire a friend or when to steer clear of an enemy. The mind will always know what is right for the human organism and how to act accordingly. When it comes to obtaining positive regard, the child will, however, deny or sacrifice his/her true self in order to ensure that he/she can please significant others. The child will instinctively know that the carer's acceptance or approval of him/her will be crucial to his/her survival. It will be as if the child has been pro-grammed to be one person but he/she will reprogram himself/herself automatically in order to become a conformist people-pleaser and, in doing so, can ensure his/her acceptability in society. During the early years of life, the child will soon start to realise that his/her survival will hinge on the way in which he/she is perceived by his/her primary carers. The child can deduce that the love and attention that he/she receives from his/her parents will be conditional upon his/her good behaviour, obedience and compliance with their wishes. The commodity of unconditional love, therefore, will seem barely attainable for the vulnerable child. External experiences that the child will undergo may be unconsciously perceived as threatening and he/she will, of course, have little unconscious discrimination between what is, in fact, right and wrong in terms of ethical behaviour. The client, thus, will tend to make adjustments to his/her true organismic personality by being what his/her primary carers would like him/her to be or by behaving in the ways in which he/she believes they will approve in the absence of a better alternative. Hence the locus of the client's self-evaluation will be invested in the external world and not in himself/herself.

The child will also develop a means of reality-testing by assessing his/her actions in terms of either success or failure. If the child's actions tend to please others, then he/she will record a success rating. If, on the other hand, the child's actions tend not to meet with external approval, then he/she may view such actions as a failure in the social climate. It will, of course, be this failure-rating from which the client will tend to form a poor self-concept. When conflicting messages of success and failure are received by the child, conflict will arise in his/her psyche – conflict between the real self and the organismic self. It will be this lack of reconciliation between the distorted self and the organismic self that the client-centred therapeutic process will seek to address. The corruption of the organismic self will lead to a form of denial of the client's own reality. This, in turn, will engender confusion and tension within the child's psyche and, from this position, maladaptive behaviours will be generated. The client will then perceive the world as a threatening place and his/her perceptions will shape his/her behaviours. A vicious cycle may now become entrenched whereby the client will find that his/her maladaptive behaviours are unacceptable both to himself/herself and to others, and this will, of course, further debase his/her already meagre self-concept.

> By taking over the conceptions of others as our own, we lose contact
> with the potential wisdom of our own functioning, and lose confidence
> in ourselves.
> – Carl Rogers

Self-concept

> The self-concept develops over time and is heavily dependent on the
> attitudes of those who constitute the individual's significant others. It
> follows that where a person is surrounded by those who are quick to
> condemn or punish (however subtly) the behaviour which emanates
> from the experiencing of the real self, he or she will become
> rapidly confused.
> – Brain Thorne

Client-centred theory looks in depth at the concept that the client has of himself/herself, how this was acquired and what effect a poor self-concept will have on his/her psychological health.

> The experiencing organism senses one meaning in experience, but the
> conscious self clings rigidly to another, since that is the way it has found
> love and acceptance.
> – Carl Rogers

The child who has been summarily condemned, harshly punished, censored, misjudged, put down, neglected, ignored or abused will almost inevitably develop a poor self-concept. If severe limitations or inhibitions are placed on the child's freedom, then this, too, will engender a poor sense of self-worth. Often the child's poor self-concept will develop as a result of his/her having been brought up by others who, similarly, have a poor self-opinion. A poor sense of self will lead the client to develop a low self-esteem, a low self-image, a mistrust of his/her own judgment and a lack of self-identification. Often the client may also be a poor decision maker because of his/her reluctance to trust his/her own thoughts and feelings. The client's self-concept will have been developed when he/she gauges the approval or disapproval that he/she receives from others. If the client has been well received, then a good self-concept will emerge. If the client cannot obtain approval or finds it an illusive commodity, then his/her self-image will be dented accordingly and he/she will develop a low self-regard.

The child's self-concept will be based on his/her perceived conditions of self-worth acquired from his/her parents and from significant others throughout childhood. The client's self-concept will develop as he/she tries to mould himself/herself into the map of the conditions of self-worth that he/she perceives are imposed upon him/her by significant others. The client's sense of self will develop though his/her personal perception of experiences, through interaction with others and by becoming aware of his/her own being and functioning. The client's unconsciously generated self-concept will be based on social evaluation because of his/her need for approval and formed through introjected beliefs, judgments, attitudes and the values of others. Because the client may have a desperate need for approval, this can mean that his/her self-concept will become virtually indestructible and he/she will perpetually need to fulfil the contracts that he/she has devised for himself/herself. The maladjusted client, therefore, may be defensive, may endeavour to maintain the status quo in life and may avoid seeking life-enhancing activities. This client may also have a preconceived life plan, may constantly feel manipulated and may frequently conform to, obey and comply reluctantly with the wishes of others.

What is meant by such phrases as "psychotherapeutic change", "constructive personality change"? This problem also deserves deep and serious consideration, but for the moment let me suggest a commonsense type of meaning upon which we can perhaps agree for purposes of this paper. By these phrases is meant: change in the personality structure of the individual, at both surface and deeper levels, in a direction which clinicians would agree means greater integration, less internal conflict, more energy utilisable for effective living; change in behaviour away from behaviours generally regarded as immature and toward behaviours regarded as mature.

– *Carl Rogers*

The Fully-Functioning Self

> The implication is that therapy is more than "adjustment to norms", and
> this approach does not stop with merely solving problems. Instead,
> practitioners with a humanistic orientation aim at challenging their
> clients to make changes that will lead to living fully and authentically,
> with the realisation that this kind of existence demands a continuing
> struggle. People never arrive at a final or a static state of being self-
> actualised; rather, at best they are continually involved in the process of
> actualising themselves.
> – *Gerald Corey*

With client-centred therapy, the client should aim to realise
his/her unique and trustworthy, fully functioning self with its
inherent growth potential. The fully functioning true self will be
the client's underlying personality without a superimposed,
people-pleasing, survivalist programme. This will result in psychological freedom for the client that will mean that he/she can
have a positive self-regard and can also gain positive regard from
others. This situation can then lead the client to a healthy, organismic self-evaluation that, in turn, will make him/her congruent
with his/her own experiences.

The fully functioning self will develop when the client regards
himself/herself as acceptable principally from his/her own opinion and, incidentally, in the eyes of others about him/her. When
the client's self-concept has improved and his/her true self has
been revealed, then his/her value in the eyes of the world will, as
a matter of course, increase. There will, thus, develop a degree of
congruence between the client's view of himself/herself and
his/her perceptions and experiences. The fully functioning client
can then utilise his/her unique talents and abilities and can realise
his/her own potential. The client will not feel threatened by others, will be empowered to trust his/her own experiences, can be
creative and intuitive and can make independent choices. The
client, furthermore, will not be imprisoned by circumstances, fate
or convention and will not be manacled by the past. The client
should aim for a satisfactory life as a continually-evolving process
rather than a state of being and should endeavour to regard life's
journey as a direction and not a destination. Full psychological
adjustment will mean that the client can be open to new experi-

ences, can trust his/her own organismic evaluation and will regard others as equals.

> To be psychically ill is therefore to have been injured in one's primal integrity, to be a person whose original self-congruence has been traumatised. In such a person the ability to live consciously and function fully is impaired.
> – *Konrad Stettbacher*

In the case-study example given below, let us consider the way in which the client was beset by a people-pleasing inclination that was stultifying her existence.

Case-study example – overbearing responsibility
This female client complained of having too much responsibility and bemoaned the fact that her family and friends were not supportive.

The client reported that her husband and her two daughters did nothing to help her in the running of the household despite the fact that she had a full-time job. The client also admitted that she was a perfectionist in terms of providing meals and doing the ironing and, therefore, was reluctant to delegate these tasks. The client, furthermore, found herself listening to the troubles of other relatives and friends and this was also impinging upon her precious time resources. Finally, the client confessed that she had no time to devote to herself and had not been able to take up a place on a pottery evening class because of the calls on her time.

The client was invited to consider her childhood environment. She told of the way in which her parents had expected her to do well at school and yet she had failed them. The client spoke of ways in which she had been bullied at school and of how this continual worry had impaired her concentration when she was studying for examinations. The client, thus, had received pressure from both home and school and was trapped by being unable to talk of her difficulties with her dismissive parents. Once the client had acknowledged that her mother had not been there for her as a supportive listener, she was able to see her life in perspective. For example, the client realised that her parents had made her vulnerable to being bullied at school and yet had not been able to help her when this situation had occurred. The client, moreover, realised that her parents had given her conditional love, and she was then able to express her resentment and sadness at this major flaw in her childhood development.

Client Profiling

The analytical hypnotherapy practitioner may wish to ponder the following points when formulating a profile for the client.

- Can the client feel that he/she is the most important person in the therapeutic environment?
- Can the client feel sure that the therapist has an unshakeable trust in his/her ability to progress in therapy?
- In what ways has true empathy been fostered with the client in therapy?
- Has the client's progress been, in any way, hampered by a judgmental stance taken by the practitioner?
- Is the client able to obtain self-congruence from the practitioner's example?
- Is the client embracing self-actualisation as part of his/her therapeutic journey?
- In what ways has the client's organismic self been distorted in childhood?
- In what ways has the client's self-concept been damaged by his/her life-experiences?
- What survivalist tactics might the client have employed during his/her childhood?
- What form of pretence or façade has the client tended to maintain in the past?
- What needs does the client have for safety and personal security?
- What needs does the client have in terms of social interaction?
- In what ways has the client aspired to peak experiences?

Chapter 7

Existential Therapy

Always, Sir, set a high value on spontaneous kindness. He whose inclination prompts him to cultivate your friendship of his own accord, will love you more than one whom you have been at pains to attach to you.

– Samuel Johnson

What Is Existential Therapy?

The basic dimensions of the human condition, according to the existential approach, include (1) the capacity for self-awareness; (2) freedom and responsibility; (3) creating one's own identity and establishing meaningful relationships with others; (4) the search for meaning, purpose, values, and goals; (5) anxiety as a condition of living; and (6) awareness of death and non-being.
– Gerald Corey

Existentialism is a philosophical approach to the therapeutic encounter in which the client will examine his/her freedom of choice in making the most of life's circumstances. The existentialist will believe that the client is responsible for all his/her own choices and actions in life and that he/she can be the architect of his/her own destiny rather than being a helpless victim of circumstances. The client can be free to choose the way in which he/she interprets events either by making the most of opportunities or by giving way to despair and inevitability.

The existential approach – based on the work of Viktor Frankl (1905–1997), Rollo May (1909–1994) and Ronald Laing (1927–1989) – will encourage the client to reflect on his/her life, to recognise those options that are available to him/her and then to act accordingly. The therapist will invite the client to identify the ways in which he/she has relinquished control of his/her life or has passively accepted unpleasant events as being inevitable. This philosophical stance will allow the client to evaluate his/her own existence and to search for the meaning in his/her life. Life can be put into a fresh perspective in the therapeutic context when the client keeps an open and enquiring mind about those things that life has thrown at him/her.

Existential therapy is, of course, a phenomenological approach, that delves into the subjective world of the client in order to identify areas for personal growth. The existentialist will acknowledge that expansion can be a painful process and that the client must leave behind the illusory security of the past in order to attain the goal of self-development. The existential persuasion will, therefore, entail a process of identifying the client's defensive strategies that serve to prevent him/her from confronting realistic limitations and existential guilt (see Chapter 11 – "Defensive Strategies"). The client will also be encouraged to remove wishful thinking and, in so doing, to pave the way for productive decision-making about his/her own destiny. Existential therapy puts the responsibility for the client's recovery solely on his/her own shoulders. It is, after all, the client who must decide to enter therapy, to undergo the process and to marshal the necessary internal resources in order to pull himself/herself through his/her difficulties. The existential approach can be extremely valuable in empowering the client to relinquish the trauma of the past and to consign it to its appropriate place of insignificance.

> The existential approach is first and foremost philosophical. It is concerned with the understanding of people's position in the world and with the clarification of what it means to be alive. It is also committed to exploring these questions with a receptive attitude, rather than with a dogmatic one. The aim is to search for truth with an open mind and an attitude of wonder rather than fitting the client into pre-established frameworks of interpretation.
> – *Emmy van Deurzen-Smith*

The Philosophy of Existential Therapy

> A truly scientific psychology must treat its subject matter as fully
> human, which means acknowledging individuals as interpreters of
> themselves and their world. Behaviour, therefore, must be understood in
> terms of the individual's *subjective experience,* from the perspective of the
> actor (a *phenomenological* approach, which explains why this is
> sometimes the "humanistic-phenomenological" approach). This
> contrasts with the *positivist* approach (of the natural sciences) which tries
> to study people from the position of a detached observer. Only the
> individual can explain the meaning of a particular behaviour and is the
> "expert" – not the investigator or therapist.
> *– Richard Gross & Rob McIlveen*

The philosophy of the existential approach to therapy will focus
on the deeper meanings of life in terms of those challenges that life
has to offer and the ways in which the client can rise to and be
inspired by such challenges.

Personal Challenges

> Existential therapy seeks to take clients out of their rigid grooves and to
> challenge their narrow and compulsive trends, which are blocking their
> freedom. Although this process gives individuals a sense of release and
> increased autonomy, the new freedom does bring about anxiety.
> Freedom is a venture down new pathways, and there is no certainty
> about where these paths will lead.
> *– Gerald Corey*

The existential practitioner will observe that the client is continually engaged in an internal struggle with personal challenges, that
confront him/her regularly in a constantly changing world. The
main challenges that will be presented to the client will be to find
the meaning and purpose of life, to cope with ill-health and psychological suffering, to undertake an occupation or other form of
work activity and to pursue love. The client's existence can never
be fixed because he/she will continually be re-creating himself/
herself through activities that will always be in a state of flux, evolution, transition and emergence. The client's future, moreover,
can never be predicted, although it can be shaped by his/her own
active participation in life. Other life challenges that the existential
approach will advocate are that the client should come to terms
with issues such as death, freedom, isolation and meaninglessness.

In facing life's challenges, the client can relinquish self-deception and face up to his/her own limitations.

Existential choices may mean that the client will need to forgo the security of being dependent on others and so face the anxiety of having to make his/her own decisions. This psychological U-turn may, then, mean that the client will need to self-affirm rather than to seek approval from others. This stance, in turn, may entail inviting the client to change his/her viewpoints and reactions and to find an alternative way of organising his/her life. This change of direction may involve encouraging the client to reshape the future rather than being condemned to abide by the past. This may entail inviting the client to think about living rather than being preoccupied with dying or decaying. This important transition may, therefore, mean that the client must accept that he/she can sometimes be imperfect and can occasionally feel somewhat unworthy. This may, then, mean that the client must live in the present and relish current circumstances rather than live with the regrets and bitterness associated with the past or the dreams and fantasies of the future. This may, furthermore, mean that the fruits of the client's aspirations do not come to him/her instantly but must be built up gradually before finally coming to fruition. All such realisations will form the client's growing and blossoming self-awareness.

Existential therapy will aim to empower the client to have the courage to face the real world, to struggle with life's problems and to uphold the core of his/her being. Sometimes, for the client, the world will be a frightening place when he/she has to stand on his/her own two feet without the support of others. It will be as if the client were afraid of himself/herself because he/she has never had to decide, to think, to calculate or to act alone.

> That which does not kill me makes me stronger.
> – *Friedrich Nietzsche*

Existential Propositions

He who has a why to live for can bear with almost any how.
– Friedrich Nietzsche

The existential philosophy puts forward a number of propositions that the client can be invited to realise in the therapeutic context. These existential propositions cover questions of self-awareness, freedom of choice, personal responsibilities, the meaning of life and the client's unique purpose within the scheme of things.

Self-awareness

As human beings we can reflect and make choices because we are capable of self-awareness. The greater our awareness, the greater our possibilities for freedom.
– Gerald Corey

Existential philosophy postulates that the client will be constantly striving to expand his/her general awareness and, in particular, his/her self-awareness. To obtain self-awareness, the client will need to accept that he/she has certain personal rights and can be free to make his/her own choices unaided by others. Because the client's time on this planet will not be unlimited, he/she can choose either action or inaction in order to shape his/her own destiny. This can be achieved when the client discovers his/her own unique purpose, increases his/her personal choices, develops his/her sense of responsibility and seizes opportunities to relate to others and to the world about him/her. Existential psychotherapy will, of course, acknowledge that the client may be subject to feelings of loneliness, isolation, meaninglessness, emptiness and guilt. It will be, however, by a growing self-awareness of such feelings that the client can overcome any negative inclinations and can put himself/herself on the right path in life. The client, therefore, will be encouraged to take the decision to expand his/her self-awareness as the fundamental pivot of the human capacity.

Freedom and responsibility

A characteristic theme of existential literature is that people are free to choose among alternatives and therefore have a large role in shaping

their destinies. Even though we have no choice about being thrust into
the world, the manner in which we live and what we become are the
result of our choices. Because of the reality of this essential freedom, we
must accept the responsibility for directing our lives.
– Gerald Corey

Existential freedom will be created when the client can accept that
he/she is responsible for his/her own destiny by choosing from
the alternatives available to him/her. The client may elect to
believe that he/she cannot control events because of past encum-
brances but can be encouraged by the therapist to relinquish such
negatively fatalistic beliefs. In adopting this policy, the client will
take responsibility for his/her own actions or for his/her own failure to act. A commitment, therefore, to taking his/her own decisions and acting upon them will be the basis for beneficial change
in the client.

Identity and relationships

People are concerned about preserving their uniqueness and
centredness, yet at the same time they have an interest in going outside
of themselves to relate to other beings and to nature.
– Gerald Corey

Existential theory claims that life is a voyage of self-discovery
rather than an inevitable process that the client needs to endure.
The client can shape his/her own identity by relating to others and
to the world about him/her by simply giving of himself/herself.
The client can strive to relate and connect to others in a meaningful way. If the client fails to achieve this state, he/she will almost
certainly experience feelings of loneliness, isolation and alienation
because of a lack of stability and a dearth of reference points. The
client, therefore, may soon realise that he/she may have spent all
his/her childhood and most of his/her adult life attempting to live
according to the expectations of significant others. The client may,
for example, have learned to rely too heavily on others in order to
resolve problems and to provide the answers in life. The client
may also have been directed exclusively by others and, in consequence, may have learned not to trust his/her own inclinations
and inner resources in order to overcome personal conflicts in life.
The client, however, can move away from regarding others as
merely objects who can assist him/her and can move towards hav-

ing a healthy regard and a respect for others as separate individuals. The client, thus, can move from fostering object relationships (or I–It relationships) to developing subject relationships (or I–Thou relationships) in line with object-relations theory (see Chapter 5 – "Object-Relations Psychology").

The therapeutic process in existential philosophy will begin by allowing the client to identify the introjection that he/she has obtained from his/her parents and to muster the courage to relinquish it in order to find his/her own true self and to stand alone and unaided in the world (see Chapter 11 – "Defensive Strategies"). As the client begins to find his/her singular identity, he/she will be in a much better position to form fulfilling relationships from a position of internal strength.

Existential meanings

A distinctly human characteristic is the struggle for a sense of significance and purpose in life. In my experience the underlying conflicts that bring people into counselling and therapy are centred in the existential questions "Why am I here? What do I want from life? What gives my life purpose? Where is the source of meaning for me in life?"
– *Gerald Corey*

The existential client can be invited to explore the meaning of life as part of the therapeutic process known as *logotherapy*. The client may be asked to question whether he/she is content with current circumstances, whether he/she enjoys his/her occupation and whether the direction in which he/she is moving is, in fact, appropriate for him/her. During this process, the client may choose to discard old beliefs, values and attitudes and to substitute those that are more in keeping with his/her veritable requirements. The existential therapist will encourage the client to re-evaluate all aspects of his/her life and to make changes accordingly. In making such adjustments, the client can develop the confidence to trust that what he/she is actually doing is truly in keeping with his/her own inner sense of values.

Within logotherapy, the concept of the *will to meaning* comes into operation. Creating a meaning in life will be an important motivator for the client who will be breaking away from past conditioning and who will wish to avoid entering a vacuum. The existential practitioner will, therefore, steer the client towards an engagement in life so that he/she can take an active part in seeking and shaping his/her own destiny. This engagement in life will be the client's commitment to creating opportunities, to forming loving relationships, to working and to building on his/her achievements.

Existential anxiety and guilt

> Anxiety, arising from one's personal strivings to survive and to maintain and assert one's being, must be confronted as an inevitable part of the human condition. Existential therapists differentiate between normal and neurotic anxiety, and they see anxiety as a potential source of growth.
> – *Gerald Corey*

The client's existential anxieties and feelings of guilt will be explored during the therapeutic process in order to expose him/her to his/her innermost fears.

Existential anxiety may be classified as either *normal anxiety* or *neurotic anxiety*. Normal anxiety will be an appropriate response to change and, in existential terms, can become a conscious motivator in itself for this client. It can be said that a certain amount of normal existential anxiety can provide a healthy balance between complacency and challenge. Neurotic anxiety, conversely, will be an unconscious force that will be an irrational, over-the-top response to circumstances and events on the client's part. The client can endeavour to reduce neurotic anxiety by facing up to his/her negative emotions and thoughts under therapeutic guidance. Neurotic anxiety, of course, may represent the client's feelings of uncertainty about confronting his/her inner psychic distress and about relying solely on his/her own resources.

Existential theory also speaks of *normal* and *neurotic* forms of guilt as a product of psychological distress. Normal guilt will engender ethical behaviour and will create a responsible individual. Neurotic guilt, on the other hand, will manifest when the client magnifies his/her feelings of wrongdoing. Often the client will imagine that he/she has grievously sinned against his/her parents, friends or colleagues, or against society. Perhaps the client will believe that he/she has failed to live up to what is expected of him/her or has somehow failed to realise his/her own potential.

Often the client will distort reality by imagining what others require of him/her and then undergo the anguish of not delivering the goods.

Death

> The existentialist does not view death negatively but holds that awareness of death as a basic human condition gives significance to living. A distinguishing human characteristic is the ability to grasp the reality of the future and the inevitability of death. It is necessary to think about death if we are to think significantly about life.
> – *Gerald Corey*

The existentialist will maintain that acknowledging the inevitability of death can give richness and significance to the client's life. If the client can accept the inevitability of death, then he/she will be facing reality and can live to the full in the present. It can be the very prospect of life as being of limited duration that can serve to motivate the client into taking action and taking responsibility in a creatively beneficial manner.

Existential Therapy Concepts

> The existential approach considers human nature to be open-minded, flexible and capable of an enormous range of experience.
> – *Emmy van Deurzen-Smith*

The existential philosophy observes the client from a holistic viewpoint and as a product of his/her environment. Existential thinking will, therefore, look at the client as a physical, social, psychological and spiritual being who has been the product of his/her upbringing. We shall now consider some concepts on which the existential premise has been founded.

Existential Dimensions

Because the client can be considered to be in a constantly evolving state, existential therapy will reflect on the levels of experience in which he/she has been involved and the way in which he/she views these past experiences. The client's life experiences will be described as existential dimensions in existential parlance and the human organism can be considered to have a physical, a social, a psychological and a spiritual dimension to his/her existence.

The physical dimension

> On the physical dimension (*Unwelt*) we relate to our environment and to the givens of the natural world around us. This includes attitude to the body we have, to the concrete surroundings we find ourselves in, to the climate and the weather, to objects and material possessions, to health and illness and to our own mortality.
> – *Emmy van Deurzen-Smith*

The physical dimension will relate to the way in which the client perceives himself/herself in the material world in terms of his/her physical being and his/her possessions. The physical dimension encompasses the client's personal body-image and his/her attitudes to health and to ill-health. How aware is the client, for instance, of his/her biological needs, his/her drives and his/her instincts, that are subject to daily cycles? Sometimes the client will find himself/herself struggling with these elements by attempting to keep himself/herself fit or by adhering to a healthy diet. The client may need to come to terms with contradictions such as the extent or the limitation of his/her own physiological capabilities.

This dimension will also consider the value that the client places on possessions and wealth. How does the client, for instance, view those things that give him/her the illusion of that very unstable commodity known as security? Does the client struggle to amass possessions or to accumulate outward appearances of wealth in a vain attempt at grasping security?

The social dimension

> On the social dimension (*Mitwelt*) we relate to others as we interact with the public world around us. This dimension includes our response to the culture we live in, as well as to the class and race we belong to (and also those we do not belong to).
> – *Emmy van Deurzen-Smith*

The social dimension will encompass the way in which the client can relate to others. Does the client, for example, interact more successfully on a one-to-one basis or with groups of individuals? The social dimension will embrace cultural traditions and attitudes and the way in which the client will react to such entrenched convention. Sometimes the client may feel rejected by or isolated from society, and this can either prompt him/her to withdraw from company or can motivate him/her to make an extra effort to be accepted and welcomed by society.

Society can also depict the client's public face and outward image. Does the client wish to follow the crowd or become a trendsetter? Does the client wish to keep up appearances at any price or play the social game at any cost? Does the client wish to acquire power and fame? Can the client's public image be upheld, or will it be easily shattered – and how will he/she react to these opposing elements? How can the client, therefore, reconcile the contradictions of acceptance or rejection and the juxtaposition of success or failure in his/her life?

The psychological dimension

> On the psychological dimension (*Eigenwelt*) we relate to ourselves and in this way create a personal world. This dimension includes views about our character, our past experience and our future possibilities.
> – *Emmy van Deurzen-Smith*

The psychological dimension will embrace the way in which the client can relate to himself/herself by creating a unique identity. What does the client think of himself/herself? How does the client conceive of his/her past? What aspirations does the client have for the future? What personal meaning does the client attach to things or to people with whom he/she is in regular contact?

The client may need to come to terms with his/her own personal strengths as well as any inherent weaknesses, with his/her activity or inactivity when participating in life and with the inevitable realisation that death will eventually destroy him/her. It will be as if self-awareness can become self-consciousness according to the client's concept of whether he/she is important and valuable or whether he/she is unimportant and worthless. For the client who feels indispensable, it may be that coming to terms with death will be a great struggle.

The spiritual dimension

> On the spiritual dimension (*Ueberwelt*) we relate to the unknown and
> thus create a sense of an ideal world, an ideology and a philosophical
> outlook. It is here that we find meaning by putting all the pieces of the
> puzzle together for ourselves.
> – *Emmy van Deurzen-Smith*

The spiritual dimension will be concerned with ideology and philosophy. This dimension will relate to those aspects of the client's
existence that have an unknown quality about them. Does the
client wish, for instance, to follow a religious path or a spiritual
teaching because it can give greater meaning to his/her existence?
Does the client wish to adopt a value system that will give a purpose to his/her actions? The client, inevitably, will need to come to
terms with contradictions such as hope or despair, significance or
void and validity or meaninglessness.

Ontological Security and Insecurity

> Existentialist theory argues that if we are fully to understand human
> existence, we also need to understand the choices which we make.
> Existentialists see people as being directly responsible for their life-
> choices, on the grounds that we are always free to say "no" and take the
> consequences.
> – *Nicky Hayes*

The concept of ontological security and insecurity – put forth by
Ronald Laing – will be a means of explaining the ways in which
the client's family history will have affected him/her. If the client's
life history has been nurturing and positive, then he/she will feel
ontological security – or family-oriented security – and will have a
good sense of identity and purpose. If the client's life history, on
the other hand, has been one of disturbance, owing to his/her having been reared in a dysfunctional family environment, then
he/she will feel ontological insecurity. A malfunctioning family
environment will trap the child in an ontological double bind –
perhaps by making him/her a scapegoat. The child will have been
placed in a victim role in the dysfunctional family setting,
whereby whatever steps he/she took would have been wrong in
someone's eyes and there would inevitably have been no means of
escape. The ontologically insecure client will, therefore, feel that
he/she faces several kinds of psychological threat. The client,

however, can choose to face these threats in the therapeutic context and can endeavour to break free of the significance that such an oppressive tyranny has exerted on him/her in the past. Let us now examine the types of ontological threats from which the client may have suffered as outlined in existential philosophy.

> Anyone who has had the opportunity to observe how a baby responds
> to its experiences will understand just how sensitive he or she
> actually is.
> – *Michael Kern*

Engulfment
A feeling of engulfment will occur when the child in the family setting fears becoming overwhelmed or swamped by the circumstances in which he/she finds himself/herself. This burden of being overwhelmed, then, will become so unbearable that psychological disturbance will result in the adult.

Implosion
A feeling of implosion will occur when the child in the family environment feels an emptiness due to the fact that he/she has been unable to formulate any concept of himself/herself. The client will then continually question his/her identity and his/her place in the world.

Petrification
A feeling of petrification will occur when the child becomes petrified of other family members and powerless to interact with significant others on an equal basis. The client will then be unable to act assertively when faced with demands or requests from others. The client, for example, may feel unable to decline even an impossible request and may prostrate himself/herself in the service of others. The client, thus, can be easily manipulated and downtrodden because of his/her inability to be assertive against the demands of others. This will be the people-pleaser syndrome taken to its extremes.

Depersonalisation
The feeling of depersonalisation will occur when the child becomes a kind of psychological automaton in the family circle in that his/her true self will become so heavily disguised that it appears to be nonexistent. Usually, depersonalisation will occur when the threat of engulfment, implosion and petrification have been an inevitable consequence of the child's upbringing or family circumstances. It will be as if the child felt so threatened that he/she could not safely be himself/herself and, therefore, psychologically lost sight of the way in which the real self could act. Here there will be a discrepancy between the client's inner world and his/her outer world whereby the inner self will remain obscure while the outer self will take command of the personality. This manifestation will, of course, be the basis of a severe psychotic disturbance of the personality, that will usually be outside the province of the analytical hypnotherapist.

Let us now turn to a case-study example that will serve to illustrate the way in which a client can become the product of a dysfunctional upbringing.

Case-study example – worry and anxiety
This female client entered therapy because she had a surfeit of anxiety and was prone to continual worrying. The client spoke at length about the ways in which merely travelling to work, doing the shopping and standing in queues could reduce her to a quivering wreck.

When the client spoke of her childhood, however, she discovered that her beloved father's frequent absence from home had caused her to question her existence. The client revealed that her father had left home without notice on several occasions in order to live with his mistress and that she was never sure when he would return. The client was told little about the situation by either her mother or her father and was, therefore, left to sit and wait in the hope of his return. The client described a vivid scene in which she was sitting on the stairs and feeling the anxiety and worry that she now experienced in adult life. Gently the client was invited to comfort herself as a young child in order to allay the child's fears of the unknown and fears of being abandoned by the parent whom she adored. By comforting the inner child and explaining the situation to her younger self, the client was then able to reconcile her conflicts and the uncertainty that had manifested in early life.

Client Profiling

The analytical hypnotherapy practitioner may wish to ponder the following points when formulating a profile for the client.

- Does the client take a philosophical approach to his/her journey through life?
- Is the client able to delve into his/her subjective world and to view it realistically?
- Is the client able to take up the challenge of undergoing therapy?
- Has the client identified his/her purpose in life?
- Is the client realistically self-aware?
- Has the client accepted that he/she can be the author of his/her own destiny?
- Does the client continually live his/her life according to the expectations of others?
- Does the client feel unable to make a move without the approval of significant others?
- Does the client consider that to stand on his/her own two feet would be an admission of failure?
- Does the client dread isolation, loneliness and personal rejection?
- Does the client suffer from the searing pangs of anxiety and guilt as a result of his/her childhood upbringing?
- How does the client view his/her standing in the social world?
- How does the client regard himself/herself in terms of his/her psychological and spiritual development?
- Has the client become stultified by his/her childhood upbringing?
- Has the client become terrified of displeasing or offending his/her parents?
- In what ways have the client's family members manipulated or distorted his/her personality?

Chapter 8

Gestalt Therapy

O how full of briers is this working-day world!

– *William Shakespeare*

What Is Gestalt Therapy?

Gestalt therapy, a powerful synthesis of differing ideas and outlooks, has
a central idea that human beings are in constant development. Our life
situations are always evolving and we do not exist independently from
the surrounding "field". The person is not regarded as a fixed,
categorizable entity but as an exploring, adapting, self-reflecting,
interacting social and physical being in a process of continuous change,
evolving throughout life towards greater maturity.
– *Malcolm Parlett & Judith Hemming*

Gestalt therapy has its roots in the psychological laws of gestaltian
perception and cognition. Gestaltian psychologists originally studied perception in order to discover the ways in which the individual attributes meaning to his/her experiences. Gestaltian concepts
identify the laws of perception that operate according to principles
of similarity, proximity, closed shapes or figures and nonfragmen-
tation of sensory stimuli. Gestaltian philosophy embraces the concept of figure-and-ground perception, whereby the client will have
a tendency to organise his/her sensory images by seeing figures or
shapes in the foreground against what lies behind it in the background in order to interpret what he/she perceives. From these
concepts, Fritz Perls (1893–1970) developed gestalt therapy that
has been based on the client's concept of awareness of experiences
and his/her perception of whole units of experience known as
gestalts. Gestalt therapy can be said to be a humanistic therapy but
with its roots in psychoanalysis, in that it is a phenomenological
approach that strongly adheres to a holistic doctrine and views the

client as a meaningful part of his/her environment. Gestalt therapy also has leanings towards transpersonal philosophies which appreciate that the client has a meaningful and purposeful soul.

The gestalt therapist will regard any state of distress or distortion as a *dis-ease* in the organism or a growth disorder rather than an inherent weakness or flaw in the client. The task of the gestalt therapist, therefore, will be to facilitate the reduction of impediments to the client's self-growth, self-actualisation and self-regulation rather than to concentrate on symptom removal. The gestalt therapist will imbue the client with self-deterministic qualities by regarding him/her as proactive rather than reactive in relation to his/her environment and will endeavour to make him/her aware of these intrinsic qualities. In keeping with humanistic doctrine, gestalt therapy acknowledges the ways in which the client can be affected by his/her experiences and that his/her recovery process may be an extremely painful one. Gestaltian theory dissects the ways in which the client will have been affected both at the time of the originating incident that caused disturbance and subsequently. Gestalt therapy, therefore, will enable the client to re-experience his/her distress or his/her traumatic past and then to appreciate the ways in which his/her personality, behaviours and motivations have been shaped accordingly.

> When people are "dis-eased" they are not experiencing themselves as whole persons in psychological and physiological relationships with their environment. They are not effectively going through the awareness cycle with ease, grace and efficiency.
> – *Petrüska Clarkson*

The Philosophy of Gestalt Therapy

> We can think of each gestalt having a life-cycle of its own. Whether it is a street encounter, or having a baby, or taking an exam, or making a complaint, there are discernible phases in how the cycle unfolds; and they relate to both energy and time.
> – *Malcolm Parlett & Judith Hemming*

The philosophy behind gestaltian thinking hinges on the fact that the client's life experience and awareness will have an effect on him/her according to whether his/her experiences have been completed or have remained fragmented. The gestalt therapist will be interested in enabling the client to complete those experiences that have left him/her with unfinished business and with an incomplete resolution of events in life.

The Gestalt Cycle

> The gestalt can be a faithful representation of an actual event or it can just as easily be a rendering consisting of unrelated data from several different events – in other words, a mosaic. This is why eye-witnesses often give surprisingly different descriptions of the same incident.
> *– Peter Levine*

A gestalt cycle of experience will be one in which the client will actively construct, organise and finally complete a meaningful experience. This can be achieved by completing a cycle that will take the client through a number of stages from initial awareness of a need that requires satisfaction to a state of equilibrium once that need has been satisfied. The satisfaction of hunger, for example, may start with a physiological change in the body, followed by a conscious awareness of hunger, followed by a decision to have a meal, that will prompt the client's action, and then culminate in the preparation of that meal and, finally, its consumption and digestion. The next gestalt may arise when a need to take a short nap or to go out to play is activated within the client. The client may have many and varied needs according to his/her priorities within the humanistic hierarchy of needs from those of survival to that of self-actualisation (see Chapter 6 – "Client-Centred Therapy"). The client's needs may, for instance, be survivalist in nature in order to satisfy hunger or thirst. The client may also have material needs for comfort, wealth and convenience. The client will, of course, have emotive needs for love, attention and harmony as well as spiritual needs for artistic pleasure or a peaceful existence.

A healthy gestalt cycle will flow uninterruptedly and fluently from a gestalt formation to its ultimate destruction – each stage being discrete but barely delineated. A gestalt will be an inherent life force akin to the human breathing cycle of inhalation and exhalation. Each stage will become a focal point of awareness and/or a concentration of energy in order to ensure that the client can pass harmoniously from one stage to the next. Contained within the idea of the gestalt cycle of awareness will be the concept of connecting

Figure 3: The Gestalt Cycle of Experience

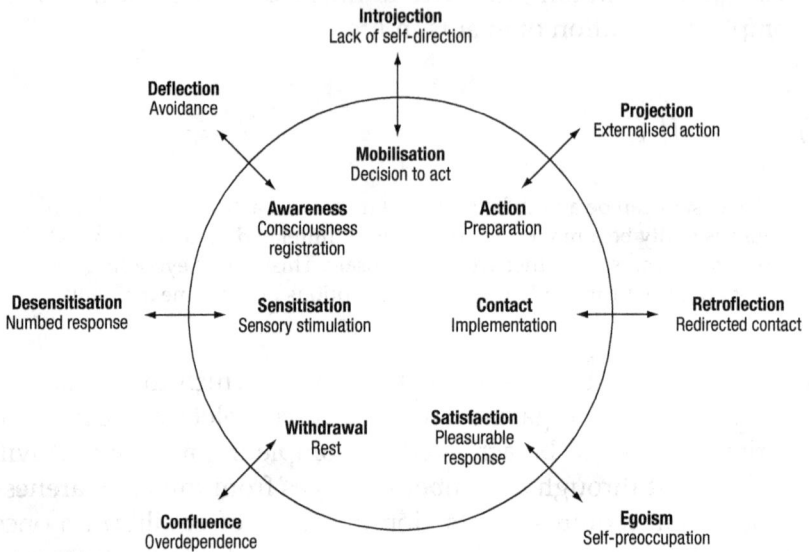

with the boundary between the self and the environment. The concept of a contact boundary will indicate that the client may elect either to make contact or to fail to make contact with his/her surroundings and circumstances. If a gestalt cycle is interrupted, however, the client will suffer distress and psychological disturbance because the cycle will have been completed only in a distorted or unsatisfactory manner and his/her need will not have been satisfied. The client will, therefore, develop disturbances or interferences when he/she fails to connect with the contact boundary that will lead to the formation of defensive strategies and this, in turn, will hamper self-actualisation (see Chapter 11 – "Defensive Strategies"). We shall now consider the various stages of the gestalt cycle of experience and awareness and look at ways in which the client may have left unresolved his/her cycles of experience (see Figure 3: "The gestalt cycle of experience").

> The basic tendency of every organism is to strive for balance. The organism is continually faced with imbalance that is disturbing through either external (demands from the environment) or internal (needs) factors. Life is characterised by a continuous interplay of balance and imbalance in the organism. Homeostasis or organismic self-regulation is the process by which the organism satisfies its needs by restoring balance when faced with demand or need which upsets its equilibrium.
> – *Richard Nelson-Jones*

Sensitisation or desensitisation

> The organism (or person) cannot remain at rest for an indefinite period.
> New organismic deficits or surpluses must arise in the living person.
> Either internal or external disturbances in the form of a living need
> which is striving for gratification or a demand made upon us will
> impinge upon the homeostatic balance of organism and environment.
> – *Petrüska Clarkson*

At the *sensitisation* stage, the client's sensory organs will be stimulated in order to enable the human brain to receive the stimuli. This may be an internal excitation such as hunger or fear or an external registration of sensory awareness such as a reprimand from a colleague or a feeling of warmth. The client's autonomic nervous system may, for example, prepare him/her to receive food or to begin the alarm response when an external threat has been posed.

A failure at the sensitisation point of the cycle can result in *desensitisation*, whereby the client will shut off or nullify his/her reactions to internal stimuli or external provocation. The client may, thus, be minimising sensation by numbing himself/herself and/or denying his/her experiences by diluting, diffusing or disregarding his/her cognition, emotive responses and sensory impressions. Does the client in need of food, for example, deny his/her hunger pangs or simply not have an appetite? Does the client who should feel afraid in the face of danger simply not react appropriately?

> In "desensitisation", the neurotic avoids experiencing himself or the
> environment. The concentrating self feels anaesthetised and deadened.
> This is where sensations and feelings of the self are diluted, disregarded
> or even neglected.
> – *Petrüska Clarkson*

Awareness or deflection

> We may gradually or suddenly become aware of any of these events
> impinging sensorily or proprioceptively on our free-floating
> consciousness.
> – *Petrüska Clarkson*

At the *awareness* stage, the client will bring the experience into conscious awareness. The experience now can become a focal point of attention for the client and, to a greater or lesser extent, the need to take appropriate action in order to satisfy the need will become apparent. The client may now feel the pangs of hunger approaching or may feel the effects of fear or uncertainty once an awareness of threat has been consciously registered.

A breakdown at the awareness stage can result in *deflection*, that will reduce the impact of the client's awareness. Deflection will be the act of turning away from involvement in life and from interaction with others by avoiding sensation or meaningful impact. Does the client, for example, attempt to distract himself/herself from the thought of food? Does the client hoodwink himself/herself into believing that he/she will be brave when the threat looms closer?

> "Deflection" means to turn aside from direct contact with another person. It is a way of reducing one's awareness of (the impact of) environmental contact, making it vague, generalised or bland.
> – *Petrüska Clarkson*

Mobilisation or introjection

> Awareness of a need is usually followed by excitement and mobilisation of self and resources. At this state of emotional and/or physiological arousal the object-figure or need becomes sharper and clearer, generating energy and images of possibilities for satisfaction.
> – *Petrüska Clarkson*

The *mobilisation* stage will occur when the client elects to take action as a result of his/her excitation. The client's body will be prompted to react or will be rendered in a state of readiness for movement and energy will be generated. When the client's emotions have been mobilised, he/she may also envisage possibilities of satisfaction. The hungry client may now contemplate preparing a meal or the threatened client may now begin to shake, sweat or jump to his/her feet in readiness for action.

An interference in the cycle at the mobilisation stage can result in *introjection*. Introjection will occur when the client absorbs the values and attributes of others and imprints these within his/her own personality. Introjection will usually lead to a lack of self-direction and self-regulation. Will the hungry client, for example, now state that he/she is on a diet and feel virtuous for declining sustenance?

Will the client confronted with threat now announce that he/she is a helpless victim of circumstances or then chastise others for feelings of fear? Perhaps this client may also expect someone else to feed him/her or to protect him/her from perceived harm.

> "Introjection" is the initial mechanism by which we take in food, ideas and rules from significant others in our environment.
> – *Petrüska Clarkson*

Action or projection

> Another punctuation point in the process of contact (or figure formation) as a single whole can be identified as the "contacting" phase of choosing and implementing appropriate action.
> – *Petrüska Clarkson*

At the *action* stage, the client will elect to implement the appropriate action by marshalling perceptual, behavioural and emotional resources. Here the client may transit a decision-making or problem-solving process in order to bring the satisfaction of his/her needs to fruition. This will be the reaching-out stage, whereby the client will have a clear aim in view and will be prepared to overcome any obstacles to its fulfilment. The hungry client may now set about preparing a meal or going out to a restaurant. The threatened client may decide to stay put, to flee or to fight off the threat to his/her person or self-image.

Disturbance at the action stage of the cycle can lead the client to forgo action in favour of *projection*. The client may attribute to others those qualities that he/she cannot yet recognise in himself/herself. A positive projection may mean that the client will see good qualities or attributes in others, yet will not acknowledge such qualities in himself/herself. A negative projection may mean that the client will accuse others of rejection or selfishness when, in fact, he/she fears being rejected or displaying selfish traits. A negative projection may also confine the client to a tyranny of rules and restrictive or stifling behaviour. Does the client who has declined food, for instance, then castigate other dieters for a lack of self-control or criticise others for greed? Does the fear-stricken client admire courageous qualities in others or scoff at such recklessness?

> Projection can be used in healthy and constructive ways in planning or anticipating future situations. All kinds of creativity involve some projection of the self into the work of the imagination. Sometimes people see fine qualities such as honesty or intelligence in others without being able to acknowledge that they already possess these qualities too.
> – *Petrüska Clarkson*

Contact or retroflection

> Choosing and implementing the appropriate action based on energetic consideration of the possibilities, both in reality and in imagination, is naturally followed by full and vibrant contact or what Goodman called "final contact".
> – *Petrüska Clarkson*

At the *contact* stage, the client will implement his/her chosen action either in reality or in imagination. Contact may involve sensory-motor functioning, interaction with others, engagement of memories, visualisation and full emotional expression. The contact stage will be the high point in the cycle when the client will be able to experience the process to the fullest extent of his/her capabilities. The hungry client may now eat his/her meal with relish while the threatened client may contact his innermost fears and react accordingly.

If the client fails to make contact at this stage in the cycle, the result can be *retroflection*. Retroflection will occur when the client undertakes activities for others – usually of a caring and comforting nature – that he/she would secretly like others to do unto him/her. Often the client who overcares for others in a self-sacrificial manner will be indulging in retroflection. The danger for this client may be to develop tendencies that can be grossly inconvenient for him/her to such an extent that he/she will put the needs of others before his/her own. Retroflection will, therefore, be a form of aggression and castigation turned inward because the client will help others when he/she should, in fact, be helping himself/herself. Alternatively, retroflective action may mean that the client will be excessively attentive to himself/herself by wallowing in self-pity or restrictive self-indulgence. Does the dieter finally start to binge-eat or to resort to near-total starvation? Does the anxious client form a society to assist the underprivileged, putting in hours of work for those in need and so neglecting his/her own needs?

> People may learn to retroflect when their feelings and thoughts are not
> validated in their families of origin or when they are punished for the
> expression of the natural impulses.
> – *Petrüska Clarkson*

Satisfaction or egoism

> The next identifiable phase is that which Perls et al called post-contact. It
> refers essentially to satisfaction and Gestalt completion. This is the phase
> where the person experiences deep organismic satisfaction, and can be
> compared to the "afterglow" following full and complete experiences of
> intimacy or creative expression.
> – *Petrüska Clarkson*

At the *satisfaction* stage, the client will derive pleasure from the fulfilment of his/her needs, having provided the human organism with gratification. This will be the lull-after-the-storm phase, when the client will be bathed in the glory of his/her achievement. This post-contact stage will imply that the aim of forming the gestalt has been completed satisfactorily. The client who has just eaten his/her meal may feel the warm glow of comfort while the fearful client may rest and feel relief after his/her ordeal.

If the cycle is broken at the satisfaction stage, the client may indulge in *egoism*. The egotist will be consumed by his/her own self-importance and will be preoccupied with his/her own needs to the exclusion of others. Egoistic qualities also generate an emptiness in the personality and a possible isolation from others. Usually the desire for control that will be exhibited by the egotist will result in a lack of spontaneity and a consequent tempering of participation in life. Does the dieter really feel virtuous or does he/she have that empty feeling inside? Does the supposedly brave client actually feel relief or invulnerability even when he/she boasts proudly of a possession of such qualities?

> "Egotism" in Gestalt is characterised by the individual stepping outside
> of himself and becoming a spectator or a commentator on himself and
> his relationship with the environment. This neurotic mechanism gets in
> the way of effective action to get one's needs met, and disturbs the good
> contact with the environment.
> – *Petrüska Clarkson*

Withdrawal or confluence

> In this resting phase the person can be balanced or centred between
> Gestalt formation and destruction. There is no clear figure and the
> organism is in a state of homeostasis or perfect balance – it's neither too
> hot nor too cold; the person is neither in a state of sexual excitation nor
> in a state of sexual deprivation; neither anxious nor excited.
> – *Petrüska Clarkson*

The *withdrawal* phase will be the resting stage at which the human organism will return to the homeostatic state in readiness for the formation of the next gestalt experience. This will be the neutral transitional state when one gestalt has been completed and the client can make ready to start another cycle once more. The client who has satisfied his/her appetite or confronted and dealt with his/her fear can now rest and regenerate resources in readiness to face a different aspect of life.

When the withdrawal phase has been interrupted, the client may experience *confluence*. Confluence will be a dysfunctional closeness or an overdependence on others. This emotional blurring of boundaries in relationships will mean that the client will lose some of his/her own identity in his/her desire to merge with others. Inherent within confluence will also be the tendency to shun decision-making and self-sufficiency. The dieter may now complain about his/her eating disorders or the timid client may now become overly dependent on others for support and guidance.

> "Confluence" is the condition where organism and environment are not
> differentiated from each other. The boundaries are blurred as between
> the foetus and the mother. Two individuals merge with one another's
> beliefs, attitudes or feelings without recognising the boundaries between
> them and the ways in which they are different.
> – *Petrüska Clarkson*

Gestalt Therapy Concepts

Fundamental to gestaltian philosophy is the concept of unfinished business, whereby the client has left unresolved or unattended those aspects of his/her past experience that need to be addressed before harmony and balance can prevail. Gestalt therapy, therefore, will seek to investigate the client's incomplete experiences and the disturbance that such experiences have created with a view to resolving the past and freeing him/her to concentrate on the present.

Unfinished Business

> The idea of "unfinished business" is a core notion in the Gestalt approach to explain how energy becomes blocked or "interrupted". It refers to the fact that the only constant flow is the forming of "Gestalten" – wholes, completeness, or organic units. Every urge or need which arises drives us to do something to complete the organismic cycle.
> *– Petrüska Clarkson*

Unfinished business will arise when the client's gestalts have largely been ill-formed, distorted or completed unsatisfactorily under stressful conditions. Because human energy will have been expended but then regained in the successful completion of a gestalt, an incomplete gestalt, conversely, will drain the client's precious energy resources. This energy deficiency will interfere with the formation of new gestalts that will, consequently, have a knock-on effect by inhibiting the client's functioning as a whole. If the client has been subjected to situations or to events in which experiences have been left incomplete in some way, he/she will be likely to experience psychological disturbance.

The gestalt therapist will endeavour to enable the client to re-experience gestalts to the fullest extent and to complete mal-formed gestalts by becoming aware of his/her past experiences. As disturbance may arise on many levels – psychological, affec-tive, cognitive or behavioural – the practitioner will aim to bring about closure of gestalts on all these levels. In this way, the client's emotional problems, psychosomatic ailments, irrational thinking processes and maladaptive behavioural traits can be altered or rec-tified during the therapeutic process. On the emotional front, unfinished business can relate to unexpressed or unacknowledged emotions resulting from a fear of abandonment or rejection (see Chapter 7, Volume 2 – "Fear and Anxiety Disorders"). The practi-tioner will encourage the client to acknowledge and to fully express subdued feelings about the past that are often related to memories and fantasies. From the psychosomatic viewpoint, the client may also have found alternative physiological outlets for unfinished business that have resulted in somatisation and conversion symptoms (see Chapter 11, Volume 2 – "Psychosomatic Disorders"). Maladaptive reactions or immature behaviours, similarly, may be displayed by the distressed client who has unfinished business. The client may also harbour resentment about the past and this resentment may build up into a well of guilt-provoking debris that will permeate his/her every thought (see Chapter 8, Volume 2 – "Guilt and Shame Disorders").

A surfeit of unfinished business may cause an *impasse* or *stuck-point* of frustration within the client. This can then mean that the client will have a tendency to manipulate others or to manipulate his/her environment in order to satisfy unquenched needs. The client may indulge, for example, in negative role-playing or portray a self-distorting quality that can impair his/her enjoyment of life. The client may come to understand that an impasse will block his/her personal growth but that such impasses can be challenged in therapy. Dealing with unfinished business can bring about valuable personal insight for the client – a theme central to the gestaltian philosophy. Gestaltists believe that gaining insight will lead the client towards restoring balance and harmony in his/her existence through total self-acceptance. Insight will allow the client to gain an awareness of his/her environment, to experience the richness in life and to interact rewardingly with others. The client can also learn to appreciate that he/she alone should be responsible for his/her own choices in life and that control can, in fact, remain in his/her own hands. The client can also learn to focus on the here and now in order to appreciate the opulence of every moment of current experience rather than being dragged down by the past.

> Unfinished business represents an incomplete Gestalt. However, the completion of wholes is such a rudimentary fact of human nature that human beings *do* complete them even if in a warped, distorted or pathological way.
> – *Petrüska Clarkson*

Avoidance

> A concept related to unfinished business is avoidance, which refers to
> the means people use to keep themselves from facing unfinished
> business and from experiencing the uncomfortable emotions associated
> with unfinished situations. Because we have a tendency to avoid
> confronting and fully experiencing our anxiety, grief, guilt, and other
> uncomfortable emotions, the emotions become a nagging undercurrent
> that prevents us from being fully alive.
> – *Gerald Corey*

Gestaltists acknowledge that the client will want to avoid dealing
with dis-ease and psychological disturbance. The therapist will
appreciate that the client may wish to avoid uncomfortable emotions and will do this, for example, by making excuses and by
resorting to a fantasy world. Gestalt therapists will speak of several layers of disturbance through which the client may pass –
some or all of which may be experienced in order to avoid
unfinished business. Gestaltists use the analogy of peeling an
onion when discarding the various layers in order to reveal the
client's true self beneath the shields (see Figure 4: "Gestalt layers
of avoidance").

Figure 4: Gestalt Layers of Avoidance

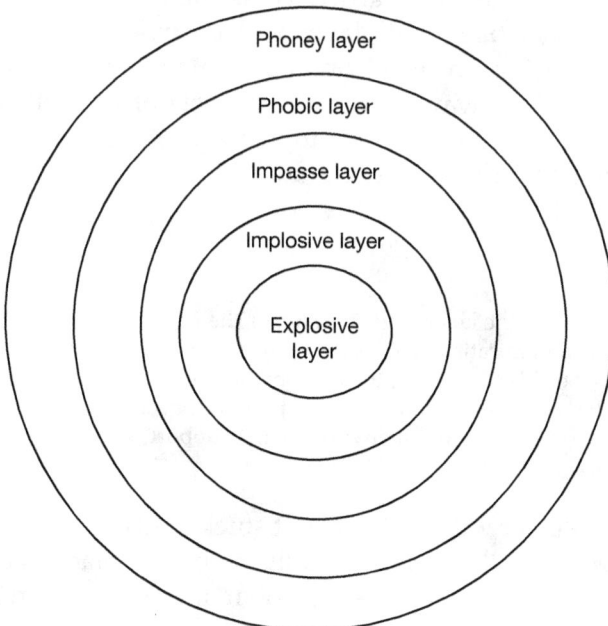

The phoney layer

> The first layer we encounter, the *phoney layer*, consists of reacting to others in stereotypical and inauthentic ways. This is the level where we play games and get lost in roles. By behaving *as if* we were a person that we are not, we are trying to live up to a fantasy that we or others have created.
> – Gerald Corey

The phoney layer will depict the client's stereotypical and inauthentic roles that he/she has adopted in society. Often the client will try to live up to a self-created fantasy or to live with a self-image that he/she believes others will require of him/her. The client may act out a role by assuming behaviour appropriate to that role. This will be a kind of game-playing in a social context that will get out of hand and will take over the major part of the client's personality.

The phobic layer

> The next layer we encounter is the *phobic layer*. At this level we attempt to avoid the emotional pain that is associated with seeing aspects of ourselves that we would prefer to deny.
> – Gerald Corey

The phobic layer can be regarded as the client's meagre attempt to avoid emotional pain. This layer will provide the client with a means of focusing on misattributed elements of himself/herself and can become a way of denying aspects of the self. Here the client will display a resistance to self-acceptance, a fear of self-recognition and a dread of rejection.

The impasse layer

> Beneath the phobic layer is the *impasse*, or the point where we are stuck in our own maturation. This is the point at which we are sure that we will not be able to survive, for we convince ourselves that we do not have the resources within ourselves to move beyond the stuck point without environmental support.
> – Gerald Corey

The impasse layer will see the client stuck in his/her own maturation process. This layer will usually be put in place because the client will be unsure of his/her own internal resources when dealing with progression to the next phase of his/her life. Because avoidance will normally be a defensive strategy for the client, that will be employed in order to help him/her to survive, relinquishing avoidance tactics will be an intrepid step for him/her (see Chapter 11 – "Defensive Strategies"). In preserving the impasse layer, the client will usually manipulate his/her environment in order to shield himself/herself from any perceived distress. The client, for instance, may expect others to see, hear, feel and think for him/her and may gain some form of solace from this protection. The impasse layer will usually also generate a sense of deadness and a hopelessness that the client may feel compelled to resolve when seeking therapy.

The implosive layer

> If we allow ourselves to fully experience our deadness, rather than denying it or running away, the *implosive level* comes into being. Perls writes that it is necessary to go through this implosive layer in order to get to the authentic state.
> – Gerald Corey

The implosive layer will be peeled off when the client finally elects not to deny his/her pain and not to run away from suffering any more. When this layer has been shed, the client will expose his/her defences, will make contact with his/her numbed side and will begin to abandon inauthentic traits and roles. Here the client will be contacting his/her genuine self, may become reflective and may begin to gain valuable insight.

The explosive layer

> When we contact the explosive layer, we let go of phoney roles and pretences, and we release a tremendous amount of energy that we have been holding in by pretending to be who we are not.
> – Gerald Corey

The explosive layer will be the time for letting go. The client can now let go of phoney roles and pretences, can release energy, can become alive and authentic. It will be as if the client has exploded into a realm of both pain and joy when anguish has been released and the ecstasy of psychological freedom takes its rightful place. Life for the client can now become enriched and joyous because of the pain and suffering that he/she has resolved successfully. The client will have earned for himself/herself a licence to live life to the full through self-discovery and honesty.

The following case-study example will serve to illustrate the way in which the client can pass through the various layers of avoidance in order to complete unfinished business when undertaking therapy.

Case-study example – erectile dysfunction

This client sought therapy in order to cure his embarrassing problem of sexual dysfunction at an age when he would normally be able to perform perfectly satisfactorily with a new and exciting partner.

The client reported that he had been impotent when he had been unhappily married but that he had now entered a new relationship that was entirely satisfactory and, therefore, he wanted to overcome his sexual dysfunction. The client assured the therapist that he strongly desired to form a new relationship and that no pressure was being put on him to perform by his new partner. The client, of course, admitted to being embarrassed about his problem but had not bothered to seek therapy until he had found a partner. In this sense, the client had been, of course, avoiding confrontation with his difficulties. The client also admitted that he tended to withdraw from male company because of his sexual difficulties and, therefore, had not discussed the question with any of his male friends. The client, furthermore, feared that he might lose his partner if he failed to restore his manhood. Hence, the preliminary layers of avoidance were in place for this client.

Therapeutic investigation revealed that, in childhood, the client had originated from a strictly religious background and that he had been forbidden to masturbate in his early teens. The client, thus, read this dictum as being a means of forbidding himself to enjoy normal sexual relationships with others. If sex was pleasurable, therefore, the client was not allowed to feel such emotions and would fear punishment if he did indulge. Finally, the client gained the necessary insight into the workings of his psyche by giving himself full permission to enjoy his body and the delights it had to offer. By ridding himself of the guilt-complex and gaining a degree of maturity, the client was able naturally to resume pleasurable sexual relations with his new-found love.

Client Profiling

The analytical hypnotherapy practitioner may wish to ponder the following points when formulating a profile for the client.

- In what ways does the client exhibit dis-ease?
- What aspects of the client's early experiences have remained incomplete or distorted?
- In what ways does the client detach or reduce the impact of his/her involvement in life?
- In what ways does the client expect others to spoon-feed him/her?
- In what ways does the client make himself/herself a doormat for others?
- Does the client display any tendencies towards self-importance or self-aggrandisement?
- Does the client portray an unnatural stereotypical role when in the social context?
- Does the client adopt an unrealistic fantasy about his/her life?
- In what ways does the client feel frustration at being stuck in a self-imposed rut?
- Does the client in any way avoid emotional interaction with others?

Chapter 9

Cognitive Therapy

There is nothing either good or bad but thinking makes it so.

– William Shakespeare

What Is Cognitive Therapy?

In the cognitive model, psychological disturbance is seen as a result of
some malfunction in the process of interpreting and evaluating
experience. In psychological health our schemata are sufficiently
consistent to allow us to predict likely occurrences, but also flexible
enough to allow changes on the basis of new information.
– Stirling Moorey

Cognitive therapy originated largely with the work of Aaron Beck
(1921–), who saw the client as an active agent who interacts with
his/her own environment. Beck's forethought has also been con-
siderably enhanced by the work of William Glasser (1925–) and
Albert Ellis (1913–). Cognitive doctrine considers that the client's
interaction with his/her environment will provide the key to
human motivation. The client, therefore, will use personal interpretation, inference and an evaluation of his/her environment and
his/her experiences in order to form conscious thoughts and
images.

Cognitive therapeutic intervention will be based on the premise
that the client has the potential to change cognitive processes (see
Chapter 5, Volume 2 – "Therapeutic Resolution"). The cognitive
therapist will believe that the client has the ability to be a rational
problem-solver when tackling his/her own dilemmas because of
his/her innate higher-order intellectual processes. This theory
accepts that the client's behaviour will have been learned behaviour but that biological factors can set limits to learning and that

he/she will need to develop innate abilities. The psychologically healthy client, therefore, will assess circumstances objectively and will apply an objective evaluation when adversity has been encountered. The psychologically distressed client, however, may view life through a mist that prevents him/her from being an effective problem-solver. A client with a perpetual failure syndrome, for example, may adopt rigid, global or judgmental thinking and may apply primitive attitudes to all situations. Success will, consequently, breed success and failure will inevitably engender failure in the client. While it will be essential for the analytical hypnotherapist to relate to the root cause of the client's disorder, it may also be a useful exercise for him/her to appreciate the cognitive perspective.

The Philosophy of Cognitive Therapy

> The main goal of cognitive counselling is to re-energise the client's reality-testing system. Cognitive counselling teaches clients how to evaluate and modify their thinking. In addition, counselling focuses on symptom relief and on helping clients to develop adaptive behaviours.
> – *Richard Nelson-Jones*

Cognitive therapy will be concerned with what makes the client tick. This discipline, therefore, will be concerned principally with motivation and with irrational thinking patterns and attitudes.

Motivation

> Cognitive therapy itself takes the view that it is how we perceive things which determines how we act toward them. According to this view, abnormal behaviour, or "mental illness", occurs because the individual has distorted perceptions, producing an unnecessarily disturbing interpretation of what is going on around them. These affect the person's behaviour in ways which are maladaptive or damaging. Cognitive therapy aims to identify and change these distorted cognitions, so that the person can begin to deal with their life more positively.
> – *Nicky Hayes*

The cognitive therapist will examine various aspects of the client's personality in order to identify those elements that are limiting, destructive or damaging to him/her with regard to motivation.

The client may be motivated by internal biological needs or by cognitive factors. Cognitive factors may include the client's anticipation of future outcomes based on past experience, a need for pleasurable sensory stimulation, a requirement for social acceptance and a compulsion for social position. The client, of course, may also be motivated by his/her own internal standards and his/her own personal code of conduct. This self-regulatory process will be derived from the client's self-observation and self-evaluation, from self-judgment of acceptable performance standards and from the way in which he/she expects he/she will react in a given set of circumstances. The cognitive therapist, therefore, will consider the client's motivational drives in terms of his/her expectations, appraisals, attributions and beliefs.

Expectations
The client's expectations may be governed by the likely outcome of his/her behaviour and the extent to which he/she believes in himself/herself. The client's self-efficacy beliefs, for example, will determine the success of a given outcome. If the client believes in himself/herself and in his/her capabilities and abilities, then he/she will achieve his/her objectives. The client who believes he/she will fail for any reason whatsoever will do so because of a lack of confidence in his/her own internal resources and in his/her abilities to deliver the goods.

Appraisals
If the client makes a negative or self-defeating appraisal of a situation, then the outcome may be doomed to failure. Such an evaluation will induce anxiety in the client and this factor, in turn, will exaggerate his/her problems. In this sense, the client will usually act out his/her own self-fulfilling prophecies.

Attributions
Cognitive therapy will examine the ways in which the client employs reasoning with regard to events or the outcome of events. The client may give any number of reasons about why things turn out the way they do or why things happen. The client's beliefs about the outcome of events will depend on the way in which

he/she makes deductions – known as *attributions* – about unknown quantities. The client may, for example, make an internal attribution about his/her personal abilities, his/her efforts and his/her lack of motivation. Similarly, the client may make an external attribution about certain circumstances that may be perceived as being beyond his/her control. The client's negative attributions, again, will set up a failure syndrome, will manifest his/her anxiety and will often lead to demotivation. Often the extent to which the client feels that he/she has control over circumstances will dictate his/her success. Positive attributions about circumstances, on the other hand, will reduce unpleasant effects and maximise the client's control facilities.

Beliefs
The client's beliefs and general theories about the world will be heeded by the cognitive therapist, who will seek to amend any negative beliefs. Often the cognitive therapist will focus on long-term beliefs that have become entrenched in the client's thinking processes and have had a seriously destructive or limiting effect on his/her true potential.

Cognitive Errors

> Beck particularly identified negative styles of thinking as the important factors producing depression. These negative thinking styles focused on what Beck described as the cognitive triad: beliefs about the patient's own self, beliefs about the person's life-experience and beliefs about their future. Beck showed that depressed people respond selectively to things that happen to them.
> – Nicky Hayes

The cognitive practitioner will examine the client's styles of negative thinking and any faulty cognition that has caused him/her to develop a negative outlook on life. Cognitive therapy will examine what the client believes about himself/herself, what he/she believes about his/her life experiences and what he/she believes about the future. This tripartite arrangement of the client's cognition is known as the *cognitive triad*. The practitioner will seek to eliminate the client's self-defeating cognitive strategies by helping him/her to recognise such thinking processes. The client who indulges in negative thinking patterns may make serious errors of judgment, that will, in turn, have a negative effect on his/her performance and success. Let us now examine some of the negative thinking patterns to which the client may be prone.

> Both social and cognitive processes are central to understanding
> motivation, emotions and actions.
> – *Richard Nelson-Jones*

Arbitrary inference

With arbitrary inference, the client may habitually jump to a negative conclusion based on little or no evidence. Here the client will suspend logic and intellectual reasoning in favour of a negative emotive response. The client may, for example, believe that he/she will continually fail at any enterprise or project that he/she undertakes.

Selective abstraction

With selective abstraction, the client may refuse to look on the bright side of things by concentrating on minor negative details and by ignoring positive indications of success. The client may, for example, have a pessimistic outlook and may habitually remember his/her failures and, simultaneously, disregard any of his/her successes.

Generalisation

With generalisation, the client may become susceptible to making sweeping negative statements and can also harbour accompanying feelings of guilt and self-blame. The client may, for example, exaggerate his/her lack of ability or worthlessness.

Magnification

With magnification, the client will tend to catastrophise his/her predicament by amplification. The client may, therefore, evaluate circumstances and ascribe an abnormally high level of disaster to an event that he/she perceives as being catastrophic.

Minimisation
With minimisation, the client will tend to play down his/her expectations. The client may, for example, believe that his/her chances of success are out of the question and that his/her propensity to failure will be inevitable.

Personalisation
With personalisation, the client will tend to take offence easily and to take things personally. Here the client will usually attribute the outcome of an external event to his/her own agency. The client may, for example, declare that his/her failure in a project was wholly his/her fault and not take into account any factors such as difficult conditions or circumstances.

Dichotomous thinking
With dichotomous thinking, the client will tend to indulge in extremes of polarised cognition. The client will, therefore, often see only black or white with no grey areas in between. The client may, for example, see only total failure or complete success rather than envisage any partial success or progress.

Cognitive Therapy Concepts

> Schemas are relatively stable cognitive patterns that influence through people's beliefs how they select and synthesise incoming data. Schemas are not pathological by definition – they may be adaptive or maladaptive.
> – *Richard Nelson-Jones*

Let us now examine the criteria by which the client may judge his/her performance and view his/her personal world.

Cognitive Schemata

Schemas may be general or specific. People may even have competing
schemas. Schemas are organised by both content and functions. The
content of schemas ranges from personal relationships to
inanimate objects.
– *Richard Nelson-Jones*

One of the fundamental premises on which cognitive therapy is
based is the notion that the client will devise for himself/herself a
set of personal cognitions known as *schemata*. Schemata are rather
like sets of personal rules or basic personal beliefs that the client
will adopt in order to interact in his/her environment. A *schema* is
a cognitive structure that will dictate the client's experience, influence his/her beliefs and organise his/her behaviour at an unconscious level. The client will be deemed to act in accordance with
his/her beliefs and will adopt beliefs in keeping with the way in
which he/she has reacted to certain past experiences. The client,
thus, will process information according to beliefs that have been
embedded in his/her cognitive schemata. Cognitive schemata
may involve the client's higher intellectual processes, although
their formation may have been unconsciously initiated. The formation of schemata will be part of the client's survival system and
his/her means of reality-checking. A problem may arise for the
client when his/her schemata are at variance with society at large
or his/her immediate social group. The client, for example, who
wishes to get a divorce from his/her spouse may find that such
conduct is condoned by the government of his/her country yet
frowned upon by his/her religious persuasion or culture. The client
will now be serving two masters – his/her own personal inclinations and needs and those of the external world – that will,
inevitably, lead to psychological distress and present a significant
resistance to the therapeutic process (see Chapter 12 – "Resistance").

Schematic processes will involve the client in the sifting and sort-
ing of data by abstraction, interpretation and evaluation of him-
self/herself and others. The schematic process will also involve
the client's memory, whereby he/she will react to his/her environment and to those about him/her in keeping with his/her past
experiences (see Chapter 10 – "Memory"). The content of a schema
will be formed by the client either by *assimilation* of information,
whereby new information can be absorbed, or by *accommodation* of

information, whereby an original schema will be expanded or developed in order to enable the client to cope with a fresh set of circumstances. Unhelpful schemata can usually be detected by monitoring the client's automatic thoughts, that can arise when he/she makes frequent self-evaluations and prejudgments and when he/she gives himself/herself a set of instructions by which to rigidly run his/her life.

Schemata may, moreover, vary according to the degree of impact, flexibility and prominence in the client's cognitive structure. If a high degree of energy has been invested in a given schema then it will be deemed to be *hypervalent* and, consequently, can easily be triggered by the client. A low degree of energy invested by the client in a schema will, however, result in psychic latency. The client in distress may readily activate inappropriate schemata, that will have an inhibitory effect because the inappropriate schema will utilise his/her precious energy resources.

Schemata may be of various types according to the way in which the client has been affected by his/her past experience. *Affective schemata* will be responsible for generating the client's emotive reactions and for dictating the emotional impact of his/her environment. *Motivational schemata* will generate the client's wishes and desires. *Instrumental schemata* will dictate the client's power of action in realising his/her aspirations. *Control schemata* will involve the ways in which the client will assess himself/herself and, when he/she undertakes self-monitoring, the result of his/her observations may inhibit, modify and/or direct his/her actions.

By way of illustrating the concept of cognitive schemata, we shall now examine a case-study example in which the client's progression was seriously hampered by her beliefs and understanding at an unconscious level.

Case-study example – infertility

This female client sought therapy because she was unable to conceive a child and because she had suffered from several phantom pregnancies. The client had also had an ovarian cyst but this had been surgically removed. In all respects, therefore, this client was young, healthy and happily married, so there was no obvious impediment to conception that could be detected.

When the therapist invited the client to investigate her past, it was discovered that she had lived abroad under a military regime. Under this regime, people frequently disappeared and were never seen again. The client recalled watching her elder sister as a pregnant teenager leaving home in order to go shopping in the city. Subsequently, the client's sister had been killed by soldiers in a military skirmish. The client's childish unconscious mind had, therefore, associated the act of becoming pregnant with certain death because when she saw her sister for the last time she had been pregnant. The client's childish logic, thus, had provided her with a reason for her sister's mysterious and rapid disappearance. Once this startling realisation had been made, it was an easy step for the client's unconscious mind to give her permission to become fertile again because the cognitive schemata that supported her inability to conceive had been circumvented.

Reality Therapy Concepts

> Clients live both in the external world (or the real world) and their own
> internal world (or perceived world). Glasser stresses that it is not the
> way reality exists that influences our behaviour but the way
> we perceive it to exist.
> *– Gerald Corey*

Control theory and its accompanying counselling approach – known as *reality therapy* – is a significant contribution to cognitive philosophy put forward by William Glasser. Reality therapy is also closely adjoined to the *theory of control* or the *theory of choice* and it is sometimes referred to as *control theory/reality therapy* (or CT/RT) for this reason. We shall now consider some of the premises of reality therapy that will be of significance to the analytical hypnotherapist.

Control Theory

> In common with the existential approach, CT/RT is based on the
> assumption that we do not have to be a victim of our past or our present
> unless we choose to be. Nor are we at the mercy of unconscious
> motivations. We have more control over life than most of us believe. The

> more effectively we exercise our control, the more fulfilled we will be. In
> short, we are almost never the victims of circumstances outside of us, for
> the capacity to change is within ourselves.
> – *Gerald Corey*

Theories of personal control are based on the premise that human behaviour will originate from within the client rather than from external forces or external influences. This approach will be concerned with the client's phenomenological world and his/her internal locus of evaluation (see Chapter 6 – "Client-Centred Therapy"). Control theorists explain that the client will make choices in his/her life in an attempt to satisfy his/her needs, to improve the quality of his/her life and to become creative and imaginative. This notion will be, of course, in keeping with self-deterministic, humanistic and existential philosophies.

Control theory contends that all the client's behaviour will be internally motivated, as opposed to viewing him/her as being at the mercy of external agencies. The client's behaviour, therefore, will be his/her best attempt to satisfy one or more of his/her basic needs. This theory also purports that the only person whose behaviour the client can control will be his/her own. The reality therapist will believe that the client has an element of choice or self-determination in electing to adopt a given symptom. Control theory, therefore, puts the responsibility squarely on the shoulders of the client to improve his/her life, to satisfy his/her intrinsic needs and to eliminate unwanted symptoms or behaviours. Responsibility will be regarded by the reality therapist as the quality that will allow the client to become autonomous by actively fulfilling his/her own needs without being hampered by self-criticism. This premise also means that the client will not allow himself/herself to be manipulated by others who are using him/her selfishly as a means of satisfying personal needs. The client who can take control of his/her life, therefore, will be applying the concept of a *success-identity* in reality therapy terms. The client's success identity will be a healthy cloak that he/she can wear in order to view himself/herself from a position of strength. The client with a success identity will be able to accept himself/herself, will feel powerful, will have a robust sense of self-worth and will satisfy needs without inconveniencing or harming others. The client with a success identity can also be deemed to have a positive addiction to being successful in his/her own eyes.

To summarise then, control theory asserts that all we ever do from birth to death is behave, and every total behaviour is always our best attempt to get what we want to satisfy our needs. In this context behaviour is purposeful because it is designed to close the gap between what we want and what we perceive that we are getting.
– *Gerald Corey*

Need Satisfaction

Control theory sees humans as driven by basic needs that are genetic in origin. All human behaviour represents an attempt to control the world to best satisfy these needs. People have no rest from their needs. Once aware of a need they have no choice but to attempt to satisfy the need and, when any particular need is satisfied, other needs emerge. Human life is a constant struggle to satisfy these different needs and to solve the ever-present conflicts between them.
– *Richard Nelson-Jones*

Reality therapy will also embrace the idea of need satisfaction as being the basis of human behaviour, that, of course, will follow the humanistic principles of the hierarchy of needs (see Chapter 6 – "Client-Centred Therapy"). The client's basic needs are defined in reality philosophy as being basic needs for survival, for belonging, for power and for freedom and fun. The human organism will have a need to stay alive and to be able to reproduce. These needs will be essential for the survival of the species and the client will have been genetically programmed to react physiologically in sur-vivalist ways. The client will also have a need to belong, a need to love and be loved, a need to share and to cooperate socially with others. Often such needs can be satisfied within family or social groups and when the client takes an interest in hobbies and leisure-time activities with a social element. The client will also have a need for power in that he/she will seek status, will aspire to recognition and will solicit the compliance of others. Sometimes this need will conflict with the need to belong when the client seeks to control or to manipulate others with whom he/she has entered into a relationship. The client will, of course, have a strong need for freedom of choice, for expression and for mobility. Sometimes this need can conflict with the client's need to belong, when, for example, a need for his/her own space may not be in harmony with what a partner or a spouse may expect from a rela-tionship. Finally, the client will have a vital requirement to bring enjoyment, fun and play into his/her life. It can be said that the child learns through play and that this learning process will, in turn, assist the survival process. Because the client will have intellectual faculties, he/she will, moreover, have a desire to minimise tedium and drudgery from his/her existence in order to enhance his/her motivation and personal achievement.

> A major reason that people maintain their choosing to stay miserable behaviour is that they remain unaware that they are doing so. They do not want the responsibility of doing something about it if they were to accept that their misery is a choice.
> – *Richard Nelson-Jones*

Total Behaviour

> Glasser uses the analogy of total behaviour as a four-wheel drive car, with each component as one wheel of the car. The front wheels are the acting and thinking components and the rear wheels are the feeling and physiology components. The needs are the engine and the driver steers in the direction closest to the picture most wanted from his or her special world album.
> – *Richard Nelson-Jones*

Control theory also incorporates the concept of total behaviour in that human behaviour is considered to be a total experience consisting of acting, feeling, thinking and physiological components that can interact harmoniously. Total behaviour and experience may be viewed in terms of each of these components coming into play when the client exhibits his/her symptoms or when he/she acts out his/her experiences. The phobic client, for example, may actively avoid the phobic object, may experience terror at the sight of the object, may imagine that the object appears in front of him/her and may shake and sweat when he/she encounters the fear source. The *acting component* of total behaviour will consist of the client's active behaviours that will involve both voluntary and involuntary physical movement. The *thinking component* will consist of the client's experience that will generate thoughts, dreams and self-statements, whether voluntarily or involuntarily. The *feeling component* will consist of the client's impressions which can generate both pleasurable and painful emotions. The *physiological component* will consist of the client's sensations that can involve voluntary and involuntary bodily mechanisms and systems. The client's heart rate, breathing mechanisms and digestive system, for example, may be actively involved in a fearful response.

Choice theory also proposes that the client can choose misery by developing painful behaviours that are the enactment of strategies for obtaining the satisfaction of his/her desires. Such behavioural strategies may be employed because the client will consider that he/she will be able to keep anger under control, to control himself/herself, to control others and to attract the attention of others. Behavioural tactics can also be used by the client as a means of opting out of taking more responsible action. The reality therapist will also see the client as having good reasons for prolonging misery and, thus, he/she will earnestly avoid taking the necessary responsibility for rectifying unwanted situations or for eliminating symptoms. The reality therapist will contend that the client may overreact to short-term pain by employing a long-term feeling. The client may, for example, react by using major depression in order to deal with a slight disappointment or a minor hurt (see Chapter 9, Volume 2 – "Sorrow and Grief Disorders"). The client may, furthermore, become unconsciously accustomed to making painful choices automatically and so misery will become a well-entrenched habit. When the client chooses misery as an ally, of course, this may also be a means of keeping control (see Chapter 12 – "Resistance"). If the client were to have to admit to being a misery merchant, then the dent in his/her self-esteem could be too much to bear. The client, however, can be encouraged to concentrate on the acting and the thinking components rather than to persist in complying with the feeling and the physiological components of his/her behaviour. In this way, the client can gain more control of the reality of his/her life and usually the first step in this process will be to elect to enter therapy.

> Reality therapy differs from the existential, person-centred, and Gestalt
> approaches in that Glasser teaches that behaviour is total; that is, it
> involves the four components of doing, thinking, feeling, and
> physiology. This means that clients are responsible for choosing not only
> what they are doing but also what they are thinking, feeling, and
> experiencing physically.
> – *Gerald Corey*

Rational-Emotive Behaviour Therapy Concepts

> The theory of rational emotive behaviour therapy has from its inception
> stressed the importance of the interaction of cognitive, emotive and
> behavioural factors both in human functioning and dysfunctioning and
> in the practice of psychotherapy.
> – *Windy Dryden*

The theory of rational-emotive behaviour therapy (or REBT), a practice devised by Albert Ellis, asserts that the individual can choose between rational reasoning and irrational thinking. REBT theory has been based on the premise that irrational beliefs and emotive reactions will prevent the client from attaining his/her all-important life goals. Such blockages to goal attainment will then set up within the client cognitions that will further prevent his/her self-actualisation and will, consequently, create psychological disturbance.

Rational and Irrational Thinking

> In REBT, "rational" means primarily that which helps people to achieve
> their basic goals and purposes, "irrational" means primarily that which
> prevents them from achieving these goals and purposes.
> – *Windy Dryden*

The therapist's role in REBT will be to help the client to dispute his/her irrational thinking and to achieve flexible, open-minded reasoning. When rational cognition has been achieved by the client, this will bring to him/her a balance between self-interest and altruism and between pleasure and discipline. When the client adopts appropriate emotive responses, he/she will portray a sensible expression of positive and negative emotion and will maintain a balance between short-term and long-term hedonism. From this standpoint, the client can then become creative, can develop, can self-actualise and can indulge in healthy goal attainment. Irrational thinking, on the other hand, will engender a self-destructive and self-sabotaging predisposition for the client. When the client exhibits inappropriate emotive expressions, these will interfere with achieving a balanced life, will manufacture irrational thinking and will often generate some insane beliefs. From this stance, however, the client will tend to implement irrational cognitions, display inappropriate emotive responses and exhibit dysfunctional behaviours.

REBT therapy acknowledges, however, that the client will be intrinsically prone to irrationality that can be exacerbated by an unfavourable environment and early external influences and that irrationality can be maintained throughout life. In REBT theory, the client will be believed to have *biological tendencies* towards irrationality that will predispose him/her to vigorously maintain unhealthy reasoning. On top of this, the client will have *emotive tendencies* towards irrationality that will support irrational cognitions and negative beliefs and will enable such elements to remain unchallenged. Finally, the client will have *cognitive tendencies* towards irrationality that will encourage him/her to think unscientifically, will reinforce emotive reactions, will put stress on negative cognitions about unwanted behaviour, will emphasise his/her past behavioural conditioning and will encourage him/her to remain in disbelief about his/her potential to change.

REBT theory attaches importance to self-dialogue that can reflect the client's emotive responses and can influence his/her behaviour. REBT therapy contends that the client will frequently retain negative cognitions about being stupid, ignorant and lacking perception. This theory also states that the client will have a tendency towards rigidity, denial and defensiveness that can render him/her unwilling to face irrational beliefs (see Chapter 11 – "Defensive Strategies"). The client may, unfortunately, also be unwilling to change personal circumstances, although he/she may be willing to indulge in distraction techniques such as drug-taking or religious practice.

Goal Attainment

REBT sees these basic goals as choices or preferences rather than needs or necessities. Rational living consists of thinking, feeling and behaving in ways which contribute to the attainment of the chosen goals, whereas irrationality consists of thinking, feeling and behaving in ways which block or interfere with their attainment.
– *Richard Nelson-Jones*

REBT also presents a theory of motivation that will govern change within the client. Ellis advocated that the factors that will mould the client's personality are those that are based on personal experiences. The nature of the client's experience of events in life will, thus, activate his/her ability to think rationally or irrationally. These so-called *activating events* will then either promote or sabotage the realisation of the client's fundamental and primary goals. The client will, thus, become subject to preferential thinking, whereby the consequences of his/her past experience will impinge upon his/her ability to rule or be ruled by his/her irrational beliefs. The nature of the client's irrational beliefs will then have emotional and behavioural consequences for him/her. The client may, for example, be prompted to act out his/her belief code, to re-enact aspects of his/her past and/or to avoid given situations. Therapeutic intervention, therefore, may focus on identifying and disputing irrational beliefs and, in so doing, carve out for the client an effective new philosophy for life.

REBT theory distinguishes between the client's fundamental survivalist goals and his/her personalised primary aims for need satisfaction. The client will have *fundamental goals* for survival, for freedom from pain, for satisfaction and contentment. Over and above these basic needs, the client will then have personalised sub-goals or *primary goals* which will engender personal happiness. These goals may, for example, facilitate a contentment about being alone, a contentment when being with others, a need for intimacy with a selected few and a satisfaction with regard to personal education, vocation and financial security. The principle of goal attainment is, of course, linked to the Adlerian teleological principles contained within individual psychology (see Chapter 3 – "Individual Psychology").

> In trying to help clients to overcome their emotional difficulties and achieve their self-enhancing goals, rational emotive behavioural therapists have clear and well-defined goals.
> – *Windy Dryden*

Client Profiling

The analytical hypnotherapy practitioner may wish to ponder the following points when formulating a profile for the client.

- In what ways is the client motivated or demotivated in his/her existence?
- In what ways do the client's biological elements, emotive reactions and behavioural tendencies interact?
- What are the client's expectations of himself/herself in the therapeutic context?
- Does the client tend towards realistic self-appraisal and attribution?
- What does the client fundamentally believe about himself/herself?
- In what ways does the client commit himself/herself to making cognitive errors?
- What erroneous cognitive schemata has the client constructed for himself/herself?
- In what ways does the client seek to be in control of his/her emotive or behavioural responses?
- Can the client's personal needs be identified in terms of needing to belong and to be loved by others?
- Does the client's need for freedom ever conflict with the emotional needs of others in his/her intimate circle?
- Does the client display any manipulative tendencies when dealing with close family members?

Part II

Therapeutic Methodology

In Part II, we shall examine the therapeutic techniques and methodology that will be of the greatest importance to the analytical hypnotherapist and that can assist him/her when working with the client. This section will cover those elements of therapeutic practice that will comprise the tools of the practitioner's trade. The aim of this section will also be to empower the therapist to gain a rudimentary understanding of the psychological background of the client who seeks therapeutic assistance.

Chapter 10

Memory

When to the sessions of sweet silent thought
I summon up remembrance of things past,
I sigh the lack of many a thing I sought,
And with old woes new wail my dear time's waste:
Then can I drown an eye, unus'd to flow,
For precious friends hid in death's dateless night,
And weep afresh love's long since cancell'd woe,
And moan the expense of many a vanish'd sight:
Then can I grieve at grievances foregone,
And heavily from woe to woe tell o'er
The sad account of fore-bemoaned moan,
Which I new pay as if not paid before.
But if the while I think on thee, dear friend,
All losses are restor'd and sorrows end.

– *William Shakespeare*

What Is Memory?

One of the great mysteries which has puzzled neuro-scientists is how the
brain actually stores memory. Even though various parts of the brain
may be damaged or even removed by surgery, memory can still remain
intact. This shows that there is not any one particular physical location in
the brain which carries out the function of memory. It seems that
memory is enfolded throughout the whole brain.
– *Michael Kern*

The way in which the memory functions will be of particular interest to the hypnoanalytical therapist because it will be the client's
perception of distressing or traumatic events from the past that
will dictate his/her current reactions and resultant symptoms.
Memory, therefore, may be the only real raw material on which the
client can work. Everything the client perceives will, hence, be a
product of his/her memory faculties because he/she will be drawing

147

on past experience in order to be able to experience the present. In essence, the client will retain in the present an imprint of his/her past experience, both psychologically in the form of emotive reactions and maladaptive behaviours, and physiologically in the guise of physical manifestations and sensory experiences.

The human memory facility is such an indeterminate and illusive commodity that there are no hard and fast rules by which to define it, to recognise it or even to prove its existence. Many writers and theorists, of course, have made statements about the physiological functioning of the memory but no-one has actually arrived at a conclusive experiment that has proved beyond doubt what we are all itching to know – and that is how the memory actually works! The only thing that can really be relied on about the phenomenon of human memory is that it is notoriously unreliable. The facts may be indisputable but the interpretations that different individuals will place on them based on a recollection of events may be vastly different.

> It is popularly believed that memory operates as a video recorder with events being recorded and stored, awaiting recovery essentially as they were laid down. Memory is, however, a much more complex and less efficient process. Bartlett showed that biographical memory is essentially a reconstructive process in which only some elements of past experience are stored and are retrievable. Far from being recovered unchanged, he demonstrated that memories may be reconstructed and elaborated by all kinds of subsequent influences.
> – *Sydney Brandon*

Each memory that the client can recall will be the product of his/her personal perception, belief structures, past knowledge, convictions and fleetingly vague impressions. A memory of a given event, furthermore, may change in the client's mind on each occasion when that episode is recalled because of the reconstructive element of recollection and his/her fluctuating perception of life as a transitory set of experiences. It will be as if the client were continually firing at a moving target when recalling the same past experience. A traumatic memory, for example, may change in terms of emotive content during the therapeutic process after the client has discharged unpleasant thoughts or feelings about the distressing experience. The client may often exaggerate or distort an unpleasant memory, owing to his/her genuine feelings of terror.

The client may also play down a dramatic memory because he/she may believe that his/her participation in an event has been blameworthy. The client, conversely, may desire to protect the reputation of another and similarly dilute the impact of the memory. Memories of experiences that have occurred in the preverbal period of the client's life, moreover, may be subject to massive distortion because his/her perceptions, linguistic skills and comprehension were, at that time, grossly underdeveloped or impaired.

> Depending on how it feels at the time, the mind selects from colours,
> images, sounds, smells, interpretations, and responses with similar
> arousal and feeling tones, then brings them to the foreground in various
> combinations to produce what we call memory.
> *– Peter Levine*

There are, however, several assumptions that can be made about the phenomenon of memory, despite the fact that no-one has really been able either to prove or to disprove these suppositions. Most people would agree, for example, that the human memory can be infallible and frequently inaccurate. Memory will generally let the thinker down when he/she most needs it and will tend to fail when he/she is trying hard to recall a fact. The client's memory facility will be constantly active and will certainly be prone to fantasy and imaginative symbolism. Imaginative wandering will, indeed, be an activity that will hold a special fascination because it can transport the client away from the rigours of his/her humdrum existence. Anything more than these vague conjectures about the behaviour of memory, however, cannot really be substantiated in the scientific laboratory. Hence, when certain theories cannot be proved, the race will usually be on in order to try. There has been, however, much controversy over the question of what the memory can and cannot actually do. The question of what an adult is capable of recalling from childhood experiences has, of course, been one that has given rise to much vehement controversy. This question, furthermore, continues to generate heated debate around the issue of whether the client can rely on his/her recollections of childhood experiences. From this premise, let us now discuss the dubious topic of memory characteristics.

> Not every detail of our experience of an event is stored in memory.
> When the record of an event is retrieved, then, it will be incomplete and
> might need elaborating before it is intelligible to our consciousness.
> *– John Morton*

Memory Processes

> There are multiple steps involved not only in the sequence of forming a
> memory, but in remembering it later. Simplistically, these steps are
> (1) sensory registration of a stimulus; (2) organising the information into
> meaningful units; (3) storing the information; and (4) retrieving the
> information. This multiple-step model of the workings of memory is a
> simple composite of several of the most widely accepted perspectives
> about memory, and is meant to highlight the fact that memory is
> complex and multidimensional. No one understands all of it.
> *– Michael Yapko*

The therapist should be aware of the way in which the memory
storage and recall process works in principle. Although the mechanism will be a difficult one to identify, a four-stage process will be
described below for the sake of convenience. To use the analogy of
a computerised filing system, the practitioner can regard the
process of storage and retrieval of a memory as having to transit
four distinct phases: namely, the recording or registering of the
experience, the organisation or processing of the information
received, the storage of the processed data in either long-term or
short-term memory and the ultimate retrieval process.

> The unconscious and conscious experiences we have recorded and
> stored become the vehicles and components of the totality of
> impressions contained in our inner map. This inner map, which is
> endowed with value by being linked to our sensations and feelings,
> forms the basis of our stance toward life.
> *– Konrad Stettbacher*

Registration of Memory

> The first level of memory is known as "sensory memory". It is memory
> of an extremely short duration – only about one-half second.
> *– Michael Yapko*

Memory registration will be triggered by a sensory reaction to a
stimulus. Initially the client's senses will need to be stimulated in
order to allow information to be grasped by his/her mind. The
client's mind will react to what it sees, hears, touches, smells or
tastes via his/her senses. The client will also have a sensory reaction of some kind to every stimulus that he/she perceives either

through conscious awareness or unconscious subliminal perception. This sensory reaction may be somatic, emotive, cognitive or psychosomatic in nature. The registration of a memory in the client's mind will invariably be affected by a continual sensory overload. It has been claimed that the human mind tends to delete, distort and generalise when absorbing information in order to avoid being bombarded with excessive data for processing. Many researchers believe that the client's conscious mind can only take in about seven units – plus or minus two units – of information at any one time despite receiving about 2 million messages per second.

The client's attention will usually be caught by what captures his/her interests, what excites him/her and what personally involves him/her – either by design or by accident. The client may also be incapable of ignoring certain forms of stimuli even though he/she may earnestly wish to forget a given experience. The distress victim, for instance, may be forced to register a given set of circumstances when trauma has been thrust upon him/her. A starving person will be so consumed with his/her need for sustenance that no possible form of distraction from this urge could be accomplished. Each memory that the client has, therefore, will contribute to the development of his/her character and self-image.

No one knows, nor can anyone know, what the truth is.
– *Burt Hotchkiss*

Organisation of Memory

The next step, organisation, refers to the necessity of making meaning
out of sensations we experience, a process known as "perception".
Sensory experiences remain simply transient neurological impressions
unless they are organised into something with meaning.
– *Michael Yapko*

The organisation of incoming memorised material would next be undertaken by the client's perceptive processes. Having acquired the information, the client will now need to make an interpretation of what has been received. The information that has entered the client's mind will need to be understood and interpreted according to his/her perception of that stimulus. The client's perception of his/her experiences will provide a means of making sense, to a greater or lesser extent, of what he/she has registered via his/her senses. Some degree of order and organisation, therefore, will need to be achieved within the client's mind – however primitive and unsophisticated this organising process may be. The client, for example, may grade experiences according to emotive content, may prioritise that which needs to be readily retrieved and may decide whether matter should be consigned either to short-term or to long-term storage. Such organisation will be influenced by the amount of information that the mind receives at any given time and to what extent the client's attention has been focused on his/her experiences. Human memory organisation will also, of course, be related to the client's past experience or its relevance to social context.

> Who you think you are, and what you believe to be true, is something
> that you have made up.
> – *Burt Hotchkiss*

Storage of Memory

> In the third stage, storage, the memory is "coded". Is the information to
> be stored as a visual image? A physical sensation?
> – *Michael Yapko*

Storage of information in the human memory may be consigned either to the client's short-term memory or to his/her unconsciously-resident long-term memory. The client's long-term memory will be used in order to store important information perhaps for the sake of human survival and self-development, while the short-term memory will be designed for immediate needs, that may be of only transitory interest. The client's unconscious mind may consign matter, for example, to his/her long-term memory in order to assist with the learning process and to ensure a source of reference. Matter received may, however, be discarded by the client's memory and, thus, forgotten by being classified as irrelevant.

Information that has been stored in the client's memory will need to be encoded and referenced in readiness for retrieval. When the client consigns information to his/her memory banks, therefore, there will need to be some form of referencing system in place in order to allow for matter to be retrieved as appropriate. A link will, thus, be made between the material stored, the client's perception of events and its accompanying emotive and physical effect. This referencing process has been described as a *memory-trace*. This will be because the client's mind will be able to trace a given item of information stored by means of a link or a key in the unconscious mind, that will allow the matter to be retrieved into full conscious awareness when necessary.

Experiences consigned to long-term memory will usually be those that have had the greater impact on the client in terms of emotive responses. For the recipient of distress, therefore, the severity and unpleasantness of a traumatic experience will ensure that such information cannot be forgotten. The process of encoding memories, however, may well be thwarted in the mind of the trauma victim – the result of which will be debilitating symptoms and intense distress (see Chapter 13, Volume 2 – "Post-Traumatic Stress Disorder"). The client's long-term memory, of course, will hold the contents of his/her biographical and episodic memory, that will ensure his/her survival by aiding the learning process, by assisting his/her understanding of events and by developing his/her awareness of danger. This will be the reason why experiences with a high emotive content will remain permanently etched in the client's long-term memory. Such memories can, consequently, act as a means of warning the client not to repeat or to court similar danger. This works on the once-bitten-twice-shy principle, that will aim to ensure the continuing survival of the human species. For information to be retained in the client's long-term memory, of course, repetition and reinforcement will be required in order to ensure that it stays there intact. If the client wishes to remember some factual information, for example, he/she will need to ensure that the matter is reinforced. Similarly, if the client wishes to remember events of a highly emotive nature, he/she will need to ensure that the emotion does not lose its potency. When working with the client in therapy, therefore, the practitioner will attempt to defuse or to depotentiate the emotive content of a disturbing memory in order to ensure that the client can consign the horror of his/her experience to emotional insignificance. The client, in this way, can remember the experience but without distress and can change his/her beliefs about himself/herself in order to view the reality of the experience.

> Nothing happens in life faster than the mind's ability to grasp it.
> – *Burt Hotchkiss*

Retrieval of Memory

> The final stage of memory is retrieval, the actual recovery of the
> information that has been sensed, interpreted, and stored. Memory
> retrieval is a process vulnerable to many influences.
> – *Michael Yapko*

Memory retrieval will be a process of re-creation, reconstruction and representation of what has been previously stored from the client's past experience. Recollection will be deemed to be reconstructive and not faithfully reproductive and during the reconstructive process a memory may, of course, become highly distorted. The passage of time and subsequent experiences will also influence the client's ability to recall matter and may, therefore, tamper with the accuracy of such recollection.

When retrieving material, the client may find that something will jog his/her memory in order to aid retrieval into his/her conscious awareness. There will, therefore, be a trigger that will connect to the memory-trace and allow the recollection to be retrieved. The mind will then need to reconstruct the original memory in order to retrieve it. It will, of course, be at this stage of reconstruction that memory distortion and malformation can and will occur. The client may also, simultaneously, retrieve the accompanying emotive content and physical sensations associated with the recollected experience. The recollection of past information from the client's mind, therefore, may be subject to a number of convoluted processes. A memory may, for instance, be retrieved by direct recollection, by means of a comparison with similar experiences, by way of recognition of something suggested by another person and through an association of ideas – a facility on which the technique of free association capitalises (see Chapter 2, Volume 2 – "Therapeutic Investigation").

> Your mind does not let you see what does not fit.
> – *Burt Hotchkiss*

Memory Influences

Factors that influence the degree of reconstruction include: the personal
significance of the event, its emotive content, the amount of time elapsed
between the event occurring and it being remembered, the reasons why
the person is remembering the event, and the circumstances of recall.
– *John Morton*

We shall now consider those factors that influence the client either
to remember or to forget his/her past experiences, be they pleasant or unpleasant episodes in his/her life. The practitioner may
constantly endeavour to decipher why a client remembers a given
experience or why he/she appears incapable of doing so.
Although this may be an insoluble question, perhaps some of the
following factors connected with recollection and forgetting can be
considered by the practitioner.

The issue of whether memory is enhanced in hypnosis or leads to
appreciably distorted recall is one that is heavily debated in the literature
of the mid-1980s. Theorists in the field assert that hypnotic memory is
both reliable and significantly enhanced in its accuracy, while others
claim that hypnotic memory is dependably in error.
– *Peter Sheehan*

Recollected Memories

Events that are personally highly significant evoke deep beliefs, attitudes
and emotional reactions and may lead to a narrowing of attention. As a
consequence, memories for peripheral details of such events may be
more vulnerable to reconstructive error. Central details are likely to be
remembered better but may still be in error.
– *John Morton*

The client will generally remember experiences that capture
his/her interest, in which he/she has actively participated and in
which he/she has become emotionally involved. Important occasions in the client's life – such as getting married, having a child,
winning a prize or the death of a close relative – are those that will
be indelibly written into his/her long-term biographical memory.
The client, for this reason, will be unlikely to forget his/her most
distressing experiences because the memory of such experiences
will have been retained long-term. The client's inclination to

re-examine such memories will, of course, become another ball game, but the memory will still be resident in his/her mind.

Sometimes when the client makes a conscious effort to remember something – such as the lines from a speech or material for an examination – he/she will need to be highly motivated or to set matter in context in order to secure its recollection. Once the incentive to remember is no longer pressing, of course, the client's mind may then decide that it has too many other things with which to concern itself. If the client attempts to cram too many things into his/her memory then the chances are that he/she will achieve very little because of the overload. Every memory, when being installed in the client's mind, will need a settling-in period before it can be classified as a permanent, long-term memory.

Memory recollection will also be influenced by repetition of matter and continuity of experiences as well as the client's personal beliefs, attitudes, values and convictions – all of which will help to seal the permanence of a given memory. The memory of a specific event may be triggered in the client's mind by the recollection of similar situations or experiences, a repetition of a given experience, similar associations, sensory stimulation and frequency of occurrence. The client may often make a conscious effort to recollect something but, at other times, his/her memories will merely float into his/her conscious mind unrequested. Recollections can be triggered spontaneously and dramatically when the client finds himself/herself plunged into a matching experience that models the past. The distressed client, for example, may open up memories of his/her unhappy experiences from the past when additional distress occurs in the present. If the victim of childhood abuse were attacked or raped in adulthood, for example, this can set in motion a recollection of his/her childhood experiences (see Chapter 15, Volume 2 – "The Effects of Childhood Abuse"). If a mugging victim encounters a person with characteristics similar to his/her robber, then such repetition and the symbolic re-creation of the past may be sufficient to allow his/her disturbing memories to surface. The emotional distress attached to such memories will, of course, also surface and this may be the reason why the client has sought therapy. Memory triggers may also appear in the form of objects that are associated with the original memory. The client who has previously been stabbed, for example, may recoil at the sight of a knife and may relive the trauma as a result – consciously or otherwise. Similarly, physical or tactile sensations and other sensory stimulation may activate the client's sensory memory. The sexual abuse victim, for instance, may react to being touched in a sexual manner or may find sexual arousal a disturbing experience because it will activate the memory-trace of the original sensation. The recollection of a traumatic event may, furthermore, be subject to spontaneous regression back to the time when the client's development was halted (see Chapter 11 – "Defensive Strategies"). A current-day event may, therefore, trigger a reaction to past distress in childhood on which the client has fixated when a highly charged snapshot was taken. This trigger may well then have an impact on the client's emotive responses, interactions, behaviour and motivations.

> It is not important whether memories are objectively accurate. Of prime importance is whether the associated activation escalates or resolves.
> – *Peter Levine*

Forgotten Memories

> Repression is only the precondition for the construction of symptoms. Symptoms, as we know, are a substitute for something that is held back by repression.
> – *Sigmund Freud*

Sometimes the client will have a marked propensity to forget information that he/she desires to remember or may be important for him/her to remember in the interests of his/her psychological health. Forgotten or partially forgotten memories, therefore, may often be manifested in the client's psychological and physiological symptoms, language patterns, behaviours and premonitions and such manifestations can be evidence of a suppressed, a repressed or a preconscious memory (see Chapter 3, Volume 2 – "Unconscious Communication").

With a nontraumatic memory, the client may simply forget matters or not be in the habit of remembering. Perhaps the client's mind will have become conditioned not to bother to make a mental note of events or he/she may not be particularly interested in doing so. It will be as if the human mind, in such circumstances, had adopted a blueprint for forgetting. The client, moreover, may be too concerned with the present to be at all interested in remembering the past. The present, for instance, may be full of excitement and interest or worry and tedium for the client and, therefore, recent experiences may appear to outweigh the effects of the past. Finally, time and advancing years may serve to help the client to forget. The client may possess a mind clouded with time distortion, that will put the events of the past into perspective – the result of this being that the past becomes insignificant in terms of his/her ability to recollect it. A traumatic memory, on the other hand, may not be remembered or encoded properly in the memory because of the nature of the client's experience. The client's memory will then be held in neural pathways rather than being stored ready for normal and accurate retrieval. This may, of course, cause a dissociative state or a depressive disorder in the client or could lead to post-traumatic stress disorder (see Chapter 13, Volume 2 – "Post-Traumatic Stress Disorder"). In such cases, factors such as suppression and repression may creep into the workings of the client's memory (see Chapter 11 – "Defensive Strategies").

Memory Classifications

> Our favourite and most popular metaphors emphasize the accuracy and efficiency of memory. Memories, we imagine, are catalogued in ever-expanding ultra-microscopic libraries. Or perhaps they are carefully stored as bits of information on a limitless supply of infinitesimal computer chips, or even recorded on blank video-cassettes, properly labelled and filed away for future use. These modern, technological metaphors reveal a deep need for order and consistency. We would like to believe that our minds work according to a method, that there is a strategy to be discovered somewhere in the brain's chemical stew, even if we can only begin to imagine what it might "look" like. We would like to think that something, somehow, somewhere, is always in control.
> – *Elizabeth Loftus & Katherine Ketcham*

In an attempt to explain the workings of the memory, a number of memory functions have been identified by researchers and, thus, we can tabulate a number of memory classifications that may be of interest to the practitioner. The memory classifications listed below are independent of whether the memory has been recalled as an experiential memory, an emotive memory or a somatic memory (see Chapter 2, Volume 2 – "Therapeutic Investigation").

Repeated events lead to a schematic, generalised representation which is
used as a framework for recall of these events. As a result, individual
events are liable to become confused.
– *John Morton*

Explicit Memory

Explicit memory is what we usually mean when we use
the term "memory".
– *Babette Rothschild*

Explicit memory (or *declarative memory*) will be the client's memory of the events in his/her life that can be readily recalled into
consciousness. With this type of memory, the client can easily
declare or articulate his/her thoughts about such recollections. In
this category will fall the client's *autobiographical memory*, his/her
event memory and his/her *episodic memory* that will collectively tell
the story of his/her life. Although explicit memory can be readily
recalled by the client, recollections of the past may often have been
dimmed by the passage of time, by subsequent events and by a
general overcrowding of experiences that have occurred more
recently. The client's memory of episodes or events in his/her life
may frequently be patchy and it can, therefore, be mystifying for
the practitioner to observe that the client will readily recall certain
occasions but completely forget others. Sometimes the client will
remember the happy times and sometimes the not-so-happy occasions. Sometimes the client will remember events vividly and
accurately and sometimes not.

Individual autobiographical memory is unreliable; people will
sometimes have startlingly accurate memories of some events yet be
unable to remember considerable parts of their past experiences. Newly
acquired facts may alter personal memories through reorganisation,
reappraisal and revision.
– *Sydney Brandon*

Often the therapist will need to probe the client's explicit memory
in order to unearth matter that forms the substance of his/her
therapeutic journey. The client should be invited to access aspects
of his/her explicit memory in order to acknowledge the way in which
he/she has perceived his/her existence. From this vantage point,
the client can then appreciate what effect such perceptions have

had and how his/her life has been shaped accordingly. The subject of an unhappy childhood, for example, will need to appreciate the way in which his/her life has been moulded by his/her distress, how its occurrence has coloured his/her thinking and the way in which it has controlled his/her behaviour or manifested symptoms.

> Episodic memory is the system associated most closely with traditional approaches to learning and memory and is that most readily disrupted by brain damage. It is normally associated with awareness of the learning process and strongly influenced by the degree of concentration and organisation.
> – *Sydney Brandon*

Implicit Memory

> Where explicit memory depends on language, implicit memory bypasses it. Explicit memory involves facts, descriptions, and operations that are based on thought; implicit memory involves procedures and internal states that are automatic. It operates unconsciously, unless made conscious though a bridging to explicit memory that narrates or makes sense of the remembered operation, emotion, sensation, etc.
> – *Babette Rothschild*

Implicit memory (or *nondeclarative memory*) will be the client's unconscious, subliminal perception of his/her experiences. With this type of memory, the client will be unable to voice given aspects of his/her experience. This subliminal memory, therefore, will involve the client's emotive responses, intuition and physical sensations. This part of the client's memory will, thus, be everything that surrounds the explicit-memory process. The practitioner will often talk of *cell memory*, *imagistic memory* and *feeling memory* and these concepts are a subcategory of implicit memory. When the client recalls an event in therapy, he/she can often access the event via the implicit memory rather than directly connecting to the explicit recollection. The impact of the client's implicit memory will often be far greater than the recollection of the experience itself but this part of his/her memory will also, of course, be susceptible to distortion and confabulation. The notion of implicit memory will be the one that holds most credence for the clinician who subscribes to the notion of memory repression and memory recovery because he/she will feel that the client can access buried memories via an implicit memory-trace.

Baddeley argues that implicit memory is a cluster of learning systems
independent of episodic memory.
– Sydney Brandon

Preconscious Memory

Processes of preconscious organisation and selection are critically
important in creative thinking. Somehow, by free association or by the
confluence of many simultaneous streams of thought, preconscious
processes enable us to leap to intuitive conclusions that we are able to
verify or disprove consciously only after slow, tedious, step-by-step
argument and deduction.
– George Miller

The human organism's preconscious memory will retain material
that can usually be fairly readily retrieved although, most of the
time, the client will keep it on the back burner in his/her mind.
The client's preconscious memory can be thought of as a halfway
house residing between his/her unconscious mind and his/her
conscious awareness. A preconscious memory, therefore, will not
be entirely removed from the client's conscious awareness but will
merely remain dormant until it is obliged to be retrieved. Often
this type of memory will comprise those aspects of life that the
client would rather not think about or has shelved owing to
his/her leading an active and eventful life. Memories stored in
preconsciousness, therefore, will constitute a form of temporary
forgetting or suppression of reality.

A preconscious memory that surfaces in therapy for the client will
generally contain elements of psychic distress. Such manifestations of unconscious conflict may surface in speech, in behaviours
or in premonitions about what may be likely to occur. The client,
for example, may use expressions in daily speech containing
phrases such as "I am afraid" or "I am sorry", that can denote
some minor inner distress when his/her conflict remains unresolved (see Chapter 3, Volume 2 – "Unconscious Communication"). Similarly, the client may have a feeling of impending
doom or despondency if a preconscious memory has been causing
discord within his/her psyche. Elements of the client's preconscious memory may also surface in dreams and manifest as forms
of symbolism (see Chapter 14 – "Dreams and Symbolic Imagery").

Preverbal Memory

> Most people's memory for early childhood experiences is nearly non-
> existent before around ages two to three, and is quite sparse and only
> episodic until around ages six to eight. To assume, however, that the
> reasons for this *must* be emotional (rather than due to other, less
> sensational, reasons such as the biology of the brain's development)
> again leads therapists to conduct a search for "the reason".
> – *Michael Yapko*

Preverbal memory will be that part of an infant's memory that manifests prior to the materialisation of his/her language skills when he/she had little or no means of verbal communication with those about him/her. Some theorists would even advocate that infantile amnesia would prevent any recollection of personal experiences prior to the establishment of the client's verbal communication skills. Other clinicians would insist that the child still has his/her innate intelligence and instincts and that, therefore, he/she will be able to recall the essence of his/her experiences, in some respect, from a very early age and, even, from birth or prebirth.

There has been, of course, much controversy over the question of how reliable the client's memory could be prior to his/her being able to express himself/herself in speech. It is felt that, when the brain is not sufficiently developed for the infant to formulate words, the record of his/her experiences cannot be proved and, therefore, the validity of preverbal memory will be seriously in dispute. Many practising clinicians, on the contrary, take the view that several of their clients have accurately recalled memories from this preverbal period that have later been adequately substantiated by relatives when questioned. Physical manifestations or sensory experiences, for example, may be registered by the client unconsciously during the preverbal period of his/her life and such experiences can then be reiterated, in some way, during therapy. Perhaps the issue to consider here might be whether preverbal explicit memory is reliable and, if so, can this same reliability be attributed to implicit memory? The therapist, of course, could be hamstrung by being unable conclusively to prove or disprove such theories. The practitioner must, therefore, rely on his/her own beliefs and clinical experience when considering the client's reported recollections. Another factor in the equation that may have been overlooked by critics is the extent to which distorted recollections and imaginative imagery may still be of value to the client in the therapeutic context. The preverbal child will, of course, not have developed linguistic abilities and intellectual prowess and, therefore, will think only in symbolic imagery (see Chapter 14 – "Dreams and Symbolic Imagery"). It may well be, however, that this very fact can be used by the practitioner to advantage in order to aid the client in arriving at unconscious realisations without the interference of conscious logic.

> Normal event memory is largely accurate but may contain distortions
> and elaborations.
> – *John Morton*

Occluded Memory

> In psychoanalytic treatment we are invariably faced by the task of filling
> up these gaps in the memory of childhood; and in so far as the treatment
> is to any extent successful – that is to say, extremely frequently – we also
> succeed in bringing to light the content of these forgotten years of
> childhood. Those impressions had never been really forgotten, they were
> only inaccessible, latent and had formed part of the unconscious.
> – *Sigmund Freud*

Occluded memory (or *screen memory*) will be that part of the client's memory that will tend to block out those aspects of the past that he/she would really rather not address. This can be achieved by creating a screen behind which the truth can hide. It will be as if this screen memory were a defensive strategy designed to protect the client from facing his/her own traumatic past (see Chapter 11 – "Defensive Strategies"). It will also be the client's occluded memory that will conceal any memory repression. Occluded memory can obliterate parts of the client's biographical memory or episodic memory as a means of obscuring his/her painful past. The highly distressed client, for example, may often have little or no recollection of any or all of his/her childhood and it will be in this part of the memory's deficiency that repressed memories are believed to reside. A screen memory may take the form of a *composite memory*, that will consist of a number of fragments of recollections, an *incomplete memory* (or *fuzzy memory*), that will have been malformed or deficient, and a *generalised memory* (or a *nonspecific memory*), that will neglect to register any fine details of an event.

Freud was responsible for coining the term *screen memory* in order to explain the way in which the human mind condenses memorised information and displaces it with imagery and symbolism in order to prevent the client from facing those unpleasant aspects of his/her life experiences (see Chapter 1 – "Psychoanalysis"). Freudian theories have, as most people would acknowledge, given rise to endless controversy about the way in which the memory functions. There are those practitioners who believe in the existence of screen functioning and there is that school of thought that utterly rejects such hypotheses.

> Anyone who has no recollection of large periods of childhood is
> certainly repressing the memory of a traumatic and painful time that
> often includes sexual abuse.
> – *Ken Graber*

The Memory-Repression Controversy

> The mental health profession is angrily and bitterly divided over the
> phenomenon of repressed memories of childhood sexual abuse. A
> repressed memory is one that has been buried in a person's unconscious,
> usually for decades, which may then surface, often in dramatic ways.
> Repression is a natural psychological defence mechanism that serves to
> keep painful and traumatic material out of your awareness. (Repression
> can't be studied directly, it can only be inferred. You can't ask someone,
> "Are you repressing memories of abuse?" If he or she knows about it, it
> isn't repressed.) Despite the past trauma being out of your awareness,
> though, its lingering effects on your thoughts, feelings and behaviour
> can be dramatic. Some very severe symptoms can be a direct
> consequence of repressed traumas.
> – *Michael Yapko*

The main concept that has been in dispute ceaselessly for decades about the functioning of the memory is, of course, that of memory repression and how accurate or reliable the client's recovered memories can actually be. Another question that sparks off contention will be how far back in time the client can go when recalling life events. This question often hinges on whether one can accept the existence and veracity of preverbal memory.

On one side are the "True Believers", who insist that the mind is capable
of repressing memories and who accept without reservation or question
the authenticity of recovered memories. On the other side are the
"Skeptics", who argue that the notion of repression is purely
hypothetical and essentially untestable, based as it is on unsubstantiated
speculation and anecdotes that are impossible to confirm or deny.
– Elizabeth Loftus & Katherine Ketcham

In the therapeutic community, of course, bloodthirsty war has
been waged between the two camps of those who support the concept of memory repression and those who decidedly do not. Let us
consider now why there are two schools of beliefs – one school
supporting the concept of memory repression and memory recovery and the other denying its existence and subscribing to the
notion of a false-memory syndrome (or FMS). In the psychological
community, one can generally distinguish between clinical practitioners who tend to support the memory-repression theory and
experimental practitioners who tend to subscribe to the notion of
false-memory syndrome because of wanting to see proof of memory repression, that has been virtually impossible to obtain. The
practitioner who, time and time again, watches his/her clients
unearth memory repression on virtually a daily basis may be
likely to argue that this is proof enough. Other practitioners may
feel, however, that this belief can be dicing with death if it is taken
literally. Let us now consider these two opposing viewpoints.

Ever since Freud, the psychology profession has split itself into two
camps – the experimental and the clinical – each viewing the other with
suspicion, condescension, and, quite often, contempt.
– Mark Pendergast

The Memory-Repression Viewpoint

> On one side are clinicians and researchers who believe that the existence
> of repressed traumas due to sexual abuse can and should be readily
> identified from a set profile, in the form of a symptom checklist. They
> believe that treatment should involve first lifting the veil of repression
> with a variety of memory recovery techniques, then working with the
> newly discovered material. They believe that memories recovered in
> therapy are essentially true, and need to be acknowledged as such in
> order for treatment to succeed. They are also concerned that perpetrators
> of sexual abuse not be given a new basis, legitimised by professionals,
> for evading responsibility for their actions.
> – *Michael Yapko*

Many clinical therapeutic practitioners and their supporters would normally regard the recovery of repressed memories as a commonplace occurrence. Such clinicians will believe that because they work at the chalk face with distressed clients they can provide first-hand testimony that memory repression and memory recovery have been proved many times, but always behind closed doors.

> The clinicians, on the other hand, complain about their experimental
> colleagues, hiding in their Ivory Tower labs, trying to draw conclusions
> from timid, limited experiments on college students. What do they know
> about real life? The clinicians pride themselves on their active
> involvement with individual clients whose life stories pour out during
> therapy sessions. Sure, the therapists sometimes read about experimental
> evidence, but it seems worlds away from their practices, from the real
> needs of their patients.
> – *Mark Pendergast*

This dilemma for the therapist who deals with cases of childhood abuse and neglect may, of course, be significant. If the practitioner subscribes to the concept of memory repression and recovery of repressed memories, then he/she can be of assistance to the client who requires this type of treatment. If, on the other hand, the practitioner cannot accept this phenomenon, then he/she may feel unable or unwilling to treat clients whose past demands a thorough investigation. The therapist, in this case, may find himself/herself at a loss to know how to proceed. The clinician will be restricted to dealing only with the client who can claim that he/she can consciously remember every aspect of his/her childhood. This choice must be a personal decision and should be taken by every therapist without external pressures. In the main, however, the analytical hypnotherapist will tend to subscribe to a belief in the existence of memory repression and its ability to be unearthed effectively and beneficially in the therapeutic context.

> The True Believers claim the moral high ground. They are, they insist, on the front line, fighting to protect children from sexual predators and assisting survivors as they struggle through the arduous healing process.
> – *Elizabeth Loftus & Katherine Ketcham*

It will, of course, be a significant fact that no proof can ever be made available either to substantiate or to deny the existence even of the unconscious mind and the way in which it works, and this will include the notions of memory repression, the recovery of repressed memories and, indeed, the false-memory syndrome.

> This is obviously more than an academic discussion about the mind's ability to bury a memory and then bring it back into consciousness years later. The issues evoked by the simple notion of repression are among the most controversial concerns of cognitive and clinical psychology: the role of hypnosis in therapy and courts of law; the power of suggestion; social influence theory; the currently popular diagnosis of post-traumatic stress disorder (PTSD) and multiple personality disorder (MPD), labelled in the fourth edition of the American Psychiatric Association's Diagnostic and Statistical Manual as a dissociative identity disorder (DID); the inner child and the dysfunctional family; pornography; satanic cults; rumour mills, moral crusades; alien abduction; media-inspired hysteria; and, of course, the question of political correctness.
> – *Elizabeth Loftus & Katherine Ketcham*

The False-Memory Viewpoint

> On the other side of the issue are those clinicians and researchers who
> are sceptical of anyone's professed ability to diagnose repressed
> memories of trauma on the basis of symptoms that might be just as
> readily explained by other means. These clinicians and researchers
> further believe that by forming a conclusion that an individual has been
> abused and is repressing memories to that effect, a therapist can
> intentionally or unintentionally influence that person to reach that same
> conclusion, when it may not be true. They recognise that people can be
> influenced, especially in vulnerable situations like therapy, to believe
> damaging things that may have no basis in fact. They are concerned that
> innocent people will be falsely accused, and that many people's lives
> will be all but destroyed in the process.
> *– Michael Yapko*

Many experimental psychologists and their research supporters
are those who will tend to want everything proved with watertight certainty. This will be the camp that largely rejects any suggestion that memory repression is a fact because it cannot be
proved. This school will consider that anything that purports to be
a recovered memory will, in fact, be one that has been implanted
in some way in the client's mind by the therapist or has somehow
been fabricated by the client. This school of thought will consider
that the client can retrieve a so-called memory because of a self-
imposed pressure that may manifest in the therapeutic context.
The client, therefore, may be attempting to comply with the wishes
of the therapist by doing what he/she believes is expected of
him/her and, in the process, this may include retrieving a memory
that the practitioner would find acceptable.

> The experimental psychologists conduct research in controlled
> conditions, attempting to prove or disprove particular hypotheses
> regarding mental phenomena. By changing one variable at a time, they
> try to isolate particular cause-and-effect sequences. In trying to explore
> the human psyche, however, they are largely hampered by ethical
> constraints. No-one, for example, would look with favour upon a
> scientist who raised a human child without any touch or affection, just to
> see how it fared.
> *– Mark Pendergast*

The concept of memory repression was first mooted by Freud
when he put forward his theories of psychoanalysis (see Chapter
1 – "Psychoanalysis"). As some of Freud's theories have been dis-

credited or fiercely repudiated by latter-day psychologists, it stands to reason that the notion of memory repression should come under fire. Those who subscribe to the view that memory repression is an unverifiable phenomenon, of course, will often also reject as unproved many of the other Freudian concepts, including the phenomenon of the unconscious mind itself.

> The Skeptics attempt to evade these accusations with talk of proof, corroboration, and scientific truth-seeking, but they are not afraid to hurl some deadly grenades of their own.
> – *Elizabeth Loftus & Katherine Ketcham*

Theories of Memory-Repression

> The life-saving function of repression in childhood is transferred in adulthood into a life-destroying force.
> – *Alice Miller*

It may be worthwhile for the practitioner to consider some of the implications that lie behind the assumption that repressed memories of childhood abuse can be unearthed in a therapeutic context while, at the same time, keeping an open mind on the subject (see Chapter 15, Volume 2 – "The Effects of Childhood Abuse"). The repression of a memory or a series of memories has been described as the human act of involuntarily excluding information from conscious awareness. The memory – in the form of the record of an experience and its accompanying emotive effects – will, thus, become buried in the client's unconscious mind. Memory repression is believed to occur as a direct result of perceived or actual trauma that the client undergoes and the consequent conflict into which his/her mind will be thrust as a result of that traumatic experience. A clear distinction should, of course, be made between what is understood as repression that will be totally unconscious amnesia for an event, and denial or suppression that will occur when the client simply pushes aside material that the mind would rather not think about. The client's mind may, however, suppress matter so assiduously that it can, in fact, become virtually excluded from instant recollection.

The theory obtains that memory repression is a defensive strategy as well as being a coping-strategy (see Chapter 11 – "Defensive Strategies"). This, therefore, will mean that the client will not only have a device for handling the traumatic incident at the time but also will have a facility that will ensure that the unconscious record of the given event will still be retained below the surface of consciousness. This is undertaken because, if it were known consciously by the client, it would bring about a recurrence of that original traumatic state. The victim of trauma, therefore, will have a primary defence that will allow him/her to survive the danger at the time of its distressing occurrence but the client will then adopt a coping-strategy that will prevent him/her from having to think about the horrors of the experience subsequently. It will, however, be the client's defensive strategies that will bring about his/her symptoms and will control his/her consequent behaviour. If an adult had a near-miss scrape with death through no fault of his/her own, for instance, the last thing he/she would want to do would be to repeat that particular episode in his/her life or to dwell upon it endlessly in his/her thoughts unless forced to do so. Childhood repression can have a similar effect on the client but the theory states that the information will be utterly or partially buried until, by chance, it manages to surface or has been purposefully triggered to surface by some means.

> Most incest victims reach adulthood bearing their secrets intact. It is not
> known how many successfully bury their past and go on with their
> lives, and how many continue to suffer the effects of their victimisation.
> There is reason to suspect that a substantial proportion, perhaps even the
> majority of incest victims, feel lastingly scarred by their childhood
> experience.
> – *Judith Lewis Herman & Lisa Hirschman*

Another factor in the equation purports that repression will manifest itself as will the client's unpleasant symptoms and, thereby, provide an indicator to its existence. Adherents to this theory claim that because of the phenomenon of repression, the client will subsequently suffer from conversion symptoms that will be indicative of the nature of the memory repression together with any accompanying psychological reactions and physiological sensations (see Chapter 11 – "Defensive Strategies"). The principal issue in the question here, of course, will be whether the client can, in fact, utterly obliterate from his/her memory a traumatic event that has occurred in childhood and that can, subsequently, surface in adulthood. This type of memory repression is sometimes known as *robust repression* or *massive repression* in order to distinguish it from other types of memory suppression, denial or simple forgetfulness.

> Most discussions of repression focus on the hypothesised active
> inhibition of previously clear conscious memories for events, whether as
> a result of a conscious or an unconscious process.
> – *John Morton*

The controversy in the clinical community about relying on memory repression as a phenomenon will often pivot on whether or not the client's surfacing memories can be substantiated by a checklist of symptoms. One school of practitioners believe that it should be possible to establish reliably whether or not what the client uncovers and divulges to the therapist is justifiable. The opposing school, conversely, believes that memory repression is a misnomer and that, at best, the client will be misguided and, at worst, he/she will be misrepresenting the truth. The adherents to this philosophy, therefore, will heavily criticise the therapist who makes a diagnosis on the basis of a checklist of symptoms and then proceeds to investigate the client's background according to this diagnosis. It has also been claimed that such practices are inherently damaging to the client because the mind can be so receptive to suggestion – particularly in the therapeutic context.

> People who have memory blanks of a year or several years during their
> childhood *and* have several symptoms are typical examples of people
> who have repressed abuse memories. This usually happens when
> trauma experienced during childhood is so threatening that the child
> shuts off all memory of it as a coping mechanism. May I also point out
> here, if someone has memory blanks but shows no symptoms of abuse,
> please don't feel obligated to search diligently for abuse or announce
> with the flair of Sherlock Holmes, "Aha! Memory blanks, just as I
> suspected, childhood abuse!"
> – *Penny Parks*

The therapist in the memory-repression camp will often claim that he/she can verify the client's claims of recovered memories of abuse or neglect by identifying symptoms that are typical of cases of childhood abuse and by observing the level of psychological distress. If the client suffers from amnesia, for example, for long periods of time during his/her childhood, it may often be felt that there would be a good reason for the mind to have blanked out any significant life period. When searching for corroborative data, the client and the therapist may need to take into account what is already known about an alleged abuser and/or the client's family environment. Indeed, some therapists may feel that an element of disbelief on the client's part can be proof, in itself, of the validity of claims of childhood abuse because of the motives of guilt and fear that frequently underlie memory burial.

> To sum up the central message in a few words: incest is epidemic,
> repression is rampant, recovery is possible, and therapy can help.
> – *Elizabeth Loftus & Katherine Ketcham*

It has also been claimed that the subject of any form of memory repression will exhibit certain symptoms that are indicative of what could be termed the repressed-memory syndrome. This theory advocates that the client will, in some way, be drawn towards the source of his/her trauma by being either attracted to it or repelled by it. In both cases, the underlying emotion will usually be that of fear or guilt. The sexual abuse victim, for example, may be fascinated by pornography but become a campaigner against it (see Chapter 15, Volume 2 – "The Effects of Childhood Abuse"). Alternatively, the sexually-molested client may become a prostitute because of a need for sex yet utterly loathe such a way of life. It has been said that, in this way, the victim will exhibit conscious behaviours that are unconsciously motivated. Other indicators of a repressed-memory syndrome may be that the client will experience intrusive thoughts and emerging memories in the form of dreams, flashbacks and bodily sensations. The client may suffer, for instance, from forms of dissociation such as feelings of numbness or feelings of unreality (see Chapter 13, Volume 2 – "Post-Traumatic Stress Disorder").

> Belief in the concept of repression comes down to – well, just that: *belief*.
> Because there is no way to verify it, and because the stakes are so high,
> both sides of the debate over repressed memories tend to become
> polarised, angry, vociferous, and dogmatic.
> – *Mark Pendergast*

Theories of False-Memory Syndrome

There is no question that sexual abuse in "civilised" countries is far more prevalent than anyone was willing to admit just a decade ago. Despite the immense amount of publicity given to the subject in recent years, it is still likely that real incidents of sex abuse are woefully under-reported, because victims are often too fearful or ashamed to reveal it. At the same time, however, there is growing evidence that illusory memories of sexual abuse are being unintentionally promulgated and "validated" by misguided therapists, resulting in devastating grief and irrevocably damaged family relations.
– *Mark Pendergast*

A false memory will be regarded as the supposed recollection of an event or an experience in the client's life that did not, in fact, occur. The client will then strongly believe in the validity of such a memory and will reshape his/her personality and lifestyle accordingly. This school of thought will claim that the client can then become resistant to any attempts either to challenge or to disprove such confabulations.

A growing body of research indicates that partially or completely inaccurate memories are not uncommon. Memory is vulnerable to suggestion. Implanted false stories can be "adopted" and subsequently "remembered" as actually experienced events whose recollections are vivid and subjectively indistinguishable from recollections of actual events.
– *Sydney Brandon*

The debate over false-memory syndrome has considered whether false memories – disguised as repressed memories – can be implanted in a client's mind. The exponents of the false-memory syndrome are, understandably, concerned that dangers can arise if the practitioner undertakes memory-recovery techniques with the client after diagnosing that childhood sexual abuse, for example, had actually occurred. Therapeutic practice involving the use of hypnosis, of course, has come heavily under fire in this respect.

Again and again women found that their own entirely genuine memories of sexual abuse were discounted or denied by psychotherapists. Again and again the factual accounts of distraught and distressed children were dismissed as fantasies. This massive denial of the experience of women and children provided the essential conditions without which the recovered memory movement could never have grown and flourished in the way it did.
– *Richard Webster*

Given that the mind will be open to suggestion and can be prone to imaginative fantasy, it seems entirely possible for the client in therapy to believe implicitly in any theories that the clinician may expound, whether knowingly or unknowingly. In fact, the client – often much in need of help and guidance – will have a vested interest in utterly believing the therapist (see Chapter 13 – "Transference and Countertransference"). If the practitioner were, albeit inadvertently, to make a pronouncement about the nature of the client's problem, then he/she may well be inclined, therefore, to believe what has been put forward. Thus, a false memory can be born and, if the belief takes hold ferociously, it may then take some time for the glue to melt, and some say that, once it adheres, the superglue may never dissolve.

> Considerable research has been done on hypnosis as an investigative tool, and it generally yields conflicting conclusions about hypnosis as a reliable memory retriever. Some studies suggest that hypnosis can be used to enhance recall, while others demonstrate that it only increases the tendency to accept suggested memories or create confabulations and incorporate them into firmly held beliefs as if they were true.
> – *Michael Yapko*

The result of having had a false memory implanted can then be the total destruction of the client's life – especially if this results in confrontation with an alleged abuser or entails estrangement from his/her family. False accusers are those people who have been the victims of implanted false suggestions – implanted usually during therapy – who have developed a false-memory syndrome and who have then wrongly accused family members or others of childhood sexual abuse. In some cases, of course, the subject of the false-memory syndrome will realise that his/her memories are inaccurate and will then retract his/her accusations but, in the interim, much psychological damage may have been done to both the victim and to his/her family.

> Accused families have formed themselves into societies to proclaim their innocence, raise awareness of a new problem and promote research and education. More than 18,000 families have sought information from the False Memory Syndrome Foundation (FMSF) established in Philadelphia in 1992. False memory societies have since been formed in Australia, Canada, The Netherlands, New Zealand, Sweden, Israel and the UK. The British False Memory Society (BFMS), founded in 1993, has received requests for information from nearly 900 families.
> – *Sydney Brandon*

The false-memory syndrome camp will also regard childhood amnesia as an explanation for the birth of a false memory. The client, for example, might appear to have a memory loss in the guise of infantile amnesia, that might be ripe for flowering into a recovered memory when this period of his/her life has been probed. This school of thought will believe that it is biologically impossible for an infant to remember anything at all during the first three to five years of life because his/her mind will not yet have sufficiently developed.

> However, a number of recent accounts of infantile amnesia do not require the concept of repression. Rather they rely on normal cognitive or social mechanisms and imply that memory is in some way organised later. The consequence of this is that early memories either cannot be accessed or do not exist in an accessible form. Infantile amnesia becomes a natural consequence of the development of the memory system. Within this framework, then, we can see how abuse which takes place before the age of four or thereabouts and does not continue beyond that age might not be retrievable in adulthood in a narrative form.
> – *John Morton*

The Power of Suggestion

> Does repression, or defensively motivated forgetting, exist? Despite some extreme views to the contrary, the wealth of cumulative clinical experience suggests that it does. However, repression is not the only reason why people forget. The ability to forget is, in some ways, as biologically necessary as the ability to remember, and there is a variety of mechanisms for forgetting that have nothing to do with trauma or repression. But a therapist who believes that if someone forgets, it automatically means there is something negative associated with the memory, will likely initiate a search for the sources of the presumed repression. This is a major reason why therapists unintentionally ask leading or suggestive questions of their clients.
> – *Michael Yapko*

We shall now consider the question of suggestibility as a human trait because it will be the client's susceptibility to the power of suggestion that can aid him/her during the therapeutic process on the one hand, or can exert a destructive influence on the other.

Human Suggestibility

> More serious would be remembering an event that has not taken place.
> This would be an instance of a false memory. There are one or two
> preliminary, research-based examples of where adults have been
> persuaded that particular things have happened to them.
> – *John Morton*

It seems undeniably clear that the client's mind will be susceptible to suggestion. Although the human organism should be a rational and thinking entity, anyone and everyone will be susceptible to suggestion. Every individual has – at least once in a lifetime – concurred with a majority decision, been swayed by an advertising slogan, been influenced by public opinion or followed a trendy pursuit. Most people have used the latest catchphrase, subscribed to a ridiculous fashion or kept abreast of a facile soap opera. The alternative would be for the client to become a hermit and to withdraw completely from society. Susceptibility to suggestion, therefore, will be part of mankind's instinctual nature and part of his heritage, and, because the human organism is a relatively primitive being, the client will tend to feel that there will be safety in numbers. Maybe this will be because mankind has animal instincts that make the client feel that he/she needs to be part of the herd for survivalist reasons. Maybe it will be because people are, by nature, social animals. Maybe it will be because man has learned to depend on others for safety and support. Maybe it will be because the client will need to acquire knowledge from others in a social group. Maybe it will be because the client can learn from others who may guide him/her and/or challenge him/her to strive for his/her existence. Maybe it will be because individuality can cause embarrassment and can damage the client's self-image. Maybe it will be because the client will have a need to belong and feel that he/she is a valuable and integral part of the society or the culture to which he/she subscribes. There may be many reasons for the client's susceptibility to suggestion, but the point at issue here will surely be that he/she will have this quality sensitivity amplified in the therapeutic context.

> In the absence of any specific memories of abuse, it is up to the
> individual to decide whether to accept the interpretation of abuse and
> whether to get absorbed in the hunt for whatever "evidence" is assumed
> to lie under a blanket of repression, waiting to be uncovered. As we have

seen, this is a time when a client is quite vulnerable to the suggestions of
the therapist.
– *Michael Yapko*

What Do You Suggest?

The social and sexual conflict which has been caused by recovered
memory therapy is already considerable. My impression is that this very
serious conflict is likely to continue unless we can face up to the
disturbing history of psychoanalysis and to the cultural influences which
shaped it. For only if we do this, is it likely that we can begin to grasp
how pervasive and powerful patriarchal attitudes are, and how easy it is
for those who genuinely and courageously seek liberation from them to
become ensnared by them themselves.
– *Richard Webster*

For the hypnoanalytical therapist it will be imperative that he/she
tread the therapeutic path very carefully and observe the golden
rules when using the powerful weapon of suggestion. The practitioner should not get carried away by his/her own convictions
and assumptions – however sound they may appear to be. The
therapist should not, unaided, reach any conclusion about the
client's background. The practitioner should not, by word or by
deed, suggest or imply any theories of abuse, neglect or maltreatment to the client. Once these sacrosanct rules and procedures
have been rigidly followed, the therapist will then be admirably
placed to tackle therapy with the client who has been a victim of
any form of abuse, neglect or ill-treatment. The clinician can then
act in the best interests of the client whether or not he/she upholds
the theory of memory repression and its recovery and/or the existence of the false-memory syndrome.

Most responsible therapists working with survivors of childhood
maltreatment, for instance, would agree that to make suggestions
to the client would be acting outside the boundaries of a healthy
therapeutic relationship and will inherently be infringing the practitioner's professional code of conduct. The therapist may have
his/her suspicions and may even be sure that he/she is correct in
his/her assumptions, but on no account should his/her opinions
be expressed to the client by means of a conclusive diagnosis. The
practitioner may have a checklist of indicators that imply that a
client has been sexually victimised, for instance, but, until the

client reveals his/her own evidence, such suspicions should remain steadfastly unvoiced. Suggestion will be dynamite in the analytical hypnotherapist's consulting room and a lethal weapon not to be employed indiscriminately. This point cannot be reiterated too strongly.

When dealing with any client who may have been a victim of childhood abuse, a number of rules should be adhered to without exception. The therapist should not make any assumptions at all as to the nature of the client's disorder. The therapist should not devise a checklist of symptoms in order to make a concrete diagnosis. The practitioner should not voice any suspicions of childhood abuse in the form of sexual, physical or emotional abuse. The clinician should not set himself/herself the task of discovering childhood abuse. The therapist should not encourage the client to believe that he/she has been a victim of childhood abuse in any form. The therapist should not search for repressed memories. In principle, these rules should be applied generally to all clients. A prescriptive diagnosis will be a presumptuous suggestion to make and will, in fact, be labelling the client with a condition that he/she might not even be aware of having. The therapist should endeavour, therefore, to relieve the client of his/her symptoms but not add to them by spouting psychological jargon or inventing a new disorder.

> Once a trend in beliefs is established, it gathers a momentum all its own. It attracts followers, but it also creates a backlash. In the case of sexual abuse, at one extreme there are alarmists who seem to see evidence of abuse almost everywhere they look. At the other extreme, are those who hide their heads in the sand because they believe that abuse is only a nasty figment of someone's perverse imagination. Such radical positions rarely represent reality.
> – *Michael Yapko*

When using investigative therapy with a client, it will be the therapist's job to listen and to withhold comment (see Chapter 2, Volume 2 – "Therapeutic Investigation"). If the client relates any abusive experiences, then the therapist should listen and offer professional assistance. Anything that even smacks of dictatorship or advice-giving will be professionally unethical. The client should be encouraged but not exploited. The client should, therefore, be provided with a vehicle for freedom of speech devoid of judgment and criticism. The client should not view the therapist as a colluder or as a conspirator in his/her quest for revenge on an abuser. The golden rule may possibly be: If in doubt, remain silent!

> Some people appear to be more susceptible than others to suggestion and people under hypnosis are particularly vulnerable to suggestion both that false things did happen and that real things did not happen. Authority figures would be more likely to influence memory. Much of the attack from the False Memory organisations is on therapists who strongly suggest to their clients that they have suffered CSA. However, it is the case that people traumatised as children are more suggestible as well as susceptible to hypnosis.
> – *John Morton*

The client in the therapeutic context will not only be susceptible to suggestion as a human being but will also be liable to believe, at face value, whatever the therapist may say because of the intense nature of the therapeutic relationship and the likely manifestation of transference (see Chapter 13 – "Transference and Countertransference"). The client will often see the therapist as a trusted mentor with a greater knowledge and an incomparable understanding of the workings of the mind. Often the client will have a desire to please the therapist because of the caring relationship that will have developed and because he/she may have a desire to be sympathetically received by the therapist. In an atmosphere in which the client has been encouraged to share all his/her feelings in a safe environment and to talk through personal problems, he/she will be likely to be more than willing to trust implicitly anything the therapist may suggest. The client, thus, will be open to suggestion and more than willing to comply with it. After all, some clients will go to see a hypnotherapist for a commodity known as *suggestive therapy*. It has, of course, not been unknown for a victim of childhood sexual abuse to consult a hypnotherapist and to expect to receive suggestive therapy in order to help him/her to forget all about it!

The competent therapist should, at all times, take a neutral stance, thereby allowing the client to be himself/herself and to express his/her thoughts accordingly. Sometimes it will be necessary for the client to feel that the therapist sincerely believes him/her and, on other occasions, his/her role will be to make no comment. The practitioner will need to exercise professional judgment and to adopt a responsible attitude towards the client and his/her predicament in such circumstances. It will be essential for the client to feel that he/she can trust the practitioner to believe his/her tale of woe, but the therapist should not use this validation as an excuse to express his/her personal opinions on the matter. If the practitioner finds that his/her position with the client has become untenable, then it might be wise for the therapist to discuss the matter in depth with a competent supervisor.

> It is necessary to distinguish (1) those cases in which someone knows *and has known all along* that he or she was abused from (2) those cases in which someone independently remembers repressed memories from (3) those cases in which a therapist facilitates recall of repressed memories from (4) those cases in which a therapist *suggests* memories of abuse.
> – Michael Yapko

Exploring the Client's Recollections

> The idea that memory is not an accurate recording device turns our conventional notions upside down and backwards. In doing so, it offers a reprieve to traumatised people who are caught on the endless treadmill of trying to piece together a coherent movie of what happened to them.
> – Peter Levine

The therapist may elect purposefully to undertake memory exploration and abreactive discharge with the client in an effort to resolve traumatic conflict or psychic distress. The analytic process can be a means of unveiling suppression and lifting repression and, in doing so, can allow the client to discharge his/her accompanying emotions cathartically when he/she locates the originating cause of his/her dilemma (see Chapter 1, Volume 2 – "The Hypnoanalytic Approach"). The practitioner should, of course, be aware that the client may unearth repressed material almost without any therapeutic intervention and may well do so merely by the application of the trance state when emotive responses may surface. The basis for the effectiveness of hypnoanalytic therapy will be underpinned by the premise that emotive responses are the human organism's controlling force in the interests of mankind's survival.

One salient factor that both the client and the therapist should bear in mind will be that total recall may not be an essential factor in the client's recovery process. The therapist need only deal with what the client presents and not search endlessly to recover memories that may not have been recorded or are not of significance to his/her recovery. When dealing with the client's emerging memories, the therapist may well also encounter the inevitable inhibition to reveal suppressed or buried material (see Chapter 12 – "Resistance"). When handling the client who may be undergoing the ordeal of resisting the memory-recovery process, the therapist may wish to consider a number of factors that may be responsible for such reticence. Let us consider some questions that the therapist might ponder in order to identify the reason for the client's understandable self-restraint.

- Does the therapeutic setting provide a congenial environment in which the client can feel free to disclose the intimate details of his/her past?
- Does the client consider that the therapeutic context is safe enough for him/her to reveal his/her innermost thoughts and feelings?
- Does the client have confidence in the therapist?
- Could the client believe that the therapist might reject him/her once he/she has revealed his/her deadly secrets?
- Is the therapy conducted at an appropriate pace for the client as an individual?
- Does the client feel generally relaxed and comfortable?
- Has the client cleared sufficient emotional baggage of a mildly distressing nature in preparation for shifting his/her major repressive material?
- Will the client lose his/her precious secondary gains once his/her problems have been resolved?
- Will the client's mind eventually become tired of resisting?
- Can the client cope with the knowledge revealed – particularly if this is likely to be of a highly distressing nature?
- Does the client feel fear or guilt that might be so profound that he/she would find the disclosure of psychic material even more disturbing than living with his/her symptoms?
- Is the client's unconscious resistance caused by the belief that he/she must not know consciously what happened for fear of causing further psychic damage?

Let us now take a case-study example that can illustrate the dangers for the practitioner of making a premature assumption when probing the client's memory in the therapeutic context.

Case-study example – insecurity
This client sought therapy because of her feelings of insecurity and a low self-esteem.

During the first session, the client mentioned that she had a suspicion of having been sexually abused by her father. The therapist also quietly noted that the client had a minor skin disorder around her mouth. The client stated, furthermore, that she felt withdrawn but had always sought to be with people in order to assuage her feelings of loneliness. The idea of being on her own created a great discomfort for the client and, for this reason, she had endeavoured to find herself an intimate partner.

In hypnosis, the client was invited to explore her childhood memories and she initially recalled events from her junior-school and senior-school days that had contributed to her debased self-esteem. One central theme of the client's recollection, however, inevitably caused her to reach an impasse. The client would claim that everything had gone dark in her mind or that she could not recall anything. The scene at which the client became stuck was one of herself at around the young age of seven years when she was in the bath at home. The client had been playing with the water and generally enjoying the pleasant experience of bathing. At some point, however, her father had walked into the bathroom. He stood over the toilet, undid his zip, took out his penis and began to urinate. The client then recalled excreting into the bath, although the order of events was fragmented. When this episode was recounted, however, the client would then experience an abre-action and manifest a great deal of fear. The client, however, would express fear merely at the idea of recalling the event. In addition, no matter how frequently the client spoke of the event, she continued to experience a significant fear reaction as if something existed that was beyond her conscious grasp.

The client was then asked to focus on the moment when she had experienced the greatest degree of fear. It transpired that this moment was just before she discharged her bowels into the bath.

The client was then asked to let her mind guide her to the original place where this fear had been initially experienced. The client's scene now shifted dramatically and her facial expression changed with relief. The client remembered being at school at approximately the age of five years during a break in the school playground. Distress began to manifest in the client's breathing pattern and she shifted her position in the chair several times. When asked what was happening to her, the client reported that she was being beckoned by a man who was standing at the school perimeter by the metal railings. What happened next was a complete shock to the client. The client had been pulled towards the fence and she had been sexually abused through the playground's railings. The abuser had forced her to perform oral sex and had also touched her genitals. The abuser had ejaculated over her face and then had swiftly left her. In the distance she could see the other children but no-one had paid any attention to what had been going on. The event, therefore, had left the client traumatised but she had never spoken about it to anyone because she believed that it had been her own fault. The client's unconscious mind, in fact, had reasoned that the event would not have happened if she had not gone over to the playground's railings.

When the client saw her father urinating a few years later, she had then, by association, unconsciously connected the previous event and her mind had then gone blank. Subsequently, the young client had then gone through a period of not wanting her father to hold her, to hug her or, even, to contact her in any way. The client, in addition, now confessed to feeling compelled to have oral sex whenever she went out with a new boyfriend and yet she felt dirty for having done so. The client, thus, was able to resolve the root cause of her insecurities and feelings of low self-esteem and, of course, to resume a healthy relationship with her father and her current partner.

Client Profiling

The analytical hypnotherapy practitioner may wish to ponder the following points when formulating a profile for the client.

- In what ways does the client manifest memories of his/her past experience?
- Does the client manifest emotive memory together with event memory and somatic memory?
- Is the client in touch with physical sensation when recalling past experiences?
- Is the client able to express emotive reactions when recalling past experience?
- In what way does the client organise perceptive processes?
- Can the client recall past experiences with ease and facility?
- Does the client evade recollection of traumatic or distressing episodes in his/her life?
- In what ways have the client's memory storage processes been influenced?
- In what ways have the client's recollections been distorted or scrambled?
- Does the client have a tendency towards forgetfulness?
- Can the client distinguish between explicit memory and implicit memory recollections?
- Has the client indicated any manifestations of preverbal memory?
- Has the client ever experienced intuitive or predictive qualities that might emanate from his/her preconscious memory?
- Does the client tend to screen off unpleasant memories or associations?
- Has the client ever suffered from any form of false memory?
- Is the client particularly susceptible to influence from others?
- Does the client too readily take up suggestions that the practitioner might casually pose?
- Is the practitioner in any way inclined to impose his/her opinions or personal values on the client?

Chapter 11

Defensive Strategies

Her childhood, then her adolescence, had taught her patience,
hope, silence and the easy manipulation of the weapons and
virtues of all prisoners.

– *Gabrielle Colette Sidonie*

What Is a Defensive Strategy?

Defence is not useful as a long-term solution. The distressing ideas
disappear only from *conscious* awareness: they do not go out of existence.
Because they are rooted in the inextinguishable biological drives of the
id, unconscious ideas exert continual pressure upon the mind, finding
expression in dreams, irrational actions, moods and so on. When the ego
becomes overloaded and is consequently unable to handle the pressures
engendered by defence, unconscious ideas erupt in the form of
psychological symptoms.
– *David Smith*

A defensive strategy (or an *ego-defence mechanism*) will be an unconscious or partially unconscious trait that the client will employ in a
feverish endeavour to keep traumatic or conflict-laden psychic
material locked up in a secure and impenetrable corner of the
mind. The defensive strategy will act in a protective capacity when
the client has been faced with an overwhelming or unmanageable
psychic crisis. The defensive strategy will often manifest at an
unconscious level when the bucket is full and the client's psychological being cannot take any more and concludes that there is no
other way of coping with prevailing conditions. Keeping unpleasant memories and negative emotive expression out of conscious
awareness will give the client the illusion of psychic homeostasis
by not exposing him/her to the rigours of his/her own psychological trauma. Essentially the function of a defensive strategy, therefore, will be to distort reality in the best survivalist interests of the

client. The defensive strategy will also enable the client to relieve immediate distress or to allay anxiety by retreating from reality. The defensive strategy, moreover, will be a type of neurotic coping device rather than being solely primitive in nature, but often the mechanism will be the only agency that the client's mind will have at its disposal in times of distress.

Self-deception will, of course, arise when a defensive strategy has been created because the client will start to believe that his/her life can really be simpler because he/she can avoid the pain of lifting the lid on reality. The defensive strategy, however, will distort the client's view of reality by generating irrational thinking and chaotic reactions, that will hamper his/her psychological development, impair clear thinking, dilute true feeling, overshadow realistic perception and, of course, disturb his/her peace of mind. A psychic-defence strategy will also give the client a distorted sense of self. It will be as if the client will seek to protect himself/herself by hiding from his/her own innermost nature and, furthermore, his/her mind will find a means of shielding him/her from the perceptions of others. In the long term, however, such a contrivance will not serve as the client's friend although his/her mind may still be attempting to protect him/her from psychological pain.

Once a defensive strategy has been employed by the human psyche, of course, it will then need to be maintained by the client in the long term. This long-term maintenance programme, however, will give rise to inevitable psychological difficulties and to overt symptoms with which the client will have to contend. Defensive strategies, furthermore, will dictate the client's behaviour and motivation and will influence his/her personal beliefs, attitudes and convictions. When there has been a struggle to keep a defensive strategy in place and when the client's symptoms become too intolerable, he/she will be likely to seek therapeutic assistance because his/her defence may really have outlived its usefulness.

The therapist will need to be able to identify the client's defensive strategies and general coping abilities when these become evident. The practitioner should also guide the client into fathoming the impact of his/her distress and encourage him/her to relinquish any related behavioural strategies or tendencies of a defensive nature.

Defensive Strategy Formation

> Hypnotic techniques can be employed to facilitate access to material and processes normally inaccessible to the individual's "ego", by providing strategies which by-pass "ego-defence mechanisms" such as repression, displacement, reaction-formation, intellectualisation and rationalisation.
> – *Helmut Karle & Jennifer Boys*

The main defensive strategies that fall within psychodynamic theory in general can be classified according to function and can be considered in terms of the reasons why the client might adopt such a scheme. A defensive strategy will be employed by the human organism from an unconscious origin in order to allow the client to conceal the distress, trauma and self-doubt that have resulted from psychological disturbance. It will be as if the client has become a victim of his/her own inability to cope with the external world and the psychological commotion that his/her experiences have engendered. Most defensive strategies will significantly distort the client's personality, principally, in order to conceal the reality of his/her internal turmoil and, secondly, in order to mitigate the effect of his/her interaction with others in the social world and, in doing so, to safeguard his/her self-concept. The client's defensive strategies may well have been around for a long time and, even, may have been formed in childhood. It would be as if the child knows too little while the adult knows too much, and this adage would serve to underlie the reasons for the formation of a defensive strategy as a survivalist function. Let us now turn to the reasons why the client may adopt a given defensive strategy.

Primitive Strategies

A defensive strategy may be adopted as a primitive means of survival or because the client has a deep-seated need to survive in the social world. Primitive defences are desperate measures that the client's psyche will grab hold of in times of extreme crisis. The intention of a primitive defence will be vigorously to suppress traumatic experience registered within the client's unconscious mind. In this category will fall defences such as repression, denial, dissociation and conversion.

Self-distorting Strategies

The adoption of a defensive strategy may result in a deformity of the client's personality because, if his/her personal truth were revealed to his/her conscious awareness, such knowledge would be deemed to cause serious disturbance. The client may, in some cases, utilise the powers of his/her intellect in order to fabricate his/her personal truth. Examples of this phenomenon are negation, rationalisation, projection, displacement and reversal.

Redirective Strategies

A defensive strategy may also serve to rechannel the client's psychic energies into more socially-acceptable areas or supposedly-mature activities. Socially-acceptable defences are high-minded actions such as identification, sublimation, reaction formation and compensation.

Nonconformist Strategies

Finally, strategies that may not be acceptable to society at large and may, therefore, constitute a form of rebellion are those that display immature tendencies such as introjection, regression and acting out.

> Held within the symptoms of trauma are the very energies, potentials, and resources necessary for their constructive transformation. The creative healing process can be blocked in a number of ways – by using drugs to suppress symptoms, by over-emphasising adjustment or control, or by denial or invalidation of feelings and sensations.
> – *Peter Levine*

Defensive Strategy Classifications

> The hypnotic dissociation makes it possible for either the content or the affect, or both, of relevant memories to by-pass ego-defences.
> – *Helmut Karle & Jennifer Boys*

We shall now take a close look at each of the most common defensive strategies and consider the ways in which such contrivances can manifest in the distressed client (see Figure 5: "Defensive strategies").

Figure 5: Defensive Strategies

Strategy	Description	Function
Repression	Client will unconsciously bury memories, psychological and physiological distress	*Primitive strategies* Client will undergo a primitive response to psychological trauma
Denial or **disavowal**	Client will preconsciously discard memories, psychological and physiological distress	
Dissociation or **isolation**	Client will detach from psychological and physiological distress	
Conversion	Client will convert psychological distress into a psychological or physiological symptom	
Negation or **minimisation**	Client will create a false self-belief which plays down reality	*Self-distorting strategies* Client will undergo self-distortion, which will be designed to conceal unacceptable reality
Rationalisation or **justification**	Client will intellectually excuse his/her own behaviour or the conduct of others	
Projection	Client will imbue others with his/her own traits	
Displacement	Client will shift emotive expression to an alternative target	
Reversal	Client will internalise blame which should rightly be attributed to another	
Identification	Client will ally himself/herself with acceptable people or worthwhile causes	*Redirective strategies* Client will undertake a socially acceptable practice, which will be designed to improve self-image
Sublimation	Client will divert unpleasant desires into socially-acceptable forms of behaviour	
Reaction formation	Client will form a negative reaction to something to which he/she is actually attracted	
Compensation	Client will overdevelop in one area in order to conceal perceived weakness in another	
Introjection	Client will adopt the unhealthy values of others	*Nonconformist strategies* Client will indulge in immature behaviour, which will be intended to relieve psychological distress
Regression	Client will spontaneously relapse into an immature psychological state	
Acting out or **re-enactment**	Client will behave impulsively in order to materialise an inner fantasy	

When considering such strategies, the practitioner will note that often the distinction between one definition and another is rather thin. Essentially, the therapist should not get bogged down with precise definitions when dealing with the client but merely get a flavour for the ways in which he/she will avoid or conceal his/her personal truth.

Repression

> The impulses in the entrance hall of the unconscious are out of sight of the conscious, which is in the other room; to begin with they must remain unconscious. If they have already pushed their way forward to the threshold and have been turned back by the watchman, then they are inadmissible to consciousness; we speak of them as *repressed*. But even the impulses which the watchman has allowed to cross the threshold are not on that account necessarily conscious as well; they can only become so if they succeed in catching the eye of consciousness. We are therefore justified in calling this second room the system of the preconscious.
> – *Sigmund Freud*

Repression will occur when an event has been perceived by the client as a major trauma and will then be placed totally out of his/her conscious awareness. When the client undergoes repression, it will be an unconscious act of burying memories and emotive responses in order to obscure these elements from his/her conscious awareness as a means of protecting him/her from the perception and the reality of his/her own trauma (see Chapter 10 – "Memory"). Repression will be the unconscious mind's way of ensuring that the client can survive the critical traumatic experience by erecting barriers that prevent recollections of distressing life events. Repressed information, in short, may be described as unconscious material that has been debarred from the client's conscious awareness, and, as a result, a disturbing symptom and/or an uncharacteristic behaviour will surface as a substitute and a compromise. Repression may, therefore, be a precondition for the existence and emergence of a symptom. Psychic repression will manifest due to the client's mental inhibition when images and memories are blocked by the withdrawal or redirection of attention. A repressed memory will usually be buried deeply within the client's unconscious mind and may need to be unearthed with a hypnotic pitchfork in order to ensure that the client can gain lasting relief from his/her distress. The emotive responses that have been buried during the act of repression will be those of an intensely painful nature – the realisation of which will often be traumatic, in itself, for the client.

The phenomenon of repression has been deemed to be a natural occurrence, that will assist the human organism's instinctive need for survival. When the client finds himself/herself either psychologically or physiologically ill-equipped to cope with a situation that he/she has perceived as traumatic, he/she will then automatically select an alternative means of defending himself/herself from the impending danger. The client may instinctively bury the memory of the event in order to ensure his/her continued survival because unconsciously he/she will consider that he/she could not live with the fear or the guilt associated with the memory of the dire traumatic experience.

> Freud believed that we repress those thoughts that are simultaneously highly exciting and riddled with guilt or shame. Chief among these are sexual and aggressive impulses. Freud believed that pressures of socialisation cause us to hide aspects of our sexuality that contravene social mores and to suppress our tendency to obtain pleasure through harming and exploiting others. We all, therefore, possess a store of highly charged unconscious sexual and aggressive fantasies.
> *– David Smith*

Repressed material may, however, emerge or become evident, for example, when the client is attracted by or is repelled by certain types of event. The client who has been severely punished as a child, for example, may have an abhorrence of violence or may delight in indulging in it. The client's conscious behaviours will be, by this means, unconsciously motivated in the form of either avoidance or attraction, that will serve as an underlying reminder of the primary source of his/her distress. The client's repressions may, in many cases, surface in the form of dreams, mysterious flashbacks, unaccountable physical sensations, dissociative numbness, feelings of unreality and amnesia for long periods of time fully covering the time when the source of the traumatic experience occurred in his/her life.

> Forgetting is one of the most common and effective ways children deal with sexual abuse. The human mind has tremendous powers of repression. Many children are able to forget about the abuse, even as it is happening to them.
> *– Ellen Bass & Laura Davis*

The therapist should be aware that the term repression does not refer only to repressed memories but that it includes all permutations of that which can be placed below the surface of consciousness and, thus, can become inaccessible to the client's conscious awareness. Repression can, therefore, embrace all the client's emotive responses, perceptions, attitudes, beliefs, motivations and physical sensations that he/she experienced at the time of the original distressful occurrence. The longer the client has endured his/her distress may, on some occasions, increase the intensity of his/her suffering. The client may, in some cases, feel more of a psychological impact while, in other instances, he/she may be affected primarily on a physiological level. The act of unearthing such material will, consequently, mean that the client can gain a realisation and an enlightenment of that which he/she has been hitherto unaware. Such realisation will then have the effect of bringing much-needed insight as well as symptomatic relief for the client.

> Psychotherapy is much more than "uncovering", and the latter is only the first step in a process of re-working the uncovered material in such a way as to reduce traumatic impact, resolve conflicting feelings and attitudes, and above all to work through the manifold and complex ways in which such traumata have become woven into the life of the patient and, indeed, the very structure of his personality.
> – *Helmut Karle & Jennifer Boys*

Denial

> It is obvious that this ego is not a trustworthy or impartial agency. The ego is indeed the power which disavows the unconscious and has degraded it into being repressed.
> – *Sigmund Freud*

Denial (or *disavowal*) and other forms of memory suppression will occur when an event has been perceived by the client as a minor trauma and will then be placed partially out of his/her conscious awareness. Memories that have been subject to this form of distortion may surface from the client's preconscious memory during the therapeutic encounter (see Chapter 10 – "Memory"). The client may be able to remember a semi-forgotten experience in conscious awareness but the recollection will have been virtually lost from view until a search – possibly under hypnosis – can be instituted with some degree of resolve.

Denial and amnesia are not volitional choices that the person makes;
they do not indicate weakness of character, personality dysfunction, or
deliberate dishonesty. This dysfunctional pathway becomes patterned in
our physiology. At the time of a traumatic event, denial helps preserve
the ability to function and survive. However, when chronic, denial
becomes a maladaptive symptom of trauma.
– *Peter Levine*

Denial will be an unconsciously motivated device that the client
may use for papering over the cracks of the past by a pretence or
a self-delusion. The mechanism of denial will operate in a manner
similar to that of repression. Data will be buried in the client's
mind at a semiconscious or preconscious level but will not be
debarred totally from his/her conscious awareness. Disavowal
will, therefore, concern material that the client can remember but
would rather not think about and so it tends to get swept under
the carpet accidentally on purpose. Sometimes the victim of
trauma will have denied his/her experiences because they were
extremely unpleasant but – unlike the case of total amnesia –
he/she will still be aware that a disaster has occurred. The client
may well admit to being distressed but will have only a vague
notion of its existence and certainly may have little or no idea of
the impact that his/her trauma has caused. The client, for example, may often appear to believe sincerely that the effects of sus-
taining a dysfunctional childhood were only minimal. On
investigation, however, the client may well discover that his/her
past has, in fact, taken a ruthless toll.

Denying is turning your head the other way and pretending that
whatever is happening isn't or what has happened didn't. It's a basic
pattern in alcoholic families. It's almost universal where incest is
concerned. "If I just ignore it long enough, it will go away."
– *Ellen Bass & Laura Davis*

Dissociation

Isolation is the process of detaching thought from feeling. One might, for
instance, recollect an important childhood loss without any sense of grief
or rage.
– *David Smith*

Dissociation (or *isolation*) will be the client's bring-down-the-iron-
curtain syndrome whereby he/she will lock his/her emotive

expression away in a watertight casket. Dissociation can be a form of emotional numbing that may indicate that the client has undergone a traumatic experience (see Chapter 13, Volume 2 – "Post-Traumatic Stress Disorder"). Sometimes the dissociative state can be described as an out-of-body experience because the client will feel as if his/her mind were not inhabiting his/her body. If the client has closed off his/her emotive expression and/or physical sensations as a shock reaction, this way of coping with life can then become an in-built tendency. The client, for instance, may then have a low-level threshold for emotive reaction. The client's dissociation may, similarly, lead to a numbing of physiological sensation – perhaps to the extent that he/she cannot feel any physical pain.

Hypnosis can be an ideal vehicle for initiating the reconnective process for the client because he/she can be given an opportunity to revisit that place where the separation of mind and body occurred and then be invited to resolve the original conflict. The client, in this way, can release the emotive reactions that caused the conflict and can then initiate a subtle reintegration whereby the parasympathetic nervous system can be pacified and physiological malfunction can be rectified.

> Symptoms had a meaning and were residues or reminiscences of those emotional situations.
> – *Sigmund Freud*

Conversion

> Conversion is the process of turning a distressing idea into a physical disorder. For example, the sense of dependency (being unable to "stand on one's own two feet") might lead to incapacitating leg pains.
> – *David Smith*

Conversion will be the method by which the client's being will convert conflict, trauma or distress into a psychosomatic or psychogenic symptom (see Chapter 11, Volume 2 – "Psychosomatic Disorders"). Often a conversion symptom will utilise the mind's capacity for symbolic representation (see Chapter 14 – "Dreams and Symbolic Imagery"). An itching-skin disorder, for example, may denote emotional irritation for the client or an eating disorder may depict his/her inability to speak about the truth. The victim of childhood sexual abuse may develop a genital infection as a form of conversion from what he/she perceives as the contamination of his/her body (see Chapter 15, Volume 2 – "The Effects of Childhood Abuse"). The henpecked husband may develop a pain in the neck when he thinks about his wife. The overstressed employee may be too ill to go to work but may be well enough for a round of golf. The client's mind, in such cases, may be signalling the source of his/her distress, that the therapist can often highlight in a quest for beneficial change.

> It introduced a dynamic factor, by supposing that a symptom arises through the damming-up of an effect, and an economic factor, by regarding that same symptom as the product of transformation of an amount of energy which would otherwise have been employed in some other way.
> – *Sigmund Freud*

Negation

> Negation means forming a false belief that one does *not* hold some distressing attitude. For example, it is possible to adamantly hold that one does not have any homosexual inclinations to avoid the homosexual side of one's nature.
> – *David Smith*

Negation (or *minimisation*) will be the means whereby the client can deceive himself/herself into believing something that he/she will regard as being socially acceptable, that, therefore, will not isolate him/her from the crowd. The client who displays a tendency to negation will form an unconsciously-driven false belief about his/her past traumatic experiences, that will serve as a cover-up in order to deflect attention away from reality. If, for example, the client feels that he/she is, in some way, abnormal or different from others, he/she may actively engage in emphasising his/her normality. Similarly, the client uncertain of his/her sexual identity may strive to develop that which he/she regards as being agreeable to society at large (see Chapter 12, Volume 2 – "Dysfunctional Relationships"). The client who may have been regularly maltreated by a violent intimate partner may perhaps make excuses for his/her partner's conduct rather than confess to the world that he/she has been seriously ill-used.

> Minimising means pretending that whatever happened wasn't really
> that bad. It means saying "My dad's a little pissed off" when in fact he
> just smashed an armchair to bits. Kids growing up surrounded by abuse
> often believe that everyone else grows up the same way. Doesn't every
> father tuck his daughter into bed like that?
> *– Ellen Bass & Laura Davis*

Rationalisation

> Socially acceptable reasons are given for thoughts and actions based on
> unacceptable motives. An example would be eating an entire chocolate
> cake because we "didn't want it to spoil in the summer heat".
> *– Richard Gross & Rob McIlveen*

Rationalisation (or *justification*) will be the personal argument that
the client uses to deceive himself/herself about an absurdly-obvi-
ous fact. The client will be economical with the truth and will manufacture a whole catalogue of excuses, that seek – often
preposterously – to conceal his/her own personal truth. Rationalisation will be the client's way of intellectually excusing his/her
own behaviour, and yet he/she will still feel the need to justify
his/her actions to others.

> Rationalisation in this special sense means that, on a conscious level, we
> believe we are acting or thinking or feeling for a particular reason, a
> reason that seems rational. But the true reason is something we would
> rather not face because, perhaps, it puts us in a bad light, or shows us
> something about ourselves we'd rather not know or is painful to us.
> *– Margaret Reinhold*

The client may also, of course, unjustifiably excuse the conduct of
others who have wronged him/her. The victim of violence may,
for example, state that his/her perpetrator really did not know
what he/she was doing or did not mean to act in such a manner.
The rapist, for instance, may say that he/she had to carry out the
violation because he/she was upset or deprived of an alternative
sexual outlet. Rationalisation, hence, can often display a kind of
sour-grapes quality and the astute therapist can usually quite easily spot such lame excuses.

> Rationalising is the means by which children explain away abuse. "Oh
> he couldn't help it. He was drunk." They invent reasons that excuse the
> abuser. "Four kids was just too much for her. No wonder she didn't take
> care of me."
> *– Ellen Bass & Laura Davis*

Projection

Unacceptable motives or impulses are transferred to others. For example,
a man who is sexually attracted to a neighbour perceives the neighbour
is being sexually attracted to him.
– *Richard Gross & Rob McIlveen*

Projection will be a means of perceiving in others those traits that the client will find unacceptable in himself/herself or, in some way, may not wish to acknowledge in himself/herself. It will be as if the client will need to externalise those characteristics that he/she can recognise as being unacceptable, yet will hesitate to acknowledge. By ascribing misdemeanours to others, the client will be diverting the attention of society away from his/her own perceived antisocial behaviour. The client, on the other hand, may imbue an acquaintance with laudable qualities as a form of hero worship. The client, in this case, will fear to recognise these praise-worthy qualities in himself/herself by putting someone else up on a pedestal in order to make himself/herself feel safe. Projection, therefore, will often occur when the client fears to acknowledge himself/herself as a worthy human being (see Chapter 12, Volume 2 – "Dysfunctional Relationships").

Projection will, of course, be the abusive parent's licence to abuse and the rapist's charter to attack (see Chapter 14, Volume 2 – "The Nature of Childhood Abuse"). The perpetrator of childhood abuse, for instance, may blame his/her victim for encouraging him/her to strike. The rapist may vehemently maintain that the victim was acting in a seductive or a tantalising manner and that, therefore, he/she became powerless to resist temptation.

Displacement

An emotional response is redirected from a dangerous object to a safe
one. For example, anger towards one's boss might be redirected towards
the family dog.
– *Richard Gross & Rob McIlveen*

Displacement will be the means by which the client can shift his/her unpleasant desires on to that which he/she considers to be a more appropriate target. Displacement will be a redirection of unacceptable emotive responses from one person to another or towards an object. This may be the means by which the client can shift from threat to safety by discharging his/her disagreeable emotive expression elsewhere. Displacement will be the kick-the-cat syndrome in practice, whereby the client, in fact, will feel angry with someone else but will find it easier to take it out on a defence-less pet. The client, for example, who feels rejected by a lover may seek solace by abusing a child or visiting a prostitute who may not be inclined to reject him/her. Similarly, a victim of childhood violence may feel irresistibly attracted to or repelled by a person who reminds him/her of his/her own violator.

> Much of the violence that plagues humanity is a direct or indirect result
> of unresolved trauma that is acted out in repeated unsuccessful attempts
> to re-establish a sense of empowerment.
> – *Peter Levine*

Reversal

> Reversal is the process of directing an attitude towards oneself rather
> than towards someone else. Resentment towards one's mother might, for
> example, be transformed into impulses towards self-harm.
> – *David Smith*

Reversal will be the way in which the client punishes himself/herself rather than express his/her inner negative reactions to others. With reversal, the client will unconsciously set in train an unacceptable attitude towards himself/herself. Often reversal will be seated in an internalisation of blame (see Chapter 8, Volume 2 – "Guilt and Shame Disorders"). Reversal can be a way for the client to avoid blaming others by putting the reproof on his/her own shoulders. The client who indulges in self-mutilation may, in fact, be expressing an unconscious wish to harm others while his/her social conscience will consider that the expression of such wishes would be unacceptable.

Identification

> Although identification is part of the developmental process by which
> children learn sex-role behaviours, it can also be a defensive reaction. It
> can enhance self-worth and protect one from a sense of being a failure.
> Thus, people who feel basically inferior may identify themselves with
> successful causes, organisations, or people in the hope that they will be
> perceived as worthwhile.
> *– Gerald Corey*

Identification will be the act of forming an alliance with acceptable
groups of people and worthwhile causes for the purpose of bol-
stering the client's self-regard and making him/her feel safe in
society. The client may become a flag-waver or a passionate campaigner in his/her attempt to gain self-worth. The rape victim, for
instance, may campaign for the justice of all other rape victims.
The abandoned child may open a children's home. The victim of a
travel disaster may operate a helpline for bereaved survivors. The
wounded-healer syndrome may also, of course, apply to the clinical therapist. It will be as if the client can acknowledge that he/she
has experienced distress and will then want to make certain that
no-one else will suffer in an identical manner.

Sublimation

> From the Freudian perspective, many of the great artistic contributions
> resulted from a redirection of sexual or aggressive energy into creative
> behaviours. Sublimation involves diverting sexual or aggressive energy
> into other channels, ones that are usually socially acceptable and
> sometimes even admirable.
> *– Gerald Corey*

Sublimation will involve diverting the client's unpleasant
thoughts or actions into more acceptable forms of behaviour. The
client may, for example, channel aggressive energy into sporting
activities or redirect sexual energy into artistic ventures. The client
will, in many cases, be venerated for his/her achievements
because they are designed to be socially acceptable and praise-
worthy. The potential child-molester may, for example, pursue a
caring profession in which children are protected (see Chapter 14,
Volume 2 – "The Nature of Childhood Abuse"). The danger, of
course, will reside in the fact that the potentiality to abuse will

remain dormant but could, therefore, be triggered under certain conditions. The headlines are full of gossip about those who have unsuccessfully buried their sublimated desires.

Reaction Formation

> The opposite of an unacceptable wish or impulse is expressed. For example, a person strongly drawn to gambling may express the view that gambling is repulsive.
> – *Richard Gross & Rob McIlveen*

Reaction formation will be a response that the client can form to events that are diametrically opposed to his/her true inclinations or wishes. The client, for example, may habitually form an intensely negative reaction to something to which he/she is, in fact, drawn. Reaction formation will, in a way, be a form of active denial of unconscious desires. With this strategy, the client's mind will be attempting to avert threat and to hide his/her true feelings by expressing opposite impulses in order to put others off the scent. This may be the client's way of guarding against succumbing to his/her deepest motivations and, thereby, alienating himself/herself from society. The potential child-molester, for example, will denigrate or even campaign against child-abuse. The client who is overtly homophobic may often fear the reality of his/ her own sexual identity and may fear the consequences of public disclosure (see Chapter 12, Volume 2 – "Dysfunctional Relationships").

Compensation

> Compensation consists of masking perceived weaknesses or developing certain positive traits to make up for limitations. Thus, children who do not receive positive attention and recognition may develop behaviours designed to at least get negative attention. People who feel intellectually inferior may direct an inordinate degree of energy to building up their bodies; those who feel socially incompetent may become a "loner" and develop their intellectual capacities.
> – *Gerald Corey*

Compensation will result when the client overdevelops in one area in order to compensate for a perceived personal weakness in another. The client may, for example, undertake a punishing keep-fit programme in an attempt to compensate for his/her perceived intellectual inferiority. Alternatively, the client may become an intellectual recluse in order to counterbalance perceived social inadequacy.

Introjection

> The mechanism of introjection consists of taking in and "swallowing" the values and standards of others. For example, in concentration camps some of the prisoners dealt with overwhelming anxiety by accepting the values of the enemy through an identification with the aggressor. Another example is the abused child, who assumes the abusing parent's way of handling stresses and thus continues the cycle of child beating.
> – *Gerald Corey*

Introjection will come into play when the client emulates or adopts the values, beliefs, attributions, convictions and/or actions of those who have done him/her harm. Introjection will involve unconsciously emulating those standards of behaviour that would normally be unacceptable practice for the client. The process of introjection will engage the client in identifying with another, then internalising this identification and, finally, incorporating what has been taken on board into his/her own actions and outward perceptions. It will be as if the client can feel safe only if he/she gives solid credence to the actions of those who have hurt him/her and, in doing so, can avoid any form of rejection (see Chapter 7, Volume 2 – "Fear and Anxiety Disorders"). The client will, in many cases, be unconsciously protecting those who have wronged him/her by joining their team. The victim of childhood abuse, for example, who himself/herself becomes an offender will be employing the mechanism of introjection. The parent who thrashes his/her own child and then protests that he/she has been disciplining the child for his/her own benefit will be engaging in this dangerous form of self-deception.

> The man who was hit as a child will feel compelled to hit as an adult. The energy behind his need to strike out is none other than the energy contained in his traumatic symptoms. This unconscious compulsion can only be conquered by great acts of will until the energy is discharged.
> – *Peter Levine*

Regression

> Responding to a threatening situation in a way appropriate to an earlier
> age or level of development. For example, an adult has a "temper
> tantrum" when he/she does not get his/her own way.
> – *Richard Gross & Rob McIlveen*

Regression will be the means by which the client can recapture the past by spontaneously regressing to a former, immature psychological state. Regressive reactions will often be the client's passport to coping with distress by opting out of a situation and, perhaps, marshalling some sympathy in the process. The client may well reenact a previous scenario by returning unconsciously to an earlier time in his/her life whereby he/she will display childish behaviour, may have flashbacks or may indulge in baby-talk. Regression will, thus, be a sort of cry for help from the client's unconscious mind, that will manifest as an impulsive behavioural reaction.

Acting Out

> Acting out means taking some impulsive action to pre-empt awareness
> of distressing inner states. One might, for example, go shopping to ward
> off a sense of grief or depression.
> – *David Smith*

Acting out (or *re-enactment*) will be the medium through which the client assuages his/her own pain by behaving spontaneously or compulsively. It will be as if the client has a fantasy and that, by partially bringing this fantasy into reality, the act will relieve his/her distress by bringing him/her as close as possible to that place where he/she wishes to be. Retail therapy will be a form of acting out when the shopaholic compulsively overspends for the sake of it or buys commodities that he/she may never use.

> The phenomenon that drives the repetition of past traumatic events is
> called re-enactment. It is the symptom that dominates the last turn of the
> downward spiral in the development of trauma symptoms. Re-
> enactment is more compelling, mysterious, and destructive to us as
> individuals, as a society, and as a world community.
> – *Peter Levine*

Exploring the Client's Defensive Strategies

> Obviously, the real issue has nothing to do with the fear itself, but,
> rather, how we *hold* the fear. For some, the fear is totally irrelevant. For
> others, it creates a state of paralysis. The former hold their fear from a
> position of power (choice, energy and action), and the latter hold it from
> a position of pain (helplessness, depression and paralysis).
> – *Susan Jeffers*

The therapist's role will be to gently expose the client to the fact
that he/she may have built up some impenetrable defensive
strategies in the course of his/her life as a reaction against his/her
psychic distress. The therapist may need to highlight those strategies that the client has been employing and provide some reasons
why these mechanisms have served a very useful purpose in the
past. From this standpoint, the client can then be encouraged to
relinquish his/her defensive strategies because they are no longer
viable.

Identifying the Client's Defensive Strategies

The practitioner can often identify the client's defensive strategies
by intuitively reading the messages that he/she unconsciously
conveys in the therapeutic setting. The astute therapist can often
cleverly learn to interpret the client's unspoken messages. The list
below illustrates some examples of ways in which the client may
inadvertently communicate his/her defensive tactics in the form
of unconsciously-derived thoughts without ever putting such
messages into words. From these examples, the practitioner may
be able to formulate his/her own phrases that may fit precisely
into the client's frame of mind. Once the client's strategies have
been identified, the practitioner will then be admirably placed to
tackle the task of assisting him/her to overcome them.

- I'll wear a mask
- I'll run away and escape
- I'll be a loner
- I've got all I need
- I'll disguise myself
- I'll do a disappearing act
- I'll wear a bulletproof vest

- I'll bury my head in the sand
- I'll hide so that no-one will notice me
- I'll make you want me
- I'll be so irresistible
- I'll cuddle my teddy bear
- I'll be a doormat
- I'll punish myself
- I'll make everyone laugh
- I'll fight back
- I'll be the boss
- I'll build an empire
- I'll live dangerously
- I'll be a rebel
- I'll be a dropout
- I'll blame you
- I'll be a brilliant academic
- I'll be ever so clever
- I'll be an overachiever
- I'll live by the rules
- I'll look after myself really carefully
- I'll feel sorry for myself
- I'll find someone to love me at any price
- I'll care for everyone
- I'll be a cynic
- I'll be a masochist
- I'll be a sadist
- I'll live in a fantasy world
- I'll court lady luck

Overcoming the Client's Defensive Strategies

Once the client has been able to identify his/her defensive strategies, this realisation can, in itself, encourage him/her to relinquish them – particularly after investigation has revealed the need for the original formation of a given strategy. In order to ensure a more permanent resolution, however, the therapist may wish to actively set about helping the client to overcome his/her defensive manifestations.

The therapist might wish to consider a number of ways of utilising questioning techniques that can help the client to resolve his/her defensive psychic mechanisms. Some suggested questions are given below, that can provocatively stimulate the client's thought processes and can encourage self-analysis. The practitioner will, of course, be advised to pose all questions in a subtle manner so that the client will be hardly aware of having been asked a question.

- Do you tend to minimise your feelings and emotions?
- Do you have a tendency to put on a brave face even for the family and friends?
- Do you find that you are desperate to uphold the right image when others are present?
- Do you find yourself wanting to be seen in all the right places, wearing the latest gear and using the correct jargon?
- Do you have a tendency to withdraw into your own shell?
- Do you make it a rule never to allow anyone else to take control in any situation?
- Do you invariably put the feelings of others before your own?
- Do you tend not to want to get involved when things go wrong?
- Do you speak only when you are spoken to?
- Do you cheerfully hand over the responsibility for decision-making to others?
- Do you endeavour to be the life and soul of the party?
- Do you bury yourself in academic books or intensive study or political debate?
- Are you an avid collector of rare or precious artefacts?
- Do you feel passionately about a cause or a campaign?
- Do you take a philosophical attitude to most aspects of life?
- Do you usually take a what-will-be-will-be attitude to life?
- Do you believe that the universe will solve all your problems?
- Do you immerse yourself in an idyllic fantasy world where no-one else can reach you?
- Do you avoid social gatherings as much as possible?
- Do you devote much of your life to caring for others?
- Do you find yourself unable to commit to an intimate relationship?
- Are you good at climbing on to the soapbox?
- Do you constantly bluster and bumble about generally?

- Do you frequently let the world go by without really taking part?
- Do you often think that fantasy is reality?
- Do you frequently drift off into a daydream in order to avoid the tedium of living?

In answering the above questions, the client may also wish to rate his/her responses. A high, medium or low rating could be assigned to each of the client's responses or he/she may be asked to use a rising scale providing a 1-to-10 rating for each answer. When asking the client to give a rating, the practitioner, of course, should employ the same degree of subtlety as he/she would utilise when posing the question. In the case-study example below, the client gave a rating to a number of questions that allowed him to identify his defensive strategies and, ultimately, enabled him to find a means of resolving such tendencies.

Case-study example – social phobia

A male client who had suffered from a fear of social occasions was asked by the therapist some subtly-worded questions about his defensive strategies.

The therapist's questioning revealed that the client had a very secure social mask – the brave face that he donned whenever he could not possibly avoid social functions. The client worked in the advertising industry and, therefore, found increasingly that he was required to go to public functions when entertaining clients. The client admitted that he would smile frequently – particularly when he was nervous – and that he would tend to talk to individuals at parties rather than to remain with a group and that he had become adept at cracking jokes. He also confessed that he often declined invitations to business functions or found someone else in his department to deputise for him. The client was, naturally, scared that his lame excuses for nonattendance at such functions would be detected by his colleagues and that, as a result, he would be exposed to ridicule because of his phobia. On one occasion when the client was openly accused by a colleague of being party-shy, he was vehemently dismissive of this claim by the co-worker but secretly felt very ashamed at not being able to admit the truth. Following this confrontation, the client then began to work over-time more frequently in the hope that he could use this as an excuse for not attending social functions.

When the therapist highlighted the tendencies that the client had adopted, he was then able to gain insight into his avoidance tactics and his resultant lack of confidence. The client now had the framework from which to investigate his past experiences. Free association was used by the therapist in order to identify the fact that the client had been caned at school in front of the class and ridiculed by his fellow classmates. The client's parents, furthermore, had reprimanded him for his misconduct at school and this had reinforced the client's fear of others.

Once the client could see that his defensive strategies were in place in order to protect him as a young schoolchild and the originating cause had been addressed, both his symptoms and his defensive strategies began to dissolve.

The suggested metaphors in the next few paragraphs can assist the client to understand the nature of his/her defensive strategies and can invite him/her to dissipate them.

How do we protect ourselves?

Our protection strategy will be our mind's way of anaesthetising itself from any perceived danger. When we are overwhelmed by life's experiences in childhood and cannot understand the world about us, we need to resort to measures that will mitigate the shock. We, therefore, employ the very limited resources we have with which to protect ourselves from harm at all times. The baby cries when danger of starvation is nigh or when loneliness or boredom is threatening or when teething is a painful experience. Baby's protection mechanism is his/her lung capacity or his/her ability to throw that rattle out of the pram.

In early childhood years, our protection mechanism is likely to be our imagination because it may be the only device we have at our disposal. We, therefore, put on that imaginary bulletproof vest, that face mask or that wall of silence in order to hide our feelings from others – because we believe that our feelings will do us harm if we express them. The pattern of bringing down the stone wall or the iron curtain will continue into adulthood. We will shut shop on our emotions in the hope that we will not suffer. When we are severely distressed, moreover, we bury our recollections deeply within our unconscious mind so that we hardly even know that they exist. We may deny ourselves the right to thoughts or to feelings. We may cover up our perceived wrongdoings or we may justify our actions or those of others. We put on a brave face and tell ourselves that we are all right but these tactics do not, unfortunately, deceive our own inner self.

We sometimes employ compensatory techniques in order to redress the balance. If we have learned to be extrovert, we often seek an introverted partner or friends. The shy, retiring type at work can sometimes be discovered as the life and soul of a wild party after working hours. The drinker tries to drown his/her sadness or to compensate for the stress in his/her life. The kind nurse may throw a temper tantrum that tyrannises the household when he/she returns from work. We often use our creativity or our intellect to escape from reality. The eccentric artist and the mad professor are examples of people who have learned to utilise internal resources in order to struggle through life. Ask yourself, perhaps, how you have survived growing up and adjusting to life as an adult. What have you done to protect yourself? What steps have you taken to buffer yourself against the impact of the real world? What have you sought to cushion the blow of living? We discover, sometimes, that our protection strategy is merely a means of worsening the damage already done by driving it more deeply inwards.

Have you ever experienced the pressure-cooker effect? The more you bury your distress – the more it will rear its ugly head in order to get noticed! The water in the pressure cooker heats up and then turns to steam. The steam begins to exude from the pressure cooker valve. When all the steam has been released, the pressure cooker itself begins to heat up. With the increase in heat and the lack of steam in the pressure cooker, nature takes the only course it can. Explosion!

Sometimes we find that the past catches up with us when we least expect it and then the penalty finally has to be exacted. Have you ever experienced the boomerang effect? The more you push your distress away – the more it will return to haunt you! You throw a boomerang out into space. You forget all about it. The boomerang circles the earth. When you are least expecting it, the inevitable happens. The boomerang returns and hits you in the face!

Client Profiling

The analytical hypnotherapy practitioner may wish to ponder the following points when formulating a profile for the client.

- In what ways are the client's defensive strategies impinging upon his/her existence?
- Does the client exhibit signs of having adopted primitive defensive strategies?
- Has the client in any way distorted his/her personality when adopting a defensive strategy?
- Does the client indulge any form of self-deception?

- To what extent does the client act in accordance with socially-acceptable principles?
- Does the client appear incapable of recalling his/her childhood years?
- Does the client tend towards denying his/her problems?
- Does the client suffer from an abundance of psychosomatic symptoms?
- Does the client appear to justify his/her actions or to rationalise his/her behaviour?
- Does the client tend to blame others or to blame himself/herself when things go wrong?
- Is the client passionate about lost causes?
- Is the client intellectually-oriented rather than being in touch with his/her natural emotive responses?
- Does the client constantly feel inclined to justify or to condone the poor conduct of others?

Chapter 12

Resistance

No mask like open truth to cover lies,
As to go naked is the best disguise.

– William Congreve

What Is Resistance?

A man who has gone to the dentist because of an unbearable toothache
will nevertheless try to hold the dentist back when he approaches the
sick tooth with a pair of forceps.
– Sigmund Freud

Resistance will be the unconscious mind's way of endeavouring to avoid having to deal with the aftermath of the client's traumatic experiences in life. Every client, without exception, will undergo some form of resistance to the therapeutic process. It may sometimes be difficult for the therapist to comprehend the reasons why a client may elect to undergo therapy and be so desperate to gain relief from his/her crippling symptoms and yet will still fight like hell in order to resist the process. Once the therapist has been apprised of this mysterious phenomenon, however, he/she can then arm himself/herself with the ammunition with which to dissolve it.

The patient, who is suffering so much from his symptoms and is causing
those about him to share his sufferings, who is ready to undertake so
many sacrifices in time, money, effort and self-discipline in order to be
freed from those symptoms – are we to believe that this same patient
puts up a struggle in the interest of his illness against the person who is
helping him?
– Sigmund Freud

Because it will be the main function of the human organism to maintain a psychological and physiological status quo, the client will strive at all times to guard against unnecessary change in order to ensure that no anxiety-provoking agency will upset the delicate balance of his/her mind. Resistance, therefore, may be the only means by which the human organism can maintain a fine balance that will give the client an illusion of peace and harmony. Even when the client has been suffering intensely, the mind will still believe erroneously that change will bring about further disaster. All change, therefore, will be registered in the client's unconscious mind as having a potential to upset the fragile system. Although the client may consciously believe, therefore, that change will be beneficial, he/she may still unconsciously feel unwilling to take even minute risks in order to instigate any improvement. The client's mind will, hence, strenuously resist any attempts to investigate his/her psychic trauma because this act will inevitably result in the dreaded change.

> When we undertake to restore a patient to health, to relieve him of the
> symptoms of his illness, he meets with a violent and tenacious
> resistance, which persists throughout the whole length of the treatment.
> – *Sigmund Freud*

Resistance Manifestation

> One hardly comes across a single patient who does not make an attempt
> at reserving some region or other for himself so as to prevent the
> treatment from having access to it.
> – *Sigmund Freud*

Resistance manifestation will usually be reasonably obvious to the therapist who knows what clues to look for in the client. The therapist should, of course, bear in mind that resistance will manifest unconsciously but will still be evident in the client's behaviour. The client may, for example, be mysteriously late for an appointment without a valid excuse or may completely forget to attend a regularly-kept meeting. The client may appear unsusceptible to hypnosis or may claim to have a blank mind when asked a question in hypnosis. The client may also claim that he/she is an unsuitable candidate for hypnosis, that he/she is unable to visualise or to use his/her imagination as a therapeutic medium. Often the truly resistant client will show a preference for merely chatting about his/her problems or symptoms rather than getting down to the task of examining what lies beneath them. The client may also bring in too much intellectual reasoning or may feel unable to think from his/her unconscious mind. The client may fight the process using intellectual argument, may employ critical objection and may, even, endeavour to engage in debate with the therapist. It will be as if, by doing so, the client will be sure to create a diversion from the task in hand.

Freud contended that the client would put up some form of unconscious resistance against uncovering disturbing material when exploring aspects of his/her past, perhaps by free association (see Chapter 2, Volume 2 – "Therapeutic Investigation"). Such resistance may mean that the client will put up a critical objection to the process or may report a representative image or substitutive association for the material to be unearthed. The client, for example, may appear unable to use free association or unwilling to report his/her thoughts. Such a client will usually pose objections to examining the past and claim that he/she is simply seeking the nonexistent quick-fix route. If the client continues in this vein, he/she will merely be surviving his/her analytical process rather than participating in it and embracing its benefits. Analytical hypnotherapy should endeavour to attain an unconscious resolution to the client's distress and not merely an intellectual understanding of his/her past. The client will, furthermore, need to revisit the emotional pull of pent-up distress directly connected with his/her recollections before he/she can ever effect or even contemplate any permanent change within himself/herself. The client who is a newcomer to therapy may well fail to appreciate that logical and deductive thinking will be of utterly no use to him/her when dealing with an unconsciously-derived problem. In short, the client will often wish to spare himself/herself the emotional pain yet still wish to give himself/herself the illusion that he/she will be dealing with his/her disorders by simply coming to therapy. In order to secure success, of course, the client must divest himself/herself of such self-deception. Logic solves nothing and never has in the therapeutic context. If logical reasoning about his/her symptoms could solve the client's problems, then there would be no need to seek therapeutic assistance and the therapeutic profession would cease to exist. Moreover, the beleaguered client would simply need to go down to Woolworth's, buy half a dozen relaxation tapes and his/her symptoms would then magically disappear!

The client's resistance, in some cases, may be so strong that he/she will be unable to overcome it – even with the help of a highly skilled therapist. The client may, for instance, simply not turn up for a session one day or may cancel a prearranged session and delude himself/herself with the belief that he/she can no longer afford either the time or the money to continue. Sometimes the client may submit to pressure from his/her immediate family, who may serve to convince him/her that therapy is not the answer. The client, of course, will merely be caving in because he/she does not have the necessary stamina and internal resources to stay the course in order to overcome his/her unconscious resistance.

Let us now identify the reasons why resistance manifests in the client in terms of the ways in which he/she will benefit from sabotaging the therapeutic progress. These self-sabotage mechanisms will have strange advantages that can be identified as either primary gains or secondary gains.

> Psychological symptoms are perpetuated because of the advantages
> that they provide.
> – *David Smith*

Primary Gains

> Primary gain is the main "reinforcer" of psychological symptoms and is
> entirely intra-psychic. As symptoms are substitutes for repressed
> conflicts, the perpetuation of a symptom enables us to avoid facing
> devastating personal truths. The pain and distress occasioned by the
> symptom is more tolerable than the pain of recognising one's own
> forbidden wishes.
> – *David Smith*

Primary gains are those benefits that the client will supposedly derive as a means of self-protection at the time of the original trauma or psychic conflict. Essentially, a primary gain will be a self-protective or survivalist mechanism, that will be utilised by the client in order to ensure his/her personal safety. A primary gain will be the principal reason for the birth of the client's symptoms as well as the manifestation of his/her defensive strategies (see Chapter 11 – "Defensive Strategies"). The function of this type of device will, thus, be to ensure that the client can avoid addressing his/her own personal truth about a perception of devastating consequence. The primary gain – even though it may, in itself, be highly unpleasant as a symptom – will, perhaps, be more tolerable for the client than facing his/her internal conflict and accepting reality.

> Only when these conditions have been fulfilled is it possible to recognise and to master the resistances which have led to the repression and the ignorance.
> – *Sigmund Freud*

Secondary Gains

> Secondary gain is less causally significant. Once a symptom is established, it may be used to provide other advantages. It may be used, for example, as an excuse to avoid unpleasant responsibilities or as a means of obtaining special privileges.
> – *David Smith*

Secondary gains are those compensatory benefits that the client will derive as a result of exhibiting his/her primary symptoms. A secondary gain will be rather like a form of psychological fringe benefit for the client who may hate his/her job but will not resign because he/she will lose the company car. A secondary gain, for example, may assist the client to unconsciously avoid unpleasant responsibilities in life. This facility may aid the client in attracting much-desired attention from others, in obtaining special privileges and in maintaining a desirable status or a high profile from which he/she will derive pleasure and admiration from others.

There are many different reasons why the client will hang on to his/her psychological and physiological symptoms. In order to understand the retention of a secondary gain, one fact will be of primary importance: however miserable a client may be made by his/her symptoms or however downright dangerous a symptom may be for his/her health or wellbeing, there will be a valid reason for keeping such a condition. At the deepest levels of the client's unconscious mind, essentially, the reason for retaining a symptom and its accompanying secondary gain will be one of self-protection and self-preservation. For the client, there will be a perceived safety in certainty and an intrinsic fear and uncertainty of the unknown that his/her primitive being will seek to deflect at all costs. Fundamentally, the client will perceive this form of self-protection as being less damaging and less dangerous than the underlying element from which his/her unconscious mind has been seeking to protect him/her. The adoption of a self-preservative factor, in other words, will be the lesser of two evils and will provide a sweetener for any additional psychological damage that the client may suffer as a result of maintaining the secondary gain. This form of protection will also have an additional benefit in that the client will know that it works to some extent. So, unless and until the practitioner can show the client's mind that there can be a better way of managing his/her psychic distress or that this particular form of self-defence will no longer be necessary, the client will elect to maintain a steadfast hold on his/her faithful servant.

A secondary gain will, of course, develop when the client has been influenced by distressing circumstances. When fear and uncertainty beset the client in overwhelming proportions, he/she may often spontaneously regress to a former childhood stage (see Chapter 11 – "Defensive Strategies") or adopt a childish personality (see Chapter 16 – "Personality Development"). This phenomenon will also be part of the client's valuable psychic armour, that will have supposedly ensured his/her safe passage through childhood on a damage-limitation basis. A sound appreciation, therefore, of what may be manifesting in the client's mind will help the practitioner to steer delicately yet effectively through any resistance to the therapeutic process. Secondary gains can take many forms and can manifest for a myriad reasons. The most important thing for the therapist to do will be to expose the client to the nature of his/her secondary gains and their functions within his/her psyche. When the client's unconscious mind refuses to relinquish a symptomatic manifestation of a secondary gain, then a reduction of its impact may need to be negotiated if, indeed, it cannot be resolved or dissolved entirely.

Multiple secondary gains

The practitioner can assist the client by helping him/her to discover the reasons why his/her unconscious mind will feel that it needs to protect him/her. It will also be important for the practitioner to bear in mind that, in some cases, there will be more than one contributory factor. There may, for example, be two or more different elements from which the client's unconscious mind may be protecting him/her in a particular manner. The client will, in these circumstances, need to realise that the reason for producing a given symptom is currently no longer valid.

When the root of the client's secondary gain has many combinations, the important thing for the therapist to consider will be whether all contributory factors need to be revealed in order to deal effectively with the presenting problem. The formation of a secondary gain may, for instance, have many contributing factors formed over a number of years in the client's life. Evidence for this may be detected when the client's symptom either appears not to shift at all or shifts very slightly and then stabilises again or, even, becomes worse. Let us now consider a typical case-study example of a client who reached such an impasse because she had a complex number of secondary gains.

Case-study example – obesity
An obese female had identified several reasons for her massive weight gain yet was unable to rectify her problem.

Firstly, the client identified that her excess weight was protecting her body following two periods of sexual abuse as a child and as a young teenager. The client's unconscious mind had rationalised: "If I'm fat, my abusers will look for a more attractive body to abuse."

Secondly, the client realised that her secondary gains were endeavouring to protect her from painful emotional expression in connection with intimate relationships. Her intimate relationships in adulthood were nearly always with men who would use her and then, ultimately, reject her. The client's unconscious mind understood this as: "If I'm fat, my partner will not be interested in me and so I can't get hurt."

Thirdly, the client was being protected from hunger after having experienced a time of extreme poverty as a child when food was scarce and she dared not leave anything on her plate in case there was no meal available later. The client's unconscious mind read this fact as: "If I eat it all now, I'll be less likely to be hungry later."

Fourthly, the client identified the fact that she feared being rejected by her mother, who was herself very overweight. The client's unconscious mind interpreted this as: "If I'm more like her, she might love me more."

Lastly, this client possessed a fear of success that could put her in the public eye. Her mind rationalised this by saying: "The pretty girl always gets the job." The client, furthermore, had been told this when being passed over for promotion earlier in her career.

Protective secondary gains

When a secondary gain has been employed by the client for protective reasons, he/she may wish to explore the ostensible reason behind this need for protection. Let us now consider a case-study example in which the client indulged in binge eating in order to conceal his psychic distress.

Case-study example – eating disorder

A grossly overweight male client tended to eat excessively and to overimbibe with alcohol.

The client identified the fact that his aunt used to slip her hand into his trousers and, cupping one of his buttocks, would tell him that he had "such a lovely bum". The client found this intrusion very uncomfortable. When this aunt habitually compared his bum with her husband's fat bum, the client unconsciously took on board the idea that putting on weight would be a means of removing this unwelcome attention. This realisation led the client to lose a considerable amount of weight and he was then content until his progress came to a grinding halt.

On further therapeutic investigation, the client recalled his fifth birthday party when his mother had made his favourite pink blancmange. When this was put on the table, his older bullying brother pushed in and helped himself. The client was furious, as it was his birthday and his favourite blancmange. The client then had a temper tantrum and his mother locked him in his bedroom in order to allow him to cool off and to learn not to be so selfish. As soon as the child was released, he went straight to the blanc-mange and ate every remaining scrap in order to ensure that no-one else could take it from him. Interestingly, as an adult, when the client's wife nagged him about his weight, he would immediately go into rebellion mode by eating and drinking even more in secret.

The client, thus, had three reasons for hanging on to his symptom: (a) protection from the discomfort of being touched intimately by another person; (b) protection from the physical invasion of having his intimate parts interfered with; and (c) the right to rebel against dictators.

Damage-limitation secondary gains

Another form of secondary gain might be described as a psycho-logical damage-limitation or damage-control device. The case-study example below shows the way in which a client with arthritis could be assisted with the dissolution of a secondary gain.

Case-study example – arthritis

A male client was suffering from a disabling form of arthritis in his ankles.

Therapeutic probing initially would not reveal the reason why this client exhibited this condition. When the therapist, however, asked the client what would be the most important reason for him to remove his arthritis, the client replied spontaneously that he would immediately go back to jogging ten miles a day! In this case, the client's arthritis was preventing him from further damaging not only his ankles but also his knees and lower back. The client's mind, therefore, had unconsciously feared developing knee prob-lems when jogging. The client felt that, because he had a poor run-ning posture, his lower spine could suffer damage. Negotiation with the client's unconscious mind then allowed his level of dis-comfort to be reduced even though he feared that complete removal of any symptom could endanger his physical health still further. Resistance, thus, was rife in this case in the interests of the client's survival.

Self-punishing secondary gains
A client may also develop a secondary gain for reasons of self-punishment. This strategy would be designed to prevent the client from repeating actions that were deemed to be so terrible and so guilt-provoking. The mechanism can ensure that the client will never ever repeat the behaviour or reconstruct the anxiety-inducing circumstance. Let us now consider a case-study example that ably illustrates this concept.

Case-study example – panic attacks
A man consulted a therapist about panic attacks that were accompanied mainly by his throat closing up and by strong feelings of nausea.

This client had a protruding jaw and had suffered a great deal of teasing about this in his teenage years. Although the appearance of his jaw and his pop-eyes was nowhere near as grotesque as the client believed, the problem had been severe enough that, on reaching full physical growth, he had considered undergoing surgery in order to reduce the size of his lower jaw. The client eventually decided not to submit to surgery because he was afraid of the long-term pain that he would suffer in the wake of surgery and because his consultant could not assure him about his final appearance.

During therapy, the client revealed that, when he was eleven, a slightly older cousin who had lost both his parents was fostered by his family. These young boys had experimented sexually together – mainly because the client was dominated by his cousin – but he had, to some extent, enjoyed the experiences. The client, however, had felt uncomfortable with the experimentation and had believed that what he was doing was wrong. One day, the client's cousin had asked him to lick his penis, which he had done, even though this act had made him feel nauseous. The next day at church the priest had delivered a fire-and-brimstone-like sermon on the evils of homosexuality. The protruding jaw then started to manifest within weeks of this sermon!

Attention-seeking secondary gains

Another reason why a client may employ a secondary gain is that of seeking and gaining attention from others. In the following case-study example, this concept is well illustrated in the case of a client who experienced a nervous form of paralysis.

Case-study example – paralysis

A female client suffered with paralysis in her legs, that had developed after she had returned from a trip to Brazil.

The client had moved to Brazil with her Brazilian boyfriend but, after three months, she had decided that she hated living there and wanted to return home. The client's partner, however, did not accompany her back and did not follow her subsequently, as she had expected. The client had experienced a bout of weakness in her legs in Brazil but this had turned to paralysis four months after her return to England and had eventually confined her to a wheelchair. When the client realised that her boyfriend was not going to return to England, she began to recover but, although she was no longer wheelchair-bound, she still experienced immense difficulty in walking.

Sometime later, the client met someone else and her condition began to improve still further. The client then fell pregnant. The client, however, took to her bed two months before the child was due to be born and remained there for nearly six months after giving birth. Coincidentally, a friend of hers gave birth at the very time when the client had first taken to her bed. The client, therefore, had been quite upset about the amount of attention her mother had been giving to her friend and her baby.

During therapeutic investigation, the client realised that, primarily, she was gaining much-needed attention from her mother by confining herself to bed. The client recalled the time when, at the age of thirteen, she had taken her mother's attention away from her two-month-old sibling when she had hurt her foot. In addition, the client discovered that her partner would not go out to work or even leave her for more than two hours in the evening because she was reportedly so helpless. As badly as the client wanted to walk properly again, she needed the attention of her mother and her partner even more. The client has now unconsciously realised that her symptoms were beneficial in this way and that her mind had previously not been prepared to give up this symptom until this realisation had been made.

Comfort-seeking secondary gains

A secondary gain that can be very difficult to recognise will be one in which the client can derive comfort from retaining a symptom. The therapist may continually feel that there can be no real reason for the client to hang on to his/her symptom and yet it persists. The obvious assumption here will be that the root of the client's symptom has not yet been reached. When such an impasse has been encountered, symptoms may tend to be of a psychological nature rather than a physiological manifestation. The case-study example below considers a client who was a compulsive nail-biter.

Case-study example – nail-biting

A female client had made several attempts in therapy to stop her habit of biting her nails.

The client had identified numerous reasons why she continued with this embarrassing and irritating habit. The client had, for instance, discovered that her habit was mainly the result of feeling fear when her mother had ranted and raved at her when she was a child. The client had, furthermore, identified the fact that she despised herself for being afraid of her mother when she was young even though she had stood up to her in adulthood.

Finally, it transpired that the client considered that her habit was a means of seeking comfort at times when she was afraid, bored, frustrated, uncertain or feeling lonely. Having unearthed these comfort-seeking mechanisms, the client was then able to acknowledge how inappropriate this need for comfort was today. The client came to appreciate that her habit had been useful in the past but that it was now no longer relevant.

Exploring the Client's Resistance

> There are patients who from the very first hours carefully prepare what
> they are going to communicate, ostensibly so as to be sure of making
> better use of the time devoted to the treatment. What is thus disguising
> itself as eagerness is resistance. Any preparation of this sort should be
> disrecommended, for it is only employed to guard against unwelcome
> thoughts cropping up. However genuinely the patient may believe in his
> excellent intentions, the resistance will play its part in this deliberate
> method of preparation and will see to it that the most valuable material
> escapes communication.
> – *Sigmund Freud*

It could be said that the sole remit of the therapist will be to
encourage the client to overcome his/her inevitable resistance to
the process of dealing with psychic trauma and his/her disincli-
nation to change his/her existence. Sometimes it will be politic for
the therapist to explain in elaborate detail the forms that the
client's resistance can take and, on other occasions, it may be wise
for him/her to remain silent on the subject. For the therapist, this
decision can be taken only on the basis of intuitively understanding the client and by working from experience.

> His initial trust or distrust is almost negligible compared with the
> internal resistances which hold the neurosis in place.
> – *Sigmund Freud*

Identifying Resistance

> The hypnotic dissociation makes it possible for either the content or the
> affect, or both, of relevant memories to by-pass ego-defences.
> – *Helmut Karle & Jennifer Boys*

Resistance to change will be a possibility that the practitioner will
almost certainly need to be alert to when working with the client.
Resistance will be the means by which the client can obstruct or
hinder the therapeutic process, can fight against the procedure and
can significantly impede his/her own progress. The client may
also seek to avoid dislodging his/her defensive strategies and
may, therefore, resist evoking change in his/her life (see Chapter
11 – "Defensive Strategies"). The client may not only have a vested
interest in keeping his/her defensive strategies in place in order to

ward off the evil day whereby he/she may be obliged to address his/her psychological disturbance, but also may seek to bury any accompanying psychological responses and physiological sensations. The more traumatic the incident that the client seeks to conceal, the more unwilling he/she may be to divulge the memory of its occurrence and to discharge any accompanying pent-up emotive responses.

The hypnoanalytical therapist can, however, regard resistance as a two-edged sword. On the one hand, the client's resistance can be a phenomenon that will often be a necessary part of therapy, as it can provide a clue to the root of the conflict. On the other hand, of course, this obstacle must be surmounted before any resolution of the client's psychological distress or relief from symptoms can be successfully and permanently attained. The therapist should, of course, be keenly aware that the client will be facing the depths of his/her greatest fears and deepest distresses in uncovering unconsciously buried or concealed material. The psychological pain that the client may have to face may be for him/her of life-threatening proportions and, therefore, will be enormously severe from his/her unique perspective. Every client, for this reason, should be handled with understanding and tenderness because of the fact that he/she will personally be reliving his/her own horrifying past as he/she has perceived it. Too much latitude, however, may not, of course, be in the client's best interests. Allowing the client to arrive late and then extending session time, for example, may not be doing a service to the client. Permitting the client too much time to chat prior to inducing hypnosis and instigating therapy may, similarly, not ultimately be of benefit to him/her.

Problems, of course, will arise in therapy when the client resists a workable solution to overcoming his/her resistance strategies. The client will eventually come to realise that he/she must be prepared to abandon all preconceived notions and to engage on a voyage of self-discovery in order to progress both in therapy and in life. When this realisation occurs, the client will either opt to forgo his/her resistance or may, regrettably, elect to terminate therapy – no doubt providing himself/herself with a justifiable reason for why he/she would not be willing to continue.

We urge him to follow only the surface of his consciousness and to leave
aside any criticism of what he finds, whatever shape that criticism may
take; and we assure him that the success of the treatment, and above all
its duration, depends on the conscientiousness with which he obeys this
fundamental technical rule of analysis.
– Sigmund Freud

The therapist should seek to uncover the reasons why the client elects to resist the therapeutic process or why progress has been halted. The following questions, for example, can be posed in order to facilitate the process of overcoming the client's resistance. Perhaps the practitioner can use these questions in order to undertake his/her own brand of soul-searching on the client's behalf.

- Is there any evidence of a lack of fruitful communication between the therapist and the client?
- Has rapport been well established or is the therapeutic relationship built only on a shaky foundation?
- Has the therapist neglected to explain to the client what is expected of him/her during the therapeutic process?
- Does the client have a false or unrealistic expectation of the nature or purpose of therapeutic intervention?
- What is the practitioner's intention when undertaking therapy for this client?
- Has the therapist employed an inappropriate form of therapeutic technique for the client?
- Is the therapeutic process proceeding either too rapidly or too slowly for the client?
- Has the therapist failed to recognise that there is an underlying cause and that the client may have a higher order of anxiety than that which is superficially evident?
- Has the therapist failed to isolate the underlying cause and the nature of the client's beliefs about the source of distress?
- Is the client engaged in bringing to fruition a self-fulfilling prophecy?
- Does the client have an underlying belief that he/she cannot succeed in therapy?
- Does the client have a fear of failure with regard to his/her therapy?
- Does the client have a complex and/or interlaced wealth of active secondary gains that are inhibiting his/her success in therapy?

- Will the outcome of the client's therapy produce results unfavourable to his/her intimate associates or his/her external circumstances?
- Is the client being thwarted by misguided friends or family members?
- Do the client's family or friends appear to be helping when, in fact, they have a hidden agenda or alternative masterplan of their own?
- Is the outcome of therapy for the client worth the cost in terms of time, money and effort involved?
- Is the client also suffering from additional physiological, biological or neurological problems that can hinder progress?

Overcoming Resistance

Once the practitioner has identified in his/her own mind the possible reasons why the client may be resisting the therapeutic process, he/she will then be in an advantageous position to steer the ship on its best course.

The passage given below may be of use to the therapist when inducing hypnosis in the resistant client. This passage has been designed for the client who may have difficulty letting go of the controls. Although this passage is slightly authoritarian in tone, it has been presented in the first person in order to enable the client to feel as if he/she is, in fact, in control of the process.

I and I ...

I want you to just listen to the sound of my voice and to repeat what I say in your mind. I want you, therefore, to do the very thing that you are thinking – to repeat everything in your mind that I am saying to you.

Perhaps you can hear yourself saying "I am going to begin to breathe deeply." "As I breathe in, I can feel relaxation being drawn into my body." "As I breathe out, I begin to feel calmer." "I can become very aware of my breathing and maybe I can begin to relax each part of my body." "If I focus on the crown of my head, I can find it so easy just to let my muscles relax." "Maybe I can now relax my forehead – relaxing the muscles even more this time." "If I concentrate now on my face, my eyes, my mouth, my jaw and my chin, I can deepen this feeling of relaxation." "I am drifting deeper down into relaxation." "As I concentrate on my neck now, perhaps I can say the word 'relax' to myself and loosen the muscles even further – pondering on how relaxed my body is becoming." "I breathe so easily ..."

"As I begin to feel my mind relaxing, too, I am wondering just how deep this relaxation can go as I focus on my back and let all the muscles there relax from the top of my back, down – all the way down – my spine." "There is a sort of heavy feeling flowing down through my body and a calmness." "Maybe this still, quiet kind of feeling can go even deeper." "As I now relax every part of my shoulders, can this relaxed, peaceful feeling grow and flow down through my arms?" "I can feel a kind of heavy feeling in my arms as the muscles let go." "I am so curious now to see if this feeling can flow through into my lower abdomen." "I can release all the tightness there easily – curious to feel how easy it is to relax my legs." "If I focus on my thighs possibly that heavy, sleepy kind of feeling can flow down into my knees and ankles and feet."

"Maybe I can also feel my mind beginning to relax." "Maybe as I feel so peaceful in my body, my mind can drift even deeper into relaxation – just pondering on how deep I can go, how deep I can drift." "I find myself wondering just how easy it is to let go of those everyday things – wondering how much deeper I can drift down, noticing how easy it is to just drift – a sleepy sort of feeling." "I feel drowsy." "I'm so deep, I'm not even sure that my body is still here." "Those everyday things are drifting away as I ponder on how much I can learn and will learn by going just that little bit deeper and how much I will benefit from drifting further still into this peacefulness."

The following case-study example shows the way in which the practitioner can be creative in assisting the client to overcome blatant resistance.

Case-study example – controlling tendencies

This male client was so beset by inner fears that he adopted control-freak strategies even in his dealings with the therapist. Initially, the client had come willingly into therapy because two other members of his family had been successfully treated by the same therapist. After the first session, however, the client had left swearing oaths at the therapist for asking too many impertinent questions.

After several months had elapsed, the client rang the therapist again demanding that therapy be continued. The therapist stated clearly that the client would be allowed to have four sessions, after which the therapist would decide whether the client could continue. When the client then returned to therapy, the practitioner pretended that she had come to the consulting room on her day off in order to see him. This unbeatable combination of strict adherence to time, on the one hand, and a demonstration of a sincere commitment to him, on the other, served to provide the client with the opportunity to relinquish his reservations about investigative analysis. The client was, thus, made aware of the strict boundaries and yet given the safety to reveal his innermost distress once the name of the game had been pronounced.

Client Profiling

The analytical hypnotherapy practitioner may wish to ponder the following points when formulating a profile for the client.

- In what ways does the client resist his/her therapeutic journey?
- In what ways does the client show resistance towards the therapist?
- In what ways does the client attempt to maintain the status quo in his/her life?
- Does the client studiously avoid discussing any particular aspects of his/her past life?
- Is the client in any way defensive about his/her activities or his/her relationships?
- What is the primary reason for the manifestation of the client's disorder?
- In what ways does the client seek to protect himself/herself from unpleasant psychic material?
- In what ways does the client endeavour to mount any damage-limitation exercises?
- Does the client appear to have any self-punishing mechanisms at work?
- Does the client indulge in attention-seeking or comfort-seeking ploys?
- Which types of symptoms would the practitioner associate with the client's guilt-provoking or anxiety-provoking activities?
- Which types of symptoms would the practitioner associate with the client's comfort-seeking activities?

Chapter 13

Transference and Countertransference

Brutus:
And whether we shall meet again I know not.
Therefore our everlasting farewell take:
For ever, and for ever, farewell, Cassius!
If we do meet again, why, we shall smile;
If not, why then, this parting was well made.

Cassius:
For ever, and for ever, farewell, Brutus!
If we do meet again, we'll smile indeed;
If not, 'tis true this parting was well made.

– *William Shakespeare*

What Is Transference?

The analytic encounter can become as complex as any intimate
relationship. Unconscious fantasies stemming from vital needs tend to
arise between the partners. Sometimes they are not intense but quite
subtle, and thus escape being noticed at all by either analyst or patient.
Yet they may influence the analysis by causing resistances, provoking
strong illusions about the analyst or the patient, or tending to sexualise
the relationship. All this is well known by now, and the technical term for
these unconscious projections is transference or counter-transference,
depending on the direction of the projections.
– *Mario Jacoby*

The act of transference is the means by which an individual will
transfer attitudes and emotive manifestations from one person to
another as a form of displacement (see Chapter 11 – "Defensive
Strategies"). The transference phenomenon, therefore, will be,
firstly, a reconstitution of impulses that the client once experienced
for a significant other in earlier days and, secondly, an unconscious

redirection of those impulses towards another. The client, thus, will unconsciously project emotive responses, thoughts and attitudes from the past on to people in his/her current life. The client, for instance, may have an intimate partner who may treat him/her in much the same way as did a parent, and this will prompt him/her to react accordingly.

In the therapeutic context, transference will be the process by which the client transfers childlike patterns of relating to others on to the practitioner. The client can, for example, imbue the therapist with qualities and characteristics of any person connected with his/her psychological distress. Any sublimated wishes or unsatisfied needs from childhood that the client possesses, moreover, may tend to be transferred to the practitioner because the client may automatically expect him/her to fulfil such desires. It will be as if the client superimposes on to the therapist an image of those significant others whom he/she has been most profoundly affected by in the past – either positively or negatively. The therapist, for instance, may become positively recognised as a caring guardian and a powerful protector or, alternatively, negatively identified with a neglectful parent or a dictatorial parental substitute.

> Classically the term is used to denote the relationship between patient and therapist that develops as the patient begins increasingly to project on to the therapist perceptions, feelings and attitudes which have nothing to do with the therapist as a real person nor derive in any way from the interactions that have overtly taken place between patient and therapist, but arise from the background of the patient's early life and experiences, usually of people who have played a significant part in his personal development.
> – *Helmut Karle & Jennifer Boys*

The Freudian View of Transference

Intellectual resistances are not the worst: one always remains superior to
them. But the patient also knows how to put up resistances, without
going outside the framework of the analysis, the overcoming of which is
among the most difficult of technical problems. Instead of remembering,
he *repeats* attitudes and emotional impulses from his early life which can
be used as a resistance against the doctor and the treatment by means of
what is known as "transference".
– *Sigmund Freud*

Freud first identified the phenomenon of transference as a therapeutic tool when encouraging his clients to retrieve material that
had been unconsciously buried. He noticed that the feelings projected on to the therapist during therapeutic investigation were
related to the disorders that the client experienced. Anger or frustration directed at the therapist, for example, might be linked to
repressed anger for a parent.

Freud concluded that transference manifestation was, in fact, a
necessary part of psychoanalytic treatment because it will be born
out of a form of dependence on the therapist (see Chapter 1 –
"Psychoanalysis"). He observed that the client would often regard
the therapist as a surrogate parent and, therefore, could strenuously resist efforts to become independent. The client might, for
example, endeavour to impress the quasi-parent, might seek to
emulate him/her or might contrive to thwart him/her. The client,
moreover, could appear unwilling to burden himself/herself with
a perceived debt of gratitude towards his/her helper – thus displaying a degree of resentment towards the therapist. The transference, in these circumstances, would become a manifestation of
the client's resistance to dealing with his/her problems (see
Chapter 12 – "Resistance"). Freud also concluded that, when the
client and the therapist are of opposite sexes, the client may decide
to use sexual guile in the hope of attaining affection from the therapist or to control him/her in some way. The client could also then
display jealousy if he/she perceived that the therapist's attention
had been taken up elsewhere.

Freud believed that the client's emotive responses to the therapist
were simply replicas of his/her original childhood experiences
and that his/her motivations for forming the basic transference

relationship would reveal the nature of his/her psychic distress. The hypnoanalytic practitioner, therefore, should endeavour to identify the source of the client's transference manifestation as a means of assisting him/her. In order to foster transference, moreover, the practitioner should guarantee that he/she will adhere to a strict pattern of noninvolvement with the client. The therapist should also remain neutral and faceless in his/her approach to the client in order to ensure that a full and free interpretation of events can be achieved.

> I would define transference in psychoanalysis as the irrational relatedness to another person which can be analysed in the analytical procedure, while transference in other situations is one which is just the same, depending on the rationality of the person, but it is not open to analysis, it is not on the table of operation.
> – Erich Fromm

The Jungian View of Transference

> In all circumstances the prime rule of dialectic procedure is that the individuality of the sufferer has the same value, the same right to exist, as that of the doctor and consequently that every development in the patient is to be regarded as valid, unless of course it corrects itself of its own accord.
> – Carl Jung

Jung took matters a stage further than Freud in that he became interested in the meaning – as opposed to merely the cause – of the therapeutic transference relationship (see Chapter 2 – "Analytical Psychology"). Jung claimed that archetypal imagery from the collective unconscious will also influence the transference relationship (see Chapter 14 – "Dreams and Symbolic Imagery"). Projections, Jung maintained, are actually part of the client's psychic structure, although such elements may be perceived as external experiences. The client who becomes hypercritical of others, for example, will often, in effect, be criticising himself/herself. As the client's projections will change during the course of treatment, the practitioner should be aware that such changes may highlight areas where further analytical work might be needed.

Jung advocated that the self-realisation process of analysis could be brought about by a careful observation of therapeutic transference manifestations. A flexible and creative approach would, therefore, be required by the therapist in order to facilitate an understanding of the client's transference relationship with the practitioner, that may manifest in dreams and in his/her fantasy-world imagery. The astute therapist should also be able to detect pockets of resistance to change depicted in transference and should be able to tease out the precise nature of the client's transference manifestation, that will constrain his/her true self from surfacing (see Chapter 12 – "Resistance"). Jung, too, subscribed to the view that the therapist should attempt to detect any evidence of the development of a parent–child relationship during the therapeutic encounter.

Jung also identified the fact that the most subtle forms of transference and countertransference will occur when both parties are communicating unconsciously. Unconscious communication may take place, for example, when the therapist despairs of his/her ability as a healer because the client doggedly resists change. In these circumstances, the practitioner may become disappointed and, as a result, may unconsciously blame the client for resisting change because of a psychological need to be successful that remains unfulfilled. When each party is unconsciously detecting and reacting to the thoughts of the other – almost as if telepathy were at work here – both transference and countertransference will have unconsciously manifested within the therapeutic relationship.

Projection Manifestation

> It is often tragic to see how blatantly a man bungles his own life and the lives of others yet remains totally incapable of seeing how much the whole tragedy originates in himself, and how he continually feeds it and keeps it going. Not consciously, of course – for consciously he is engaged in bewailing and cursing a faithless world that recedes further and further into the distance.
> – Carl Jung

Both projection and transference are unconsciously spontaneous and automatic phenomena. Neither will be a voluntary act of will. A subtle form of distinction, however, can be made between these two phenomena, that it might be prudent for us to discuss.

Jung regarded projection as a general psychological mechanism whereby the client will subjectively view an object, whereas transference can occur only between individuals. A child, therefore, may form an attachment to and project feelings on to a cuddly toy, but transference can occur only between the child and other human beings. Projection may dissolve, therefore, when the child discovers that his/ her object can be viewed objectively. When the client – perhaps as an adult – realises the function of his/her cuddly toy, therefore, the role of projection may disintegrate. The client may, however, be aware of his/her projected feelings but not of their extent, because a certain portion of his/her projection will remain unconscious.

Transference, on the other hand, will be an extension of the projection phenomenon and will be of an emotive and compulsory nature for the client. The emotive content of transference will tend to form an unbreakable bond for the client and this attachment will then exercise a compulsory influence on his/her emotive expression. The value of transference in hypnoanalytic therapy will, therefore, be of paramount importance to the client. Because of the emotive content of such an unshakeable attachment, a dynamic relationship between the client and the practitioner can manifest. In entering into any form of therapeutic relationship, of course, both the client and the therapist will experience emotive responses in that relationship – however detached the clinician may be from the psychology of the client. This mutual and unconscious experience may be confusing for both the client and the therapist. When the therapist, however, has been the subject of his/her own intensive self-analysis, this confusion will not be so daunting or so entirely unrecognisable that it cannot be dealt with successfully by him/her in supervision.

Transference Manifestation

> Transference: Most generally, the passing on, displacing or "transferring"
> of an emotion or affective attitude from one person to another person
> or object.
> – *Arthur Reber*

During the course of the therapeutic encounter, transference will manifest, to a greater or lesser extent, in a number of different ways. For the client, of course, transference will simply be an illusion brought about by his/her own inner state. The client, for example, may feel suspicion, mistrust, jealousy, hostility, resentment or fear of the practitioner, on the one hand, or an overwhelming affection for him/her, on the other. The client may often, of course, feel guilty about harbouring such feelings towards the therapist. The practitioner, however, can assist by informing the client quite candidly that he/she may feel anything from love to hate during the course of therapeutic treatment. This stance will then give the client permission to experience transference to its fullest extent for his/her own benefit. Transference manifestation, therefore, will be an invaluable tool in the therapeutic context because it will give the client carte blanche to unload his/her psychological baggage – in a totally judgment-free ambience – on to a complete stranger whom he/she does not know personally and will never meet again. This, indeed, will be a rare opportunity for the client and, as such, can be one of the greatest gifts that hypnoanalytic therapy can bestow on him/her. When effective transference can develop naturally, therefore, this may often mean that the analytical therapist will be the last port of call for the client – a culmination of all other counselling, therapy and healing techniques combined. This factor alone can often make a significant difference to the client's therapeutic progress and will propel him/her towards that vital major shift.

Transference may either take an ostensibly active conscious form or be a more passive unconscious occurrence between the two parties. Let us now consider the various ways in which transference can develop either naturally or with a generous helping of encouragement from the therapist.

Transference as Active Projection

> Jung spoke also of active projection or empathy, where one enters
> actively and consciously into the inner situation of the other person, as
> opposed to passive projection, in which I unconsciously "find" a part of
> myself that really belongs to me in another person.
> – *Mario Jacoby*

Active projection will occur when empathy and rapport are intentionally cultivated between the therapist and the client. This will usually be purposely engendered by the therapist in his/her role as facilitator of the therapeutic process. In the therapeutic context, active projection will usually foster an environment in which the client's transference can be allowed to manifest naturally. The practitioner, therefore, may purposely develop the transference relationship by consciously endeavouring to build rapport and empathy with the client.

Transference as Passive Projection

It is as if the guidance of life had passed over to an invisible centre ...
and there is a release from compulsion and impossible responsibility that
are the inevitable results of *participation mystique*.
– Carl Jung

Passive projection will occur when two parties unconsciously identify with each other and both indulge in a form of mutual projection of feelings. Passive projection can occur spontaneously when the therapist and the client naturally identify with each other and an unconscious communicative link will naturally evolve. Jung spoke of the phenomenon of *mystic participation* (see Chapter 2 – "Analytical Psychology") whereby what the client experiences internally will also manifest externally in his/her subjective world. This idea lies behind the theory of passive projection. It will be as if the client's inner state will continually be reflected outwards and he/she will then recognise a part of himself/herself in the therapist and vice versa.

Transference as Resistance

But in general human terms resistance and transference are among the
most powerful emotional forces which exist.
– Erich Fromm

Psychoanalytic thinking also advocates that transference can be a form of resistance in terms of the relationship between the client and the therapist (see Chapter 12 – "Resistance"). The astute therapist can utilise to great benefit this form of resistance, that can be observed in a plethora of ways. Does the client, for instance, have a tendency to rebel against the therapist in the same way as he/she had a desire to rebel against his/her parents? Does the client exhibit a lack of trust in the therapist just as he/she failed to trust those carers who have betrayed him/her? Does the client feel unsafe with the therapist just as he/she felt unsafe in a former situation? Does the client wish to please the practitioner as he/she might have wished to please significant others? Does the client fear any loss of the therapist's approval just as he/she might have feared not being good enough when compared with other children in childhood? Manifestations of this form of transference can, of course, overwhelm the client, who may elect to discontinue therapy as a result. If, however, the practitioner can skilfully ride the storm and can engineer the situation in order to allow the client to realise the significance of his/her emotive reactions, then the arduous battle will have been won. The vital ingredient in the equation will be that the client will need to move in a given direction – however sluggishly. No movement will signify an impasse. Sometimes the shift may occur when the client's symptoms get worse. It may be that the client will need to feel the pain strongly enough before it can budge. Failure to effect a shift will, of course, not be a reflection of the therapist's competence but may well be the result of an overwhelming resistance on the client's part, that he/she cannot, unfortunately, find the means to overcome.

> In a very real sense, the patient–therapist "dyad" becomes a stage on which the patient re-enacts formative experiences and reactions, and so brings directly into the interactions between the patient and the therapist the very processes by which his personality developed.
> – *Helmut Karle & Jennifer Boys*

Transference Classifications

> Transference takes place when clients resurrect from their early years intense conflicts relating to love, sexuality, hostility, anxiety, and resentment; bring them into the present; re-experience them; and attach them to the analyst.
> – *Gerald Corey*

When the client and the therapist first meet they will both have a specific objective in sight when forming a relationship – namely that of working together with the sole intent of alleviating the client's symptoms or other manifestations of his/her psychic disorder. During the course of the therapeutic encounter, therefore, transference may manifest itself in an infinite number of ways and in varying degrees of intensity. In all cases, the form of transference that will manifest in the client's mind will almost invariably be an illusion – provided that the practitioner can maintain a professional stance throughout. We shall now examine some of the forms that transference phenomena can take in the therapeutic context.

Positive Transference

> In a positive transference, the patient transfers on to the therapist idealised, dependent feelings which commonly derive from the relationship with his parents but which may also signify an unresolved, intra-physic conflict and a dependent style in relationships.
> – Mark Aveline

Positive transference will occur when the client can benefit from the nature of the relationship formed with the practitioner. With positive transference, the client will usually have an implicit trust and confidence in the therapist, that should have a noticeably cumulative effect on the progress of therapy. The client could, for example, view the therapist as a professional carer who will, perhaps, compensate, in some measure, for any dearth of care and consideration that he/she lacked in childhood. The client who can regard the therapist as an ideal mother, a model father or a trusted confidant will, of course, be making an effective use of positive transference. Ideally, positive transference may be the form of transference that will develop for the client, as this may secure his/her passport to success in therapy.

> Transference can only serve a positive, self-affirming function if it is carried out at a conscious level. Otherwise, destructive and/or positive experiences are blindly transferred.
> – Konrad Stettbacher

Negative Transference

> Hostile feelings are the product of negative transference, but clients may
> also develop a positive transference and, for example, fall in love with
> the analyst, wish to be adopted, or in many other ways seek the love,
> acceptance, and approval of an all-powerful therapist. In short, the
> analyst becomes a current substitute for significant others.
> *– Gerald Corey*

When negative transference manifests, the client may evoke a number of negative characteristics or psychologically unhealthy reactions towards the therapist. Negative transference has sometimes been described as a transference neurosis because it evolves as a form of dependence on the therapist, that, in fact, the client would have had for his/her primary carers from whom his/her psychic distress has emanated.

Negative transference will often develop because the client will be opening up his/her soul to the therapist and will be divulging his/her most intimate secrets to a relative stranger. Negative transference may, for example, result in a mistrust of the practitioner, a contempt for him/her or a lack of confidence in his/her abilities. The client may also feel afraid that the therapist will not be taking his/her job seriously. This form of transference may, in turn, develop into a dislike for or even a hatred of the practitioner. The client may, furthermore, exhibit a feeling of frustration or irritation towards the therapist. Perhaps the client may even feel a degree of jealousy or suspicion of the therapist. The client may also feel a fear of ridicule or rejection by the therapist. The client may experience a fear of shocking the therapist because of the nature of the information that he/she will reveal about himself/herself during therapy. The client, in this instance, may fear that the therapist will be offended by his/her shameful revelations or confessions of dishonesty. The client may, conversely, display an intense love or erotic feeling for the therapist, that may, in turn, lead to a fear of loss of sexual independence. This form of transference may, in addition, develop into an overdependence on the therapist and can manifest as the client's unwillingness to discontinue therapy long after his/her symptoms have abated.

The therapist should console himself/herself with the fact that, although negative transference may not be a comfortable state to negotiate, it may be the only way in which the client can express certain aspects of his/her traumatic past. For this reason, the therapist should be able to handle any negative transference with equanimity because, ultimately, it may be of great benefit to the client. If the practitioner finds that a difficult negative transference with the client has become too hot to handle, then he/she should promptly, of course, seek supervisory backup.

> Transferences influenced by the unconscious anticipation of pain or anxiety hamper our ability to form relationships and can, under certain circumstances, be critical to our survival.
> – *Konrad Stettbacher*

Mirror Transference

> The mirror transference, according to Kohut, arises from a basic and vital human need for "empathetic resonance". We all need mirroring in order to recognise ourselves, as we need empathetic resonance in order to feel real, accepted and therefore valuable to others and in turn valuable to ourselves.
> – *Mario Jacoby*

Mirror transference will be a means of providing the client with a reflective mirror through which to view himself/herself. With this form of transference, the practitioner should provide sensitive mirroring (or *empathetic resonance*) for the client in order to assist him/her to maintain a healthy psychological balance and to create a realistic degree of self-esteem. When mirror transference manifests, the client will often regard the therapist as an extension of himself/herself.

Mirror transference may be employed by design, when the practitioner will be required to deal with a narcissistic personality disorder whereby the client has suffered as a result of having been rejected or harshly overcriticised in childhood and subsequent years (see Chapter 7, Volume 2 – "Fear and Anxiety Disorders"). The client, for example, may have previously been given a distorted mirror and, consequently, will have developed an overcompensatory self-admiration. The practitioner's role here would be to hold up a realistic psychological mirror as well as to help the client to understand that he/she can have a value in his/her own right.

Object Transference

Becoming conscious means for the most part *separating*: separating the
qualities which belong to my own person from those that belong to my
partner. I have to make my own inner tendencies – the dynamics of the
relationship as felt by me – and the needs of my partner into an It, an
object of some kind of reflection.
– Mario Jacoby

Object transference will manifest when the client regards the therapist as an object or a vehicle through which to attain his/her own
ends (see Chapter 5 – "Object-Relations Psychology"). Often, this
form of transference will be a necessary product initially in the
therapeutic setting because the client may be re-enacting his/her
early relationship with a parent. As this form of transference
dissolves and the client can begin to mature, however, he/she will
usually come to regard the therapist as a human being in his/her
own right rather than merely as a means of needs-accommodation.

Coercive Transference

Patients who suffer from a traumatic syndrome form a characteristic
type of transference in the therapy relationship. Their emotional
responses to any person in a position of authority have been deformed
by the experience of terror. For this reason, traumatic transference
reactions have an intense, life-or-death quality unparalleled in ordinary
therapeutic experience.
– Judith Lewis Herman

Coercive transference will be derived from one individual's ability
to manipulate another by means of threat or punishment. The
practitioner, for example, may be seen by the client as a parental
figure or an authoritative figure. The client may, therefore, exhibit
fears, anxiety and/or guilt in the presence of the therapist. The
client may also live in dread of offending the therapist or become
fearful of soliciting his/her disapproval. The client, moreover, may
be overanxious to please the practitioner in an attempt to avoid
being manipulated. The average client who may be in desperate
need of help may literally strive to gain approval from the therapist and, of course, this dependency issue should be sensitively
handled.

Rewarding Transference

If, by contrast, we encounter a person who signals positive experiences,
we will do all we can to gain from it by repeating the experience.
– *Konrad Stettbacher*

Rewarding transference can be derived from the therapist's ability to give benefit to or reward the client. The therapist, for example, may be perceived by the client as being equipped to render comfort or to provide a feel-good factor. The client may, therefore, become overly cooperative and may become very obliging towards the practitioner in the interests of his/her own passage towards recovery.

Legitimate Transference

Transference is a result of the failure in one's own freedom and thereby
is the result of the need to find an idol to worship, to believe in order to
overcome one's fear and uncertainty about the world. The adult human
being is in a way no less helpless than the child.
– *Erich Fromm*

Legitimate transference will be derived from the client's perception of the practitioner as being in an exalted position. The therapist, for example, may be perceived by the client as a chosen person – one who has been especially selected for the important work of effecting his/her cure.

Expert Transference

Transference expresses a need of a person to have somebody who takes
over the responsibility, who is a mother, who gives unconditional love,
who is a father who praises and punishes, and admonishes and teaches.
– *Erich Fromm*

Expert transference will be derived from the client's perception of the therapist as possessing greater knowledge in a given area. The practitioner, for example, may be regarded by the client as a wise mentor who should command respect and deference.

Referred Transference

> Transference is not a simple repetition; but what we are dealing with is the need of a person to have another person to fulfil his need. For instance, if I feel weak, uncertain, afraid of risks, afraid of decisions – I may want to find a person who is certain, who is prompt, who is powerful, in whom I can take refuge.
> – *Erich Fromm*

Referred transference will be derived from the client's perception of the therapist as someone with positive personal characteristics. The client, for example, may genuinely admire the practitioner for being friendly, amiable and, intrinsically, an interesting personality. The client, in this case, may feel that the therapist is a person worth knowing in his/her own right and may even seek to cultivate his/her friendship. In such circumstances, of course, the practitioner should ensure that the client's overtures are not met with curt rejection while, simultaneously, a healthy distance can be maintained.

Love Transference

> It goes without saying that countertransference-love may also arise in the analyst in a more or less intense form. It may even happen that the mutual emotions become so strong that a concrete sexual relationship seems to be indicated. This puts a heavy weight of responsibility and conflict on the analyst.
> – *Mario Jacoby*

Love transference (or *erotic transference*) will be derived from the fact that the client may hold the therapist so dear that the emotive reactions stirred up within him/her are likely to involve love and/or sexual desire. This form of transference can possibly be the most dangerous of any type of transference because intense emotive and primitive needs will be involved. When the client has been severely emotionally neglected or sexually abused, for example, he/she may well develop an erotically-tinged attachment to the therapist (see Chapter 15, Volume 2 – "The Effects of Childhood Abuse"). The practitioner, of course, will need to apply great skill in keeping the client at a distance if such transference develops yet not show any sign of rejecting him/her. At the same time, of course, the therapist will need to help the client to work through the love transference and to understand the reasons for its generation. It may well be, for example, that the client can only make a relationship with another person that has a sexual connotation.

Idealising Transference

> Omnipotence, for instance, is an archetypal quality which in general is attributed to a godhead. Idealising transference is therefore in my opinion, as already mentioned, a projection of an archetypal content upon the analyst. The gradual disappointment in the analyst is part of the general process of "taking back projections".
> – *Mario Jacoby*

Idealising transference will occur when the client has a need to put others on a pedestal and may perceive the therapist as the epitome of a superhero. By this means, the client will give importance to himself/herself by having an ideal person to emulate. The client, in this way, may attempt to compensate for his/her own perceived lack of self-worth.

> If somebody is impressed by power, somebody wants to be protected by a powerful person, you will have the same worship and the same overestimation of his analyst as he has of his professor, or of a governmental figure, or he has of his minister or priest or what's not what. It's always the same mechanism.
> – *Erich Fromm*

Illusional Transference

> The illusional form of transference shows itself by a certain amount of flexibility. It leaves room for being questioned, interpreted and eventually transformed.
> – *Mario Jacoby*

Illusional transference will occur when the client regards the practitioner as a godlike creature. The client may become consciously aware that the therapist is similar or broadly identical to a supergod. The client, thus, will create for himself/herself an illusion that will attempt to make his/her own life worthwhile because of his/her association with such a being.

Delusional Transference

Pure delusions are found of course in psychosis and have to do with loss
of reality. But there is a sliding scale between illusional and delusional
transference experiences. In any analysis, episodes of delusional
transference may pop up. They often create difficulties since the patient
at any time may not be able to distance himself from the delusional
aspects of his experience.
– *Mario Jacoby*

Delusional transference will occur when the client actually regards
the therapist, in reality, as being a godlike incarnation. The client,
in this case, will have totally deluded himself/herself – even if for
only a short while – into sincerely believing that the therapist possesses this superhuman identity.

Chaotic transferences take place at the unconscious level, the resultant
outbreaks of rage, anger, distress, and fear usually have little or nothing
to do with the real situation.
– *Konrad Stettbacher*

Exploring the Client's Transference

The therapeutic process involves detailed exploration, within the
transference, of the mechanisms of projection and displacement and
therefore of their origins. The pathogenic elements and processes in the
patient's formative years may be directly reflected in and expressed by
the symptoms displayed and are sought in the reactions of the patient to
the therapist, when they can be analysed with an immediacy that is
unobtainable when exploring behaviour outside the consulting room
and appointment time.
– *Helmut Karle & Jennifer Boys*

The therapeutic experience will consist of an interrelationship
between the therapist and the client that will be unique. It will be
a relationship that may change on each occasion when the two
protagonists meet. The therapeutic relationship, consequently, will
fundamentally differ from normal social interaction in that it will
have an element of falseness about it when compared with normal
relationships. The therapeutic environment, therefore, will be an
ideal setting in which the practitioner can make full use of the phenomenon of transference as an agent for change within the client.

Let us now examine the ways in which transference can be fully utilised by the practitioner.

Fostering Transference

> Transference typically goes through a positive phase of emotional
> attachment to the analyst followed by a negative and critical phase;
> according to Freud, this reflects working through the ambivalence
> experienced in the child's relationship with their parents.
> – Richard Gross

The therapeutic environment will be a fertile breeding ground for the development of transference and the practitioner can, therefore, capitalise on this opportunity in order to utilise an important therapeutic tool. In order to assist the client with natural projection and transference, the therapist should elect, at all times, to remain aloof from the client. The client should not be provided with any personal details about the therapist and no attempt whatsoever should be made to form a personal relationship with him/her. A strict pattern of noninvolvement with the client may well be the pivot on which therapeutic intervention hinges. It will be essential, however, that the practitioner can develop a rapport and empathy with the client. Rapport and empathy will allow for a full and fruitful communication between the two parties and will afford the client the opportunity to maximise his/her chances of a free interpretation of events whereby transference can develop.

The more opportunity the client will have to project his/her illusions on to the therapist without interference from a significant other, the more speedily he/she will be able to address his/her psychic disturbance. It will, therefore, be essential that the analytic practitioner undertake strictly one-to-one therapy with the client. Including a third party during a therapy session will dilute, if not stultify, the effectiveness of the client's transference manifestation. If the client earnestly requests that a third party be present, however, it may well be that he/she will have some transference issues to address with that third party or, alternatively, that he/she wishes to avert any arising transference issues with the therapist. If the practitioner cannot avoid including a third party (for example, if a language barrier necessitated the presence of an interpreter), then, of course, a close relative would not be a good idea if the practitioner wished to be effective in fostering transference with the client.

The nature of transference will usually naturally metamorphose during therapeutic intervention as treatment progresses. Initially the practitioner may be seen as an object to be utilised in order to fulfil the client's inner needs if object transference has been invoked. Towards the end of the therapeutic period, the client may then progress to seeing the therapist as a person in his/her own right with a distinct personality when he/she has attained a more mature attitude towards others. When the client can manage to regard his/her therapist as an equal, this will, in itself, be indicative of his/her increasing self-awareness and consequent respect for the personality of others.

The following metaphorical passage could be employed by the practitioner in order to enhance the development of constructive transference. This passage will encourage the client to develop transference by becoming imaginative and to interpret symbolic imagery in an appropriate manner. The aim of using this form of methodology would be to create a bridge in order to allow the client to identify with the practitioner and the therapeutic environment via an inanimate object – thus making the development of rapport and the manifestation of transference a more palatable entity. This passage will also allow the consulting room chair to serve as a hypnotic anchor if it can be used during the induction process.

The therapy chair ...

And I wonder if you can take a moment and allow that relaxation to take you still deeper into a greater feeling of comfort. And, as you do, perhaps you can ponder on the comfort that that chair is providing you with right now. You could even think about how much time and care the designer took to design that chair, that would give all the necessary support – ensuring that whoever would use that chair would receive a level of support that would allow a complete letting go. Hours of work and thought were necessary to create a place of support and comfort and, in designing that chair, the designer put all that creativity towards ensuring that the appropriate materials were used.

Chair, having only one purpose, having only one thought in mind, was designed, therefore, to provide a place of comfort and support, allowing you to sit and let go. So perhaps now you can give chair an opportunity to do what chair does best – to provide a resting place that allows you to completely relax and to accept everything that chair has to offer. Giving you, in the right environment, the time for both mind and body to rest and to reflect – and at the right time and not before – allowing chair to give you back to yourself, rested and refreshed.

Utilising Transference

> Why is this cool, unresponsive attitude of the analyst to the benefit of the patient? Because transference is a form of neurosis, a wish to stay dependent on the doctor and not to become independent. Therefore any demand of the patient which is fulfilled by the analyst keeps the patient longer in dependence.
> – Mario Jacoby

The aim of analytical hypnotherapy will be to allow the client to undergo a process of development and maturation whereby he/she can be awakened to the realisation that there have been certain impediments to his/her psychological growth. Often immaturely-seated relationships will form a major obstruction in this respect for the client. By investigating transference manifestations, however, the client can find his/her own true nature and the reasons for his/her motivations and compensatory behaviour, that have hitherto controlled his/her existence. If the client can identify and resolve unsatisfactory past relationships, usually with significant others, he/she will then be free to form more productive relational associations (see Chapter 12, Volume 2 – "Dysfunctional Relationships"). The practitioner's role in these proceedings will be gently to allow the client to become aware of any transference manifestations that have been evoked as a result of unresolved issues with significant others in childhood. The therapist should endeavour to interpret any forms of projection or transference, therefore, as a means of enlightening the client about his/her inner self. Whenever possible, of course, the therapist should bring transference issues to the client's attention in a subtle manner.

The client would need to identify the motivations behind any of his/her transference manifestations and then to resolve these issues in order to ensure his/her therapeutic progress. The therapist should, of course, be constantly alert to the subtleties of the transference relationship between himself/herself and the client and should be aware of the ways in which clues can be utilised in order to bring about improvement or furtherance of treatment. Often transference manifestation will appear very subtly because the genuine and human part of the relationship between the client and the practitioner may partially obscure the transference relationship. Transference will manifest itself not only in terms of the way in which the client interacts with the therapist and others in his/her current life but also in the guise of dreams, that can be a direct thoroughfare to his/her unconscious mind (see Chapter 14 – "Dreams and Symbolic Imagery").

Once treatment has been completed, it will, of course, be essential for the sake of the client's recovery to ensure that the transference relationship formed for the purposes of treatment can be terminated. It will be necessary for the client to sever any temporary dependence on the therapist once traumatic experiences have been explored and resolved. Failure to achieve this resolution may, on the one hand, result in an impediment to the client's future progress or, in extreme circumstances, could, on the other hand, lead to an irreconcilable impasse for him/her. To assist this breaking-free process, the practitioner may decide that a period of separation following therapy will be deemed necessary in order to allow the transference relationship to dissolve naturally. Alternatively, if the client can be encouraged to regard the therapist simply as a human being in the later stages of therapy, the relationship can then gently drift on to a more adult footing whereby saying good-bye will not be a painful experience for the client. Any dependency aspects of the transference relationship will, thus, tend to diminish. Resolving transference phenomena will also be part of an inevitable process whereby the client will be reintegrated into society with his/her new-found insight and psychological freedom.

In extreme cases, the development and resolution of transference may turn into a testing experience for the practitioner. The client, for example, may become obsessively involved in the transference relationship, as in the case-study example below. In such circumstances, it will be essential that the practitioner can remain impartial and in charge of the situation and that he/she does not render himself/herself susceptible to being manipulated or controlled by the client.

Case-study example – negative transference

A female client developed an obsessive transference manifestation for her male therapist.

The client sent the therapist photographs of herself and wrote several letters to him after each weekly session. These letters recounted her dreams and thoughts in infinite detail. The client was also offended when these letters were not received with acclaim because she had expected the therapist to study them in detail. At one point during the therapy, the client would regularly park her car outside the therapist's practice in the hope of catching a glimpse of him in order to attract his attention. Finally, the client confessed a love for the therapist and then threatened suicide when the therapist did not reciprocate this affection.

At all times, the therapist remained rational and unemotional when confronted with this client's obsessive manifestation of transference and, indeed, any deviation from this course might well have been fatal for the client. By this means, it was the therapist who acted responsibly and in the best interests of the client by not engaging in any dialogue or game-playing.

Eventually the client came to the startling realisation that she had been overdependent on her father, who had shown her little or no affection in childhood. This client was, therefore, living with an illusion and projecting this manifestation on to the one person in her life who had ever shown her any real consideration. Resolving the transference manifestation was, in this case, an earth-shattering experience for the client but marked a major turning point in her personal development and freedom from disturbing influences.

What Is Countertransference?

Trauma is contagious. In the role of witness to disaster or atrocity, the therapist at times is emotionally overwhelmed. She experiences, to a lesser degree, the same terror, rage, and despair as the patient. This phenomenon is known as "traumatic counter-transference" or "vicarious traumatisation".
– *Judith Lewis Herman*

Countertransference can occur during the therapeutic encounter when emotive responses are unconsciously transferred or projected from the therapist on to the client. Countertransference, however, can be used to advantage by the therapist, who can monitor his/her own feelings and reactions towards the client in order to be able to make adjustments to the therapeutic approach. Countertransference, moreover, can provide the practitioner with valuable feedback about the client's progress. If the therapist finds himself/herself becoming too apologetic about his/her treatment methodology, for example, this may well be an indicator that the client has been resisting any form of therapeutic intervention.

The practitioner's own psychological disturbances can, of course, be activated in the presence of the client but, if the therapist reacts in an inappropriate manner, then the client's advancement in therapy will suffer. The client's transferred illusions may, therefore, be even more contagious when the projected contents are identical with the therapist's own unconscious negative issues. The client's progress may be halted or he/she may even sustain further psychological damage owing to any mishandling in this respect. Passive countertransference, that may take place unconsciously, can, of course, be potentially damaging for the client and should be avoided at all costs. This form of negative countertransference materialisation can, of course, be reduced to a minimum when the therapist undertakes his/her own personal therapy successfully (see Chapter 1, Volume 2 – "The Hypnoanalytic Approach"). Undergoing personal therapy can help the practitioner to ensure that he/she will strive constantly to monitor personal conflicts, behavioural motivations, psychological weaknesses and inadequacies as a result of his/her own personal psychic disorders. It will, of course, be of utmost importance that the dedicated professional can render nonjudgmental guidance and impartial evaluation of the client's needs, and self-investigation will be the first step along this somewhat treacherous road.

Countertransference will, of course, manifest in subtle ways. Any hint of unconscious motivation on the part of the therapist, furthermore, may cause the client to react unconsciously in order to fulfil the desires that he/she perceives the therapist might demand. The client may endeavour to gain approval, for example, from the practitioner if he/she gains the impression that he/she should act in a prescribed manner. If the therapist could be susceptible, in any way, to employing any manipulative tactics in such circumstances, then he/she should without delay consult a supervisor who is reliably experienced in handling negative countertransference manifestations.

> *Theoretically* the training analysis lessens the danger of wild projections from the side of the analyst because through it he becomes more conscious of what happens in himself.
> – Mario Jacoby

Countertransference Classifications

> Likewise, therapists have feelings towards their clients, and they do not react uniformly to all clients. So it is not precise to contend that all positive and negative feelings of therapists toward their clients are merely countertransference. Countertransference is the phenomenon that occurs when there is an inappropriate affect, when therapists respond in irrational ways, or when they lose their objectivity in a relationship because their own conflicts are triggered – specifically, when they relate to the client as if this person were mother, father, or lover.
> – Gerald Corey

An awareness of the ways in which countertransference can manifest itself will be of importance to the dedicated hypnoanalytic therapist. The practitioner can utilise both positive and negative forms of countertransference at his/her command rather than let the situation get out of hand. Constant self-investigation on the part of the therapist will enable this form of healthy self-control to occur naturally.

Positive Countertransference

> The analyst has all sorts of irrational attitudes toward the patient. He is
> afraid of the patient, he wants to be praised by the patient, he wants to
> be loved by the patient. It's too bad, it shouldn't be that way, he should
> by his own analysis have achieved a position where he doesn't need all
> that love, but this is really not always the case.
> – Erich Fromm

Positive countertransference will occur when the therapist has been motivated to act in an exemplary manner in his/her professional dealings with the client, owing to an underlying social conscience and a genuine regard for the wellbeing of his/her charge. A positive form of countertransference, therefore, can assist the client with his/her healing journey because it can be utilised for his/her benefit. Positive aspects of this type of transference can be seen when the therapist endeavours to be received by the client as a genuine and caring professional who is acting as a guide and a mentor. The practitioner, in this sense, will be maintaining a high standard of clinical practice even though his/her motivations may have been unconsciously-driven. The client can, thus, via countertransference, receive the therapist's true empathy and then feel able to confide in one who truly understands his/her plight as no other can.

Negative Countertransference

> I have some brief examples of so-called neurotic or illusory
> countertransference, where the analyst feels rather stupid or blocked,
> and unable to arrive at any meaningful insight.
> – Mario Jacoby

Negative countertransference (or *neurotic countertransference*) can occur as a reflection of the therapist's own negative thoughts and projections. Negative countertransference can often manifest when a knowledge of the client's problems serves to activate the therapist's own childhood trauma. A negative form of countertransference, therefore, can be seriously detrimental to the client's progress in therapy. The most common form of negative countertransference can occur, for example, when the therapist finds himself/herself reacting passively like a parent to the client's childlike behavioural projections. Negative features of countertransference can occur, however, in a number of circumstances. The therapist may be flattered, for example, by the positive image that the client may have of him/her and may, in addition, want to elicit praise. The client, thus, will be being manipulated in order to pander to the therapist's vanity. The practitioner may also be overzealous in his/her desire to effect a cure in the client and/or may feel impatient with him/her for resisting treatment or for not progressing quickly enough while in therapy. The therapist may be overly inquisitive about the client's background and, as such, may ask irrelevant or intrusive questions in order to satisfy his/her morbid curiosity. If the practitioner feels that he/she could not possibly treat the client for a given disorder – sexual abuse being a prime example – then it may well be that the therapist will need to look into his/her own background in order to identify those aspects of his/her personal past that might still contain elements of psychological distress. If the therapist, in any way, shies away from a given territory, it could well be an indicator of underlying fear, guilt and shame, that will prevent him/her from helping such a client. Overcoming such reluctance to investigating the client's past will be the analytic practitioner's passport to success and a sincere reward for undertaking such uplifting and worthwhile work.

Being ever watchful for negative manifestations of countertransference, the therapist should monitor his/her own thoughts and dreams and, if any negative countertransference signs are detected, adequate steps should be taken to resolve the source of the conflict. The therapist will also need to suppress any conscious negative reactions that he/she may have towards the client in order to ensure that such feelings are not unconsciously conveyed to him/her. Negative countertransference may be experienced, for example, if the therapist harbours a distaste of the client's physical appearance or a dislike of his/her personal disposition. Suppression of such feelings will ensure that empathy and rapport are maintained at all times from a neutral standpoint when the client is under therapeutic care. If such feelings become unmanageable, then the therapist must seriously consider investigating such a dilemma with the aid of a supervisor or personal therapist.

Syntonic Countertransference

> Racker has proposed the term countertransference proper in distinction
> to neurotic countertransference.
> – *Mario Jacoby*

Syntonic countertransference (or *countertransference proper*) will manifest when the therapist can become truly in tune with the client's inner conflicts and, hence, will become fully able to empathise with his/her feelings and problems. With this form of positive countertransference, the practitioner may also become adept at detecting any forms of subtle resistance that the client may display towards the therapeutic encounter (see Chapter 12 – "Resistance"). Syntonic countertransference will, of course, be the ideal to which all genuine therapists will aspire.

Concordant Countertransference

> I am probably experiencing concordant countertransference when I can
> allow myself to be spontaneous with the patient whenever he really
> needs me to be, and when I can be open and flexible to allow him to
> "use" me to a wide extent, according to his needs within the symbolic
> framework of the therapeutic situation.
> – *Mario Jacoby*

Concordant countertransference will be a positive form of counter-transference characterised by a high degree of mirroring, rapport and empathy. Such countertransference will exhibit features of an openness and a spontaneity within the therapeutic relationship, a flexible approach, an intuitive and a near-telepathic quality. A high degree of what Jung described as mystic participation will also occur with concordant countertransference. This form of counter-transference will be of enormous benefit to the client who can truly be himself/herself in the consulting room. The client can, thus, be free to express feelings, thoughts and opinions in the sound knowledge that these sentiments will be received with under-standing and, even, acclaim.

Complementary Countertransference

> With this woman I obviously acted out countertransference impulses of
> the kind Racker calls complementary. I virtually became the patient's
> mother, the most important figure of her past, an image or complex
> which was still operating within her at present.
> – *Mario Jacoby*

Complementary countertransference will be a positive form of countertransference that portrays the characteristics of complementary behaviour. The therapist, for example, may actively exhibit parental qualities by purposefully evoking a characteristic reaction in the client in order to allow him/her to identify his/her childlike motivations. In this instance, however, the therapist will not be fulfilling any inner needs but will be engineering the situation in order to achieve the desired degree of enlightenment on the client's part. Essentially, when the practitioner can be the master of his/her own reactions, then he/she can be of genuine service to the client. If, however, the practitioner's reactions become uncontrollable, then the client may suffer in consequence.

> Transference onto the therapist of infantile love-expectations, as well as
> repressed hatred and aggression, was for Freud the condition for
> successful treatment. On the other hand, it was exactly the transference
> which seemed, according to Freud, to sabotage quick healing; the
> original neurosis transformed itself during analysis to a new kind of
> neurosis, which he called again transference neurosis. In other words,
> the patient gets tied to the analyst and this dependence can remove him
> from all personal responsibility. He can feel himself to be the beloved
> infant of the analyst-father or mother and unconsciously does not want
> to give up this dependence. The healing of his neurosis would mean at
> the same time giving up his dependence on the analyst, and therefore he
> unconsciously refuses to get better. Thus transference can also cause a
> resistance against the healing process.
> – *Mario Jacoby*

Client Profiling

The analytical hypnotherapy practitioner may wish to ponder the following points when formulating a profile for the client.

- In what ways does the client react to the practitioner in an immature manner?

- In what ways does the client not regard the practitioner as an equal?
- Does the client look upon the practitioner as a parental substitute?
- Does the client manifest transference via dreams and symbolic imagery?
- Does the client have a profusion of cuddly toys to which he/she has become inextricably attached?
- In what respects does the client harbour unfounded illusions about the therapist?
- Does the client in any way appear uncooperative in the therapeutic context?
- Does the client display fear or anger towards the practitioner?
- Does the client expect to be praised by the practitioner?
- Does the client regard the practitioner as a vehicle for the satisfaction of his/her personal needs?
- Does the client confess to or indicate an overaffectionate or erotically-tinged tendency towards the therapist?
- Is the client obsessive in his/her approach and attitude to therapy?
- Does the client in any way delude himself/herself about the capabilities or the role of the therapist?
- Does the practitioner in any way find that his/her motivations when dealing with the client are inappropriate?
- Does the practitioner consider that his/her conduct towards the client appears to be unprofessional sometimes?

Chapter 14

Dreams and Symbolic Imagery

In dreaming the clouds methought would open and show
riches ready to drop upon me that when I wak'd I cried to
dream again.

— William Shakespeare

What Is the Importance of a Dream?

Jung teaches that many dreams contain messages from the deepest layer
of the unconscious, which he describes as the source of creativity.
He calls this deep layer the *collective unconscious*, the "all-controlling
deposit of ancestral experiences". Jung sees a connection between each
person's personality and the past, not only childhood events but also the
history of the species.
— Gerald Corey

In examining the client's psyche, Freud was the first to draw attention to the fact that dreams are a rich source of bounty, that can enable the client to reveal what lies at the depths of his/her psychic distress. Freud broke away from the conventional object-oriented interpretation of dream symbolism, thereby handing power over to the client, who can provide his/her own interpretation of personal dream imagery. Psychoanalytic doctrine advocates that unconscious conflicts, defensive strategies, resistance and transference can manifest in a number of ways in dreams and that such elements can become apparent to the keen therapeutic observer. The therapist can, therefore, often explore the client's dream imagery and fantasy world, that may provide evidence of psychic distress when incidental elements seep through from the depths of his/her unconscious mind in various imaginative and symbolic forms.

Although there was an extensive literature on the subject of dreams
before Freud turned his attention to it, Freud is justly famous for pulling
the threads together, for making the dream into a legitimate object of
scrutiny, and for creating a theory of dreams and a technique for
interpreting them.
– *Anthony Storr*

The Freudian View of Dreams

The transformation of the latent dream-thoughts into the manifest
dream-content deserves all our attention, since it is the first instance
known to us of psychical material being changed over from one mode of
expression to another, from a mode of expression which is immediately
intelligible to us to another which we can only come to understand with
the help of guidance and effort, though it too must be recognised as a
function of our mental activity.
– *Sigmund Freud*

Freud argued that the process of hiding thoughts in a dream
would be a clear example of the same mechanism that will be at
the forefront of all the client's problems (see Chapter 1 –
"Psychoanalysis"). Freud maintained that psychological distress
will occur when the client's deepest desires have been so thor-
oughly repressed or suppressed that these conflicts can explode
internally and self-destructively. A resolution, however, can occur
when the client can – not only rationally but also emotively –
unearth the reality of such aspirations. An analysis and interpretation of a dream can, therefore, lead the client to his/her disturbing
psychic material and will allow for problem-solving activities to
be undertaken via this substructure.

Freud advocated that children's dreams are purely egocentric
desires but, as the child grows older, his/her socially-conventional
superego will want to disguise such cravings (see Chapter 15 –
"Personality Structure"). Freud also asserted that a dream will be
a disguised wish-fulfilment that may contain trauma, anxiety or
sexual desire. A wish may be taken broadly to imply the client's
desire to possess an object, to correct a transgression or to control
an unpleasant circumstance. Freud considered that the client's
dreams contain restrained wishes and expressions that can
emanate from early childhood. This form of suppression will then
lead the client to find an alternative outlet for his/her instinctual
thoughts and, naturally, dreams can provide a vehicle whereby

he/she may continue to fulfil secret wishes unhampered. The client's dreams, however, will then become distorted with what appears consciously to him/her to be mindless, nonsensical and relatively harmless imagery.

Dream Content

> It is still too soon to reach a definitive verdict on some central tenets of Freud's dream theory, but recent neuropsychological research suggests that he was at least on the right track. There is a close link between brain structures responsible for dreaming and those responsible for biological emotions and motivations.
> *– Mark Solms*

Freud spoke of the *manifest content* and the *latent content* of a dream. The manifest content of a dream will be that part of the client's dream that will be apparently evident and will superficially depict recognisable elements. The latent content of a dream will, however, be that part of the client's dream that will conceal its true meaning. The latent part of the client's dream, once interpreted, can reveal the unconsciously-suppressed material that would normally be concealed by the client's ego and, thus, consciously inaccessible. The latent content of a dream, therefore, will contain the dream's true meaning hidden from the dreamer's conscious awareness in order to avoid his/her psychic distress. Manifest dream content may, in fact, clearly express hidden wishes while latent material in the client's dreams may depict aggressive instincts, sexual desires or power-hungry yearnings. According to Freud, man's deepest instincts are often very wild and antisocial. The power instinct may, for example, want to destroy anyone who poses an obstacle to the client's accomplishment of power – even parents, siblings and close friends. A basic sexual instinct may, for instance, reveal the client's desire for an incestuous or an adulterous relationship, that society at large might find horrific.

According to Freud, latent dream content will be converted to manifest symbolism by a dramatisation process, that he termed *dream-work*. This message-scrambling, censorship process will occur in the client's dream in order to disguise the unconscious aspects of it. This form of distortion will be the means by which the client's unconscious mind can render the latent content of a

261

dream less disturbing and more palatable to him/her. Dream material can, therefore, be regarded as a roundabout way of expressing psychic conflicts because of the symbolism and imagery contained within it, but the dream-work will distort reality in order to conceal the truth from the dreamer. This distortion or censorship of conscious reality on the client's part may take a number of forms. Latent material may be condensed or abbreviated, for instance, when a series of events can be depicted in the client's dream as a single incident. Inadmissible elements may also be displaced or substituted in that the dreamer may dream of an innocuous image instead of one totally unacceptable to him/her. Dream images may also be transformed, embroidered or embellished by the dreamer in the process of distortion in order to ensure the disguise of the original, underlying thought. Freud, however, believed that free association and other investigative methods were a means of reaching the latent content of the client's dream, that would then reveal the wish-fulfilment (see Chapter 2, Volume 2 – "Therapeutic Investigation").

> We will describe what the dream actually tells us as the *manifest dream-content*, and the concealed material, which we hope to reach by pursuing the ideas that occur to the dreamer, as the *latent dream-thoughts*.
> – *Sigmund Freud*

Dream Symbolism

> Dreams are things which get rid of psychical stimuli disturbing to sleep by the method of hallucinating satisfaction.
> – *Sigmund Freud*

Freud put forward his own views on dream symbolism while simultaneously departing from conventional imagery-interpretation of dreams, whereby an object universally portrayed a specific meaning. Although the therapist would normally ask the client to interpret his/her own dream imagery, a number of symbols or images have been shown to represent certain aspects of life. Perhaps, we can now consider some of these generally-accepted interpretations of dream objects as an overall guide for the therapist. Dream symbolism can, in this way, become the therapist's slave and not his/her master.

People or objects, in general, may be a reflection of aspects of the client's psyche or his/her internal conflicts. Dreams of houses or buildings, for example, may depict the dreamer himself/herself or his/her unique view of himself/herself. The client's parents may be represented by kings and queens or heroes and heroines. The client's siblings are sometimes considered to be animals or vermin of whom he/she may be unconsciously jealous. Persons depicted in dreams, however, may provide a clue to the transference relationship that the client will be developing with the therapist (see Chapter 13 – "Transference and Countertransference"). If the client were to dream of a taskmaster or a dictator, for example, he/she may be inadvertently expressing negative transference. A kindly nurse or a guardian angel, conversely, may portray a positive form of transference in the client's dream. Sometimes the therapeutic process can be symbolically represented in a dream as either a birth or a new beginning. Similarly, the therapeutic journey may be envisaged as a death, an end of a previous existence or a pilgrimage, that may be either an enjoyable experience or a living nightmare.

Most people will be familiar with sexual connotations and symbolism – particularly that adumbrated by Freud himself – but it may be of particular relevance to the therapist who may need to detect the client's unconscious thoughts and conflicts in this area. With the sexually-abused client, in particular, it may well be that sexual symbolism and imagery will be the only means by which he/she can express his/her inner fears. An appreciation of such symbolic imagery will, therefore, be a useful tool about which the practitioner should be aware. Male genitalia, for example, can be represented by images of a pen, a tree, a weapon or a snake. An erection can be depicted by an inflatable balloon or an aircraft taking off. The female vagina can be represented by images of a cave, a box, a store cupboard or a jewel case. Female breasts can be depicted as hills, mountains or rocks, and virginity or purity may be seen as a flower or a key. The client's sexual instincts, similarly, may be represented by wild animals or evil inclinations. An orgasm can be symbolised by images of a watering can, a tap or a fountain. Sexual intercourse, moreover, may be depicted as dancing, riding, climbing or being threatened with weapons. Masturbation, too, may be symbolised as playing, gliding or climbing trees. It goes without saying, of course, that the therapist should merely note these symbolic associations and not make extravagant predictions about any supposed meaning to the bemused client.

The Jungian View of Dreams

> No amount of scepticism and criticism has yet enabled me to regard dreams as negligible occurrences. Often enough they appear senseless, but it is obviously we who lack the sense and ingenuity to read the enigmatic message from the nocturnal realm of the psyche. Seeing that at least half our psychic existence is passed in that realm, and that consciousness acts upon our nightly life just as much as the unconscious overshadows our daily life, it would seem all the more incumbent on medical psychology to sharpen its senses by a systematic study of dreams.
> – *Carl Jung*

Jung saw dreams as expansive – rather than taking the reductionist Freudian view – by regarding a dream as having some form of anticipatory or prophetic quality (see Chapter 2 – "Analytical Psychology"). Jung considered that the manifest symbolic quality and the archetypal imagery contained within a series of the client's dreams were worthy of direct analysis by analogy and comparison. Jung contended that the manifest elements of the client's dream were not a façade of deceptive distortion. He regarded such material as being ripe for interpretation by means of assimilation of both the dream's subjective and objective content. Jung also regarded dreams as the nocturnal side of the client's psyche, that contained representations of current difficulties rather than remnants of childhood traumas or conflicts. The analytical psychologist will consider that the function of the client's dreaming would be to balance his/her life by reconciling opposing factions within the psyche and to prepare him/her for future experiences. Jung also advocated detailed examination of the client's fantasy life and visions, in a similar way, because he felt that, once resistances had been overcome, this material would then contain a wealth of enlightening substance. Jung paid great heed to distinguishing between signs and symbols particularly evident in the client's dreams. A gun, for example, might be a sign of a penis according to Freud, but it could also be a symbol of masculinity, fertility and reproduction in Jungian doctrine.

The word "archetype" has passed into more or less general use; but it is
extraordinarily hard to give an adequate definition of the term as used
by Jung.
– *Anthony Storr*

Dream Symbolism

Jung views dreams more as an attempt to express than an attempt to
repress and disguise. They are a creative effort of the dreamer in
struggling with contradiction, complexity, and confusion. The aim of the
dream is resolution and integration. According to Jung, each part of the
dream can be understood as some projected quality of the dreamer. His
method of interpretation draws on a series of dreams obtained from a
person, during the course of which the meaning gradually unfolds.
– *Gerald Corey*

Jung undertook the client's dream analysis in order to identify
archetypal manifestations of transference. As the main archetypal
images are often depicted in dreams, the therapist's role would be
to interpret these images and also to observe carefully any emotive
responses that the client projected on to such identities.

Jung postulated a method of dream interpretation in which the
dream would be examined in the context of the client's lifestyle so
that the images and archetypes illustrated could be dissected
accordingly. Dream interpretation should also take into account
the client's family background and current circumstances, including his/her lifestyle and character. This form of investigation can
be achieved by questioning the client about the meaning of the figures or the personages in his/her dream. Does a mother-figure, for
example, represent good or evil, protection or neglect, power or
weakness in the client's eyes? It will, of course, be the client's interpretation that will be of importance and not the therapist's opinion in all cases. Jung recommended that a series of dreams be
analysed in this way in order to verify previous dream interpretation and to uncover recurring themes. He felt that a series of
between twenty and a hundred dreams should be analysed
because interpretation of a single dream could be accepted arbi-
trarily, whereas analysing a series of dreams will allow the therapist to monitor the continuity of the client's unconscious
processes. Both objective and subjective interpretations can be
made in this manner. With an objective interpretation, the persons
or symbols appearing in the dream may represent the client's

reality. With a subjective interpretation, people depicted in the dream may represent aspects of the client's own personality. Again, it is for the client to decide whether the content of the dream should be taken objectively at face value or not. Jung maintained that a dream does not conceal anything but that the client merely does not understand its language.

Jung's methodology in dream analysis was to amplify the dream contents, to seek parallels and to resolve the dream's context by asking the client what the dream meant to him. Jung also advocated that, in dream analysis, the practitioner should not look for a personality complex but rather for that which the client's unconscious mind was doing with that complex. Freud, on the other hand, used dream analysis in order to uncover the complex. When the client's dreams contain an archetypal image, it could be a clear indication that his/her dream goes beyond the realm of his/her personal unconscious. Jung believed that explaining to the client that his/her problem might not be purely personal but could be approaching a universally-human level would make him/her feel better about his/her difficulties. Jung theorised that when something befalls a group, the client may be able to cope far more easily than if it had happened only to him/her. The client who can learn that having anxiety is a supposedly normal and frequent occurrence in most people's lives, for instance, may feel some degree of relief at receiving this knowledge.

Jung himself underwent a stage of intense self-analysis in virtual seclusion, modelling the isolation of his own childhood. Because of this, Jung was convinced of man's ability to emerge from a crisis as part of a continuing self-regulatory process. During this phase of his life, Jung examined his own dreams, fantasies and visions by delving into the contents of his active imagination. Such a technique can often be utilised in hypnosis and during hypnotic visualisation in order to dislodge the client's imaginative essence. Jung considered that the client could utilise his/her active imagination in order to purposefully create a scenario in which events have a life of their own. These symbolic events can then be allowed to develop within the client's mind along a logical route without interference from his/her conscious mind. Since all imaginative material will inevitably be reproduced in the client's conscious state of mind, it will be far more rounded and may have much greater significance than that obtained purely from dreams. The client's feeling-values can frequently be examined, for example, in order to allow him/her to judge the content of such material. As with dreams, the material reached by this method will frequently have a strong archetypal content of significance to the client. Jung would frequently analyse the client's drawings and paintings by searching for archetypal imagery and then interpreting his/her state of mind from these pictures (see Chapter 2, Volume 2 – "Therapeutic Investigation").

> Jung agrees with Freud that dreams provide a pathway into the unconscious, but he differs from Freud on their functions. He writes that dreams have two purposes: They are prospective, in that they help people prepare themselves for the experiences and events they anticipate in the near future. They also serve a compensatory function; that is, they work to bring about a balance between opposites within the person. They compensate for the over-development of one facet of the individual's personality.
> – *Gerald Corey*

Jung's Archetypal Imagery

> The archetype in itself is empty and purely formal, nothing but a *facultas praeformandi*, a possibility of representation which is given *a priori*. The representations themselves are not inherited, only the forms, and in that respect they correspond in every way to the instincts, which are also determined in form only. The existence of the instincts can no more be proved than the existence of the archetypes, so long as they do not manifest themselves concretely.
> – *Carl Jung*

An archetypal image is a universally-accepted motif or symbolic pattern that can depict a given notion or concept. Jung maintained that archetypal imagery can emanate from the collective unconscious and can impact upon the client as a manifestation of his/her inner psychic dilemmas. The collective unconscious can, therefore, be regarded as a repository for housing myths, visions, ideas and fantasies. Jung believed that, when the client experiences primordial imagery in his/her dreams and in hallucinatory states of the mind, he/she will be beholding the collective unconscious at its most direct.

The universal consciousness will contain signs, symbols and similar imagery that may be indicative of a given culture but will be collectively accepted by all. Jung considered that myths were a fundamental expression of human nature. Myths are formed and expressed in words but the spirit, the emotive associations and a large portion of the subject matter abound from the collective unconscious. Because myths are based on the collective unconscious, moreover, they are found in similar forms across all peoples of the world and in all times. All cultures have various myths, superstitions, fairytales and folklore containing characters that are recognisable as indicative of a certain type of universal characteristic. The hero, for example, may be the metaphorical knight in shining armour. The heroine, similarly, may be a damsel in distress. The good guy may be the personification of all that is upright and praiseworthy. The bad guy may be the epitome of sin, evil and wickedness. The central figures in all religions are archetypal in nature, clothed in conscious perceptions. Examples of archetypes that are ancient in origin are typically gods and goddesses, dwarves and giants, mythical animals and other such symbolism. Modern-day archetypes, however, are seen in the guise of Superman and Batman. Several archetypal images that are of particular significance for the human race can be correlated with myths and historical figures throughout the world. Robin Hood and William Tell are known as national heroes in a number of cultures. These heroic archetypes can have a greater personal significance for the client while other images will have a larger collective-unconscious component.

Jung also emphasised that most geometric shapes such as the wheel, the square, the circle and the cross are also archetypal images. These abstract shapes can often be combined in typical ways in order to produce the mandala and other well-known designs. The Celtic cross, that consists of a circle and a cross, and the Star of David, that comprises two triangles, are examples of these combinations.

> Whereas ritual mandalas always display a definite style and a limited number of typical motifs as their content, individual mandalas make use of a well-nigh unlimited wealth of motifs and symbolic allusions, from which it can easily be seen that they are endeavouring to express either the totality of the individual in his inner or outer experience of the world, or its essential point of reference.
> *– Carl Jung*

Archetypal imagery may also be experienced by the client as emotive responses and will be especially noticeable in typical and significant human situations such as birth, death, danger, triumph, transitional stages of life and awe-inspiring experiences.

> Have you ever been thinking of somebody whom you had not seen in months, and had them arrive on your doorstep that very morning? Have you ever written to a friend after years of no communication and had your letters cross? Have you ever been singing an old song in your head and found it playing on the radio when you turned it on?
> *– Andrew Matthews*

Sometimes the client can achieve a degree of harmony and integration with his/her environment when he/she perceives archetypal imagery. This form of harmony Jung termed *synchronicity*. Jung believed that, when the client connects with the collective unconscious in this way via synchronicity, he/she will be receiving a powerful and deeply meaningful message, that cannot be ignored. It will be for this reason that archetypal imagery will exert an intensely powerful influence on the client's psyche and will be of great importance in the therapeutic setting. If the client were to succumb to the influence of any given archetype to the extent that it became dominant in his/her personality, there would be a very real danger that he/she may become swamped or inflated by this intrusion on his/her individuality. The client, in these circumstances, would be halting or interrupting the individuation process. Let us now concentrate on considering some of Jung's archetypes, that may manifest in the client's dream symbolism or his/her imaginative life.

> What I found were "coincidences" which were connected so meaningfully that their "chance" concurrence would represent a degree of improbability that would have to be expressed by an astronomical figure.
> *– Carl Jung*

The Self

> Unity and totality stand at the highest point on the scale of objective
> values because their symbols can no longer be distinguished from the
> *imago Dei*. Hence all statements about the God-image apply also to the
> empirical symbols of totality.
> – Carl Jung

The self will depict the theme of wholeness and will represent the
central balancing aspect of the client's personality. The self archetype will be the client's true self, that he/she can pursue in therapy by exploring all elements of his/her personality. The
regulation of the self archetype will be an eternal struggle on the
client's part to reconcile that which he/she will find acceptable
and that which he/she will consider to be inadmissible. Some
examples of the way in which the archetype of self has been symbolically depicted are as a child, an animal, a jewel, a flower, a religious leader and a shape, such as a circle, a wheel or a square.

> The "self" as the totality of the psyche is immanent throughout and
> functions both as the beginning and the end of all psychic activity. It
> mediates the opposites of good/evil, creativity/destruction,
> divine/human, etc., and offers the possibility of achieving wholeness or
> "individuation" through the conjunction of opposites.
> – Ann Casement

Jung regarded the self as the centre of the personality, midway
between the hard-won values of consciousness and the vitality
and power of the unconscious mind. Jung differed in this respect
from the doctrine of Freud, who regarded the ego as the centre of
consciousness.

> It appears to act as something like a magnet to the disparate elements of
> the personality and the processes of the unconscious, and is the centre of
> this totality as the ego is the centre of consciousness, for it is the function
> which unites all the opposing elements in man and woman,
> consciousness and unconscious, good and bad, male and female, etc.,
> and in so doing transmutes them. To reach it necessitates acceptance of
> what is inferior in one's nature, as well as what is irrational and chaotic.
> – Frieda Fordham

The Persona

The persona is a complicated system of relations between individual
consciousness and society, fittingly enough a kind of mask, designed on
the one hand to make a definite impression upon others, and, on the
other, to conceal the true nature of the individual.
– *Carl Jung*

The persona will be the client's social mask. During the child's
development, he/she will tend to suppress natural instincts that
are unacceptable factors in society – and will be the subject of
parental controls – such as greed, aggression and jealousy. As the
child learns to deny his/her true self in the process of growing up,
he/she may find that it will be necessary to develop a persona that
will allow him/her to assume a role in many guises. These false
roles can then satisfy the dictates of social convention and can
assist in the client's integration and acceptance into society. The
average client will have a mask to wear at work in professional
life, a mask to wear in front of the children and a mask to wear on
social occasions. Sometimes the mask may slip when the client is
alone but often it will simply stay in place out of habit or
uncertainty.

The persona is a mask, or public face, that we wear to protect ourselves.
– *Gerald Corey*

The client's persona will frequently signify a group identity rather
than a personal characteristic. When playing a role, the client will
be modelling himself/herself on other members of that group. The
client, for instance, may wear the same styles of clothes, may
adopt the same speech patterns or bodily mannerisms and may
even believe in the same doctrines. The client will, of course, be
fulfilling his/her role according to the dictates of others and what
he/she perceives to be social expectations. The client's persona,
therefore, will be a conscious or semiconscious effort to conduct
himself/herself according to the unwritten rules to which he/she
voluntarily subscribes as a society member.

"Persona" lies also in the conscious sphere and is the mask that the
individual presents to the world.
– *Ann Casement*

In order to illustrate the concept of the persona, let us observe the way in which a client expressed this phenomenon in her own narrative. This female client was a victim of childhood abuse but was adept at wearing a social mask behind which all her fears were encased. This information came from the client's journal that she kept during therapy (see Chapter 2, Volume 2 – "Therapeutic Investigation").

Client narrative – my emotional face-mask ...
My mask was that indispensable item of equipment in every abused child's wardrobe. It was that item in my child's toybox that was automatically transferred to my adult's costume collection. It was the mask that I put on when I was facing the world. The mask is what all sufferers are obliged to wear – it is their only means of protection and survival. In many cases, my mask was so firmly in place that I often forgot to take it off even when I was completely alone. In fact, in the end, I found difficulty in being able to take it off at all.

My mask was the perfect solution. The mask presented me to the outside world as the perfectly well-balanced woman, the one who was in full charge of herself, the one who was stable and placid, calm and unruffled, steady and dependable, unperturbed and unflappable. All these attributes were mine but did not show the real me beneath the mask. The real me with the demon inside!

When the mask slipped or got dislodged I suffered from a depressive disorder that would take the form of painful and seemingly endless tears. I would sob and howl and choke and wail from the torture inside. I would regularly take to my bed, wrap myself up warm and just go into myself for days. Antidepressants had no effect – except to take away from me the remnants of my virtually obscured personality. Even while I was wearing the mask, I still cried and wailed and howled inside. So there was no escape.

When I went out into the world, I would manage to get through the day without breaking down but, when the heat was off, I would dissolve into tears. The tears could come in public and, before I entered therapy, I became more and more unable to control my floods of tears in public places. No amount of determination or bloody-mindedness would enable me to keep the mask in place on these occasions.

The Shadow

> The shadow has the deepest roots and is the most dangerous and
> powerful of the archetypes. As mentioned, it represents our dark side,
> the thoughts, feelings, and actions that are socially reprehensible and
> that we tend to disown by projecting them outward.
> – *Gerald Corey*

The shadow represents all those aspects of the client that he/she would rather not acknowledge. The shadow will be that part of the client's personal unconscious mind that, in contrast to the persona, will not be the face that he/she will dare to show to the world. The shadow will contain all those negative emotive impulses and qualities that the client has been taught directly and indirectly not to express openly. These emotive reactions and inclinations will have thus been drummed out of the client while he/she was passing through childhood and submitting to social integration. The client's shadow, therefore, will be a means of shielding himself/herself from the rigours of the social adaptation process.

> By shadow I mean the "negative" side of the personality, the sum of all
> those unpleasant qualities we like to hide, together with the
> insufficiently developed functions and the contents of the
> personal unconscious.
> – *Carl Jung*

The client will often be aware of inclining towards unsociable emotive expression but he/she may strive relentlessly to suppress this tendency. The client's suppression of shadow responses, however, may sometimes result in an almost total dissociation from or denial of his/her natural responses (see Chapter 11 – "Defensive Strategies"). The client may, then, be likely to imagine such unacceptable qualities in others when these negative expressions are outwardly projected. The client's shadow qualities, of course, may surface in dreams and may, perhaps, be exaggerated in the process.

> The shadow is the personal unconscious; it is all those uncivilised
> desires and emotions that are incompatible with social standards and
> our ideal personality, all that we are ashamed of, all that we do not want
> to know about ourselves.
> – *Frieda Fordham*

The suppression of the shadow self will often be a necessity if the client wishes to interact with others in society. The danger, however, will lie in the fact that too much suppression can cause the client's shadow to erupt and then to upset his/her psychic apple-cart. The subjective components of psychic functioning will be the client's subjective reactions to objects or to people. These reactions may well be deemed inadmissible, unjust or inaccurate by the client's conscience. The client, for instance, may possess a disposition that will react in a certain way even though that way will not usually be entirely conducive to social interaction. This portion of the client's shadow-world may then become the skeleton in the closet with his/her behaviour becoming the personification of this silhouette. In order to regulate the shadow, the client must engage in a degree of self-love and self-acceptance, that will enable these socially-inappropriate qualities to be kept to manageable proportions.

> The shadow is a moral problem that challenges the whole ego-
> personality, for no one can become conscious of the shadow without
> considerable moral effort. To become conscious of it involves recognising
> the dark aspects of the personality as present and real. This act is the
> essential condition for any kind of self-knowledge, and it therefore, as a
> rule, meets with considerable resistance. Indeed, self-knowledge as a
> psychotherapeutic measure frequently requires much painstaking work
> extending over a long period.
> – *Carl Jung*

Jung believed that the client who attempts to totally negate his/her shadow-side will become only a two-dimensional personality. Moreover, if the client lives almost totally in the shadow element, he/she may personify his/her own negation. Invasion of the personality, in this way, will mean that the client's shadow-side will unconsciously take full control of his/her personality by breaking through into consciousness. Personality invasion can occur, for example, when the client suffers from a surfeit of anger, that will spill over into his/her intimate relationships. The client may, at times, become very angry and, indeed, may have difficulty in controlling such anger; but, while it remains under wraps, it will still simply be a difficulty that he/she is currently experiencing. The client's anger, in this instance, will merely be a troubling effect but not one that has got out of hand. Personality invasion, on the other hand, can occur when the client experiences vivid fantasies of mutilating or destroying the object of his/her anger. There will then be a real danger for the client that such ostensibly harmless fantasies can easily get out of control.

> The "shadow" lies in the personal unconscious and represents all those aspects that are seen to be undesirable by the ego and which are, therefore, repressed.
> – *Ann Casement*

The Anima and the Animus

> A very feminine woman has a masculine soul, and a very masculine man has a feminine soul. This contrast is due to the fact that a man is not all things wholly masculine, but also has certain feminine traits. The more masculine his outer attitude is, the more his feminine traits are obliterated: instead, they appear in his unconscious.
> – *Carl Jung*

The anima and the animus will relate to the unconscious elements of the client's opposing sex contained within his/her psyche. The anima will comprise the feminine aspects of the male personality and the animus the masculine aspects of the female personality. The client may often be desirous not to acknowledge these socially-unacceptable traits that he/she may observe within himself/herself.

> The anima and the animus represent both the biological and psychological aspects of masculinity and femininity, which are thought to coexist in both sexes.
> – *Gerald Corey*

These anxiety-provoking archetypes, that threaten to dent the client's self-image, can become personified in dreams, fantasies or visions and a study of these manifestations can lead him/her to self-knowledge and to personal enlightenment. The anima and the animus may also manifest in the client's emotive reactions and in attitudes projected on to members of the opposite sex.

275

The anima

> The compelling power of the anima is due to her image being an
> archetype of the collective unconscious, which is projected on to any
> woman who offers the slightest hook on which her picture may be hung.
> – *Frieda Fordham*

The male client may be hypersensitive to those characteristics within his personality that he regards as feminine elements. The male anima may display characteristics such as gentleness, intuition, sensitivity and moodiness, that he may feel uneasy about exhibiting publicly. A heterosexual man, for example, may not wish to appear effeminate in society.

According to Jung, the anima archetype will be derived from the male client's knowledge of women throughout his life – from the mother of early years to the sexual partner of later years. The anima will intrinsically be the client's perception of the way in which his mother was in childhood and this impression may be projected on to all other women with whom he has any contact. The image of womanhood, therefore, may depict eternal youth, wisdom, power and strength as a nurturing mother-figure for the client. The anima may also be beheld as an image of virginal purity beyond reach or the tantalisingly irresistible temptress who will lead to the client's ultimate destruction.

The animus

> The *animus* in women is the counterpart of the anima in man. He seems
> to be (like the anima) derived from three roots: the collective image of
> man which a woman inherits; her own experience of masculinity coming
> through the contacts she makes with men in her life; and the latent
> masculine principle in herself.
> – *Frieda Fordham*

The female client may be disinclined to acknowledge any masculine elements found within her personality. The female animus may contain characteristics such as aggression, single-mindedness, ruthlessness and self-aggrandisement, that the client may not wish to acknowledge socially. A heterosexual woman, for example, may not want to be seen as manly by others.

The animus can find expression in women's fight for equality and equal opportunities, in political leadership and in supervisory roles in the working environment. The childhood image of father as the ultimate provider will be the one that the female client may project on to all other men with whom she comes into contact. The image of manhood, therefore, may manifest itself as the primitive, dominant and self-seeking caveman or the spiritually uplifting guardian and protector for the client.

> "Anima" and "animus", like all "archetypes", originate in the "collective unconscious" and act unconsciously through projection when activated by an outer object, for example falling in love.
> – *Ann Casement*

The Hero and the Heroine

> The ego would thus be assured of an impregnable position, the steadfastness of a superman or the sublimity of a perfect sage.
> – *Carl Jung*

The archetype of the hero or the heroine will be that part of the client's psyche that will strive for success, fame and outstanding achievement. The hero or heroine, therefore, will appeal to the client's fantasy-oriented aspirations and yet it will be his/her way of saying to himself/herself that he/she can never reach such dizzy heights. These archetypes, therefore, can become the client's personal vote of no confidence in himself/herself.

The individuation process that Jung advocated can be depicted in heroic archetypes, symbolic of the child maturing into an adult and taking his/her place in the world, with the self archetype guiding this process. The practitioner can, of course, see heroic archetypes in classical works of literature, music, mythology and modern film and theatrical performance.

> Archetypes are felt to possess immense emotional significance. They are, if one likes to put it that way, typical human experience; but experience raised to what is felt to be of superhuman, or even cosmic significance.
> – *Anthony Storr*

The Wise Old Man and the Earth Mother

> In dreams, it is always the father-figure from whom the decisive
> convictions, prohibitions, and wise counsels emanate. The invisibility of
> this source is frequently emphasised by the fact that it consists simply of
> an authoritative voice which passes final judgements. Mostly, therefore,
> it is a figure of a "wise old man" who symbolises the spiritual factor.
> – *Carl Jung*

As Jung regarded the individuation process as a means of freeing
the client from parental control – both personal and archetypal –
he formulated the intellectual and knowledgeable wise-old-man
archetype and the bountiful earth-mother archetype. These archetypes were almost certainly based on his own impressions of his
homely mother and his nebulous father, who were perpetually in
conflict, and his desire to separate from them psychologically.

The wise old man

> This archetype represents a serious danger to personality, for when it is
> awakened a man may easily come to believe that he really possesses the
> "mana", the seemingly magical power and wisdom that it holds. It is as
> if the fascination of the anima had been transferred to this figure, and
> the one possessed by it feels himself endowed with great (perhaps
> esoteric) wisdom, prophetic powers, the gift of healing, and so on.
> – *Frieda Fordham*

The archetype of the wise old man will be a state whereby the
client may feel himself/herself to be imbued with superhuman
powers in the hope of attracting sheep to his/her fold. The wise
old man will be that force within the client that will provide the
key to his/her insight and profound self-understanding. Here, too,
will be the potential megalomaniac or paranoid schizophrenic –
the egoist blown up out of all proportion.

The earth mother

> Anyone possessed by this figure comes to believe herself endowed with
> an infinite capacity for loving and understanding, helping and
> protecting, and will wear herself out in the service of others. She can,
> however, also be most destructive, insisting (though not necessarily
> openly) that all who come within her circle of influence are "her
> children", and therefore helpless and dependent on her in some degree.

This subtle tyranny, if carried to extremes, can demoralise and destroy
the personality of others.
– *Frieda Fordham*

The archetype of the earth mother will be the client's inflated
extension of the nurturing role of the female. Here the overposses-
sive or overprotective mother role will have become an exaggerated quality built on illusion within the client. The earth-mother
archetype can, for example, turn the client into an excessively submissive and self-sacrificial carer or into a rigidly dictatorial nanny.

Exploring the Client's Dreams and Symbolic Imagery

If a person thinks he knows nothing of experiences the memory of which
he nevertheless has within him, it is no longer so improbable that he
knows nothing of other mental processes within him.
– *Sigmund Freud*

Psychoanalytic therapists will stress the importance of dream
interpretation and fantasy-life exploration as a means of identifying the client's unconscious thoughts and wishes. The therapist's
role will be to encourage the client to examine the underlying significance of imagery in order to reveal disturbing pressures or conflicting elements.

Analysing Dreams and Imagery

The client's dream-oriented and fantasy-based imagery can be an
excellent vehicle for unearthing disturbing psychic matter,
because such material will require time, patience and a safe environment before it will be ripe for retrieval. Sometimes a daydream
can be a surface-level experience for the client, while a dream may
have a more unconsciously-mysterious element and will, therefore, be a more valuable tool for psychic exploration. An excellent
practice for the therapist, therefore, will be to enquire regularly
about the client's dream life. Asking the client to record his/her
dreams will, moreover, keep his/her mind focused on the resolution of his/her dilemmas. Dream exploration may also be undertaken with the client either formally or informally in the
therapeutic context. In simply recounting a dream, for instance,

the client may well become consciously aware of the underlying significance of what he/she will be divulging to the therapist. The client can often be shrewdly made aware of his/her motivation for a dream, the wishes he/she seeks to fulfil and the problems with which he/she has been grappling, as well as the ways in which obscure material may be surfacing. The therapist's role in the process of dream exploration should, of course, be to listen to the contents of the client's dream in an impartial manner. The client, by this means, can be allowed to divulge and freely interpret his/her own dream content and imaginative imagery in a judgment-free environment. The therapist should, however, seek to question what the dream's message actually means to the client when undertaking dream analysis. It will, of course, be vitally important for the therapist to remember that it must be the client himself/herself who will provide the clue to his/her own dream interpretation. The beliefs or opinions of the practitioner will be more or less irrelevant in terms of an interpretation of the client's symbolic imagery.

> There has been a continuing to and fro debate within psychoanalytic circles as to whether externally imposed or internally imagined experiences are more important in development. Sigmund Freud had at first thought that the prime causes of neurosis were trauma and seduction, but when he realised that these may have been imagined, he considered inner psychic reality to be the more important.
> – *Dennis Brown & Jonathan Pedder*

The hypnoanalytic practitioner can also explore the importance of the symbolic representation of any conflicts that beset the client's unconscious mind. The client will, of course, have within his/her mind all the necessary resources in order to unearth the meaning of symbolic imagery both in dreams and in fantasy life. The client's self-discovery process can be assisted greatly by the therapist who utilises hypnosis. In using a hypnotic process of imagery analysis with the client, the therapist should, of course, ask him/her to provide a complete picture of his/her thoughts. Producing an edited account for the therapist will lead the client to further self-deception and may prevent an ultimate resolution of his/her problems. The practitioner should also strive to detect any forms of resistance to this process in the interests of the client's recovery and should endeavour to take advantage of resistant ten-

dencies as being fodder for analytical dissection (see Chapter 12 –
"Resistance").

> Patients will frequently bring to the therapist a recurring dream which
> they find to be emotionally disturbing and which therefore has some
> unconscious significance in relationship to their problems.
> – *Edgar Barnett*

Interpreting Dreams and Imagery

The passage below can provide the therapist with an effective tool
for dream exploration and interpretation while the client is in the
trance-state. This passage utilises a fairly direct approach but a
more open-ended or permissive method could also be adopted by
the practitioner whereby the client could construct his/her own
vehicle for dream exploration.

The dream interpreter ...

I want you to imagine a private room – a room that no other person can enter.
That's right – the right image will be created for you. Make it a safe and comfortable environment, that can help you to relax and to find stillness. In your
private room there can be several of your favourite things. But most important of all, perhaps, you will be able to observe a very large flat screen, that is
attached to a videoplayer. You may notice some additional buttons on this
particular model and it could even have an unusual colour.

At this time, perhaps you can place the videotape into the player and press
PLAY. You may, in a few moments, then begin to notice the screen light up and
slowly imagine an image of your dream coming on to the screen. Now you
don't have to do anything, just observe the dream – that's right – and it may
even appear slightly different from the way in which you described it to me
earlier – but that's all right. So just sit and observe the dream now and allow
your mind to continue to just sit and observe. Just nod your head when the
dream has come to a stop. Now press the REWIND button so that the tape can
go back to the beginning.

Now that you've seen the dream and it has been rewound, I would like you
to look carefully and notice that on the front cover of the player there is a button which is marked clearly INTERPRETER, and make sure that you have the
switch on. Now sit back once more and allow yourself just to observe the
underlying message clearly that your inner mind has been wanting to send
you in your dream. What your unconscious mind will do for you here will be
to re-present to you the very thing that it has been trying to send you through

your dreams. Simply press PLAY and this time merely observe the conversion, and when you have finished and fully understood the dream then nod your head so that I can see that you have gained the information you need in order to help your mind.

In the following case-study example, the client was able to utilise dream analysis and interpretation in order to gain an appreciation of the ways in which her anxieties had lain dormant for many years.

Case-study example – perpetual anxiety and worry

The client reported having a recurring dream whereby she saw her mother in the distance in bed with her father. The client's father appeared as if he were dead. The client then walked towards the bed and saw her father close to death. The client then became very anxious and reached over in order to touch her father. At this point the client's dream came to an end.

Some twenty years previously, the client's father had been very ill – he had contracted a virus, that was causing his doctors to be very concerned for his life. It then took some time before the doctors were able to diagnose the virus and to prescribe the appropriate medication. What was damaging, however, to the client, as a teenager, was that her mother had been continually suggesting that her father was going to die. The client's mother had kept worrying about what she would do without him and how she would manage. No matter what was said to the client's mother by relatives and others, she would walk around screaming hysterically and further perpetuating the worrying situation for the client. This situation traumatised the client. The client's mother spent little time, however, with the client in order to calm her mounting fears. As the client was reporting the event, she began to express her feelings towards her father. The client poured out the fact that she loved him and she hoped that, although he was getting older, he would not pass away. Coincidentally, the client's dream had begun two years earlier, when her father had recently been taken ill.

When this client's dream was analysed in hypnosis, she was simply asked by the practitioner to replay her dream in her mind. The client was next invited to rewrite it if she wished. The client then elected herself to change the ending of the dream so that, as she approached the bed, her father opened his eyes and smiled at her. Her father now appeared in her imagination as if he had just experienced the most beautifully refreshing sleep and was now completely energised.

The client never experienced her disturbing dream again and was able to resume normal sleeping patterns thereafter. During this therapeutic process, therefore, the client was able to appreciate the significance of her dream imagery, was able to discharge deep feelings of grief and, thus, she was able to bring about an important resolution to her conflict.

In the client narrative given below, the client had become adept at deciphering her own dreams. This interpretation of the client's dream will provide a rich source of symbolic and archetypal imagery that can be duly appreciated by the practitioner. The client's ability to carry out her own dream analysis on waking also illustrates the way in which her dilemma could be resolved without any external intervention. The client was also able to utilise this skill long after therapeutic intervention had ceased.

Client narrative – the demons and the winners ...

I had a dream in which there was an almighty war going on. There were a vast number of demons who had a lot of power and they were fighting with a small number of good spirits. Even though the good spirits were completely outnumbered, they did not back off from entering into battle.

The demons used a lot of violence and dirty fighting but the good spirits still managed to avoid being hurt or injured. Once the battle was in full swing, I experienced a lot of anxiety on behalf of the good spirits because I felt that they were at a great disadvantage. Finally, perseverance and guile enabled the good spirits to triumph because the demons simply gave up and disappeared.

On waking, I endeavoured to analyse my dream and the meaning came quite quickly. I had doubted the fact that I would ever recover from my bouts of anxiety but this dream illustrated to me that recovery was, in fact, possible but that it would not necessarily happen instantly and not, perhaps, in the way I had hitherto expected. I, therefore, derived great comfort from this apparently disturbing dream.

Client Profiling

The analytical hypnotherapy practitioner may wish to ponder the following points when formulating a profile for the client.

- Does the client appear to attach any importance to his/her dream imagery or other form of symbolism?
- In what ways can the client be encouraged to monitor his/her dream-world or fantasy-life in order to further his/her progress in therapy?
- Can the practitioner detect any evidence of conflict or distress within the client's imaginative imagery?
- In what ways can an appreciation of the client's fantasy-oriented symbolism be of use in the therapeutic context?
- Can the practitioner detect any indicators of the source of the client's distress from his/her accounts of dreams or fantasy?
- Can the therapist recognise any pockets of resistance to the therapeutic process by considering the client's dream imagery?
- Can the therapist detect any manifestations of transference in the client's dream imagery?
- Can the therapist appreciate any countertransference manifestations in his/her own dream-life when undertaking therapy with a given client?
- Can the client be encouraged to appreciate the distinction between manifest and latent imagery in his/her dreams?
- Can the practitioner identify any imbalances in the client's psyche when studying dream imagery or symbolic representational material?
- In what ways does the client depict himself/herself within his/her fantasy life?
- In what ways does the client's persona manifest itself in his/her life?
- Can the client identify his/her unacceptable qualities?
- Has the client managed to accept wholeheartedly both his/her masculine and feminine traits?

- Does the client depict himself/herself as either a hero or a heroine?
- Does the client view his/her parents in any way unrealistically?

Chapter 15

Personality Structure

The greatest pleasure I know is to do a good action by stealth
and have it found out by accident.

– Charles Lamb

Why Study Personality Structure?

The pendulum of the mind oscillates between sense and nonsense,
not between right and wrong.
– Carl Jung

Almost every psychological theorist has put forward a personal
hypothesis or made a contribution to the debate on the structure of
the human personality. We shall take time, therefore, to consider
some of these theories as an integral part of our study of psychological practice. In studying a number of theories, however, the
practitioner can learn to evaluate each but aspire to make no-one
single theory his/her master. The therapist can also learn to appreciate that there is not one single definitive or proven answer to the
structure of the personality but that a knowledge of what has hitherto been documented by writers in this field may be of assistance
to him/her when attempting to understand the client. It will be
important for the therapist to understand, however, that there can
be a temptation to interpret a personality theory too literally. There
will, perhaps understandably, be an inherent danger, therefore, in
being too dogmatic about the meanings behind theories of personality structure, that could lead to an unwarranted degree of rigidity on the part of the therapist. Such a stance will not be helpful to
the client, and so let us consider each and all of these theories as
representative of notional elements rather than as hard facts.

Freudian Personality Theories

In the Freudian scheme, psychological disturbance can be equated with
states of unmanageable severe conflict: the personality is literally torn
apart by its own contradictions. Through defending against inner
conflict, the person treats a distressing internal state as though it were an
external danger: he/she flees from it.
– *David Smith*

Freud formulated his theory of the structure of the personality and
personality types, that explains the ways in which the client's
unconscious mind can work in order to protect him/her from
danger and to ensure his/her survival (see Chapter 1 –
"Psychoanalysis").

Personality Structure

Freud saw the adult personality as having three basic components: the
id, the ego and the super-ego. The id and the super-ego were both
unconscious, but exerting pressure on the ego, which was the part of the
mind in direct contact with reality.
– *Nicky Hayes*

Freud purported that the structure of the human personality was
governed by three potentially conflicting elements. He outlined
the concept of the *id*, that will represent the client's impulsive and
instinctive desires, the *superego*, that will represent his/her moral
and social conscience, and the *ego*, that will act as the mediator and
regulator of the personality. Freud theorised that each of these systems could be in potential conflict in an attempt to control the
opposing aspects of the client's personality. This overall control
can be achieved because the client will have limited energy
resources and so a dominant aspect of the personality can sometimes take the reins. Contemporary psychoanalysis – known as *id
psychology* – also places emphasis on the client's objective to fulfil
his/her basic needs and to cope with intrapsychic conflicts as a
means of developing the structure of the personality (see
Chapter 5 – "Object-Relations Psychology").

The id

The id is the original system of personality; at birth a person is all id.
The id is the primary source of psychic energy and the seat of the
instincts. It lacks organisation, and it is blind, demanding, and insistent.
A cauldron of seething excitement, the id cannot tolerate tension, and it
functions to discharge tension immediately and return to a
homeostatic condition.
– *Gerald Corey*

The id will be that aspect of the human personality that will seek
to fulfil the client's biological needs and will accompany the
child's first stage of development in infancy. The id will govern the
client's pleasurable and instinctual drives, such as sexual desire
and aggression. This aspect of the client's personality will be
blindly insistent and demanding in its attempt to reduce tension
and to avoid pain. Because the infant will be totally consumed
with satisfying his/her own needs to the exclusion of all others,
the id has been associated with what Freud termed the *pleasure
principle*.

The id was the primeval, impulsive part of the personality, demanding
instant gratification of all of its demands. It was unrealistic, selfish and
demanding, working on what Freud described as the **pleasure principle**
– the idea that every impulse should be satisfied, immediately.
– *Nicky Hayes*

The superego

The superego is the judicial branch of personality. It includes a person's
moral code, the main concern being whether action is good or bad, right
or wrong. It represents the ideal, rather than the real, and strives not for
pleasure but for perfection. It represents the traditional values and ideals
of society as they are handed down from parents to children.
– *Gerald Corey*

The superego will be that aspect of the human personality that will
seek to fulfil the client's social and environmental needs by giving
him/her a social and moral conscience. The superego will endeavour to conform to what is expected of the child by its primary carers and what society requires of him/her. The client's superego
will monitor the way in which he/she will be expected to behave
in order to take his/her place in society and to fulfil a specific role.
This element of the client's personality will strive for idealistic perfection and will often take a moralistic stance in order to uphold

traditional values set by others. The superego, however, will reward the client's virtue with pride and self-love but will punish any perceived indiscretions with guilt.

> In its own way, the super-ego is as unrealistic as the id. Where the id is impulsive and over-reacting, for example, reacting with murderous rage rather than anger, the super-ego would demand total commitment to the most rigid demands even at the cost of health and self.
> – *Nicky Hayes*

The ego

> The ego has contact with the external world of reality. It is the "executive" that governs, controls, and regulates the personality. As a "traffic cop," it mediates between the instincts and the surrounding environment. The ego controls consciousness and exercises censorship. Ruled by the *reality principle*, the ego does realistic and logical thinking and formulates plans of action for satisfying needs.
> – *Gerald Corey*

The ego will be that aspect of the human personality that will seek to fulfil the client's psychological needs by getting in touch with what would serve him/her best in reality. The client's ego will, therefore, assume the role of censor. The ego may take an intellectual and rational approach to life's experiences by mediating between the inclinations of the client's instinctive id and the dictates of his/her surroundings as viewed by the superego. It will be the client's ego that will become dominant in order to suppress his/her instincts when defensive strategies take hold (see Chapter 11 – "Defensive Strategies"). If the ego, for example, feels that the client's id desires are unacceptable or his/her superego behaviour is inappropriate, then ego-defence mechanisms may be instituted as its means of curbing such tendencies. The ego will now defend to the death its position using all its defences in order to ensure that unacceptable matter remains out of the client's conscious awareness. Because of the ego's moderating role within the client's personality, Freud spoke of the ego as encompassing the *reality principle*.

The therapist can observe this interaction between the id, the superego and the ego in natural human behaviours and inclinations. The client may, for example, longingly wish to consume many cream cakes to the point of gluttony (an id impulse), may sternly forbid himself/herself from having any such cravings (a superego edict) but, in reality, may relent by having just one or two treats per week (an ego moderation).

> According to Freud, the ego maintained a state of **dynamic equilibrium** between these different pressures – a kind of balancing act, giving in a little to one source and then compensating by giving in a little to the other.
> – *Nicky Hayes*

Personality Classifications

Freud identified three specific character types, that he termed the *oral-schizoidal* personality, the *anal-paranoidal* personality and the *genital-hysteric* personality. The client will normally display character traits from all three classifications, although he/she will usually adhere to one predominating group. Specific psychological problems and difficulties, therefore, will tend to be connected with each group.

The oral-schizoidal personality

The oral-schizoidal personality will exhibit traits that are formed when the child is between birth and about two and a half years old. During this period in the infant's life, the mouth will become the centre of his/her focus of attention, from which pleasure will be derived. The infant will indulge, for example, in eating, sucking, tasting and making sounds. The child may, moreover, discover that smiling will bring rewards in the form of love and the security of touch from his/her primary carers. The infant may also discover that echoing the sounds that the grown-ups make will solicit further attention and reward. If the rewards and gratification are high enough at this oral stage, then the client's life may revolve around pleasing others, doing what has been asked of him/her and doing what he/she believes will be expected of him/her. The client may also learn to expect reward in the form of comfort or praise, become upset when that reward is not freely forthcoming and may have a tendency towards self-blame when he/she has been offended. The oral-schizoidal personality may, therefore, display schizoidal or dual-mindedness traits by being prone to mood swings.

The oral-schizoidal client may be identified by his/her responsiveness, his/her smiling face, his/her generally-agreeable nature and his/her cooperative disposition. The oral-schizoidal client may make a very good candidate for hypnoanalytical therapy because he/she may endeavour to please others and will do his/her very best to go along with whatever the therapist requests. This type of client, however, may also tend to blame himself/herself if the therapy is not completely effective (see Chapter 5 – "Object-Relations Psychology").

The anal-paranoidal personality
The anal-paranoidal personality will display traits that are usually formed between the ages of two and five years. During this period, the child will attempt to control his/her environment and his/her bodily functions – the most important usually being the functioning of his/her bowels and urinary system. If the child's parents reward any attempts at control during this formative period with praise and pleasure, then the client may spend his/her life trying desperately to be in control of situations.

This personality classification may also be subdivided for the purposes of refinement of the character traits associated with the anal-paranoidal type. An *anal-retentive* personality may, for example, have a tendency to weigh things up carefully before he/she makes any response and may tend not to be too concerned about what other people think. An *anal-aggressive* personality may, however, have a tendency to resent authoritative control or any form of perceived confinement. An *anal-expulsive* personality may, on the other hand, have a tendency to irrational outbursts or attention-seeking displays of temper.

The anal-paranoidal personality will usually make a good business associate but a hard-to-deal-with client for any form of hypnotherapeutic treatment because of his/her fear of being controlled and his/her paranoidal distrust of others. The practitioner, therefore, will need to gain the client's trust and may need to find some indirect means of absorbing his/her interest (see Chapter 5 – "Object-Relations Psychology").

The genital-hysteric personality
The genital-hysteric personality will form his/her major character traits from the age of five years onwards, when the majority of influence will come from other children outside the family circle. The child's major interest will usually be invested in his/her being the centre of attention, having fun and receiving instant gratification for any of his/her wishes. The genital-hysteric client, therefore, will often tend to reach adulthood with somewhat juvenile values. The client may also have a low boredom-threshold, may be inclined to be hysterically noisy, can be easily offended and may absolutely hate having to conform in any way. The client may also be histrionic, may tend to be an exhibitionist and may have questionable morals and ethics. The genital-hysteric personality, therefore, may make an extremely good hypnotic subject but will not always respond well to therapy.

Jungian Personality Theories

Fortunately, in her kindness and patience, Nature has never put the fatal question as to the meaning of their lives into the mouths of most people. And where no-one asks, no-one needs to answer.
– *Carl Jung*

Jung expounded his theories of the structure of the human personality by enquiring more deeply into the nature of mankind and the way in which the client functions. He did this by devising a number of theories about psychological types and psychological functioning (see Chapter 2 – "Analytical Psychology"). Jung examined the way in which the client views himself/herself and the world about him/her and the way in which he/she could function in that world. This investigation into human conditions and tendencies has become the basis of Jung's conclusions about personality types and human behaviour. We shall now explore some of Jung's findings in this area.

Psychological Types

> Unfortunately the two types misunderstand one another and tend to see
> only the other's weakness, so that to the extravert the introvert is
> egotistical and dull, while the introvert thinks the extravert is superficial
> and insincere.
> – *Frieda Fordham*

Jung's psychological types embrace the well-known *introvert* characteristics and *extrovert* characteristics, that are governed by the
client's attitude and his/her orientation to the world in which
he/she resides. A healthy, balanced attitude would be an equal
mix of both outgoing and introspective characteristics, but normally the client will have one attitude that will be more highly
developed than the other. Jung's work in this field may well have
been influenced by the work of Ernst Kretschmer (1888–1964), the
German psychiatrist who correlated physical constitution with
personality characteristics.

Each of Jung's psychological types will be subject to different
influences and will be dependent on differing values. It has been
said that each type will undervalue, if not despise, the other in a
competitive atmosphere of survival, whereas, in truth, the two categories will complement each other when these personality types
intermingle. The ebullient extrovert, for instance, may seek a wall-
flower type to temper his/her exuberance or the retiring introvert
may find a partnership with someone who will make all the
speeches and be a good social animal. The client will, of course, be
an amalgamation of both extroverted characteristics and introverted traits but it will be the extent to which he/she veers in one
direction that will be of interest to the therapist. According to Jung,
the tendency towards a predominant attitude will begin quite
early in the child's life and there may often be both types within
the same family. When this happens, the extrovert may tend to
outshine and overshadow the introverted child. Both types, moreover, will tend to misunderstand and undervalue each other in
childhood as well as in adulthood.

It has been claimed that Western societies tend to prefer the extrovert while those in the East prefer the introvert. This may conve-
niently explain the material and technological development of the
West in contrast with the material poverty but greater spiritual

development seen in the East. It is felt by many writers that Freudian psychology is inherently extroverted because it places determinants of character on outside people and events, while Adlerian psychology and Jungian psychology are based on intro-version (see Chapter 3 – "Individual Psychology"). Adler, further-more, tended to emphasise the significance of the client's inner attitude, just as Jungian interests have focused on the client's sub-jective inner world.

The extrovert

> Extraversion is characterised by interest in the external object, responsiveness, and a ready acceptance of external happenings, a desire to influence and be influenced by events, a need to join in and get "with it", the capacity to endure bustle and noise of every kind, and actually find them enjoyable, constant attention to the surrounding world, the cultivation of friends and acquaintances, none too carefully selected, and finally by the great importance attached to the figure one cuts, and hence by a strong tendency to make a show of oneself.
> *– Carl Jung*

The extrovert will, by nature, be habitually interested in people, events and the things that go on around him/her in the world. The extrovert will tend to be inspired by social gatherings that will recharge his/her energy batteries because he/she will be naturally gregarious and outgoing. Social isolation, however, will tend to drain the extroverted client's resources. The extroverted child will frequently develop more rapidly because he/she will be less cau-tious – perhaps showing little or no fear. This child will feel no bar-rier between himself/herself and external objects, the people with whom he/she plays and from whom he/she learns. The extro-verted child, therefore, may be more popular, may be thought to be well balanced and considered brighter by significant others because of his/her early rapid development.

Jung saw the extrovert as having an outward flow of libido, that will manifest as an interest in people and things. This type will readily form relationships, will be motivated by external factors and will be greatly influenced by the environment. The extravert will tend to accept the current norms and attitudes and will tend to favour a conventional outlook on life. The extrovert may come forward and react immediately when the need arises in a given social setting because he/she will be confident that his/her behaviour will be considered to be correct even in unfamiliar surroundings. The extrovert may well seek to impose his/her views on others when disputes arise but may also manifest a lack of self-criticism because he/she may regard reflection as being a morbid preoccupation. The extrovert, in general, will be optimistic but may become superficial and dependent on making a good impression because of a dislike of being alone or isolated from the crowd.

> The extraverted attitude is characterised by an outward flowing of libido, an interest in events, in people and things, a relationship with them, and a dependence on them; when this attitude is habitual to anyone Jung describes him or her as an extraverted type.
> – *Frieda Fordham*

The introvert

> Introversion, on the other hand, being directed not to the object but to the subject, and not being oriented by the object, is not so easy to put into perspective. The introvert is not forthcoming, he is as though in continual retreat before the object. He holds aloof from external happenings, does not join in, has a distinct dislike of society as soon as he finds himself among too many people.
> – *Carl Jung*

The introvert will, by nature, be habitually interested in his/her own inner needs and can appear to be withdrawn and self-reflective. The introvert will require his/her own space and solitude in order to generate energy. The introverted client, therefore, will find that his/her energy will be depleted by too much social interaction. The introverted client, whose immediate response may be to draw back from new experiences, may tend to display a certain negative relationship to events. A seeming lack of confidence, therefore, may be outwardly exhibited by the misunderstood introverted client who may appear unsociable and afraid of looking ridiculous because of being unpolished in the field of social graces. In intimate relationships, however, the introvert may be capable of extreme loyalty and can form sympathetic long-term friendships. The introvert may also have a tendency to be pessimistic, overconscientious and hypercritical, but may often possess unusual knowledge or highly developed talents. The introverted client will possibly withdraw from society when a disagreement arises because he/she will value his/her own judgment as being more important than conventional mores.

In Jungian terms, there may an inward flow of libido within the introvert's psyche, that will concentrate on subjective factors with the predominating influence being on the client's inner necessity. The introverted child, for example, will usually be shy and hesitant and will approach new situations, objects and people with caution and, sometimes, with trepidation. The introvert may, therefore, have few friends but can be thoughtful and often possess a rich imaginative life.

> The introverted attitude, in contrast, is one of withdrawal; the libido flows inward and is concentrated upon subjective factors, and the predominating influence is "inner necessity".
> – *Frieda Fordham*

Psychological Functions

> I distinguish four functions: *thinking, feeling, sensation,* and *intuition*. The essential function of sensation is to establish that something exists, thinking tells us what it means, feeling what its value is, and intuition surmises whence it comes and whither it goes.
> – *Carl Jung*

Jung's four psychological functions relate to the client's ways of perceiving and acquiring information. The client's means of functioning and self-orientation within the world in which he/she resides can often lead him/her to develop habitual reactions. These reactions can then be categorised according to whether the client will be more prone to sensation, to intuition, to thought or to feeling. Jung emphasised that any function can lead to an emotive response but that an emotive reaction will not, in itself, be a function. The way in which the client functions will, of course, be modified largely by his/her attitudes to life in terms of his/her character type. It can be said that the client's psychological functions, therefore, may be heavily overridden by his/her psychological classification in that his/her attitudes will modify the way in which he/she processes and handles information. The client will, in most cases, consciously exhibit one primary function but there may, additionally, be a secondary unconscious characteristic lurking. To an extent, of course, the client will consist of a combination of each of the psychological functions but in differing proportions. The client will have often developed one function to such a high degree that the others will have been neglected. The client's psychological health, in this case, will depend on developing and resuscitating his/her neglected functions. The average client will usually employ one modified function while the more psychologically-sophisticated client may utilise two and the highly-differentiated personality may employ three. The inclusion of the fourth function will then belong to the individuation process and the balancing of the opposing trends in the client's nature.

Jung classified the sensing and intuitive functions as the two opposing irrational functions and the thinking and feeling functions as the two opposing rational functions. The irrational sensitive and intuitive functions will relate to the client's perception of life's experiences. These perceptive functions are likely to lead the client to a spontaneous and flexible lifestyle because he/she will have a tendency to be open to life's experiences and to seek to comprehend the meaning of life. The rational thinking and feeling functions, conversely, will relate to the way in which the client makes value-judgments and tackles decision-making based on what he/she has perceived. Here the client will strive to regulate and to control his/her environment. In this category, consequently, the practitioner can usually observe order and method with a degree of inflexibility in the client.

> There are four functions, he considers, which we use to orientate ourselves in the world (and also to our own inner world): sensation, which is perception through our senses; thinking, which gives meaning and understanding; feeling, which weighs and values; and intuition, which tells us of future possibilities and gives us information of the atmosphere which surrounds all experience.
> – *Frieda Fordham*

The sensitive type

> Sensing is a way of perceiving through the senses of the eyes, ears, nose,
> touch and taste. These inform an individual of what is actually
> happening out there and keep one in touch with the realities of a
> situation. Sensing types tend to accept and work with what is given in
> the here-and-now, and have a realistic and practical approach to life.
> They are adept at working with facts.
> *– Ann Casement*

The sensitive client will be preoccupied with the mechanism of his/her senses. The client will relate strongly to what his/her senses can perceive and he/she will usually have a good grasp on reality. The sensitive client will also prefer to take in information consciously via the five senses and to rely on his/her conscious perceptions. The *sensitive extrovert* will favour sensory objects, as this will be his/her way of stimulating his/her senses. This client will rely on sensations provided by external objects, that will become all-important in his/her world. This type may, of course, become a sybarite or a restless pleasure-seeker who will always be looking for new thrills. The *sensitive introvert*, on the other hand, will enjoy sensory experiences, as this will be his/her way of deriving satisfaction. This client can be overcome and preoccupied by images from the collective unconscious and will frequently be difficult to understand. Many musicians and artists, therefore, may fall into this category.

The intuitive type

> Intuiting is the other way of perceiving and is directed to the meanings
> and possibilities that go beyond information given through the senses.
> Intuition takes in the whole picture and tries to grasp the essential
> patterns at work in any situation. Intuitives value imagination and
> inspiration and are expert at seeing new possibilities.
> *– Ann Casement*

The intuitive client will rely on his/her own resources and will perceive incoming information indirectly and unconsciously. This client will add inner knowledge and self-wisdom to what he/she already perceives directly. The *intuitive extrovert* will be likely to be impulsive and unconventional. This client will intensely dislike anything safe or familiar. This client will not respect custom or other people's feelings and convictions. This type, thus, will often appear to be a ruthless adventurer because he/she may tend to sow but never to reap and may squander his/her energy chasing possibilities and never seeing them through to the end. This stance will frequently carry through into the client's personal relationships. The *intuitive introvert* may, alternatively, become engrossed in his/her spiritual life, in mysticism and in the world of dreams. This client may be prone to see visions and to have prophetic revelations. This client may, in fact, often border on insanity unless he/she can find a way of relating his/her experiences to the external world. This can often be achieved when the client becomes involved in a religious sect or a spiritual community, whereby his/her vision will have some value. The intuitive client will often be able to content himself/herself solely with perception unless he/she is artistic, in which case he/she may be concerned with shaping his/her unique perceptive abilities.

The thinking type

Thinking predicts the logical consequences of any particular choice or action. Decisions are made objectively on the basis of cause and effect and of analysing and weighing the evidence inherent in any situation. Individuals with a preference for thinking seek an objective standard of truth and are good at analysing what is wrong with something.
– *Ann Casement*

The thinking client will be primarily concerned with facts and ideas. The thinker will be one who uses thought in decision-making and problem-solving. This client will usually prefer to apply objective and concrete thinking to the resolution of problems and may not give undue weight either to his/her own feelings or to the subjective opinions of others. This client may, therefore, work according to rules, procedures and moral values. The *thinking extrovert* will deal in logical facts, that can be calculated in the light of experience. Where creative ideas are lacking, however, the client will often compensate by producing masses of additional information, but may get bogged down in the sheer volume of data. By neglecting his/her feeling side, this logical and rational client will often develop an attitude whereby the end will be believed to justify the means. The *thinking introvert* will, on the other hand, be more likely to be consumed with abstract ideas and, thus, may appear absent-minded. The absent-minded professor, for example, may be interested in facts only as a means of providing evidence that will fit a theory rather than be concerned with the facts themselves.

The feeling type

> Feeling, on the other hand, considers what is important without requiring it to be logical. Values to do with the human domain are at the basis of this way of functioning and the emphasis is upon how much one cares about any situation. Individuals with a preference for feeling like dealing with people and tend to respond in a sympathetic, appreciative and tactful way to others. Feeling as used in Jung's typology is to be differentiated from actual feelings or emotions and is, instead, to do with a capacity for making judgements or decisions based on humane values.
> – *Ann Casement*

The feeling client will be driven by hunches and gut-feeling reactions. This client will also give adequate consideration to his/her own opinions and those of others when making decisions. The *feeling extrovert* may be discerning in rendering value-judgments. This client will fit into the world well, will choose the right friends and the right partner and will accept current values and norms at face value. This client will generally be a good host and a peacemaker – being sympathetic, helpful and charming. This client, however, can often be superficial and insincere and can give an impression of pose and unreliability. The *feeling introvert*, on the hand, will be more likely to provide judgment based on emotive reactions. This client will often give the impression of being cold and aloof when, in reality, the greater the intensity of feeling, the greater may be his/her outward lack of expression. The client will often be incapable of displaying affection but may sometimes show incredible powers of self-sacrifice. This client, however, will frequently be inflexible and may not be able to cope with a need to play a societal role.

Myers-Briggs Personality Theories

The mother-and-daughter team of Katherine Cook Briggs (1875–1968) and Isabel Briggs Myers (1897–1980) have been instrumental in developing Jung's theories by devising the enormously popular Myers-Briggs Type Indicator (or MBTI). This personality profile can be used as a method of assessing the different psychological types that were originally identified by Jung. The MBTI extends Jung's groundwork by attempting to understand the ways in which the client will foster self-awareness and will increase his/her appreciation of others. The MBTI model will consider a number of the client's personal inclinations and tendencies – known as *dimensions* – which will depict the way in which he/she will direct his/her energies, process information, make decisions and organise his/her life. Classifications made according to the MBTI should, therefore, be considered to be indications of the client's potential temperament rather than hard-and-fast predictions about his/her personality. Let us now consider the main personality types within this model. The practitioner should, of course, view the client in terms of a combination of types within each dimension so that a four-function personality type can unfold when any assessment is being made.

The Introverted and Extroverted Dimensions

Initially, the client can be considered in terms of the way in which he/she will direct his/her energies. The client may be classified as being either on the *introverted dimension* or on the *extroverted dimension* in terms of his/her interests, ideas and attitudes. The client on the introverted dimension will primarily be interested in his/her inner world and his/her inner thoughts. This client will be quiet and insular, will deliberate before taking action and will have a high capacity for concentration. The client on the extroverted dimension will primarily be interested in his/her outer world and in spoken thoughts. This client will be likely to be sociable, outgoing, expressive, expansive and spontaneous.

The Sensitive and Intuitive Dimensions

Next, the client can be considered in terms of the way in which he/she will process information. The client may be classified as being either on the *sensitive dimension* or on the *intuitive dimension* in terms of information processing. The client on the sensitive dimension will principally deal with known facts and familiar elements recorded by his/her senses. This client will process information on the basis of facts, past experience, practical considerations and security issues. The client on the intuitive dimension will be more interested in possibilities and potential that have been detected unconsciously. This client will be inspired by novelty, future aspirations, changing circumstances and idealism and will take a generalised broad-brush view of life.

The Thinking and Feeling Dimensions

The client can also be considered in terms of the way in which he/she will make decisions. The client may be classified as being either on the *thinking dimension* or on the *feeling dimension* with regard to decision-making and his/her evaluation of first-hand experience. The client on the thinking dimension will be motivated by logical consequences and hardened reasoning when he/she makes decisions. This client will be attracted by objective considerations, detailed analysis and objective criticism, and, as an onlooker, will take a long-term view when making choices. The client on the feeling dimension will take a personal and subjective approach to decision-making. This client will be likely to make decisions instantaneously on the basis of personal values and will be sympathetic to the needs of others rather than act in a politically-correct manner.

The Judging and Perceptive Dimensions

Lastly, the client can be considered in terms of the way in which he/she will organise his/her life and existence. The client may be classified as being either on the *judging dimension* or on the *perceptive dimension* with regard to decision-making and his/her evaluation of personal experience. The client on the judging dimension will want life to be structured and well organised. This client will normally wish to know where he/she stands, will desire to undertake sound planning and seek to gain full control of events and situations. The client on the perceptive dimension will usually be flexible and adaptable. This client will usually like to make discoveries, to explore the world about him/her, to be spontaneous, to leave things unplanned and often to alter his/her mind for no apparent reason at the eleventh hour.

Transactional Analysis Personality Theories

> "Transactional analysis is a theory of personality and a systematic
> psychotherapy for personal growth and personal change." That's the
> definition of TA suggested by the International Transactional Analysis
> Association. In fact, TA today is all this and much more. Among
> psychological approaches, transactional analysis is outstanding in the
> depth of its theory and the wide variety of its applications.
> *– Ian Stewart & Vann Joines*

Transactional analysis (or TA) was originally devised by Eric
Berne (1910–1970) as a means of understanding the client in terms
of human interaction and social communication. The client can
learn to analyse his/her social transactions with others in terms of
his/her psychological ego-states and the various psychological
programmes that may be influencing such interaction. TA will be
concerned with allowing the client to recognise his/her behavioural traits and then to modify his/her tendencies accordingly.
Many TA concepts are reminiscent of psychodynamic theories but
TA differs from psychodynamic disciplines in that it is assumed
that the client's behaviour can be conscious and deliberate and
that free will and intentionality will prevail. The client, therefore,
can be viewed as having self-determination rather than being the
victim of his/her unconscious processes, that are beyond his/her
reach.

TA consists of an ego-state theory of personality, that can help the
client to understand the ways in which his/her mind functions
and can provide a theory of communication that will enable
him/her to analyse interactive systems (see Chapter 5 – "Object-
Relations Psychology"). The philosophy of TA also provides a theory of development whereby the client is believed to replay an
earlier life script, that he/she has adopted as a coping-strategy in
his/her current life. The client, therefore, can learn to recognise
ways in which negative programming from childhood has
affected his/her social interaction. TA, thus, can provide a harmonious blend of psychodynamic principles with cognitive considerations in order to permit the client to control his/her own life in an
effective way. The principles of TA, hence, can provide the client
with practical tools for life improvement and productive social
interaction.

Transactional analysis, often referred to as TA, is a therapy which does not restrict itself to those individuals considered to be "neurotic" or "in need of help". Instead, it maintains that it has something to offer everyone, as a way of understanding their everyday interactions better.
– *Nicky Hayes*

The Ego-State Model

In his contact with patients Berne observed three different *categories* among the multitude of ego states which constitute the personality. One category is concerned with here-and-now reality (the Adult), one with the person's past experiences (the Child) and one with the introjects or internalisation of significant authority figures (the Parent).
– *Petrüska Clarkson, Maria Gilbert & Keith Tudor*

The ego-state model (or *P-A-C model*) forms the basis of the TA personality theory. The theory purports that the client will have three structural ego-states of the *Parent*, the *Adult* and the *Child*, that will influence his/her personal behaviours and social interactions. These ego-states are, of course, similar in concept to the Freudian counterparts of the superego, the ego and the id, respectively. An ego-state may be regarded as a related set of the client's behaviours, thoughts, emotive responses and physical sensations. It will be the role of the practitioner to help the client to bring to light the unconscious aspects of the Parent and the Child ego-states in order to gain self-understanding. The process of analysing the client's personality in terms of his/her ego-states and their manifestations can be used metaphorically in order to analyse the structure and function of his/her personality. The client can be taught to recognise inappropriate behavioural reactions and the resultant ego-state manifested in such actions by noting the language he/she uses, his/her tone of voice, gestures, mannerisms, posture and facial expressions. The client can, thus, discover ways in which he/she can distinguish between the executive power of an ego-state and his/her real self by detecting any incongruity that can act against his/her true inclinations.

The Adult ego-state

> And when I am behaving, thinking and feeling in ways which are a direct here-and-now response to events round about me, using all the abilities I have as a grown-up, I am said to be in my Adult ego-state.
> – *Ian Stewart & Vann Joines*

The Adult ego-state will use the "I will" and the "I can" philosophy. The client's Adult ego-state will depict the competent and effective problem-solving aspects of his/her personality. The Adult state – like the Freudian ego – can be said to react maturely to current circumstances and to tap into adult resources. In this state, the client will have the ability to evaluate present experiences rationally with the emphasis on conscious freedom of choice.

The Parent ego-state

> When I am behaving, thinking and feeling in ways I copied from parents or parent-figures, I am said to be in my Parent ego-state.
> – *Ian Stewart & Vann Joines*

The Parent ego-state will use the "I ought to" philosophy. The client's Parent ego-state will uphold sets of rules for fitting into society. Often such rules will have been gleaned from parental figures and from authority figures who have exerted an influence on the client in childhood. The doctrines that the child has derived from his/her parents were, of course, the values that were handed down from their parents respectively. In the Parent state, therefore, the client may be introjecting elements of the Parent, the Adult and/or the Child ego-states exhibited by his/her own parents (see Chapter 11 – "Defensive Strategies"). In the therapeutic context, this hand-me-down analysis will help to enlighten the client about his/her behavioural characteristics. The client's Parent state will principally use unconscious reasoning by replaying and re-enacting past experiences. The Parent state can, of course, provide wise doctrines and sound advice to the client as well as rendering overbearing and unnecessarily cumbersome rules for his/her social conduct. The Parent state – like the Freudian superego – will be primarily concerned with doing the right thing in order to maintain the continued protection of the client and to ensure his/her social survival. The Parent state will acquire a behavioural model from the client's primary carers, whom he/she sought to emulate and to please in childhood. From the Parent state, therefore, the personality can exhibit self-rejection and guilt.

The client's Parent ego-state may be further subdivided into the *Controlling Parent* ego-state, that will be authoritarian, critical and dictatorial, and the *Nurturing Parent* ego-state, that will be caring and protective.

The Child ego-state

> When I am behaving, thinking and feeling as I did when I was a child, I am said to be in my Child ego-state.
> *– Ian Stewart & Vann Joines*

The Child ego-state will use the "I want to" philosophy. The client's Child ego-state will be characterised by spontaneity, creativity and intuition. This state will essentially employ unconscious emotive reactions such as those experienced in childhood and can, consequently, be playful and mischievous. The Child state – like the Freudian id – will be concerned fundamentally with expressing emotive reactions in order to satisfy the client's immediate needs. From the Child state, therefore, the client can exhibit hurt, fear and anger.

The Child ego-state can be further subdivided into the *Adapted Child* ego-state, that will bottle up emotive expression in order to be attention-seeking or rebellious towards parental figures, and the *Free Child* ego-state, that can naturally satisfy any pressing needs.

Within the Child state, moreover, the client can also exhibit elements of the Parent, the Child and the Adult ego-states. When the Child, for example, blindly imbues his/her parents with superhuman qualities, he/she will be producing a *Magical Parent* ego-state. When the Child employs immature strategies for problem-solving, the client will be acting in a childishly adult frame of mind known as the *Little Professor* ego-state. When the Child reacts in attention-seeking ways in order to satisfy immediate needs, the client can be described as being in a *Somatic Child* ego-state because he/she will merely be reacting to the dictates of physical sensations.

> *Functional Analysis* is the sub-division of Transactional Analysis which
> relates primarily to the behavioural and social components of ego state
> diagnosis. In this model, which is most useful for communication
> training and behavioural change, *behaviours* are classified under the
> following headings: Controlling Parent, Nurturing Parent, Adult,
> Free Child and Adapted Child.
> – *Petrüska Clarkson, Maria Gilbert & Keith Tudor*

Dysfunctional Ego-States

> At times, I may mistake part of the content of my Child or Parent
> ego-state for Adult content. When this happens, my Adult is said
> to be contaminated.
> – *Ian Stewart & Vann Joines*

The client's ego-states may merge and this can result in either the
contamination or the *exclusion* of an ego-state within the client's
personality, that will culminate in the malfunctioning of certain
ego-states. Contamination and exclusion can be total or partial
according to the psychological progress of the client. The more
contamination and exclusion the client exhibits, the further he/she
will be from reality and the more in need he/she may be of therapeutic intervention.

> All people are structurally alike in that they all have a Parent, an Adult,
> and a Child. They differ in two ways: in the content of Parent, Adult and
> Child, which is unique to each person, being recordings of those
> experiences unique to each; and in the working arrangement, or the
> functioning of Parent, Adult and Child.
> – *Thomas Harris*

Ego-state contamination

> The concept of *contamination* describes the way in which effective Adult
> functioning is impeded by limiting beliefs, traumatic experiences and
> learned emotional and psychological responses.
> – *Petrüska Clarkson, Maria Gilbert & Keith Tudor*

A contaminated ego-state may become corrupted or polluted by
another ego-state. Ego-state contamination will occur, for example, when the client's Adult ego-state has become clouded by the
opinions, beliefs, values and modus operandi of either his/her
Parent state or his/her Child state. In this case, either the Parent

state or the Child state will have merged with and will have contaminated the Adult state.

Contamination of an ego-state can occur if the client exhibits *prejudice* or *delusion*. Prejudice will occur when the client's Adult state has been contaminated by the unreal opinions of the Parent state. With prejudice, in this case, the client will have inappropriately externalised Parent data to the extent that this data will have polluted mature thinking. Delusion will occur when the client's Adult state has been contaminated by the unreal experiences of the Child state. With delusion, in this instance, the client will have inappropriately externalised Child data and, thus, lost touch with reality.

Ego-state exclusion

> Sometimes, Berne suggested, a person will shut out one or more of her
> ego-states. He called this exclusion.
> – *Ian Stewart & Vann Joines*

An excluded ego-state will become cut off by or cordoned off from another ego-state. Ego-state exclusion will occur, for example, when one of the client's ego-states separates from another state. Exclusion will frequently mean that the client denies or fails to acknowledge the elements inherent in a given state, whether the content be wise or foolish. Exclusion will be a form of denial of parts of the client's personality – similar to that of ego-splitting well documented in ego-state therapy (see Chapter 4 – "Ego-State Therapy").

The client can exclude any of his/her ego-states. When the Adult state has been excluded, the client will have no means of reality-testing. The client, therefore, will listen either to the internal Parent doctrine, that will err on the side of caution, or to the internal Child dialogue, that will be engaged solely in satisfying childish needs. When the Parent state has been excluded, the client will live according to his/her own rules of conduct and will disregard the valuable teachings of society, that would normally help him/her to get through life. When the Child state has been excluded, the client will deny the spontaneous, imaginative and sensitive characteristics of his/her nature.

> Exclusion, on the other hand, occurs in situations where psychic energy becomes exclusively cathectic in a constant Parent, a constant Adult, or a constant Child. Thus one ego-state is strongly cathectic while the other two are decommissioned.
> – *Richard Nelson-Jones*

Transactional Classifications

> Berne categorised transactions into three types: complementary (predictable), crossed (unpredictable), and ulterior (with hidden or covert agenda). These divisions facilitate the easy analysis of functional and dysfunctional communication between people, so enabling people to identify those transactions that further the script and to practice new options.
> – *Petrüska Clarkson, Maria Gilbert & Keith Tudor*

Due note can be taken by the practitioner of the ways in which the client will respond to others and what communicative transactions can be established during social interaction. The aim of utilising TA principles in the therapeutic context will be to facilitate the client's means of communicating with the therapist. Ideally, communication should be free-flowing and productive and should be steered on to an Adult-to-Adult footing.

The complementary transaction

> A complementary transaction is one in which the transaction vectors are parallel and the ego-state addressed is the one which responds.
> – *Ian Stewart & Vann Joines*

A complementary transaction (or *parallel transaction*) will occur when both parties initiate and respond to each other in a complementary ego-state, whereby communication can be plentiful and continuous. An Adult-to-Adult communication, for example, would mean that both parties engage in the interaction from a rational standpoint. Both communicators in the Adult state would acknowledge the other person's viewpoint but would still be able to state a personal opinion openly. Such communication will, hence, be productive and harmonious.

A complementary transaction will, in addition, occur when both parties enter a given state either consciously or unconsciously in order to maintain the communication. A complementary transaction may occur, for example, between Parent and Parent when both parties are gossiping or setting the world to rights or, similarly, between Child and Child when both communicators elect to be playful and mischievous. A Parent-to-Child complementary communication, moreover, might result when, for example, the office manager became patronising (Parent state) to a member of his/her staff and the staff member responded by being overly apologetic (Child state). Alternatively, a woman might act as a Nurturing Parent towards her partner, who would respond as a Free Child by accepting and enjoying the experience.

The client may, however, detect that he/she tends to respond in a Child-to-Parent state to authority figures or to superiors who address him/her in a Parent state. Here the transaction will be complementary despite the fact that it does not really benefit either party. The client, of course, could be encouraged to modify his/her transactions by altering his/her Child responses and so sever the unwanted relationship that may have been created. When the client can recognise that he/she is responding as he/she would have done to a parent, this factor can serve to break the restrictive psychological bonds in such a transaction (see Chapter 12, Volume 2 – "Dysfunctional Relationships"). For social communication to be successful and productive, complementary transactions will need to take place. This will usually mean that a shift from one state to another by one party will need to be followed correspondingly by the other party in order to maintain the complementary nature of the communication. The aim in therapy, therefore, should be to strive for complementary transactions between client and therapist – ideally when both parties are in the Adult state.

> So long as transactions remain complementary, communication can
> continue indefinitely.
> – *Ian Stewart & Vann Joines*

The crossed transaction

> Formally, a crossed transaction is one in which the transactional vectors
> are not parallel, or in which the ego-state addressed is not the one which
> responds.
> – *Ian Stewart & Vann Joines*

A crossed transaction (or *noncomplementary transaction*) will occur when one party, adopting a given ego-state, will address another party, who will respond steadfastly in an opposing state and, in consequence, the communication will break down. If the client who may be in an Adult state, for example, initiates communication but the respondent continually replies in a Child state or in a Parent state, then communication will, inevitably, be curtailed. If the patronising office manager were to address the member of his/her staff in a Parent state but the employee then replied in an Adult state, a crossed transaction would have resulted. If the woman in her Nurturing Parent role addresses her partner, who replies in an Adult state or in a Parent state by deflecting her overtures, then that communication will be diminished because her partner did not uphold the Child state in order to continue the transaction.

The therapist should, of course, almost invariably adopt the Adult state when addressing the client. In the therapeutic context, therefore, the client should be encouraged to shift his/her Child reactions or Parent responses in order to ensure that any crossed transaction metamorphoses harmoniously into a beneficial complementary transaction with the therapist. The client who habitually responds as a Child when addressing the therapist – whom he/she may view as an authority figure – could be encouraged to shift the emphasis to his/her Adult state. If the client displays a tendency to respond to the therapist as if he/she were a parental figure, then the practitioner could, perhaps, subtly intervene in order to effect a shift to a more mature form of productive communication by exploring these self-denigrating tendencies. The client who tends to adopt the superior Parent response, furthermore, when addressing the practitioner could, similarly, be gently invited to alter his/her responses in order for the Adult-to-Adult communication to be established and to permit the relationship to be placed on a mature footing.

When a transaction is crossed, a break in communication results and one
or both individuals will need to shift ego-states in order for
communication to be re-established.
– *Ian Stewart & Vann Joines*

The ulterior-motive transaction

The client can also learn to recognise ulterior motives in transactions, whether they be complementary or crossed transactions.
Such recognition will help the client either to modify his/her own
behaviour or to direct his/her attention towards educating the
other party when unfruitful communication ensues. A transaction
with an underlying ulterior motive will consist of an overt or
social quality as well as a covert or psychological undertone. This
will mean that a communication may contain an overt message on
an Adult-to-Adult level while, simultaneously, containing a
Parent-to-Child or a Child-to-Parent psychological message. A
simply enquiry about the state of someone's health may, at face
value, be a message of caring concern but the question may also
carry an undercurrent of facetiousness. Perhaps the questioner
will regard the respondent as either a hypochondriac or a nuisance
for being unwell.

The stroking transaction

Strokes are positive units of human recognition, like telling someone that
they have done something well, or that you like them.
– *Nicky Hayes*

A stroke will be a unit of recognition and an acknowledgment of
the value of another person. A stroke may be a social greeting, a
compliment or a throwaway remark, but its function will be to
give value to the other person even though the communication
may not be absolutely vital to transacting any important business.
A stroke may be a verbal remark or a response or it may simply be
a wave of the hand or a nod of the head that acknowledges the
other party in the transaction. Transactional analysts believe that
most people will be stimulus-hungry for strokes because people
are generally recognition-hungry. A seemingly futile remark about
the weather, therefore, can make a person's day.

A stroke may be either positive, when the experience becomes pleasurable, or negative, when the recipient experiences distress. A *positive stroke* may be a friendly greeting. A *negative stroke* – such as a frown, a scowl or a cutting remark – can, of course, have unpleasant consequences for the recipient. Sometimes, of course, the client may feel that receiving a negative stroke will be better than nothing because of man's inherent desire to be acknowledged. Too many negative strokes delivered in childhood can, of course, make the client hungry for negative strokes and this may mean that he/she will discount positive strokes when any are, in fact, proffered. The client, for example, may habitually refuse to accept positive personal compliments or sound encouragement from others.

> Berne stressed the importance of the human infant's capacity to love and his need for love and recognition as basic to human psychological development. His concept of *stroking* grew from his appreciation of the enormous power which the provision or withdrawal of recognition can have on human behaviour, and particularly on infants and children.
> – *Petrüska Clarkson, Maria Gilbert & Keith Tudor*

Time-structuring

Time-structuring is an important element of TA practice, and considers the ways in which the client will spend time when in the company of others. A time structure will be the mode of interaction that will be adopted when people get together and group dynamics are initiated. A knowledge of such group dynamics will be useful to the analytical practitioner who may, perhaps, be interested in undertaking forms of group therapy.

Withdrawal

> Withdrawal, although it is not a transaction with another person, can take place, nonetheless, in a social setting. A man, having lunch with a group of boring associates more concerned with their own stroking than his, may withdraw into the fantasy of the night before, when the stroking was good. His body is still at the lunch table but "he" isn't.
> – *Thomas Harris*

Withdrawal will occur when the client wishes to distance himself/herself psychologically from the activities of the group. The client may contribute his/her physical presence but may not partake in group activities or may not become part of the group because his/her mind may be in the realms of fantasy or daydream.

> In withdrawal, people remain wrapped up in their own thoughts.
> – *Richard Nelson-Jones*

Rituals

> A ritual is a socially programmed use of time where everybody agrees to do the same thing. It is safe, there is no commitment to or involvement with another person, the outcome is predictable, and it can be pleasant in so far as you are "in step" or doing the right thing. There are worship rituals, greeting rituals, cocktail party rituals, bedroom rituals.
> – *Thomas Harris*

A ritual will be a familiar and acknowledged social interaction that will be preordained by society's rules. Usually societal and cultural conduct will have been learned from childhood and from the culture in which the client was reared. The ritual, thereby, will adhere to social convention, and so will be accepted by other members of the group and will, thus, will be performed with a degree of automaticity. The client may, for example, have been schooled in the ways of conducting himself/herself in the social setting and on a variety of social occasions.

> Rituals are stylised signs of mutual recognition dictated by tradition and social custom.
> – *Richard Nelson-Jones*

Pastimes

> People who cannot engage in pastimes at will are not socially facile. Pastimes can be thought of as being a type of social probing where one seeks information about new acquaintances in an unthreatening, noncommittal way.
> – *Thomas Harris*

A pastime will be a means for the client to engage in communication with others but with no strict purpose. A pastime will simply be a way for the client to pass time without putting anything into action. Idle chat, for instance, about current events may occupy the client's time at a party. A pastime has something of a conventional formula, as does a ritual, but the outcome of the interaction will not be so predictable. Light conversation or a meaningless group discussion can be an ideal way to pass time and, simultaneously, to cover up any embarrassing silences when the client interacts in a group setting. The main advantage of a pastime will be that the client will not need to subscribe to any emotive involvement with the members of the group and sometimes, of course, a pastime can be his/her means of evaluating the possibility of forming a friendship.

> Pastimes are semi-ritualistic, topical conversations which last longer than rituals but are still mainly socially programmed.
> – *Richard Nelson-Jones*

Activities

> An activity, according to Berne, is a "common, convenient, comfortable and utilitarian method of structuring time by a project designed to deal with the material of external reality". Common activities are keeping business appointments, doing the dishes, building a house, writing a book, shovelling snow, and studying for exams. These activities, in that they are productive or creative, may be highly satisfying in and of themselves, or they may lead to satisfactions in the future in the nature of stroking for a job well done.
> – *Thomas Harris*

An activity will direct the energies and attention of group members towards achieving a concrete goal or working towards a material outcome. When a group engages in an activity, each member of that group will be psychologically exposed by being expected to take a part. If each member of the group exhibits the Adult state, of course, something tangible can usually be achieved from the group activity. If, on the other hand, certain members of the group display Parent or Child attitudes, then these stances will be likely to impede the progress of the group or limit the outcome of the activity.

> Activities, more commonly called work, are not just concerned with dealing with the material means of survival. They also have a social significance in that they offer a framework for various kinds of recognition and satisfactions.
> – *Richard Nelson-Jones*

Games

> Most games cause trouble. They are the relationship wreckers and the
> misery producers, and in understanding them lies the answer to "why
> does this always happen to me?"
> – *Thomas Harris*

A game will be a series of complementary transactions with an
ulterior motive and a predictable outcome – known as a *payoff*. A
game will always be played on two levels with the protagonists
acting in stereotypical ways in order to achieve a payoff, that can
then generate discontent. The client may, for instance, complain
that no-one comes to his/her aid and, yet, he/she will still dismiss
all offers of help in whatever form. Once this situation has been
engineered, the client can then enthusiastically declare that he/she
is beyond help and so has a right to feel miserable. A game will,
thus, be a kind of heads-I-win-tails-you-lose scenario for the client.

Usually a game will be played by involving two or more people,
who will each be playing a set game. A person offering assistance
to a distressed individual, for instance, would unconsciously
realise that the complainer did not actually want to be helped. The
helper would, consequently, end up with the payoff of a feeling of
failure or a feeling of worthlessness about which he/she could
then complain himself/herself and so draw attention to him-
self/herself. In the therapeutic environment, of course, the therapist will need to be highly attuned to any unhelpful games that the
client might be attempting to play. If such game-playing cannot be
averted successfully, the therapist might find that the client will
not wish to continue in therapy because his/her game will not be
supported.

> A psychological game is a set of covert or ulterior as well as overt
> transactions which lead to a predictable outcome or payoff. Frequently
> these payoffs involve negative feelings or "rackets" such as anger and
> depression.
> – *Richard Nelson-Jones*

Intimacy

> The central dynamic of philosophy has been the impulse to connect. The
> hope has always been there, but it has not overcome the intrinsic fear of
> being close, of losing oneself in another, of partaking in the last of our
> structuring options, intimacy.
> – *Thomas Harris*

An intimate relationship will be the ultimate form of unity that the client can enter into with another individual. Intimacy will be a productive rather than a defensive form of time-structuring in that a fruitful union can hinge on the client's self-acceptance. When the client accepts himself/herself, he/she will then be able to entertain love and intimacy from another. Intimacy will depict a mutual sharing and an open spontaneity of expression, free of any social programming or destructive game-playing.

> Intimacy represents individual and instinctual programming in which
> social programming and ulterior motivations are largely, if not totally,
> suspended.
> – *Richard Nelson-Jones*

Life Scripts

> Like all stories, your life-story has a beginning, a middle and an end. It
> has its heroes, heroines, villains, stooges and walk-on characters. It has
> its main theme and its sub-plots. It may be comic or tragic, enthralling or
> boring, inspiring or inglorious.
> – *Ian Stewart & Vann Joines*

A life script will be an unconscious story that the client will write for himself/herself throughout his/her life. The client's plot will be formulated in early infancy but the theme and the details will be developed and polished up throughout his/her childhood. A life script will be the client's coping mechanism for surviving childhood and will be based on his/her emotive responses and reality-testing strategies. Once written, the life script will be consigned to the client's unconscious oblivion but will be acted out by him/her with real-life characters and situations. In conscious awareness, the life script will represent the client's regular patterns of action and thought, that can be potentially self-destructive. It will be as if the client wears the uncomplimentary labels given to him/her in childhood, believes their content and then lives his/her life accordingly. The child may have believed his/her parents when they said or intimated that he/she was worthless, idle or in any way abnormal. The client can, for example, become a winner or a loser according to his/her life script. The client, therefore, can activate his/her life script if he/she feels under stress and needs to resort to childish coping strategies. The client will also be likely to trigger a life script when the present resembles the past.

> A *script* is formed out of the child's response to the environment, particularly to her or his interaction with her or his parents and/or significant others. The combination of inherited limitations and/or predispositions interact with trauma (e.g. shock) or cumulative conditioning events (e.g. frequent criticisms) so that the infant makes survival conclusions (pre-verbal and physiological) or script decisions (e.g. never to depend on others again).
> – *Petrüska Clarkson, Maria Gilbert & Keith Tudor*

Life Positions

> Berne had a positive view of human nature, which is stated in the transactional-analytic position of "I am OK; you are OK".
> – *Richard Nelson-Jones*

Life positions centre on the theory that the client may feel content with himself/herself (or *OK*) or uneasy and insecure (or *Not OK*). Negative notions will have originated from the client's childhood, when he/she felt inferior in every way to his/her parents and significant others. The adoption of this negative feeling about himself/herself would have been the unfortunate child's only way of making sense of the world. The child would have, therefore, concluded that his/her parents were *OK* but that he/she was *Not OK*. From this standpoint, the client will bring a number of life positions into adulthood. These negative life positions are said to have been adopted by the client as a direct result of circumstances perceived in childhood. Such conditioning will then dictate the client's subsequent actions and impinge upon his/her relationships with others (see Chapter 12, Volume 2 – "Dysfunctional Relationships").

The client, in therapy, should move from negative life positions to a positive place. Often the client will proceed from the *I'm not OK/You're not OK* position, through to the *I'm OK/You're not OK* position, to the *I'm not OK/You're OK* position before reaching the healthy position of *I'm OK/You're OK*. These life positions are, of course, similar to the paranoid-schizoid position and the depressive position of object-relations theory (see Chapter 5 – "Object-Relations Psychology"). In the therapeutic setting, of course, the ideal will be for the practitioner to bring the client into the *I'm OK/You're OK* position.

I'm not OK/You're not OK

> The position "I'm not OK, you're not OK" is the most likely foundation for a losing script. This child has become convinced that life is futile and full of despair. She views herself as being one-down and unlovable. She believes no-one will help her because they are not-OK as well. Thus she will write her script around scenes of rejecting and being rejected.
> – *Ian Stewart & Vann Joines*

The *I'm not OK/You're not OK* stance (abbreviated to I-U-) will be the *futility life-position*, whereby communication will completely falter between the client and others. This client will, therefore, view himself/herself and other people as hopeless cases. The client will have learned that there will be no point in making any effort because he/she is worthless and impotent, as is everyone else in life. This client will be likely to lack true commitment in relationships and many relationships will fail as a result of his/her in-built perception of futility and hopelessness.

> Life, which in the first year had some comforts, now has none. The stroking has disappeared. If this state of abandonment and difficulty continues without relief through the second year of life, the child concludes I'm Not OK–You're Not OK.
> – *Thomas Harris*

I'm OK/You're not OK

"I'm OK, you're not OK" may form the basis for a script that seems on the face of it to be winning. But this child will have the conviction that he needs to be one-up and put others down. He may manage to do this for some of the time, achieving his wants but only with a continual struggle. At other times, the people around him will get tired of being one-down and reject him. Then he will switch from apparent "winner" to heavy loser.
– *Ian Stewart & Vann Joines*

The *I'm OK/You're not OK* stance (abbreviated to I+U-) will be the *paranoid life-position*, in which the client will wish to dismiss others by somehow sending them away. This client will have a dismissive approach to people and, generally, not enter into any fruitful communication. People may be shunned or rejected by this client both aggressively when he/she adopts a patronising stance and/or passively when he/she ignores others. Often this client will be defensive and will endeavour to stay on top in any altercation or confrontation with others. This client may, generally, appear to be overbearing and insensitive in social interaction.

A child who is brutalised long enough by the parents he initially felt were OK will switch positions to the third, or criminal, position: I'm OK–You're Not OK.
– *Thomas Harris*

I'm not OK/You're OK

If the infant takes up the position "I'm not OK, you're OK", she is more likely to write a banal or losing life-story. To fit with her basic position, she will construct her script round themes of being victimised and losing out to others.
– *Ian Stewart & Vann Joines*

The *I'm not OK/You're OK* stance (abbreviated to I-U+) will be the *depressive life-position*, in which the client will seek to detach from other people. This stance will often mean that the client will endeavour to isolate himself/herself from others and not get involved in close relationships. This position may also engender self-harming or self-destructive tendencies, because the client will harbour negative feelings and will adopt repetitive behaviours that will confirm his/her personal perception of unworthiness.

> This is the universal position of early childhood, being the infant's
> logical conclusion from the situation of birth and infancy.
> – *Thomas Harris*

I'm OK/You're OK

> The child who chooses "I'm OK, you're OK" is likely to build a winning
> script. He views himself as lovable and good to have around. He decides
> that his parents are lovable and trustworthy, and later extends this view
> to people generally.
> – *Ian Stewart & Vann Joines*

The *I'm OK/You're OK* stance (abbreviated to I+U+) will be the *healthy life-position,* in that the client will mix well with people and will progress in life because his/her perceptions will be based on reality. In this position, the client will accept himself/herself and can fully accept others. Self-acceptance will mean that the client can totally accept himself/herself, faults and all, without harsh judgment and with a degree of joy. Acceptance of self and others will also mean that the client will regard himself/herself as a winner and will act out his/her life script of guaranteed success accordingly.

> There is a fourth position, wherein lies our hope. It is the I'm OK–You're
> OK position. There is a qualitative difference between the first three
> positions and the fourth position. The first three are unconscious, having
> been made early in life.
> – *Thomas Harris*

Frommian Personality Theories

> Both Freud and Jung had seen personality as happening as a result
> partly of maturation, and partly of interaction with members of the close
> family. Fromm recognised both individual development and family as
> important, but also included society as a third factor in the formation of
> personality.
> – *Nicky Hayes*

Erich Fromm (1900–1980) – another theorist of the psychodynamic persuasion – voiced his conviction that there will be a dialectic relationship between the client, his/her family and the wider society in which he/she resides. Fromm recognised that personal relationships are not only based on the client's needs but also can be influenced by social, cultural and economic factors. Relationships, for example, that cross class, cultural and financial-status barriers are not principally the norm. Fromm posited, therefore, that the client's personality can be influenced largely by economic and social values.

Personality Orientations

> I do arrive to my concept of character as in fact to all other constructs, not from the development of the libido but from the character of the parents and from what I called the social character. By social character I mean that type of character which every society produces, because it needs men and makes men want to do what they have to do.
> – *Erich Fromm*

Fromm noted that the client's personality can be subject to change as a direct result of the climate in which he/she exists. Fromm regarded this human capacity and the inclination to change as being the client's *productive character*. A productive character will be exhibited by the client who has been lovingly nurtured in childhood. Dysfunctional family relationships, social hardship and financial impoverishment in childhood may, however, raise negative orientations in the client in adulthood. Let us now consider the negative personality orientations that Fromm devised.

The receptive character

> Receptive characters, in Fromm's theory, typically feel that the source of all good things is external – outside themselves – and that being inoffensive and lovable will bring them a positive life.
> – *Nicky Hayes*

The receptive character will be the client who believes that a positive position in life will be derived from external factors. This client will, therefore, strive to make himself/herself lovable and acceptable to others in the belief that he/she will automatically become the recipient of good fortune, peace and contentment. This client will have a tendency to display allegiance and loyalty to others, to colleagues and to employers, but may lack self-determination and may adopt a self-masochistic approach to social interaction.

The exploitative character

> Exploitative characters, by contrast, see the world in competitive, "dog-eat-dog" terms; and gain great satisfaction from outsmarting or controlling others.
> – Nicky Hayes

The exploitative character will be the client who believes that he/she lives in a hostile and competitive world. This client will be likely to derive satisfaction from winning the race and from outstripping others in the process. This will be the ruthlessly ambitious client who may trample on others in order to get to the top of the pile. This client, however, may display a sadistic tendency and may hold his/her benefactors in contempt. This client would not normally be overendowed with warmth for his/her fellow human beings.

The hoarding character

> Hoarding characters, according to Fromm, are often avid collectors, and very protective of what they have, so they do not tend to be open to new ideas or to sharing their lives with other people.
> – Nicky Hayes

The hoarding character will be the client who amasses possessions and has an intrinsic need to control his/her life. Often this need for control may become a destructive aspect of the client's personality because such a need will be so dominant within his/her psyche. This client will seldom be open to suggestion or innovation and will be disinclined to share thoughts or possessions, that he/she will regard as his/her only form of security. This client may also become a loner in his/her vain attempt to keep control of his/her life.

The marketing character

> Marketing characters, in Fromm's model, are concerned with image and style, and tend to judge their personal world in terms of social success.
> – Nicky Hayes

The marketing character will be the client who evaluates himself/herself only in terms of personal success and the accumulation of wealth. This client will seek admiration and popularity and will be continually attention-seeking. Unhappiness can result if this client is not admired and he/she may endlessly endeavour to contrive ways of gaining the approbation of others. This client will be likely to be a conformist and a trend-follower rather than an individualist because of the risk of becoming unpopular if he/she deviates from the norm.

Social Cognition Theories

> The theory put forward by Walter Mischel stated that it is people's understanding of the cognitive and social aspects of their situation which determines their personality. Rather than assuming that their behaviour is symptomatic of underlying dispositions or traits, Mischel focused on how people react to the different stimuli in their environment.
> *– Nicky Hayes*

Social cognition theory – expounded principally by Albert Bandura (1925–) – puts forward the view that personality can be determined by the client's perception and understanding of the social aspects of his/her environment. This theory stresses the importance of personal expectations and values that will dictate the client's personality and will be linked to his/her beliefs in self-efficacy and personal competencies. The client, for example, will believe in himself/herself according to his/her evaluation of past experiences. The client will also form beliefs about himself/herself when observing the performance of others. This client will carefully note the extent to which he/she is encouraged or praised by others and so act accordingly. The client, moreover, will take action only after monitoring the degree to which he/she is physiologically or psychologically ready to proceed. We shall now consider some of these concepts as a route for the practitioner towards understanding the client's underlying motivations.

Human Agency

> Human agency is the capacity to exercise self-direction through control
> over one's own thought processes, motivation and action.
> – *Richard Nelson-Jones*

The concept of human agency asserts that the client will have the ability to exercise self-control (see Chapter 9 – "Cognitive Therapy"). The client, therefore, may view himself/herself as being free in direct proportion to the extent to which he/she can influence and determine his/her own actions. Human agency may take a number of differing forms for the client according to the source of the instrument and power behind the vehicle. *Autonomous agency* will obtain when the client considers himself/herself to be a totally independent agent. *Mechanical agency* will be the agency that will be determined by the client's environmental factors. *Emergent-interactive agency* will be that which will be reciprocally determined by the client's behavioural, cognitive and personal factors and his/her environmental influences. Emergent-interactive agency is the model on which social cognitive theory has been based. Here the control of an outcome or circumstances will be said to emanate from a combination of the client's behaviour, thought processes, personal attributes and any external environmental factors.

Human Capabilities

There are five basic cognitive capabilities that will be the domain of the client. An appreciation of these human capabilities will assist the analytical hypnotherapist in understanding the client's cognitive processes. *Symbolising capability* will occur when the client is capable of processing or transforming his/her experiences into symbolism and imagery (see Chapter 14 – "Dreams and Symbolic Imagery"). The client can then naturally process information via these symbols or images. *Forethought capability* will obtain when the client is capable of contemplative forethought that will enable him/her to act after reflection rather than spontaneously. The quality of the client's forethought, of course, will regulate his/her behaviour by allowing him/her to anticipate consequences, to evaluate past experiences and to set goals accordingly. *Vicarious capability* will transpire when the client has the capacity to observe and to learn from the actions of others. Keen observation of actions and consequences will aid the client in acquiring life skills such as language skills and social skills. The client can also learn by imitation and by emulating his/her role-models. *Self-regulatory capability* will manifest when the client has the ability to develop internal standards by which to evaluate his/her own behaviour. The client will then have his/her own personal code of conduct, that will intercede and can pronounce what is right and what is wrong for him/her. Having made this adjudication, the client can then strive to act within the scope of his/her internal code of conduct. *Self-reflective capability* will come into play when the client possesses the ability to analyse his/her personal experiences and to make unbiased judgments about his/her competence and his/her general performance.

Skills Learning

Social cognition theory is also concerned with the ways in which the client can acquire and process information in order to acquire skill. According to this theory, the client will learn either by observation or from experience.

Observational learning

Most human behaviour and cognitive skills are learned by observing models. Modelling can inhibit and disinhibit behaviour already in people's repertoires and facilitate responses. Modelled behaviour can serve as prompts and cues for people to perform behaviour already in their repertoires, and it can elicit emotional responses. People can perceive and behave differently in states of heightened arousal.
– *Richard Nelson-Jones*

When learning by observation, the client will process information and will be influenced by what he/she notices. The observational learning process will mean that the client will begin by perceiving an object and then allowing it to influence him/her. After this, the client will then remember what he/she has observed and will make a symbolic representation of the viewed object. Finally, the client will translate this symbolic representation into action and can determine the way in which such representation will motivate or demotivate him/her.

Enactive learning

> Enactive learning or learning from experience is ubiquitous. A distinction exists between knowledge and skill. In many domains people need to go beyond knowledge structures to develop proficient actions. Developing performance skills requires people to have accurate conceptions of targeted skills against which to match their attempts to perform the skills. Enactment provides the vehicle to translate knowledge into skilled action.
> – *Richard Nelson-Jones*

When engaging in enactive learning, the client will learn from experience. When learning by experience, the client will learn by copying the actions of others, by plunging into new situations, by responding to circumstances as well as learning by accident. The client will then evaluate the result of his/her past experiences and the outcome of this evaluation will dictate his/her subsequent behaviour. If experiences are deemed to be pleasant and/or productive, then the client will tend to want to repeat such experiences. If experiences are unpleasant and/or anxiety-provoking, on the other hand, the client will then tend to want to avoid repetitions of similar experiences.

Client Profiling

The analytical hypnotherapy practitioner may wish to ponder the following points when formulating a profile for the client.

- Does the practitioner have a comprehensive grasp of the client's personality structure?
- In what ways does the client display childish inclinations and tendencies?
- In what ways does the client's social conscience rule his/her life?
- Does the client exhibit any depressive or paranoidal tendencies?
- Does the client sometimes act in an overtly hysterical manner?
- Could the client be classed as either an introvert or an extrovert?

- In what ways does the client relate to his/her environment?
- In what ways does the client acquire and process information?
- Does the client tend to be sensitive and intuitive or does he/she deal only in concrete facts?
- How does the client make value-judgments about others?
- How does the client handle interaction with others from a psychological standpoint?
- Does the client frequently show an ulterior motive in his/her dealings within intimate relationships?
- Is the client at all manipulative in social interaction?
- In what ways is the client re-enacting a prewritten life script for himself/herself?
- How does the client view his/her ability to cope with the working environment?
- Is the client in any way competitive or ruthlessly ambitious?
- In what ways can the client be self-sufficient?
- What are the client's capabilities and inner resources?

Chapter 16

Personality Development

The sleeping and the dead
Are but pictures; 'tis the eye of childhood
That fears a painted devil.

– William Shakespeare

Why Study Personality Development?

Two things fill the mind with ever new and increasing wonder and awe,
the more often and the more seriously reflection concentrates upon them:
the starry heaven above me and the moral law within me.
– Immanuel Kant

Because the analytical hypnotherapist will be almost exclusively concerned with the origins of the client's symptoms rather than the symptoms themselves, it will make sense for us to take time out now in order to consider the topic of childhood development. The client, of course, may have his/her symptoms only because once, as a child, he/she had been obliged to interact in the family circle and, in adulthood, he/she had then to contend with the social world. The child will, inevitably, be a product of his/her upbringing and will have suffered as a result of self-distortion. If society did not exist, for instance, then the client would not be forced to compare himself/herself unfavourably with others. If there were no crowds, the social-phobic would not find himself/herself reacting as he/she does. If, as a human race, reproduction were not a factor in the equation, then the client would not suffer from problems of intimacy or engage in destructive relationships. Life for the client would, of course, be infinitely less complex in terms of symptomology if he/she lived on a desert island but, of course, in practice no-one ever could live in total isolation indeed, if he/she expressed a desire to do so then the practitioner may wish to question his/her motives. Looking, therefore, at some developmental theories will assist the practitioner to understand the point from which the client has come, wherein may lie the source of his/her psychological and physiological distress. In this chapter we shall examine the classical theories of Freud and Jung as well as those of the neo-Freudians who considered the child as a product of his/her immediate family, social and cultural environment.

Freudian Developmental Theories

> Failure to progress adequately through the stages of libidinal development can cause fixation: attachment to objects appropriate to those earlier infantile stages. Fixated persons suffer frustrating wastes of energy because of their over-investment in past objects.
> – *Richard Appignanesi & Oscar Zarate*

Freud explained childhood evolution by identifying five stages of development, that are known as the psychosexual developmental stages and cover the client's journey from childhood into adulthood. Freud was also responsible for devising the theories behind the *oedipus complex* and the *electra complex* – the remnants of which still permeate therapeutic understanding and practice – that deal with issues of the child's attachment to the opposite-sex parent.

> We can see these early events producing three principal results. First, they steer the development of the mother–child relationship (the basic template of future relationships as well as the major influence on the child's early development). Secondly, they shape the development and expression of the child's affective reactivity. Thirdly, they lay down the framework of the child's self-image, especially his perception of the effect he sees himself as having on the outside world and the persons in it and his experience and perception of himself as withdrawing from or moving out to the world.
> – *Helmut Karle & Jennifer Boys*

The Developmental Stages

Freud believed that the conflicts and difficulties implicit in each of the psychosexual developmental stages needed to be adequately resolved in order to ensure the child's safe passage through childhood (see Chapter 1 – "Psychoanalysis"). Freud asserted that the client's psychological problems could arise at any of these developmental stages and that a disturbance at any stage would bring about symptoms such as relationship difficulties, problems of self-acceptance, an inability to express negative emotions and sexual dysfunction (see Chapter 12, Volume 2 – "Dysfunctional Relationships"). If a given stage remained unresolved, the child would then become *fixated* at that stage and, consequently, psychological distress would be installed within his/her mind. This arrested development would, of course, hinder the client's personal and social development. Because the client's fixation would have been due to an energy-stoppage when the psychic snapshot was taken, this psychic state will then give rise to the client's psychological conflicts and distressing symptoms. The pregenital stages, that govern the first six years of life, will, of course, be the most critical in terms of the child's personal and interpersonal development.

> Patients give us an impression of having been "fixated" to a particular portion of their past, as though they could not manage to free themselves from it and were for that reason alienated from the present and the future.
> – *Sigmund Freud*

The oral stage

> If an infant could speak, he would no doubt pronounce the act of sucking his mother's breast by far the most important in his life.
> – *Sigmund Freud*

The oral stage – from birth to one year old – will be the initial period of life when the infant will strive diligently to fulfil his/her survival needs using his/her mouth, either when consuming food or when crying out for assistance. Problems that can manifest at this stage of the child's development are likely to result in the need for oral gratification in adulthood. The client, for example, may seek gratification in the form of comfort-eating, smoking or drug-taking as a means of obtaining supposed satisfaction or may become a gossip or a backbiter as a means of venting anger. This will also be the stage at which problems of trust and dependency can emerge. The client can, for instance, become intensely overanxious and susceptible to developing co-dependency relationships or become unable to sustain an intimate relationship.

Problems at the oral stage of childhood development are, of course, associated with Freud's oral-schizoidal personality theory (see Chapter 15 – "Personality Structure").

The anal stage

> We conclude that infants have feelings of pleasure in the process of evacuating urine and faeces and that they soon contrive to arrange those actions in such a way as to bring them the greatest possible yield of pleasure through the corresponding excitations of the erotogenic zones of the mucous membrane.
> *– Sigmund Freud*

The anal stage – from one year to three years old – will be the time at which the toddler will get his/her first taste of independence and autonomy. The young child will also learn to deal with negative emotions usually directed against his/her parents in the process of breaking free. When the child learns that his/her parents are authority figures who must be unquestionably obeyed, he/she may seek to find a way of exerting control over such dictators by attempting to control bodily functions when engaged in activities such as toilet-training. During this period, the child may be able to monitor the reaction of his/her parents and then act accordingly. Such parental reactions may be either of pleasure or dismay at the child's performance on the potty. From the anal stage, therefore, the child may learn to be aggressive, power-hungry, self-centred, controlling, stubborn or miserly if this stage remains unresolved. Such traits may result from the child's inability to express negative emotions appropriately. The child who seeks unsuccessfully to control his/her parents may become a control-freak in later life and may be referred to as an *anal-retentive* personality because he/she had striven to disregard parental wishes during this period. The child, moreover, who takes an aggressive stance with regard to parental control may well become the *anal-aggressive* personality who later becomes cruel and disorderly. The child who sought wholeheartedly to comply with parental expectations during the anal phase may be described as the *anal-expulsive* personality, who will be characterised by being undisciplined or overproductive. Problems at the anal stage of childhood development are, of course, associated with Freud's anal-paranoidal personality theory (see Chapter 15 – "Personality Structure").

The phallic stage

> According to the orthodox Freudian view, the basic conflict of the phallic
> stage centres on the unconscious incestuous desires that children
> develop for the parent of the opposite sex. Because these feelings are of
> such a threatening nature, they are typically repressed; yet they are
> powerful determinants of later sexual development and adjustment.
> – *Gerald Corey*

The phallic stage – from three to six years old – will be depicted by the child's exploration of both himself/herself and the world about him/her. During this period of life, the child will learn to move, to speak and to think for himself/herself. A natural curiosity together with an inherent capacity for sexuality will usually result in sexual experimentation for the young child. The child will now begin to explore his/her own body and to wonder about its functions. Problems of sexual identity can manifest if the phallic phase does not progress satisfactorily for the client. This will be the stage often associated with the oedipus/electra complex, when the child begins to identify with the opposite-sex parent. This can lead the boy to become naturally attracted to his mother and the girl to be drawn towards her father.

The latency stage

> From about the sixth to the eighth year of life onwards, we can observe a
> halt and retrogression in sexual development, which, in cases where it is
> most propitious culturally, deserves to be called a period of latency. The
> latency period may also be absent: it need not bring with it any
> interruption of sexual activity and sexual interests along the whole line.
> – *Sigmund Freud*

The latency stage – from six to twelve years old – will denote the time when the child will begin to settle into a period of calm following the resolution of previous phases of development. By now the major interactive structures of the child's personality in terms of the id, the ego and the superego will have been formed (see Chapter 15 – "Personality Structure"). The child should now develop friendships and take up interests in connection with schoolwork and leisure-time activities, that are external to the home environment. The focus should also shift from the child's internal world to his/her external environment. An unresolved latency phase in the client may result in narcissistic problems and may lead him/her to become reclusive and/or preoccupied with himself/herself (see Chapter 7, Volume 2 – "Fear and Anxiety Disorders").

The genital stage

> Young adults move into the genital stage unless they become fixated at
> an earlier period of psychosexual development.
> – *Sigmund Freud*

The genital stage – from twelve to eighteen years old – will mark the period of adolescence for the client. The teenager will now be on the threshold of adulthood and should be leaving behind an immature way of life. The young adult should start to form intimate relationships with members of the opposite sex and, in doing so, begin to break free from parental dictates. Problems at this stage may hark back to problems developed by the client at earlier phases of life – particularly during the phallic stage if the oedipus/electra complex has not been resolved adequately. Adolescence will often be the stage at which the client can begin to show his/her true feelings towards parental influences – thus the rebellious-teenager syndrome may evolve or, alternatively, the young adult may be afraid of fleeing the nest. Problems at the genital stage of childhood development are, of course, associated with Freud's genital-hysteric personality theory (see Chapter 15 – "Personality Structure").

The Oedipus and Electra Complex

> In the theory of the Oedipus complex Freud has, in effect, invented a perfect theoretical instrument for explaining away allegations of sexual abuse and undermining their credibility. Since Freud's theory that all children might fantasise about sexual relations with their parents, it followed that recollection of sexual abuse by parents could be construed as fantasies. Even though Freud himself specifically pointed out on a number of occasions that memories of childhood seductions sometimes did correspond to real events, the overwhelming tendency of the psychoanalytic profession throughout most of the twentieth century has been to construe recollections of incest as fantasies. In this respect, at least, psychoanalysis in general and the theory of the Oedipus complex in particular have caused untold harm.
> – *Richard Webster*

In Greek mythology, Oedipus murdered his father and married his mother. Similarly, Electra slew her mother in order to protect her father from slaughter. The oedipus/electra complex, therefore, has been derived from these two legends in that the boy-child will entertain oedipal wishes and the girl-child those of electra. The oedipus-complex theory purports that a boy-child will have an unconsciously-repressed wish to possess his mother and that this possession may include a desire for domination and an erotically-tinged relationship with her. In his longing to possess his mother fully, the boy will also wish to fend off or to destroy all other rivals, and his father, naturally, will be the prime target for both his fears and his jealousies. The electra-complex theory, similarly, purports that a girl-child has an unconsciously repressed desire to unite with her father and to form an erotically-tinged relationship with him. The girl, too, will then seek to exterminate her mother as a would-be rival for her father's affections.

The practitioner today, however, would be advised not to take these analogies absolutely literally when speaking of the oedipus/electra complex. The oedipus/electra complex may, in essence, be taken to assert that the child unconsciously wishes to be close to the opposite-sex parent and to distance himself/herself from the same-sex parent during the phallic stage. These patterns are, no doubt, nature's way of preparing the young child for future adult intimate relationships, that are, after all, instinctive drives in every human organism. In Freud's day, moreover, homosexuality was abhorrent to the general public and, therefore, this theory may have gone some way towards discouraging the same-sex parent from forming an affectionate relationship with the young child. It should also be emphasised that as far as Freud's interpretation of sexuality is concerned, the child's feelings are merely erotically-tinged rather than being a full-blown desire for sexual intercourse – just as many overtly platonic relationships between the sexes will exhibit an element of sexual role-play. The child may only con-sciously be aware of a need for physical closeness to the opposite-sex parent but, nevertheless, unconscious guilt will be experienced – particularly in the light of prudish social mores. The child may, moreover, consciously express his/her need to separate his/her parents when they are in physical proximity, not only as a means of attempting to exclude or to eliminate the same-sex parent but also, indeed, in order to secure attention for himself/herself.

During the phallic stage, furthermore, the ground may be fertile for the child to become increasingly curious about sexual matters, to explore his/her own body, to have sexual fantasies, to develop sex-role patterns of behaviour and to indulge in masturbation or sex-play. This complex of instinctive wishes, feelings and ideas, however, can be repressed by the client's unconscious mind because such feelings will more often than not be unacceptable to consciousness awareness, even in a sexually-liberal society. Many parents, of course, have sternly discouraged their children in such natural practices at this stage of life when, in fact, the child craves to explore his/her own body.

Freud believed that the oedipus/electra complex could be resolved when the child matures in an emotionally-healthy environment. That is to say, the complex will resolve naturally if both parents are loving and supportive of the child during the phallic stage and if their attitudes have been neither prudishly prohibitive nor excessively stimulating to the delicate emotions engendered by the complex. The child will, in time, replace his/her longings for mother or for father with a more socially-agreeable form of affection and will also receive satisfaction from developing a strong identification with the same-sex parent. Freud was of the opinion that it will be the superego that overcomes the complex and that this will be the most important achievement of the mind in terms of the client's sexuality. The oedipus/electra complex, therefore, will partly be resolved by the child's appropriate identification with the same-sex parent and then fully resolved by discovering a mature adult sexual partner in later life. An unresolved oedipus/electra complex, however, will mean that the client may experience feelings of guilt. This guilt-complex may then surface to the client's consciousness as a psychogenic symptom because the child will become unconsciously fixated to the opposite-sex parent – possibly in the absence of control from the same-sex parent. Psychological symptoms that are likely to be a direct result of an unresolved oedipus/electra complex are usually deemed to be sexually-based fixations, sexual aberrations, debilitating guilt and sexual-identity crises. For the victim of incestuous sexual abuse, the resulting damage to the client's sexuality can, of course, be catastrophic during this delicate developmental process (see Chapter 15, Volume 2 – "The Effects of Childhood Abuse").

It is clear that many women have suffered immensely as a result of
orthodox psychoanalysts construing real episodes of sexual abuse as
Oedipal fantasies. To this extent the recovered memory movement was
actually born out of a reaction against some of the tyrannical
assumptions of psychoanalysis.
– *Richard Webster*

Freudian theories have, of course, given rise to much fervent
debate over the years. It was Freud who posited the theory of
memory repression with particular reference to childhood sexual
abuse (see Chapter 10 – "Memory"). Freud not only hammered the
theory of the oedipus/electra complex but also the seduction theory – both of which have fuelled the bitter fires of controversy.
Freud advocated theories and then abandoned them and, because
of this, he has been described as a patriarch for his oedipus/electra
complex theory. It has also been felt by some practitioners that an
adherence to the oedipus/electra complex theory was responsible
for a trend in which cases of incest and childhood sexual abuse
have formerly been minimised or dismissed. The therapist should,
in general, therefore, tread exceedingly carefully in accepting the
oedipus/electra complex as an utterly literal interpretation of
Freud's theories, while keeping an open mind about information
that the client may divulge in therapy about sexual practice during childhood.

For during the late 1970s and the early 1980s many feminist writers and
therapists began to recognise the frequency with which real cases of
sexual abuse were subject to denial. Quite deliberately they started to
draw back the veil of patriarchy and to reveal the reality which had been
concealed behind it.
– *Richard Webster*

Jungian Developmental Theories

Children are so heavily involved in the psychological attitude of their
parents that it is no wonder that most of the nervous disturbances in
childhood can be traced back to a disturbed psychic atmosphere in
the home.
– *Carl Jung*

Jung's observations of children led him to believe that the child
will prefer to explain and to interpret events within the realms of
fantasy rather than to understand experiences as concrete facts

(see Chapter 2 – "Analytical Psychology"). Jung observed that the child will brush aside scientific fact in favour of mythical fact. He maintained that, if the child's parents were to indulge his/her fantasy explanations, this would allow him/her to continue using and developing his/her imagination as a precious asset. Jung believed, therefore, that insisting that a child accept scientific fact would be an obstacle to the free development of his/her thinking, that would then be unconsciously suppressed. These ideas, therefore, may help the practitioner to understand the workings of the child's mind when he/she is addressing the client.

Jung inspired the work of the prominent analytical psychologist Frances Wickes (1875–1967), who also put forward important theories with regard to the world of childhood. Wickes maintained that the psychic state of the child would identify with the psychic state of his/her parents. She regarded this phenomenon as the means by which the child will be deceived by his/her parents, and that, in fact, this situation can foster a climate of unreality, dishonesty and mistrust within the child–parent relationship. Wickes also theorised that the client's identity will be derived from his/her unconscious mind when he/she was a small child, because children are primarily creatures of sensation and intuition. The child will explore the world of objects through sensation while, simultaneously, he/she will become aware of his/her inner forces – both within himself/herself and in others – via intuition.

Jung maintained that the child's separate identity will be formed before ego-consciousness. He believed that the child's antecedents are just as responsible for his/her identity as are his/her immediate parents. He reasoned that the dreams of a young child, for example, would often comprise a sizeable mythological content, that will emanate from the collective unconscious (see Chapter 14 – "Dreams and Symbolic Imagery"). The child's unconscious psyche prior to the development of ego-consciousness will be influenced, therefore, by much more than merely his/her parentage. The child will imbue his/her parents with the characteristics of the archetypes, making them larger than life and super-powerful. Jung also believed that this was the root of the oedipus/electra complex. The remnants of this child-soul in the adult client, therefore, will comprise both his/her best and his/her worst qualities.

Jung also posited that once the child had become aware of himself/herself as a separate identity – usually between the ages of three and five years – he/she would then develop memory and would start to pull together fragments from his/her unconscious mind in order to form a coherent psyche. This process will then be reinforced at school by education and cultural learning for the child and will continue until psychic puberty has been reached. Jung regarded psychic puberty as being between the ages of nineteen and twenty years for females and about twenty-five years for males. Because the young child's psyche will be so deeply involved with the psychological attitudes of his/her parents, most of his/her psychological disorders will reflect the psychological conflict of his/her parents until he/she starts school. Once the child has started school, the teacher will then become a substitute parent and, as such, some of his/her psychological attitudes will infect the child, who will project the father-image or the mother-image on to that teacher. The teacher, therefore, plays a vital role in the psychic development of the child. School will be the beginning of the process by which the child can free himself/herself from his/her parents. The child will also pass through ancestral stages during psychic development and will be educated into the current-day level of culture and consciousness.

The Developmental Stages

> The nearer we approach to the middle of life, and the better we have succeeded in entrenching ourselves in our personal attitudes and social positions, the more it appears as if we had discovered the right course and the right ideals and principles of behaviour.
> – *Carl Jung*

Jung – building on the work of Freud – suggested three developmental stages of childhood development.

The presexual stage
During the presexual stage – from birth to five years old – the infant will primarily be concerned with nutrition and growth. The child at this stage will see his/her mother merely as a care-giver and as a provider of those much-needed ingredients for survival.

The prepubertal stage
During the prepubertal stage – from five years old until puberty – the child will develop his/her interest in sexual activity, will form his/her sexuality and his/her sexual identity.

The maturity stage
Maturity will herald adulthood in terms of the client's fulfilment of his/her full sexuality when he/she will seek out a mate in order to procreate.

Object-Relations Developmental Theories

> To show pity is felt as a sign of contempt because one has clearly ceased
> to be an object of *fear* as soon as one is pitied.
> – *Friedrich Nietzsche*

Let us now examine some concepts within object-relations theory that have extended the basic philosophy of psychodynamic theory (see Chapter 5 – "Object-Relations Psychology"). Margaret Mahler (1897–1985) took up the original ideas of Melanie Klein (1882–1960) and developed additional theories with regard to childhood development that have been a valuable contribution to this body of knowledge. Mahler concentrated her research on the first three years of the infant's life, when he/she will be developing his/her senses and his/her conscious awareness. These primary developmental phases will then set the scene for later psychosexual and psychosocial development.

Mahler stressed the importance of the infant's separation from the mother-figure in the early years of life as being the foundation for the success or the failure of the individuation process. These phases of development will be an important landmark for the client, because this will be the preverbal period when the child will still be developing his/her language skills. Distress, therefore, during this time cannot necessarily be verbalised directly by the client. When the young child has an inability to express himself/herself, the result may be an accumulation of psychological and physiological symptoms.

The Developmental Stages

> The object relations school (the "British school") was greatly influenced
> by Klein's emphasis on the infant's earliest relationships with its mother.
> It places far less emphasis on the role of instincts and more on the
> relationship with particular love objects (especially the mother), seeing
> early *relationships* as crucial for later development. Fairburn, for example,
> saw the aim of the libido as object-seeking (as opposed to pleasure-
> seeking), and this was extended by Bowlby in his *attachment theory*.
> *– Richard Gross & Rob McIlveen*

Mahler outlined four developmental stages through which the infant passes, although often, in practice, one phase will overlap with or blend into the next. Each stage will carry its inherent characteristics of loss of a love-object and the accompanying separation anxiety that will inevitably result from this deprivation (see Chapter 7, Volume 2 – "Fear and Anxiety Disorders"). Any crises that manifest in one of these critical developmental stages will, of course, have a profound effect on the client's ability to form mature and meaningful relationships in adult life (see Chapter 12, Volume 2 – "Dysfunctional Relationships"). The developmental phases in object-relations theory will track the unfolding of the infant from birth, when he/she is totally self-absorbed and unable to comprehend that his/her mother is a separate being, to the time when the child will be able to function as a separate and independent entity.

> The voice of the intellect is a soft one, but it does not rest till it has
> gained a hearing.
> *– Sigmund Freud*

The infantile-autistic stage

The infantile-autistic stage of babyhood – from birth to four weeks old – will be characterised by the fact that the infant will be totally self-absorbed with his/her own needs in the interests of his/her survival. This will be the stage at which the infant will respond solely to states of tension in his/her inner world because he/she will be oblivious of everything else around him/her. When the infant is born, he/she will be unable to differentiate between his/her own existence and that of his/her mother, and will be blissfully unaware that his/her mother is a separate being in her own right. Mother may be regarded as a number of different parts or objects, such as a breast, a face, a hand or a mouth. If this stage has been characterised by crises or trauma, then the client will be likely to suffer from fears, fixations and anxiety-states.

The symbiotic stage

The symbiotic stage, when the infant is toddling – from four weeks old to five months old – will be characterised by the fact that the child will establish a pronounced dependency on his/her mother. The infant will be in a state of psychological fusion or symbiosis with his/her mother during this stage in that he/she will believe that his/her provider is merely an extension of himself/herself. At this stage, however, the child may begin to suspect that his/her mother could be a separate being and an entity in her own right. In order to bridge this gap of separation, however, the child will develop a high degree of emotional attunement with his/her mother and will strive to please her as his/her primary love-object. If this stage has been characterised by crises or trauma, then the client will be likely to develop dependency states and to become the victim of addictions and compulsions.

The separation-individuation stage

The separation-individuation stage in the life of the preschool child – from five months to three years old – will occur when the child moves away from regarding himself/herself as an extension of his/her primary care-giver. The child will now begin the process of separating from his/her mother and will begin to mature as an individual in his/her own right. The child may still feel a degree of dependence on significant others in his/her life but will not be totally reliant on such carers. The child may, however, feel a conflict between relishing independence and needing to be dependent on his/her carers. The child, for example, may tentatively experiment with being curious and adventurous at this stage but his/her confidence will grow if the developmental process can be transited without crisis.

The separation-individuation stage will also contain a number of subphases, as it will be a very complex developmental stage for the child. The *differentiation subphase* – from five to ten months old

– will occur when the infant first becomes aware that his/her mother is a separate being. The *practising subphase* – from ten to sixteen months old – will occur when the infant becomes a toddler who clings to his/her mother's skirt. The *rapprochement subphase* – from sixteen to twenty-four months old – will occur when the toddler gains more confidence in his/her ability to separate physically from his/her mother. The *object-constancy subphase* – from twenty-four to thirty-six months old – will occur when the child gains a degree of confidence in his/her own autonomy.

During this period of the child's existence, his/her mother and other primary carers will become the means by which he/she can validate himself/herself. The child, for example, will seek approval and recognition in order to engender a good sense of self. If the child's parents provide a sound reflective mirroring, then he/she will develop into a stable adult with a healthy self-esteem. Dents in the child's self-image at this stage in life due to poor empathetic resonance, however, are likely to set up disturbing personality disorders because of the insecurity manifested early in the client's life (see Chapter 7, Volume 2 – "Fear and Anxiety Disorders"). Relationships in general in adult life may suffer if this stage has been weathered unsuccessfully in that the client will learn not to trust others in intimate relationships (see Chapter 12, Volume 2 – "Dysfunctional Relationships").

The constancy stage

The constancy stage of self-development – from three years old onwards – will commence when the child fully realises that other people are indisputably separate entities. At this stage, the child will begin to accept that he/she can now function independently without being beset by fears of doing so. Now the child can start to develop his/her own identity with this new-found self-confidence. Object-relations theorists maintain that the child will progress into the oedipus or electra stages of development following this phase of constancy.

Psychosocial Developmental Theories

Erik Erikson, trained by Anna Freud as a child psychoanalyst, also
stressed the importance of the ego, as well as the influence of social and
cultural factors on individual development. He pioneered the *lifespan
approach* to development, proposing eight social stages, in contrast with
Freud's five sexual stages that end with physical maturity.
– *Richard Gross & Rob McIlveen*

Psychosocial psychology – and its accompanying theories of psychological development – was explicated by Erik Erikson
(1902–1994). Erikson considered that the client was an integral part
of his/her environment and laid stress on the importance of
his/her interaction in the social world. Erikson put forward theories of development that cover the entire span of the client's life
and this stance has provided a fresh view of human psychological
needs.

Psychosocial psychology is a branch of developmental psychology
that lays the foundations for viewing personality development in
terms of social and cultural interaction. Erikson's work was based
on the Freudian concept of the psychosexual life stages but, by
contrast, he modelled a number of social developmental stages.
Erikson's childhood and adolescent stages, however, correspond
approximately to the Freudian psychosexual stages for the childhood period, although psychosocial theories herald a significant
departure from Freudian philosophy (see Figure 6: "Psychosexual
and psychosocial developmental stages"). This branch of psychological theory makes an important contribution to the therapist's
understanding of the client, because it examines his/her life at
varying developmental stages throughout childhood, adolescence
and adulthood. Psychosocial theory also provides the practitioner
with an appreciation of the ways in which life's experiences have
formed the client's identity and the ways in which his/her inadequate self-concept may have been formed.

Erikson believed that healthy psychological development will
occur when the conflicts of each developmental stage can be
resolved in readiness for the next so that the personality will build
up like building-blocks to a position of strength. A lack of resolution or an unsuccessful resolution at one stage may, however,
mean that these unsettled scores would remain within the client's

Figure 6: Psychosexual and Psychosocial Developmental Stages

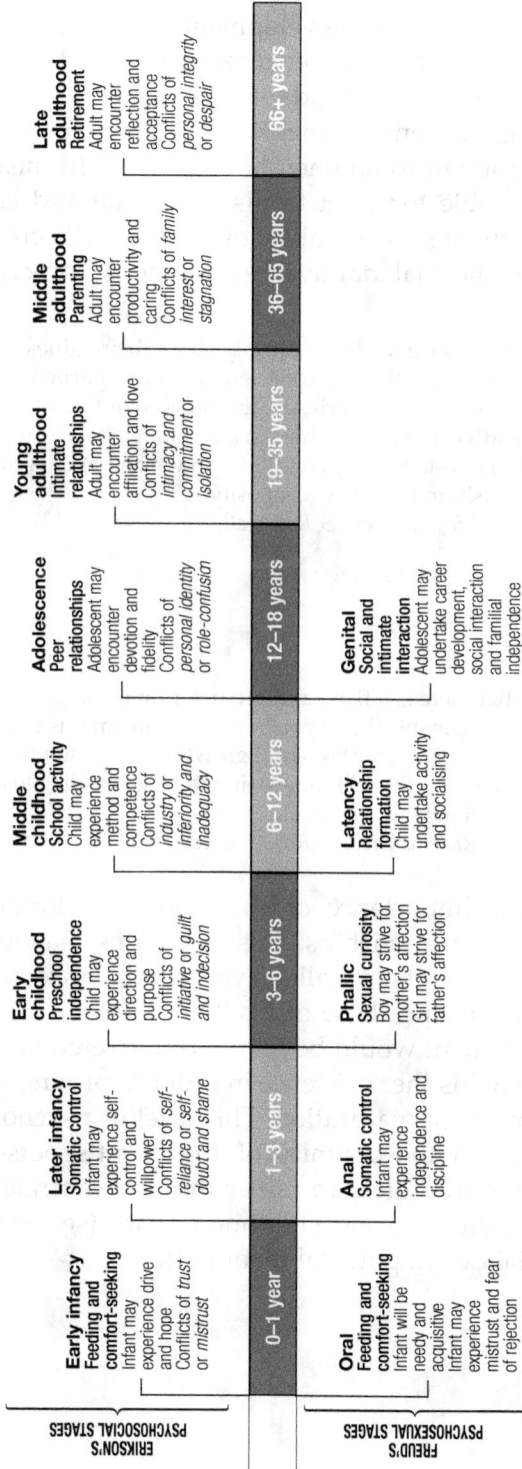

	0–1 year	1–3 years	3–6 years	6–12 years	12–18 years	19–35 years	36–65 years	66+ years

ERIKSON'S PSYCHOSOCIAL STAGES

Early infancy
Feeding and comfort-seeking
Infant may experience drive and hope
Conflicts of *trust or mistrust*

Later infancy
Somatic control
Infant may experience self-control and willpower
Conflicts of *self-reliance or self-doubt and shame*

Early childhood
Preschool independence
Child may experience direction and purpose
Conflicts of *initiative or guilt and indecision*

Middle childhood
School activity
Child may experience method and competence
Conflicts of *industry or inferiority and inadequacy*

Adolescence
Peer relationships
Adolescent may encounter devotion and fidelity
Conflicts of *personal identity or role-confusion*

Young adulthood
Intimate relationships
Adult may encounter affiliation and love
Conflicts of *intimacy and commitment or isolation*

Middle adulthood
Parenting
Adult may encounter productivity and caring
Conflicts of *family interest or stagnation*

Late adulthood
Retirement
Adult may encounter reflection and acceptance
Conflicts of *personal integrity or despair*

FREUD'S PSYCHOSEXUAL STAGES

Oral
Feeding and comfort-seeking
Infant will be needy and acquisitive
Infant may experience mistrust and fear of rejection

Anal
Somatic control
Infant may experience independence and discipline

Phallic
Sexual curiosity
Boy may strive for mother's affection
Girl may strive for father's affection

Latency
Relationship formation
Child may undertake activity and socialising

Genital
Social and intimate interaction
Adolescent may undertake career development, social interaction and familial independence

psyche and would impede later development. A positive outcome and transition from one stage of development to another would mean that the client will be able to adapt smoothly and to integrate successfully into his/her environment. A dubious passage from one stage of development to another, however, would mean that the client will be unable to adapt to his/her social and cultural environment. The client's personality, of course, will contain a mixture of adaptive and maladaptive developmental processes.

> Erikson, for example, spoke to clients directly about their values and concerns and encouraged them to consciously fashion particular behaviours and characteristics. For Erikson, the ego's cognitive processes are constructive, creative and productive. This is different from Freud's therapeutic approach of establishing conditions in which patients could "shore up" the ego's position.
> – *Richard Gross & Rob McIlveen*

The Developmental Stages

> Erikson believed that there is a fixed and pre-determined sequence of stages in human development. His *epigenetic principle* maintains that the entire pattern of social and psychological growth is governed by a genetic structure common to all humans, in which genes dictate a timetable for development.
> – *Richard Gross & Rob McIlveen*

Erikson stressed the importance of childhood development in terms of interpersonal relationships. This theory of social development postulates that the client will strive for a balance between his/her personal needs and those of his/her social environment. Erikson felt that the client would be required to overcome certain crises at each stage of his/her existence in order to progress rather than to recede in terms of maturation. This facet of psychological thinking will focus on the disunity of the client's personality throughout his/her entire lifespan rather than concentrate solely on intrapsychic conflicts during childhood years (see Figure 7: "Personal and social developmental theories").

Figure 7: Personal and Social Developmental Theories

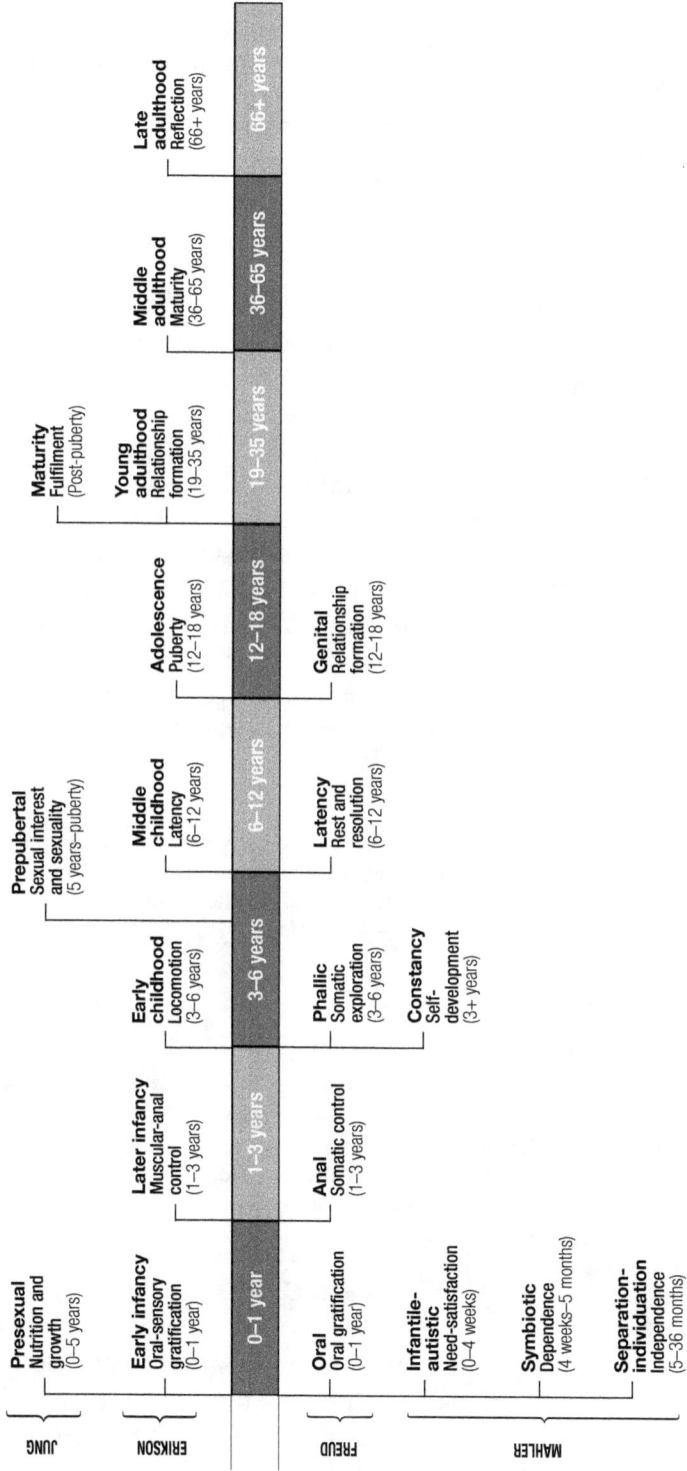

The early infancy stage

> From Erikson's viewpoint if the significant others in an infant's life
> provide the necessary love, the infant develops a sense of trust. When
> love is absent, the result is a general sense of mistrust of others. Clearly,
> infants who feel accepted are in a more favourable position to
> successfully meet future developmental crises than are those who do not
> receive adequate nurturing.
> – *Gerald Corey*

The early infancy stage (or the *oral-sensory stage*) – from birth to
one year old – will be characterised by a struggle between trust
and mistrust when the infant's overriding concerns will be those
of feeding and comfort-seeking. The infant who has been cared for
and fondled tenderly will develop a sense of trust in himself/her-
self and in his/her carers. The infant will, thus, learn to feel safe in
the knowledge that he/she will survive because he/she is being
properly nurtured. A crisis at this early stage in life can mean that
the client will encounter problems of mistrust and suspicion of self
and others (see Chapter 12, Volume 2 – "Dysfunctional
Relationships"). Interpersonal relationships will undoubtedly be
affected, moreover, and the client may feel disinclined to commit
to intimate relationships for fear of betrayal or being forsaken in
adult life.

> **Trust vs. mistrust** – To gain a balance between trusting people and
> risking being let down, or being suspicious and mistrustful and therefore
> being unable to relate to others fully.
> – *Nicky Hayes*

The later infancy stage

> According to Erikson, early childhood is a time for developing *autonomy;*
> children who do not master the task of gaining some measure of self-
> control and ability to cope with the world develop a sense of *shame* and
> *doubt* about their abilities. Parents who do too much for their children
> hamper their independence. Children who are encouraged to stay
> dependent will doubt their capacities for successfully dealing with the
> world.
> – *Gerald Corey*

The later infancy stage (or the *muscular-anal stage*) – between one
year and three years old – will be the time at which the child will
strive to develop a measure of autonomy and self-reliance or,

conversely, will become beset with shame and doubts about his/her abilities. At this stage, the child must learn to accept discipline without undue resentment. The child who has been encouraged to attain a degree of independence in accordance with his/her capabilities will transit this stage successfully. Parents who overindulge and foster dependency in the child may bring about a loss of self-power and a lack of self-confidence in the client. Problems at this stage of development may also set up in the client a sense of inadequacy and uncertainty (see Chapter 7, Volume 2 – "Fear and Anxiety Disorders").

> **Autonomy vs. shame and doubt** – To develop a sense of personal agency and control over behaviour and actions, or to mistrust one's personal abilities and anticipate failures.
> – *Nicky Hayes*

The early childhood stage

> From the social perspective, the core struggle of the pre-school phase is between *initiative* and *guilt*. Erikson contends that the basic task of the pre-school years is to establish a sense of competence and initiative.
> – *Gerald Corey*

The early childhood stage (or the *locomotor stage*) of the preschool child – between three and six years old – will be the time depicted by a clash between initiative and guilt. During this phase, the child should be encouraged to develop a sense of personal competence as well as a fluidity of movement and muscular coordination. A degree of freedom of choice and meaningful occupation at this phase of development will also assist the child. The child should, by now, be learning to initiate his/her own behaviour rather than to imitate his/her parents. If the child can be allowed the freedom to select meaningful activities, he/she will tend to develop a positive outlook on life characterised by the ability to initiate and to follow through projects. If, on the other hand, the child has not been permitted adequate freedom of expression or his/her choices have been heavily criticised or ridiculed, a sense of guilt about taking the initiative will manifest (see Chapter 8, Volume 2 – "Guilt and Shame Disorders"). Problems at this stage of the client's development will frequently spring from parental overstrictness and/or overprotection. The child can then engender a sense of guilt about striving for success and taking initiatives, and a general reluctance to attempt anything new or unusual can often accompany such feelings. In adulthood, the client may then tend to withdraw from taking the lead and will permit others to take important decisions on his/her behalf.

> **Initiative vs. guilt** – To develop an increasing sense of personal responsibility and initiative, or to develop increased feelings of guilt and doubt.
> – *Nicky Hayes*

The middle childhood stage

> According to Erikson, the central task of middle childhood is to achieve a sense of industry; failure to do so results in feelings of inadequacy and inferiority. A sense of industry is associated with creating goals that are personally meaningful and achieving them. If this is not done, it will be difficult to experience a sense of adequacy in later years, and future developmental stages will be negatively influenced.
> – *Gerald Corey*

The middle childhood stage (or the *latency stage*) of the school-age child – between six and twelve years old – will see the conflict of endeavouring to fit into the learning and studying role with a sense of achievement for the child. At this stage, the child's efforts should be encouraged and adequately praised in order to allow him/her to develop and to become competent at those tasks that he/she attempts. If the child has felt that his/her parents lack interest in his/her work or activities, then the result may be that he/she will develop a sense of failure and harbour perceptions of inadequacy and inferiority. Problems at this stage of the client's development will often lead him/her to hold a negative self-image in terms of his/her competence to perform. This may well give the child a feeling of inadequacy and inferiority, that may, in turn, lead to a lack of willingness to show initiative or to rise to a challenge in later life.

> **Industry vs. inferiority** – To learn to overcome challenges through systematic effort, or to accept failure and avoid challenges, leading to an increasing sense of inferiority.
> – *Nicky Hayes*

The adolescence stage

> According to Erikson, the major developmental conflicts of the
> adolescent years are related to the formation of a *personal identity*.
> Adolescents struggle to define who they are, where they are going, and
> how to get there. If they fail to achieve a sense of identity, *role confusion* is
> the result. Because they experience diverse pressures – from parents,
> peers, and society – they often find it difficult to gain a clear sense of
> identity.
> – *Gerald Corey*

The adolescence stage (or the *puberty stage*) – from twelve to eighteen years old – will be the time for the teenager to develop peer relationships. By now, the client should engage in forming worthwhile relationships with peers in order to secure his/her personal identity. If the adolescent struggles at this stage of life, he/she may lack a sense of identity.

> **Identity vs. role confusion** – To develop a consistent sense of personal
> identity faced with the changes in social role and expectations of
> adolescence, or simply to become overwhelmed by choices and
> expectations and to fail to develop a sense of consistent inner self.
> – *Nicky Hayes*

The young adulthood stage

> During young adulthood our sense of identity is tested again by the
> challenge of *intimacy* versus *isolation*. One of the key characteristics of the
> psychologically mature person is the ability to form intimate
> relationships. A prerequisite to establishing this intimacy with others is a
> confidence in our own identity.
> – *Gerald Corey*

The young adulthood stage – from nineteen to thirty-five years old – will be the time for the client to develop loving and intimate relationships. If the client lacks the confidence to achieve this goal then he/she may withdraw from intimate involvement and become a loner.

> **Intimacy vs. isolation** – To develop intimate and trusting relationships
> with others, or to avoid relationships as threatening and painful.
> – *Nicky Hayes*

The middle adulthood stage

Erikson sees the stimulus for continued growth in middle age as the crises between *generativity* and *stagnation*. He considers generativity in the broad sense to include creating through a career, family, leisure-time activities, and so on. The main quality of productive adults is their ability to love well, to work well, and to play well. If adults fail to achieve a sense of productivity, they begin to stagnate and to die psychologically.
– *Gerald Corey*

The middle adulthood stage (or the *mature adulthood stage*) – from thirty-six to sixty-five years old – will be the time when the client will engage in child-rearing and personal development. The adult at this stage in life should settle into the role of parent, family member, career person and one who fully partakes of an active life. The client who fails to achieve a sense of purpose and productivity at this stage may begin to lose interest in his/her existence.

Generativity vs. stagnation – To develop a productive and positive life incorporating recognition of personal achievements, or to stagnate and fail to develop or grow psychologically.
– *Nicky Hayes*

The late adulthood stage

According to Erikson, the core crisis of the elderly is *integrity* versus *despair*. Ego integrity is achieved by those who feel few regrets; they have lived a productive and worthwhile life and have coped with their failures as well as their successes. They are not obsessed with what might have been, and they are able to derive satisfaction from what they have done.
– *Gerald Corey*

The late adult stage – from sixty-six years onwards – will be the time for the adult's reflection and acceptance of the life that has gone before. The adult at this stage of life should now feel a sense of achievement on which he/she can reflect with pleasure and acceptance. The adult should now come to terms both with his/her failures and with his/her successes and should derive satisfaction from his/her past achievements. If this form of integration cannot be achieved, the client may now fall into a phase of melancholic despair with much to regret about the past.

Integrity vs. despair – To become able to look back on one's life in a
positive fashion, and to evaluate one's achievements, or to feel that life
has been meaningless and futile.
– *Nicky Hayes*

Personal Identity-Crises

Healthy resolution of these conflicts would mean that the person would
be able to adjust to the changing role demands of the period of
adolescence while still retaining a strong sense of their own lasting
personal identity. If the increasing role demands of adolescence placed
too great a stress on the individual, **identity diffusion** would result. This
means that the individual would become confused about who they were,
in view of all the different roles which they seemed to be acting out.
– *Nicky Hayes*

Erikson put forward the notion of the identity-crisis, that could be
the result of excessive stress on the client during one of the social
stages of development. An identity-crisis disorder would mean
that the client had not achieved a sense of personal identity when
passing through one of the stages of social and cultural development. Adolescence will often be cited, for instance, as being a particularly important stage in the client's life, as this station in life
will be the time when he/she will be launching himself/herself
into the social world and so relinquishing the dependency bonds
of childhood.

When considering elements of an identity-crisis, the client will, in
fact, be asking and answering the "Who am I?" question. The
client will, in the course of his/her life, be required to grapple with
issues of intimacy and with the need to intermingle with others in
the social context. The client, for example, may need to consider
his/her desire to rebel against family ties and against societal
impositions. The client may also need to struggle with doing what
will be deemed to be appropriate or inappropriate in society at different stages in life. The client will, furthermore, be forced to face
the pressures of educational achievement and the demands of
occupational obligations. Let us now consider some of the issues
with which the client will need to struggle throughout his/her
existence.

> Failure to integrate perceptions of the self into a coherent whole, results in *role confusion*. According to Erikson, role confusion can take several forms. Sometimes it is shown in an aimless drifting through a series of social and occupational roles. However, the consequences can be more severe, leading the adolescent into abnormal or delinquent behaviour (such as drug taking and even suicide).
> *– Richard Gross & Rob McIlveen*

Intimacy issues

> The adolescent who fears intimacy because of the danger of being "swamped" may become isolated from others, retreating either into stereotyped or formal relationships. Alternatively, they may become frantically involved in seeking intimacy with what Erikson described as "improbable partners".
> *– Nicky Hayes*

The establishment of intimate relationships will be a natural human desire as well as something of a social requirement for the client. An inability to form fruitful relationships would normally be considered to indicate that the client would be suffering from psychological disturbance and impaired maturation. When blending and uniting with another, however, it will be important that the client retain his/her own personal identity. If the client loses part of his/her identity when forming an intimate relationship by being overdependent on or totally dominated by his/her partner, then the value of such a relationship will be significantly reduced (see Chapter 12, Volume 2 – "Dysfunctional Relationships"). The client who shuns intimate relationships, however, or who follows dysfunctional relationship patterns may become physically or emotionally isolated. The child who may have had an inadequate relationship example from his/her parents will have been given a false concept of what is appropriate in an intimate partnership and/or may fear becoming involved with others.

Time-perspective issues

> Excessive anxieties about changing and growing into the world of
> adulthood may mean that the adolescent represses that fear into an
> inability to plan for the future, and so denies that times are changing. If
> this happens, the adolescent may not undertake the long-term projects or
> make efforts which are needed to form a secure basis for adult life.
> – Nicky Hayes

The childhood period, the adolescence period and the adult period of life should all be experienced by the client at the appropriate biological time, and that time-frame should be put into a time-perspective. The child should not, for example, be expected to become an adult before his/her time. The neglected or abused child will have been unknowingly plunged into the adult world when asked to participate in adult activities or when required to service the emotional needs of parental figures (see Chapter 15, Volume 2 – "The Effects of Childhood Abuse"). The adolescent, similarly, should not be expected to remain a child once he/she has reached puberty. The adolescent who has been molested or ill-treated will suffer from a misunderstanding about what has taken place during an abusive encounter but, at the same time, will be denied the rights of decision and choice usually afforded in adulthood. The adult, naturally, should leave the childhood citadel in order to take his/her place in society. When the client has been taken out of his/her time-perspective, the result may be a confusion that will sap his/her enthusiasm for life by putting a brake on initiative. Fear may also stultify the client, who can become insecure and unwilling to take even necessary risks.

Industry issues

> Adolescents typically have a number of tasks to do, in terms of work
> and study. These, too, represent preparation for adult life, and Erikson
> regards it as important in this stage that the adolescent should learn to
> harness their energies realistically. But doing this involves a certain
> amount of commitment to the task in hand, which some adolescents find
> anxiety-provoking.
> – Nicky Hayes

Throughout childhood, the child will be expected to play, to work and to undertake various activities in the interests of his/her development. Any faulty development can mean that the client may become overindustrious or, conversely, become unwilling to make any effort at all. The client will be trying either to compensate for internal distress or to withdraw from life in general. The victim of a dysfunctional upbringing or significant maltreatment in childhood may endeavour to become excessively powerful and industrious in order to compensate for the past. The client, alternatively, may withdraw from social interaction completely by living on the streets or by pursuing a life of crime.

Negative-identity issues

> Some adolescents will consciously choose an identity which is based on rejection of the values of others, rather than on a positive choice of their own – such as choosing an identity which is exactly the opposite to that which their parents would like them to adopt, purely in order to assert their own independence.
> – *Nicky Hayes*

The client may take a rebellious attitude or an antisocial stance when moulding an identity for himself/herself. This type of reactionary identity may be so far away from what the client truly needs that a major personality distortion will need to take place in order to satisfy these short-term aims. The victim of childhood abuse or neglect may, for example, become a delinquent, may become a criminal or could become a child-molester when a negative identity has been assumed (see Chapter 15, Volume 2 – "The Effects of Childhood Abuse").

Personal Identity-Status

> Marcia identified four *statuses* of adolescent identity formation which characterise the search for identity. A mature identity can be achieved if an individual experiences several *crises* in exploring and choosing between life's alternatives, finally arriving at a *commitment* or investment of the self in those choices.
> – *Richard Gross & Rob McIlveen*

Four developmental statuses that explain the phenomenon of identity crisis were originally defined by Erikson. These classifications of personal identity-status can often explain the client's reactions and his/her ways of coping in times of crises during the developmental phases of his/her life. Let us now consider the types of identity-status that the client may have elected to adopt in order to secure his/her passage through childhood, adolescence and adulthood.

Identity-diffusion status

The individual is in crisis and is unable to formulate clear self-definition, goals and commitments. This represents an inability to "take hold" of some kind of adult identity.
– *Richard Gross & Rob McIlveen*

With the identity-diffusion status, the client will opt out of assuming any specific identity. The client's identity will, thus, become a diverse or diffuse mixture of uncertainty and mayhem. The client with an identity-diffusion status will be likely to have a laissez-faire attitude to life and may be willing to try anything once but without any genuine prospect of commitment. The client who suffers from identity-diffusion may well not know who he/she is or where he/she is going in life. The client may, therefore, appear immature, confused and unable to move forward. This client may be reasonably willing to sign up for therapy but may not, unfortunately, have the requisite commitment needed to see it through.

Identity-foreclosure status

The individual has avoided the uncertainties and anxieties of crisis by rapidly committing him- or herself to safe and conventional goals without exploring the many options open.
– *Richard Gross & Rob McIlveen*

With the identity-foreclosure status, the client will play safe and adopt an identity that he/she perceives as the safest option. This client will probably be unadventurous and rigid in his/her thinking and will be inclined to play it safe whenever necessary. Frequently the client with an identity-foreclosure status will make choices as a result of pressure and influence from others rather than initiate his/her own decisions. This client, therefore, may be prone to assuming the identity of others and allying himself/herself with societies or groups of people with well-defined goals. The client who suffers from identity-foreclosure may also be prone to make a snap decision about entering therapy in order to grasp some form of security but may, then, display a degree of dependency on the therapist.

Identity-moratorium status

> Decisions about identity are postponed while the individual tries out
> alternative identities without being committed to any particular one.
> *– Richard Gross & Rob McIlveen*

With the identity-moratorium status, the client will assume many disguises but without a commitment to any particular single identity. This client will probably appear to be indecisive and may keep all his/her options open. The client with an identity-moratorium status will often be quite actively searching for an identity but his/her search may turn out to be fruitless. This client will often be so busy weighing up the pros and cons that he/she will never get round to action. The client who suffers from identity-moratorium may never be able to take a decision when there is more than one option from which to choose. This client, therefore, may forestall any decision to undertake therapy.

Identity-achievement status

> The individual has experienced a crisis but has emerged successfully
> with firm commitments, goals and ideology.
> *– Richard Gross & Rob McIlveen*

With the identity-achievement status, the client will have managed to ride the crisis in hand and to emerge from the storm personally stronger and better equipped. This client will have adapted well and will exhibit a strong coping-strategy for handling life. Often the client with an identity-achievement status will have found a means of coming to terms with trauma or crisis and will display a degree of success in terms of his/her social roles and values. This client will also have the ability to keep an open mind in terms of decision-making and this will, naturally, lead to healthy development. The client who has achieved a true and sound identity will find that his/her inner strength will be a great asset in addressing any trauma, distress or conflict and in pulling himself/herself through the therapeutic process.

Client Profiling

The analytical hypnotherapy practitioner may wish to ponder the following points when formulating a profile for the client.

- In what ways has the client's childhood development affected his/her current existence?
- Does the client exhibit any signs of being fixated in childhood?
- Does the client display any obvious oral traits or anal traits in his/her character?
- Does the client appear to be overly attached to or overprotective of his/her parents?
- In what ways does the client identify with parental doctrines or dictates?
- In what ways does the client exhibit childish characteristics?
- Does the client treat the practitioner with an undue degree of deference?
- Does the client appear to fear the presence of the therapist?
- Does the client appear in awe of the therapist's supposed wisdom?
- Does the client appear to be unable to stand on his/her own two feet unaided?
- Did the client suffer from being tormented or bullied at school?
- Did the client experience difficulties during his/her teenage years?
- Did the client find difficulty in adjusting to the adult world after leaving full-time education?
- Has the client made a successful transition into the working environment after leaving full-time education?
- Does the client consider himself/herself to be a success or a failure in life?
- Has the client managed to form fruitful and rewarding relationships in adulthood?
- Has the client been successful in raising a family and taking pleasure in this quest as a form of self-fulfilment?
- Has the client gained a degree of independence and autonomy?
- Has the client carved out a successful identity for himself/ herself?

Chapter 17

The Case for Therapy

The greater the difficulty, the more glory in surmounting it.
Skilful pilots gain their reputation from storms and tempests.

– *Epicurus*

What Does Therapy Achieve?

Counsellors may have different goals with different clients, for instance
assisting them to heal past emotional deprivations, manage current
problems, handle transitions, make decisions, manage crises, and
develop specific life skills. Sometimes goals for counselling are divided
between remedial goals and growth or development goals. The dividing
line between remedying weaknesses and developing strengths is unclear.
– *Richard Nelson-Jones*

Therapy can achieve change in the client's existence and psychological make-up. This change for the client may be a relief from
presenting symptoms, a relinquishment of destructive behavioural
patterns and/or a freedom from intolerable life circumstances. The
client, in tackling his/her problems, will be undertaking a journey
towards beneficial self-betterment. It will not be at all unusual for
the client to discover, moreover, that, after one step along the road,
his/her achievement will then highlight other unresolved issues
that may also require urgent attention. The client's therapeutic
voyage of self-discovery, therefore, could be regarded as a virtu-
ally-endless crusade, although not all of this journey will be, or
should be, undertaken in the practitioner's consulting room (see
Chapter 1, Volume 2 – "The Hypnoanalytic Approach").

> People go to therapists for good reasons. They are in pain, they are
> unhappy, they feel some lack in their lives. When people seek out a
> therapist one of the things they go for is to relieve the burden of their
> own memories. They may never have talked about these memories in
> any depth with another person. Tragic things have often happened to
> them, especially in childhood, which other people deny, especially those
> who caused them to happen. When we read almost any modern
> autobiography, we see that what was most painful was living in a reality
> that others did not see or would not acknowledge or did not care about.
> – *Jeffrey Masson*

An appreciation of the benefits of therapeutic intervention will
help to clarify in the therapist's mind the reasons why the client
might wish to undertake the perhaps gruelling and arduous
process of investigative psychotherapy. Both the practitioner and
the client can regard the hypnoanalytic journey as one that can
resolve the client's presenting problems by enabling him/her to
understand the way in which the past has affected his/her present
and by uncovering those aspects of his/her past experience that
have been buried beneath the layers of pretence and defence.
During this process, the client will be required to apportion blame
where blame is due in order to relieve himself/herself of the burden of guilt, to discharge accompanying emotive build-up that has
hitherto been subdued and to eliminate negative beliefs and attitudes that he/she may have held. The client will, thus, begin to
appreciate the reasons why he/she has been motivated in specific
ways and may come to realise the ways in which he/she has been
compelled to re-enact the past within the present. The client, for
example, may have acted in an irrational or neurotically-tinged
manner in the past and such behaviour may well have formed
his/her presenting symptoms.

Despite the fact that analytical hypnotherapy can undoubtedly be
used for deep-rooted problems, the client may also wish to benefit
from this approach when he/she seeks therapy for even minor ailments. The client who will avoid taking a bus to work or who will
shun a disgruntled person in the office can be treated just as effectively as the client who suffers from a multitude of presenting
symptoms because of a lifetime of unparalleled disaster. The practitioner can, therefore, regard the investigative analytic approach
as having an empowering outcome for the client when he/she can
begin to divest himself/herself of unpleasant symptoms and can
discard unwanted habits, addictions or compulsions. The client

can also seek to relinquish unfavourable coping-strategies and to eliminate any self-destructive or self-punishing mechanisms that may unconsciously be at work within his/her mind. The therapeutic process should also enable the client to raise his/her self-esteem and self-worth, to boost genuine self-confidence, to enhance his/her self-image and to utilise his/her positive attributes.

Following a period of analytic investigation, the client may also seek to form mutually-rewarding relationships and to discard relationships that are abusive, destructive, unworkable or fruitless. The client may also be freed to make his/her own decisions and choices from a vantage point of self-security. This will mean that the client can be liberated from undue self-imposed pressures, influences and persuasions that are not in his/her own interests. The client should, consequently, start to grow and to develop in ways that can assist his/her own maturation process and can create a path in life that he/she will be genuinely happy to follow. Therapy does not, of course, make the past go away or fade into oblivion, but it can help to take the heat out of the situation and nullify the emotive component of the client's past experiences that have hitherto caused distress and conflict.

> Resolving suffering means no longer being unconsciously compelled to follow, "love", or serve; not having to despair, hate, rage, or suffer. It means an end to tantrums and mournful feelings, resignation, and obedience. It means no longer being driven by fear or exhaustion. It means being able to freely, consciously, and resolutely shape our own lives and allow ourselves to love what is genuinely worthy of love.
> *– Konrad Stettbacher*

During the process of hypnoanalysis, the client may undergo a number of stages when dealing with unconscious conflict, distress or psychological disturbance. Most of these elements, of course, can usually be blended seamlessly and well-defined stages may not always be abundantly clear, either to the client or to the practitioner, because the change should take place at an unconscious level. Analytical hypnotherapy can allow the client, initially, to examine his/her perceptions and to discharge his/her emotive responses to past experiences. Once the client has confronted the workings of his/her own mind, then a degree of intellectual understanding can be applied in order to consign painful matter to insignificance. The final stages of therapy can then concentrate on allowing the client to assert his/her human rights in an unhampered fashion in order to enable him/her to be reintegrated into society with his/her new-found psyche. Let us now consider in detail the elements and stages of analytical hypnotherapy as separate entities, that, of course, combine to make a composite and holographic therapeutic experience.

> The four steps are based on our inborn, primal ability to establish relationships to ourselves and the world around us. The order of the four steps corresponds to the building blocks of our functions as they determine our interactive ability.
> – *Konrad Stettbacher*

Taking the First Step

> If you work long enough and hard enough to understand yourself, you will come to discover that this vast part of your mind, of which you now have little awareness, contains riches beyond imagination.
> – *Scott Peck*

The client's decision to initiate the recovery process and to face up to the distresses of his/her past will take an enormous amount of personal courage. To see the project through to a satisfactory conclusion will take even more courage, dedication and resilience on the part of the client. The decision to heal therapeutically will be the client's initiation stage, in which he/she will need to acknowledge, at some level, that he/she requires help and must take active steps in order to secure it. The practitioner will, of course, see some clients who are beginning the journey and others who are partway towards coming to terms with the past. It can be said that, in fact, the journey never really ends but that the decision to commence will often be an intrepid time for the client and may well have been preceded by a period of adamant opposition and disbelief. Often the client will arrive at the therapist's door because he/she cannot cope any longer with the interminable pressure of his/her presenting symptoms and because current circumstances have become intolerable.

Recovery unfolds in three stages. The central task of the first stage is the
establishment of safety. The central task of the second stage is
remembrance and mourning. The central task of the third stage is
reconnection with ordinary life. Like any abstract concept, these stages
of recovery are a convenient fiction, not to be taken too literally. They are
an attempt to impose simplicity and order upon a process that is
inherently turbulent and complex.
– *Judith Lewis Herman*

The practitioner may wish to ask himself/herself a number of
questions in order to tease out the reasons why the client has been
prompted to seek therapeutic assistance at this time along life's
path. Does the client find his/her symptoms to be so debilitating
that his/her existence can be tolerated no longer? Has the client
undergone a major life crisis such as getting a new job or getting
married or having a child? Has the client entered a critical life-
phase such as adolescence or midlife? Has the client suffered the
bereavement of a close relative? Has the client recently undergone
a relationship breakdown or separation? Has the client had to face
a devastating trauma such as being raped, mugged or similarly
violated? Has the client heard news of an intense tragedy, such as
the violation of a child or the abduction of a hostage, which might
have triggered his/her own distress? Any number of tragic or disturbing life-events can often jockey the client into acknowledging
that his/her inner pain will not cease unless action is taken. The
client, alternatively, may have settled into a happy life – perhaps
forming a rewarding relationship and contemplating starting a
family – and now he/she feels sufficiently well supported to be
able to muster the strength to tackle his/her personal problems.
Triggers may, therefore, take many forms and the list above will, of
course, not be exhaustive. It will be the practitioner's task to make
such enquiries into the client's reasons for seeking therapy in
order to appreciate the backdrop against which he/she stands
before any investigative work can ensue.

The decision to undertake therapy should not, of course, be one
taken lightly by the client. The potential client's decision may
come after much forethought – perhaps even years of delay – and
may fill him/her with a degree of terror as he/she steps over the
therapist's threshold. If the practitioner is at all unsure about
whether the client is really ready for the therapeutic engagement,
then perhaps a degree of dissuasion may be in order. Once he/she

is on the roundabout, of course, it will be disheartening and, perhaps, unwise for the client to dismount while it is in full swing.

> The decision to heal from child sexual abuse is a powerful, life-affirming choice. It is a commitment every survivor deserves to make. Although you may have already experienced some healing in your life – through the nurturing of a foster family, the caring of an intimate partner, or the satisfaction of work you love – *deciding* to heal, making your own growth and recovery a priority, sets in motion a healing force that will bring to your life a richness and depth you never dreamed possible.
> – *Ellen Bass & Laura Davis*

We shall now consider a client's account of her thought processes prior to seeking therapeutic assistance. This client was an intelligent and successful female who had suffered from depression for many years without any notion of why her symptoms had manifested.

Client narrative – considering therapy ...

As an adult I began to search for logical reasons for my distress. I engaged in a massive let's-think-hard-about-my-problems campaign that served only to intellectualise the problem rather than allowing my mind to do the necessary work. As a result I considered that I had undertaken by own psychoanalysis, with a little help from some intimate friends, because I had thought about every aspect of my life in detail and had come to the conclusion that my parents were incompetent and so I gave them the sack. This act of self-dissection was, in fact, having precisely the opposite effect because it prevented me from facing up to the very problems I was experiencing. I was in denial-and-justification mode.

I would also hook the reasons for my emotional and physical disorders on to whatever object or situation presented itself most apparently at the time. Often I was able to blame the current man in my life or lack of one. Sometimes it was lack of work or lack of job satisfaction or difficulties with work superiors. Once or twice, I felt that financial problems were the cause of my troubles. I sought to eliminate each obstacle as it reared its ugly head. Finally, I hooked my state of distress on to the fact that my central heating had packed up and that I didn't, at that time, have enough money to get it fixed. My dilemma occurred once the central heating boiler had been replaced. What the hell was I going to hook it on to now? In utter despair, my search for a therapist then commenced in earnest!

Establishing Safety

Trauma robs the victim of a sense of power and control; the guiding principle of recovery is to restore power and control to the survivor. The first task of recovery is to establish the survivor's safety. This task takes precedence over all others, for no other therapeutic work can possibly succeed if safety has not been adequately secured. No other therapeutic work should even be attempted until a reasonable degree of safety has been achieved.
– *Judith Lewis Herman*

During the initial phases of therapy, the client will be endeavouring to establish a degree of safety for himself/herself. During these crucial introductory sessions, the therapist's role will be to reassure the client that he/she can be helped if he/she wishes to take the plunge, that the therapeutic context can be a safe haven and that therapy can afford him/her a place for total freedom of expression. The client, in a stress-free atmosphere, can, thus, be himself/herself and can learn to recognise that true self. The therapist's caring, nonjudgmental and nonauthoritarian presence can help to imbue this feeling of self-freedom in the client. The client, in a conducive climate, can then be given licence to talk uninterruptedly, to discharge emotive impulses appropriately and to express opinions honestly. This will be the only route by which therapeutic progress can be made and all attempts on the client's part to sabotage therapy can be overcome. Once the client has found a sanctuary in which to retreat and to recuperate, he/she will then eventually arrive at a position from which he/she can venture out and integrate with the rest of society when the time is right.

During this feet-finding phase, the client can gradually learn that he/she can take control of his/her current life. The client can discover that he/she has the strength and the power, that he/she can, in fact, recover and that the key to the whole process will be in his/her own hands. The practitioner will merely be a facilitator, observing and nudging forward this process of the client's self-empowerment.

When the patient has been subjected to prolonged abuse in childhood,
the task of diagnosis is not nearly so straightforward. Disguised
presentations are common in complex post-traumatic stress disorder.
Initially the patient may complain only of physical symptoms, or of
chronic insomnia or anxiety, or of intractable depression, or of
problematic relationships. Explicit questioning is often required to
determine whether the patient is presently living in fear of someone's
violence or has lived in fear at some time in the past.
– *Judith Lewis Herman*

Perceptual Processes

In the first step, you will be asked to express your current state of mind,
to express in words "what is" right now. You will also be encouraged to
give voice to your most urgent perception, the problem that is currently
in your mind.
– *Konrad Stettbacher*

The practitioner may need to make a preliminary diagnostic evaluation of the client's state in order to appreciate the depth and
severity of the psychic distress to which he/she may have been
exposed. Such investigative questioning will not only reveal the
nature of the client's problem to the therapist but, more impor-
tantly, will allow the client himself/herself to identify the nature
and scope of his/her condition and its implications. The client can,
by this means, learn to appreciate that he/she can take control of
his/her own life and environment. The practitioner may, of
course, wish to take a complete background case history of the
client during the initial sessions (see Chapter 4, Volume 2 –
"Therapeutic Enquiry"). It should be remembered, however, that
preliminary case notes are only the beginning and only a means of
awakening in the client relevant thought processes that can lead
him/her to facilitate his/her own recovery.

The client should initially be invited to give a summary of his/her
reasons for seeking therapy. The client can be asked to outline
symptoms, behaviours and motivations from his/her current
viewpoint. The client should be encouraged to provide as much
information as possible about his/her condition and current thinking with regard to his/her symptoms. The client's perception of
reality will, therefore, give rise to emotive expressions, that he/she
can evaluate and grade according to their impact. This evaluation

will constitute the client's unique understanding of his/her experiences both emotionally and intellectually. The client may then be able to gain insight into the way in which he/she has formulated his/her unconscious needs. The client's neurotically-driven needs, of course, will generate his/her unwanted symptoms, dictate his/her irrational behaviours and control his/her motivations.

> In the first step, I try to describe my general condition. What am I
> sensing, noticing, seeing, hearing, smelling? What bothers me, what is
> on my mind ...?
> – *Konrad Stettbacher*

The client might also be asked to express his/her thoughts on what he/she perceives within his/her mind. This may involve describing a scene or commenting on a situation as viewed through the client's eyes. This may well be an intellectual process for the client who may, at this stage, be at a loss to understand his/her symptoms and feel powerless to control his/her behaviour. Allowing the client an opportunity to voice his/her opinions will set current symptoms in the context of his/her present life. The client may, for example, describe the effects of his/her distresses or anxieties in terms of how much his/her life has been disrupted by such disturbing factors. The client may report the way in which an overpowering social phobia or a drugs-problem has forced him/her to give up work or to withdraw from society (see Chapter 7, Volume 2 – "Fear and Anxiety Disorders"). The client with an obsession or a compulsion may describe the ways in which his/her quality of life has been impaired or his/her freedom of movement restricted (see Chapter 8, Volume 2 – "Guilt and Shame Disorders"). The client may, similarly, relate ways in which the loss of a close relative may have left him/her feeling bereft and empty (see Chapter 9, Volume 2 – "Sorrow and Grief Disorders"). The client with anger-based symptoms may also confess to violent outbursts or to criminal activities (see Chapter 10, Volume 2 – "Anger and Rage Disorders").

> Sensations occur in infinite variety. This is one of the reasons that simple
> awareness is so important. Receptivity will help you notice the nuances
> in your sensations much more easily. In the land of physiology, subtle
> sensations and rhythms are just as important as blatantly obvious ones.
> – *Peter Levine*

The therapist's role will be to listen passively and with neutrality to the client and to give him/her the opportunity to fully express his/her thoughts in an atmosphere of freedom and honesty. This may be the heaven-sent opportunity that the client has long been waiting for whereby he/she can start to unload the first consignment of his/her emotional baggage and, therefore, no impediment should be put in this path. At this stage, the client may, however, need to be assured that the therapist will be there for him/her unreservedly and will not judge, criticise, blame, chastise, censure, denounce, reproach or reject him/her. The therapist must be prepared to accept at face value everything that the client divulges without any adverse reaction. The client should be made abundantly aware of this fact as an open-door policy, that will run throughout the entire course of his/her therapeutic treatment. The therapeutic environment may well be the first opportunity the client has had in life to be able to voice his/her inner thoughts honestly to an outsider who is working in his/her own interests. The concept of the safe sanctuary will, thus, be further consolidated and fostered in the client's mind.

> Location of the critical experiences is therefore crucial to therapy, even though it is only a part of the analytical hypnotherapist's task.
> – *Edgar Barnett*

The following passage will provide a means of preparing the client for therapy by highlighting the reasons for his/her symptoms and opening the door to the instrument that can resolve them. The practitioner may wish to utilise this passage or a paraphrase of it once the preliminary enquiries have been dispensed with and the client has had ample opportunity to state his/her case in detail.

You are what you think ...

All your thoughts, impressions and ideas bubble up from that part within you that controls you absolutely – your unconscious mind. Your unconscious mind stores in your memory the important occurrences in your life. That is, the events, the emotive reactions you have had to these events and the physical result of your own reactions. If you burn your finger on a candle flame, you will remember the event, recall the physical pain and recollect the emotional anguish. Your unconscious mind will remember these things in this three-fold way so that it can influence the way in which you act in future. This information will be retained in order to help you to remember not to make the same mistake again. After all, it is a good idea to avoid getting burned alive! Your mind is, thus, endeavouring to ensure your survival.

The vital point to remember here is that the conscious mind is controlled and influenced by your unconscious mind, and herein lies the danger. A rational decision can be utterly thwarted by our emotional needs, our secret desires, our instinctive behaviour and our deep-seated motivations. In most cases, a minor blip on the horizon will cause no great distress or upset that cannot be ironed out. But for major events – or rather those events that you perceive as major – your unconscious mind can be affected for years after the event until the dilemma is resolved.

Let us take an example of the way in which a relatively minor event can have devastating repercussions. Just imagine that when you were a little child your bad-tempered primary-school teacher decided to put you in the corner and to call you a dunce for some trifling misdemeanour – like forgetting your pencil-case or drawing on the classroom wall. You may retain a picture in your mind of cringing in the corner or of surreptitiously looking over your shoulder and watching the rest of the class staring at you. You may still hear the teacher's voice loudly balling you out in front of your classmates. You may still experience that shuddering feeling, you may feel your legs wobbling with terror or you could feel your cheeks going red with embarrassment as you recall the event. You may also feel the acute shame at being made to look so small or to feel so guilty. You may feel the fear at the recollection of that nasty overpowering teacher. You may feel the injustice at having been singled out. You may remember desperately trying to choke back your tears. You may also feel angry with the teacher, who had the audacity to perpetrate such wrongs against you and then to compound them by chastising you publicly. Does any of this strike a chord with you?

Now just imagine the subsequent effects that such an event could have had on you as a small child. This episode may have been indelibly imprinted on your mind when you were innocent, naïve and impressionable, and the repercussions will echo till this day. You grow up fearing all authority figures. You grow up feeling embarrassed when others are looking at you. You grow up with a guilty feeling that you have somehow committed something terribly wrong. You castigate yourself for having sinned or despise yourself for having been found out. You feel jealous when other people do not get found out. You may also hate yourself for not having had enough courage to speak up against the injustice. You may resent the wrath of the teacher or the jeering comments of your classmates. You may learn that initiative does not pay. You may learn that others are more fortunate than you are and so you resign yourself to a life of hard luck. You may conclude that all teachers are biased and unfair and misuse their power. You may learn that it is useless ever to trust people because they can betray you when you least expect it. When you cannot trust anyone, you cannot commit yourself to any relationships. You, therefore, avoid making friends and have a catalogue of unsuccessful intimate relationships that cause you a great deal of pain and anguish. Even when you did, perhaps, try to tell someone of your plight – such as a parent or a carer – you might have met with remarks such as "Don't be so sensitive!" or "Stop worrying about it!" or "The teacher had to teach you a lesson!" These futile statements will further reinforce the fact that you cannot trust anyone ever – least of all your so-called confidants – and so you determine to keep all secrets to yourself for the rest of your life! Even though this incident may have happened long ago and you've tried not to think about it since, this single event will have affected your emotions, coloured your thinking, influenced your beliefs, constrained your actions and fuelled your reactions from that day to this. This one momentary episode – that occurred because you were naïve and vulnerable – may have dictated the whole pattern of your life, that you may now regard as a disaster. Is there something similar in your life?

Furthermore, because your past is part of your present, your mind will clumsily attempt to resolve any conflict, distress or trauma that has been stored in your memory bank. You may, perhaps, tend to dwell on those things that you would rather forget and that sometimes you do manage to disregard temporarily. Even if you do manage to bury a recollection because it is unpleasant, your mind may still go on thinking about it in dreams or in daydreams or in fantasies. These unpleasant thoughts are your mind's way of drawing your attention to the fact that something is wrong within you. This is the only way it knows of doing it. It is a nonsensical and a primitive way of trying to resolve your unconscious conflicts. It is primitive because we are primitive and instinctive beings – animals with limited intellect. Sometimes, when we give way to our fears and imaginings, we think unwanted thoughts and then we find that some unwanted things happen to us. And when we become convinced that unwanted things will always happen to us, we expect them to happen and maybe they will. Just like the self-fulfilling prophecy – if you expect it to happen, it will. Or you may get a headache or catch a cold or come out in a rash or burst into tears in the supermarket for no apparent reason. The mind will, thus, be trying to tell you something. And, if you do not listen, your mind will get desperate and may have to take some mighty drastic steps. But you can reverse the process and make things work in your favour! The good news is that you can use that powerful unconscious mind of yours to unscramble your own problems! You can use that very same mind – the one that screwed you up in the first place – to unscramble yourself.

Emotive and Confessional Processes

> In the second step, I give voice to my sensations and feelings, how they
> affect me and what they mean. What this means to me, does to me,
> causes to happen in me, leaves behind, means ...
> – *Konrad Stettbacher*

The client should, of course, be encouraged to explore his/her emotive reactions to thoughts and physical sensations that may accompany his/her perceptions. At this outpouring stage, the client may not only express a myriad emotive reactions but also may state his/her true opinions about events. Often emotive exploration will provide the key to the client's true feelings and will identify the root of his/her distress. This stage will further enhance the client's view of what he/she is currently experiencing, recalling or reliving during therapeutic investigation.

> In the second stage of recovery, the survivor tells the story of the trauma.
> She tells it completely, in depth and in detail. This work of
> reconstruction actually transforms the traumatic memory, so that it can
> be integrated into the survivor's life story.
> – *Judith Lewis Herman*

The hypnoanalytic process will be a means of empowering the client to unveil suppressed thoughts and, in doing so, to discharge cathartically the accompanying emotive impulses. This can usually be achieved by asking the client to employ a range of techniques – such as a free association of thoughts and ideas – that can lead him/her to the originating cause of his/her dilemma (see Chapter 2, Volume 2 – "Therapeutic Investigation"). Further insight can then be achieved by exploring the client's dreams (see Chapter 14 – "Dreams and Symbolic Imagery"), navigating any detectable resistance to therapy (see Chapter 12 – "Resistance") and analysing the transference and countertransference phenomena that may develop within the relationship between therapist and client (see Chapter 13 – "Transference and Countertransference").

The investigative phase of therapy will be the time when the client should allow his/her thoughts, impressions and emotive expression to flow uninterruptedly. This will be the story-telling phase, when the client should be encouraged to relieve himself/herself of the oppressive burden of his/her mind's turmoil. The client will, hence, uncover the details of his/her experiences and dredge up from the depths of his/her unconscious mind those incidents that have had the greatest impact on him/her. The client's critical experiences will be at the very nub of his/her psychological distress and the investigative process will seek to identify these key junctures. From the core of the client's conflict all other distressing experiences will often pivot. It will be for this reason that the hypnoanalytic practitioner will often speak of the root cause of the client's psychic distress and will liken other events – however unpleasant – to the branches and leaves of that same tree.

> Where uncovering has been possible, an inappropriate emotional response has always been discovered to be due to an unresolved Parent/Child conflict. In such a conflict, the expression of the individual's natural response has been repressed because of unconscious guilt due to fear of parental disapproval.
> – *Edgar Barnett*

The basis for the effectiveness of hypnoanalytic therapy will be underpinned by the premise that emotive reactions are the mind's controlling force in the interests of the human organism's survival. The infant will express himself/herself emotionally in order to ensure that his/her survival needs are met. A baby will express hurt or discomfort usually in the form of yelling or screaming in order to attract the attention of his/her primary carers with a view to securing for himself/herself nourishment, warmth, shelter and protection from apparent danger or impending harm. Any lack of protection of the child by his/her primary carers in childhood will result in painful disorders, that will take their toll in adulthood and will manifest as the client's presenting symptoms.

Emotive outbursts are likely to be the client's passport to unburdening his/her soul and the therapist's role will be to guide him/her gently through this delicate process of confession and abreaction (see Chapter 1, Volume 2 – "The Hypnoanalytic Approach"). This element will constitute the abreactive aspect of therapy whereby the client can discharge his/her subsurface, pent-up emotive expression. The client should be able to feel and to spontaneously express pain, sadness, loneliness, despair, grief, regret, remorse, anger, resentment, bitterness, frustration, indignation, fury, impatience, rage, fear, anxiety, tension, agitation and, of course, guilt and shame. In so doing, the client will be uncovering those emotive reactions that were unconsciously buried, disregarded or brushed aside at the time of his/her most critical experiences. The client may, for example, have deemed it inappropriate to express such feelings fully at the time of the seeding events and, consequently, such distress will have become imprisoned within his/her innermost mind.

During the confessional phase, the client may begin to retrieve memories of the past that are relevant to the present and represent those times when the greatest traumas and conflicts were set up in his/her unconscious mind (see Chapter 10 – "Memory"). For the client with only a vague memory of the past, the key incidents that have caused him/her the utmost distress may now begin to emerge. Perhaps the client will tell the therapist of events that have remained locked in his/her soul for decades. Often the therapist will be the only person in the world to whom the client has ever admitted the unexpurgated truth. The client's initial recollections will often be those that have had the most impact on his/her psyche and have formulated his/her personality-defects ever since.

> Beginning to deal with memories and suppressed feelings can throw
> your life into utter turmoil.
> – *Ellen Bass & Laura Davis*

When the client begins to explore his/her past emotional life, his/her current existence may be turned upside down in any number of ways, that can indicate that the unconscious mind has grasped the idea that the past can be dumped. Once agitated, it will be as if the client's mind can go into overdrive or, even, into a bemused state of shock when it starts to process traumatic memories from the past. The client's old tapes may now begin to play, intrusive and obsessive thoughts may dominate and frequent abreactions may occur both within and outside the consulting room. Breaking down the doors of denial and gnawing at the foundation of defences can be a mighty earthquake right off the Richter scale for the client (see Chapter 11 – "Defensive Strategies"). It may feel as if the very essence of the client's whole existence is being shattered in one fell blow. This may also be the time when the client may feel at his/her most vulnerable. The client may consider, however, that he/she is not yet ready to tackle his/her problems at this juncture and that he/she would rather live with unpleasant symptoms than face this brand of hell. The client's symptoms may, in fact, appear to worsen as a consequence of this dramatic healing-crisis and he/she may feel desperately in need of help from many quarters. The client, however, who can stay this part of the course will often have deep within his/her breast that inner knowing that tells him/her faithfully that success is in sight.

> Many survivors suppress all memories of what happened to them as
> children. Those who do not forget the actual incidents often forget how
> it felt at the time. Remembering is the process of getting back both
> memory and feeling.
> – *Ellen Bass & Laura Davis*

The clinician should not, in any way, underestimate the impact that self-investigation may have on the client. For survivors of childhood abuse, for example, who may be retrieving previously-repressed memories, the surfacing of such recollections may be a mind-blowing experience (see Chapter 15, Volume 2 – "The Effects of Childhood Abuse"). The cracking of the shell of repression will, on the one hand, relieve the client of an interminable burden but also, on the other, may shake him/her to the core and plunge him/her into a state of confusion. The client may also recover aspects of the past in daily life as a flashback, as a dream-sequence or as a spontaneous regression (see Chapter 14 – "Dreams and Symbolic Imagery"). All such memory-recovery vehicles will, of course, be traumatic in nature for the client, who may experience violent psychological and physiological abreactions on virtually an on-going basis. Once recollections start to open up the client's unconscious mind, the process will not, of course, be instant. The client may well find himself/herself recollecting over a period of months or even years. For each wave of recollection, the client will need to undergo the whole therapeutic spectrum in order to acknowledge, to release and to resolve the underlying conflict.

The confessional phase will usually entail a detailed reconstruction of the client's past life – scrutinising both his/her past and present. The present can supply a clue to the client's symptoms and manifestations of disturbance while the past can provide a key to the root causes of his/her distress. The client will need to view his/her life in the context of unpleasant incidents in terms of the effect that the distress has had on his/her psychological and social development. The client will need to appreciate the background to his/her childhood and family environment and what effect these influences have had on his/her vulnerability. Once the distress and the backdrop to its occurrence have been shown the light of day, however, the client can then start to appreciate the aftereffects and to resolve the personal consequences. During this important outpouring phase, the client will be delving into the essence of his/her most distressing psychological experiences and his/her innermost being. Perhaps the client will feel regret at having had to suffer in the past. Perhaps the client will feel resentment and indignation at having been deceived or ill-treated by others. Perhaps the client will feel terror at the thought of having been subjected to neglect, violence or abuse. Perhaps the client will feel that he/she has sinned and can never obliterate the shame. Perhaps the client will feel unclean and contaminated by any violation of his/her person or psyche. The practitioner should, of course, endeavour to understand the way in which the client's perceptions of events and experiences will have dictated the nature of his/her underlying emotive conflict. The client may feel terror if he/she perceives an abusive situation as fearful or if he/she was powerless to prevent its occurrence. The client may feel guilty if he/she perceives that he/she has participated willingly in shameful deeds. The client may feel anger if he/she perceives that a parental figure took advantage of his/her childish innocence or exploited him/her in any way. The unique nature of the client's distress, therefore, should be appreciated by the therapist.

> In the second step, try to spontaneously describe the feelings and sensations arising from these perceptions. Describe their effects and what this means for you.
> – *Konrad Stettbacher*

The practitioner will need to ensure that he/she works at a pace that will be suitable for the client. The client may be able to proceed quickly enough to begin feeling the benefits of his/her work but slowly enough for the experience not to be overwhelming or oppressive. The most comfortable pace can be set only by the client. If the therapist can be sensitive to the needs of the client and can gain authentic rapport with him/her, then it should simply be a matter of skilfully following his/her lead. If the client can comfortably dictate his/her own pace throughout therapy, then he/she will have a good chance of bringing it to a satisfactory conclusion. The therapist should not, of course, impose a specific rate of working on the client, as this would constitute a misuse of the therapist's privileged position.

> Patients at times insist upon plunging into graphic, detailed descriptions of their traumatic experiences, in the belief that simply pouring out the story will solve all their problems. At the root of this belief is the fantasy of a violent cathartic cure which will get rid of the trauma once and for all.
> – *Judith Lewis Herman*

The suggested passage below can introduce the client to the fact that it is permissible to express his/her emotive reactions in therapy. This passage has been designed in order to allow the client to contact his/her emotional nature and to prepare him/her for abreactive expression as part of the healing process.

Our emotional baggage ...

Let's take a holiday! You've just won an all-expenses-paid trip to your favourite place on earth – the one that you can paint in your imagination. But before you go you will need to pack a suitcase with all you will require. You will need to pack your new clothes, your swimwear, your sports equipment, your favourite toiletries and perfumes, that relaxing novel, those cuddly toys and, perhaps, your bucket and spade. But, because this is a very special suitcase, you will also need to pack your emotions. You will need love and joy and happiness. These you can bring back with you after your refreshing and exiting holiday. But you may also need to pack some emotions that you can leave on the beach or dump at the bottom of the sea or leave at the top of a mountain or simply release into the atmosphere, where they can be dispelled. These are your negative emotions of fear, guilt, anger and sadness. Notice which holds the most power for you. Put each in a special place at the bottom of your suitcase where they cannot contaminate all those other beautiful and new things you have packed.

When you arrive at your destination, the first thing you will need to do is to unpack. Make yourself at home in your luxury hotel suite. Fill your new life with love, joy and happiness. But, because you have no use now for those negative emotions, why not get rid of them? Take them out of your suitcase. Go and bury them down on the beach. Go and dump them in the deep, blue sea. Go and scatter them on the hillside. Toss them out into the atmosphere so that they can just simply float away on a cloud. Say goodbye to them for ever. Watch them dissipate into the atmosphere. Place them out of your reach. Feel that good feeling when you know they have disappeared. Gone from your life for ever. Feel a new spring in your step at having taken this great leap forward.

Now get on and enjoy your holiday. Have the time of your life. Observe your surroundings. Behold nature as nature intended it to be. Watch the day break and the sun set. Listen to the birds cry. Feel the warmth of the sun and the gentle cooling breeze on your skin. Feel the texture of the sand, the sea and the earth beneath your feet. Let your voice echo into the mountains and roll down the hillside. Enjoy your holiday as you have never enjoyed anything before in your life. What more could you want? You are now free! Free to live your life as you have never lived it before. Free of all that emotional junk. Free to get on with the business of living and loving yourself.

It may sometimes be necessary for you to revisit the past because an understanding of your past experience will empower you to cope with the present. You may, therefore, need to revisit some unhappy or painful events and to relive their accompanying negative emotions in order to come to terms with what has happened to you. The revisitation of negative emotions can, of course, be unpleasant because it can mean that you might relive those aspects of your life that you would sooner forget. Because we are inherently pleasure-seekers and pain-avoiders, our natural instinct will be to run away from our own negative emotional reactions. You may, therefore, be naturally disposed to deny or to bury or to suppress your negative feelings simply because they are unpleasant. If you feel you wish to avoid the past, however, this, in itself, will be an indication that you may have some unresolved emotional conflict with which to deal.

Furthermore, your childhood experience will often, in itself, prevent you from dealing with your own problems. If you have learned that you are valueless, you will tend not to want to devote time to yourself. If you have learned that you are a victim of misfortune, you will tend to reject success. If you have learned that you can be betrayed, you will tend to be sceptical about the value of working on yourself. The act of acknowledging and facing up to such negative emotions will be part of your healing process. After all, once the dynamite has exploded, it loses its potency. Negative emotions cannot be resolved by comfort-zone tactics because this merely serves to suppress still further that which needs to be released. You can console and encourage yourself, however, with the fact that, if you have actually survived an unpleasant incident, then you can be assured of having the necessary resources merely to revisit it in your mind. If you find this process difficult, or even impossible, however, then do not beat your bosom or proclaim yourself as a failure. Now is the time to accept that your desire for self-improvement has been the catalyst that has set you on this essential path of self-discovery.

Insightful and Reintegrative Processes

> In the third step, I critically examine the situation, the scene, and those
> involved (including myself). I demand an explanation (explain myself)
> and justification. I ask why am I doing this? What for? What good does
> it do? Where does it come from? Why? What have I done wrong? Not
> understood? Forgotten to do? Made a mess of?
> – *Konrad Stettbacher*

The client may now be invited to proffer an interpretation of
his/her thoughts, perceptions, emotive reactions or physical sensations. The client should be able to realise the way in which past
events have formed or distorted his/her personal self-image and
created negative beliefs about self-efficacy. The client, at this stage,
may reveal feelings of self-reproach, self-condemnation, vulnerability, helplessness, regret or remorse about the past. Here the
practitioner may wish to intervene in order to encourage the client
to take a realistic view of his/her part in past events and invite
him/her to relieve any self-blame that may remain. It will be
important for the client to appreciate the true picture – and not just
the gloss as painted by others who might not have been working
in his/her best interests. Any manifestations of guilt, shame or
self-blame should be brought to the surface for close scrutiny and
resolution.

> By returning to the critical experiences and reviewing them in the light
> of his present (Adult) wisdom and understanding, the patient is
> persuaded to reassess these experiences and then find the resources with
> which to formulate more effective behavioural responses to the stimuli
> previously responsible for symptoms.
> – *Edgar Barnett*

The client will need to apply some intellectual understanding to
those events in his/her life that have set in train dramatic
responses. The client will need to realise both consciously and
unconsciously that he/she will no longer need to feel fear or
worry because the danger has been averted. The client will no
longer need to feel sad or depressed because he/she felt unloved,
neglected or maltreated in childhood. The client will no longer
need to feel guilty or shameful because he/she can learn to appreciate that his/her actions were not his/her fault and that he/she
was blameless when he/she indulged in spontaneous behaviour.
The client will no longer need to feel resentment or rage because

he/she can now begin to comprehend that he/she has been a victim of his/her own suffering. It will be as if the abreactive release of emotive expression will have been a wholly unconsciously-triggered process but the resolution of the conflict, distress or trauma can be a preconscious process aided by the client's conscious intellect and cognitive processes (see Chapter 9 – "Cognitive Therapy").

> It bears repeating that the survivor is free to examine aspects of her own personality or behaviour that rendered her vulnerable to exploitation only after it has been clearly established that the perpetrator alone is responsible for the crime.
> – *Judith Lewis Herman*

Resolution can occur only when the client has fully comprehended the effect of his/her past experience on his/her whole psychic composition (see Chapter 5, Volume 2 – "Therapeutic Resolution"). The client can then learn to appreciate that his/her symptoms and behaviours have been an inevitable consequence, perhaps, of maltreatment at a tender age and that recovery and healing can now begin. This will be the stage whereby the past can become a part of the client's life-experience but it can take on a new significance so that it can be reintegrated into his/her psyche without causing further distress or traumatic conflict. It will be as if the client can form a new relationship with his/her past and with himself/herself. In this phase of the recovery cycle, the therapist can, therefore, negotiate with the client in order to allow him/her to put the originating cause of his/her distress, trauma or conflict in context. Essentially, the client should be encouraged to realise the profound effect of any maltreatment, neglect or abuse and the way in which he/she was an innocent and helpless victim of the machinations of others and unfavourable circumstances.

The key to the client's psychic reintegration will, of course, be the acquisition of insight, acceptance and unconscious comprehension. An unconscious appreciation of the reasons why the client may have felt fear and why life-events have had such a devastating effect on him/her will help him/her to resolve any fear-based symptoms such as phobic conditions, high-anxiety states or confidence problems (see Chapter 7, Volume 2 – "Fear and Anxiety Disorders"). An unconscious understanding of why the client had a need to feel guilty will help him/her to resolve any manifestations of the guilt-complex (see Chapter 8, Volume 2 – "Guilt and Shame Disorders"). An unconscious acknowledgment of the child's sense of grief, loss and remorse will, similarly, help the client to resolve any depressive disorders or comfort-seeking mechanisms (see Chapter 9, Volume 2 – "Sorrow and Grief Disorders"). An unconscious acceptance of the child's sense of indignation, resentment and fury will help to resolve any anger-related symptoms such as excessive jealousies, violent behaviour or egoistic disorders (see Chapter 10, Volume 2 – "Anger and Rage Disorders"). The client should also come to realise the subsequent knock-on effects of his/her original distress or trauma and the reasons why it has shaped his/her life, attitudes, thinking, relationships, behaviours, motivations and symptoms. In a way, the client will need to appreciate both the effect and its consequences simultaneously in order to bring about lasting psychological relief and to restore psychic homeostasis.

> In the third step, try to unearth the reasons for your problems. Think
> critically about the situation, those involved and yourself.
> – *Konrad Stettbacher*

Rehabilitative Processes

> Having come to terms with the traumatic past, the survivor faces the
> task of creating a future. She has mourned the old self that the trauma
> destroyed; now she must develop a new self. Her relationships have
> been tested and forever changed by the trauma; now she must develop
> new relationships. The old beliefs that gave meaning to her life have
> been challenged; now she must find anew a sustaining faith. These are
> the tasks of the third stage of recovery. In accomplishing this work, the
> survivor reclaims her world.
> – *Judith Lewis Herman*

Once the client has gained the necessary insight from his/her exploration of the past and dissected his/her perception of events, he/she can then act on this new-found knowledge. The client may emerge from the therapeutic encounter with a greater self-understanding but will then have the task of putting this awareness into practice. A better self-image will mean that the client can truly value himself/herself. A greater degree of confidence and self-esteem will afford the client more choices. Often the client will come to appreciate the degree of emotional strength that he/she possesses. This inner strength will have been displayed by the client not only in surviving distressing events in the first place but also in having the courage to address them in therapy. With greater confidence will come the courage to face situations that previously have invoked a fearful reaction in the client. The phobic client, for example, can now risk encountering the source of his/her fears without the danger of an over-the-top reaction or a need for avoidance.

> In the fourth step, I formulate my demands. I don't need this.
> I need that to live.
> – *Konrad Stettbacher*

At the final stage of the therapeutic process, the client should appreciate the way in which his/her personal needs and demands may have been neglected and can now allow the consequences of such neglect to be rectified. Here the client should be encouraged to put his/her distress into context by appreciating what should have happened to him/her in the past in order to ensure his/her healthy self-development. The child should have been loved and protected and, perhaps, because love was not forthcoming, the client became vulnerable to subsequent neglect, misuse or abuse. The client will now, of course, have a right to state his/her need to be loved in an appropriate manner. The client can also learn to appreciate that he/she now has a right to be assertive rather than passive or aggressive. The client can become self-confident and value himself/herself for his/her own true worth. As a child, the client may have been given a low-value rating but now he/she can regard himself/herself in the best possible light and as someone unique and special. The client can now be pampered, spoiled, treasured and even worshipped without that wretched, undeserving feeling. The therapist can assist with this stage of the process by developing the client's self-assertiveness and strengthening his/her self-image. The therapist can also help to curb any tendency the client may have to resort to self-blame or self-denigration. The client should now be free to choose partners and friends who will reflect this new self-worth. The former victim can now ensure that he/she will not become the recipient of other people's demands or the provider of other people's emotional nurturing. The client can now no longer feel obliged to service the needs of others in deference to his/her own. The client can, therefore, become free to choose relationships that will enhance his/her own wellbeing. The client should now give himself/herself a true value and can even applaud his/her own praiseworthy traits.

> In the fourth step, you will articulate, again within the context of the same situation, your needs and your *rightful* claim to that which would have prevented the initial damage and helped you to live.
> – *Konrad Stettbacher*

The client may also undergo a process of letting go of old patterns in relationships, social activities and interaction in society. Any detrimental or abusive relationships can be severed by the client at this stage. Revenge tactics can be dropped as the client's anger dissipates. The client's fear can be replaced by courage and assertiveness. Guilt-ridden behavioural traits can give way to the client's sense of belief in himself/herself. A state of maturity can be attained despite the fact that the client has experienced the loss of nurturing in childhood and in formative years. Remorse and regret, therefore, can also be suitably relinquished by the client. The client may, of course, be faced with greater opportunities when relinquishing old habits or when freeing himself/herself from neurotically-driven patterns of existence. Those old defensive stances can now be abandoned by the client and replaced with natural responses and healthy reactions. The client's own natural weaknesses and failings should, furthermore, be accepted with equanimity. This will be the process of self-discovery whereby the client can find himself/herself – and it may come as a pleasant surprise!

The client can, in general, begin to gain that feeling of being free of the ties that have hitherto bound him/her to the past. The fledgling can concentrate on the present without being dominated by the horrors of the past. This will be the time for the client to grow and to realise his/her true potential in the outside world. It will be as if the whole package of emotional junk can be dumped slowly but surely and, in dumping it, the client will find his/her true inner self and have the courage to express it without let or hindrance. Perhaps finding a new dimension to life will be the client's mission. A new spiritual dimension may be appropriate for him/her or greater strides can be taken in his/her career. Often some degree of self-advancement will accompany the client's final stages of therapy.

In one sense, of course, the self-enlightenment journey will be an endless one for the client. The client cannot obliterate the past. The client cannot say that the past never occurred. The client cannot deny what effects the past has had on his/her personality make-up and psychic development. The client can, however, come to terms with the past and learn to deal with any subsequent minor blips that may appear on the horizon from time to time. Taking therapy will provide the client with an ability to deal with any future aspects of the journey in the most appropriate manner possible and to take corrective action when necessary. In the final stages of the therapeutic process, therefore, the client will be in a much more advantageous position to decide how to act – even to the extent of seeking further therapy with another practitioner if necessary.

After therapeutic work, the client can make the necessary adjustments to his/her life with his/her new mindset. This will be the time when the client can relinquish secondary gains and replace neurotically-driven needs with more appropriate behaviour patterns. Often this will be a time of great change when the client will be moving away from the therapist and the safety and confines of the therapeutic environment. Sometimes the client will begin to build an entirely new life. A change of job or career may not be an uncommon occurrence for the client who has recently graduated from therapy. Unsatisfactory or destructive relationships will often be terminated and a more assertive stance can be taken in the client's dealings with others. The therapist can assist the client in this endeavour by encouraging him/her to be more assertive and to gently release himself/herself from any dependency that he/she may have developed towards the therapist. The client's job now – away from the consulting room – will be to shape his/her own destiny and to exercise his/her own choices in life untrammelled by the disturbances and traumas of the past.

> The analytical hypnotherapist persuades the patient to review in detail,
> through the medium of regression, those experiences which were
> responsible for the symptom-producing behaviour. Having identified
> these experiences, and all of their associated emotional responses, he
> then activates the Adult within the patient to examine the current
> inappropriateness of such responses and encourages him to discover
> improved ways of behaving in the present.
> *– Edgar Barnett*

Client Profiling

The analytical hypnotherapy practitioner may wish to ponder the
following points when formulating a profile for the client.

- In what ways has the client changed while undergoing the therapeutic process?
- In what ways has the client benefited by undertaking his/her therapy?
- Does the client feel safe in the therapeutic context?
- Is the client open and honest with the practitioner?
- Has the client fully unloaded the burden on his/her soul in therapy?
- Has the client faced his/her innermost fears and trepidation in therapy?
- Has the client undertaken a full confessional of his/her darkest secrets?
- Is the client merely seeking to survive the therapeutic process rather than to face up to his/her greatest traumas?
- Has the client fully expunged all the skeletons in his/her psychic cupboard?
- Has the client expressed the emotional effect of his/her past and understood the ways in which it has affected him/her subsequently?
- Has the client acquired an unconscious acceptance of his/her past, or does he/she merely have an intellectual understanding of it?
- Has the client's physical appearance and general demeanour changed dramatically during therapy?
- Has the client gained the necessary insight and enlightenment that he/she needs from the therapeutic experience in order to relinquish his/her symptoms?

- Is the client able to integrate his/her past traumatic experiences into his/her new-found psyche?
- Can the client learn to accept the past for what it was and now move on successfully?
- Can the client leave his/her past and his/her therapist behind?
- Does the client now have all the tools he/she needs in order to face that brave new world?

Appendix

Professional Training and Development Resources

For the therapist who may wish to develop more fully in the practice of analytical hypnotherapy, some additional training and development resources are listed below.

Further Training Resources

The International College of Eclectic Therapies

> ICET, 808a High Road, Finchley, London N12 9QU, UK
> Tel: 44 (0)20 8446 2210
> Email: info@icet.net
> Website: www.icet.net

The International College of Eclectic Therapies (ICET) runs a number of courses that may be of interest to the analytical hypnotherapist as given below.

Diploma in Clinical and Analytical Hypnotherapy with Psychotherapy
This course will equip the delegate with the skills to set up in practice as a qualified hypnotherapist and psychotherapist who can specialise in permanently resolving psychological trauma and liberating the client from psychic or neurotic disorders.

Certification and Diploma in Stress Management Counselling
This two-part course has been designed to enable the practitioner to become fully conversant with and skilled in dealing with the client suffering from the effects of both chronic and acute stress.

Diploma in Gold® Psychotherapeutic Counselling and Master-Level Gold® Creative Psychotherapy
This series of courses will offer comprehensive training in the restructuring and management of beliefs and will provide the practitioner with a unique philosophy and the necessary skills to bring about rapid change.

Diploma in Post-Traumatic Stress Disorder Therapy
This course will provide a vehicle for the practising therapist to gain an appreciation and an essential understanding of the mechanism of PTSD and its treatment.

Diploma in Victims of Childhood Abuse Therapy
This course will be for the professional therapist who seeks neither to paper over the cracks of childhood abuse nor to teach the client to forgive and forget, but rather to look at the consequences of childhood abuse and to examine really practical ways in which the client can live life after such ordeals.

Supervisory Skills Certificate
This course – which has been approved by the National Council of Psychotherapy – will examine the key role of the supervisor in assisting the practitioner to become more productive and effective within a supportive, professional and caring framework.

Professional supervision may be sought either from Jacquelyne Morison in the Kent area, whose email address is:

jacquelyne.morison@btinternet.com

or from Georges Philips in the London area, whose email address is:

gp@georgesphilips.com

A copy of a comprehensive client questionnaire that could be used by the analytical hypnotherapist can also be obtained from ICET, contact details for which are given above.

The Institute of Clinical Hypnotherapy and Psychotherapy
The Institute of Clinical Hypnotherapy and Psychotherapy (ICHP) runs a number of courses that may be of interest to the analytical hypnotherapist as given below.

Institute of Clinical Hypnotherapy and Psychotherapy
ICHP Administrative Offices
Therapy House
No.6 Tuckey Street
Cork City
Ireland
Tel: 00353 (0) 21 4273575
Fax: 00353 (0) 21 4275785
Email: hypnosis@iol.ie
Website: www.hypnosiseire.com

The ICHP offers comprehensive training programmes in all aspects of clinical and ethical hypnosis, hypnotherapy, hypno-analysis and psychotherapy. Training is from foundation level through to diploma and advanced diploma levels as distance learning and advanced practical classes held in both Dublin and Cork. For details of these training courses contact the ICHP for a free prospectus and demo audio cassette.

The primary purpose of the Institute of Clinical Hypnotherapy and Psychotherapy is the advancement of the art, science and practice of ethical hypnotherapy/ psychotherapy as a technique for the relief and rehabilitation of persons suffering from nervous disorders and emotional problems. The ICHP exists to promote widespread personal empowerment through therapeutic techniques and to promote the training of its members and education for the general public.

Further Reading Resources

Other publications by the contributor Georges Philips that deal specifically with aspects of analytical hypnotherapy are given below.

Gold Counselling: A Structured Psychotherapeutic Approach to the Mapping and Re-Aligning of Belief Systems, by Georges Philips and Lyn Buncher, Crown House Publishing Ltd (2000)

Rapid Cognitive Therapy: The Professional Therapist's Guide To Rapid Change Work, by Georges Philips and Terence Watts, Crown House Publishing Ltd (1999)

Bibliography

Adams KM. *Silently Seduced: When Parents Make Their Children Partners: Understanding Covert Incest.* Health Communications Inc, 1991.

Ainscough C, Toon K. *Breaking Free: Help for Survivors of Child Sexual Abuse.* Sheldon Press, 1993.

Amendolia R. *A Narrative Constructivist Perspective of Treatment of Post-Traumatic Stress Disorders with Ericksonian Hypnosis and Eye-Movement Desensitisation and Reprocessing.* American Academy of Experts in Traumatic Stress Inc, 1998.

Andersen SM, Miranda R. Transference: How Past Relationships Emerge in the Present. *The Psychologist,* British Psychological Society, 2000.

Andrews B, Brewin CR. Psychological Defence Mechanisms: The Example of Repression. *The Psychologist,* British Psychological Society, 2000.

Andrews B, Brewin CR. What Did Freud Get Right? *The Psychologist,* British Psychological Society, 2000.

Appignanesi R, Zarate O. *Freud for Beginners.* Pantheon Books, 1979.

Baldwin DV. 'Consequences of Early Traumatic Experiences.' Article on Trauma Information website: www.trauma-pages.com, 1997.

Ball J. *Understanding Disease: A Health Practitioner's Handbook.* CW Daniel Company Ltd, 1990.

Barnett E. *Analytical Hypnotherapy: Principles and Practice.* Westwood Publishing Co., 1989.

Bass E, Davis L. *The Courage To Heal: A Guide For Women Survivors of Child Sexual Abuse.* Vermillion, 1997.

Ben-Shahar AR. Patterns of Abuse: Application of Integrative-Massage-Therapy (IMT) to Physical, Emotional and Sexual Abuse Victims. *The Journal,* National Council of Psychotherapists & National Council for Hypnotherapy, 2000.

Bifulco A, Brown GW, Adler Z. Early Sexual Abuse and Clinical Depression in Adult Life. *British Journal of Psychiatry*, Royal College of Psychiatrists, 1991.

Blume ES. *Secret Survivors: Uncovering Incest and Its After-Effects in Women*. John Wiley & Sons Inc, 1990.

Bowlby J. *Attachment*. Pimlico, 1997.

Bowlby J. *Attachment and Loss*. Pimlico, 1998.

Bradshaw J. *Healing the Shame That Binds You*. Health Communications, 1991.

Bradshaw J. *Homecoming*. Judy Piatkus (Publishers) Ltd, 1991.

Brandon S, Boakes J, Glaser D, Green D. Recovered Memories of Childhood Sexual Abuse: Implications for Clinical Practice. *British Journal of Psychiatry*, Royal College of Psychiatrists, 1998.

Brandon S, Boakes J, Glaser S, Green R, MacKeith J, Whewell P. Reported Recovered Memories of Child Sexual Abuse. *Psychiatric Bulletin*, Royal College of Psychiatrists, 1997.

Brown D, Pedder J. *Introduction To Psychotherapy: An Outline of Psychodynamic Principles and Practice*. Routledge, 1996.

Bull T. Eating Disorders and Related Problems. *The Journal*, National Council of Psychotherapists & National Council for Hypnotherapy, 1996.

Burgess AW, Holmstrom LL. Rape Trauma Syndrome. *American Journal of Psychiatry*, American Psychiatric Press, 1974.

Burgess AW, Holmstrom LL. Coping Behaviour of the Rape Victim. *American Journal of Psychiatry*, American Psychiatric Press, 1976.

Burgess AW, Holmstrom LL. Adaptive Strategies and Recovery from Rape. *American Journal of Psychiatry*, American Psychiatric Press, 1979.

Byrne J. The Use of EMDR in Therapy. *The Journal*, National Council of Psychotherapists & National Council for Hypnotherapy, 1998.

Byrne J, Pelser SKS, Poggenpoel M, Myburgh CPH. The Underlying Subconscious Dynamics of Two Women Who Were Sexually Abused as

Children. *European Journal of Clinical Hypnosis,* British Society of Medical & Clinical Hypnosis, 1998.

Chopra D. *The Seven Spiritual Laws of Success: A Practical Guide to the Fulfilment of Your Dreams.* Amber-Allen Publishing, 1993.

Chu JA. *Rebuilding Shattered Lives: The Responsible Treatment of Complex Post-Traumatic and Dissociative Disorders.* John Wiley & Sons Inc, 1998.

Clarkson P. *Gestalt Counselling in Action.* Sage Publications, 1989.

Coffey R. *Unspeakable Truths and Happy Endings: Human Cruelty and the New Trauma Therapy.* Sidran Press, 1998.

Coles R. *The Erik Erikson Reader.* WW Norton & Co. Inc, 2001.

Conroy DL. *Out of the Nightmare: Recovery From Depression and Suicidal Pain.* New Liberty Press, 1991.

Conte JR, Shore D. *Social Work and Child Sexual Abuse.* Haworth, 1982.

Corey G. *Theory and Practice of Counselling and Psychotherapy.* Brooks/Cole Publishing Company, 1997.

Cottle TJ. *Children's Secrets.* Addison-Wesley Publishing Co. Inc, 1980.

Covitz J. *The Family Curse: Emotional Child Abuse.* Sigo Press, 1986.

Crook G. False Memory Syndrome. *The Journal,* National Council of Psychotherapists & Hypnotherapy Register, 1995.

Davies JM, Frawley MG. *Treating the Adult Survivor of Childhood Sexual Abuse: A Psychoanalytic Perspective.* Basic Books, 1994.

Dryden W(ed.). *Handbook of Individual Therapy.* Sage Publications, 1997.

DSM-IV-R: Diagnostic and Statistical Manual of Mental Disorders. American Psychiatric Press, 1994.

Durbin PG. My Tribute to Viktor Frankl. *The Journal,* National Council of Psychotherapists & National Council for Hypnotherapy, 1999.

Elman D. *Hypnotherapy.* Westwood Publishing Co., 1964.

Erikson EH. *Childhood and Society.* Vintage, 1995.

Espinosa R. Understanding the Mind Body Connection in Chronic Illness. *The Hypnotherapy Journal*, National Council for Hypnotherapy, 2001.

Farmer S. *Adult Children of Abusive Parents: A Healing Program for Those Who Have Been Physically, Sexually or Emotionally Abused*. RGA Publishing Group Inc, 1989.

Finkelhor D. *Sexually Victimised Children*. The Free Press, 1979.

Finkelhor D. *Child Sexual Abuse: New Theory and Research*. The Free Press, 1984.

Finkelhor D. *A Sourcebook on Child Sexual Abuse*. Sage Publications, 1986.

Foa EB, Davidson JRT, Frances A. Treatment of Posttraumatic Stress Disorder. *Journal of Clinical Psychiatry*, Physicians Postgraduate Press Inc, 1999.

Foa EB, Keane TM, Friedman MJ. *Effective Treatments for PTSD: Practice Guidelines from the International Society for Traumatic Stress Studies*. Guilford Press, 2000.

Fonagy P. The Outcome of Psychoanalysis: The Hope of the Future. *The Psychologist*, British Psychological Society, 2000.

Fordham F. *An Introduction to Jung's Psychology*. Penguin Books, 1966.

Foy DW. *Treating PTSD: Cognitive-Behavioural Strategies*. The Guilford Press, 1992.

Fredrickson R. *Repressed Memories*. Simon & Schuster, 1992.

Freud S. *Introductory Lectures on Psychoanalysis*. Penguin Books, 1991.

Freyd JJ. *Betrayal Trauma: The Logic of Forgetting Childhood Abuse*. Harvard University Press, 1997.

Friedman MJ. *Post-Traumatic Stress Disorder: An Overview*. National Center for Post-Traumatic Stress Disorder, 1997.

Friedman MJ. *PTSD Diagnosis and Treatment for Mental Health Clinicians*. National Center for Post-Traumatic Stress Disorder, 1998.

Fromm E. *The Art of Listening*. Constable & Co. Ltd, 1994.

Gawain S. *Creative Visualisation*. Bantam New Age Books, 1982.

Gay P. *The Freud Reader*. WW Norton & Co. Inc, 1995.

Gilvarry CM. Repressed Memories or Unleashed Fantasy. *European Journal of Clinical Hypnosis*, British Society of Medical & Clinical Hypnosis, 1997.

Goodyear-Smith F. *First Do No Harm: The Sexual Abuse Industry*. Benton-Guy Publishing, 1993.

Gorman AG. Unconscious Memory: False or Fact. *European Journal of Clinical Hypnosis*, British Society of Medical & Clinical Hypnosis, 1997.

Graber K. *Ghosts in the Bedroom*. Health Communications Inc, 1991.

Gross R & McIlveen R. *Psychology: A New Introduction*. Hodder & Stoughton, 1998.

Gross R. *Psychology: The Science of Mind and Behaviour*. Hodder & Stoughton, 1996.

Groth NA, Birnbaum J. *Men Who Rape: The Psychology of the Offender*. Plenum Press, 1990.

Gucciardi I. Hypnotherapy and Post Traumatic Stress Disorder. *Fidelity*, National Council of Psychotherapists, 2000.

Hammond DC. *Handbook of Hypnotic Suggestions and Metaphors*. American Society of Clinical Hypnosis, 1990.

Harner M. *The Way of the Shaman*. HarperCollins Publishers, 1980.

Harris TA. *I'm OK – You're OK*. Pan Books, 1969.

Harvey MR, Herman JL. The Trauma of Sexual Victimisation: Feminist Contributions to Theory, Research and Practice. *PTSD Research Quarterly*, National Center for Post-Traumatic Stress Disorder, 1992.

Haugaard JJ, Reppucci ND. *The Sexual Abuse of Children: A Comprehensive Guide to Current Knowledge and Intervention Strategies*. Jossey-Bass Publishers, 1988.

Hawkings PH, Almeida A, Hemmings M, Ranz R. Sexuality: Narrative and Hypnosis. *European Journal of Clinical Hypnosis*, British Society of Medical & Clinical Hypnosis, 1998.

Hawkins PJ. Hypnosis in Sex Therapy. *European Journal of Clinical Hypnosis*, British Society of Medical & Clinical Hypnosis, 1996.

Hayes N. *Foundations of Psychology: An Introductory Text*. Thomas Nelson & Sons Ltd, 1998.

Henri D. Eating Disorders. *The Journal*, National Council of Psychotherapists & National Council for Hypnotherapy, 1997.

Herman JL. *Trauma and Recovery: From Domestic Violence to Political Terror*. Basic Books, 1997.

Herman JL, Hirschman L. *Father–Daughter Incest*. Harvard University Press, 1981.

Hofmann A, Fischer G, Galley N, Shapiro F. EMDR Memory Reprocessing. *European Journal of Clinical Hypnosis*, British Society of Medical & Clinical Hypnosis, 1998.

Holmes J. *John Bowlby and Attachment Theory*. Routledge, 1993.

Hotchkiss B. *Your Owner's Manual*. International College of Eclectic Therapies, 1997.

Hudson J. The Epigenetic Theory of Erik Erikson. *The Journal*, National Council of Psychotherapists & National Council for Hypnotherapy, 1996.

Hunter CR. *The Art of Hypnotherapy: Diversified Client-Centered Hypnosis*. Kendall/Hunt Publishing Company, 1995.

Hunter M. *Adult Survivors of Sexual Abuse: Treatment Innovations*. Sage Publications Inc, 1995.

Hyde M, McGuinness M. *Jung for Beginners*. Icon Books Ltd, 1992.

Hyer L, McCranie EW, Peralme L. Psychotherapeutic Treatment of Chronic PTSD. *PTSD Research Quarterly*, National Center for Post-Traumatic Stress Disorder, 1993.

ICD-10: International Statistical Classification of Diseases and Related Health Problems. World Health Organisation, 1992.

Jacoby M. *The Analytic Encounter: Transference and Human Relationship.* Inner City Books, 1984.

Jampolsky GG. *Loving is Letting Go of Fear.* Celestial Arts, 1988.

Jeffers S. *Feel the Fear and Do It Anyway: How To Turn Your Fear and Indecision into Confidence and Action.* Arrow Books, 1991.

Jeffers S. *Dare to Connect: How to Create Confidence, Trust and Loving Relationships.* Judy Piatkus (Publishers) Ltd, 1992.

Jenkins DG, Newman D, Sawyer A. Hypnotherapy and Depression. *European Journal of Clinical Hypnosis,* British Society of Medical & Clinical Hypnosis, 1997.

Johannes CK. *EMDR: An Overview of Procedure and Research. The Hypnotherapy Journal,* National Council for Hypnotherapy, 2001.

Jung C. *The Development of Personality,* Princeton University Press, 1981.

Karle H, Boys J. *Hypnotherapy: A Practical Handbook.* Free Association Books, 1987.

Kern M. *Wisdom in the Body: The Craniosacral Approach to Essential Health.* HarperCollins Publishers, 2001.

Kirschenbaum H, Henderson VL. *The Carl Rogers Reader.* Constable & Co. Ltd, 1990.

Lake F. *Clinical Theology.* Longman & Todd, 1986.

Levine PA, Frederick A. *Waking the Tiger: Healing Trauma.* North Atlantic Books, 1997.

Lew M. *Victims No Longer: A Guide for Men Recovering from Sexual Child Abuse.* Cedar, 1990.

Lindenfield F. *Self Esteem.* Thorsons, 1995.

Lindsay DS, Read JD. Memory, Remembering and Misremembering. *PTSD Research Quarterly,* National Center for Post-Traumatic Stress Disorder, 1995.

Living Without Fear: An Integrated Approach to Tackling Violence Against Women. Women's Unit, Cabinet Office, 1999.

Loftus E, Ketcham K. *The Myth of Repressed Memory: False Memory and Allegations of Sexual Abuse*. St Martin's Press, 1994.

Lüscher M. *The Lüscher Color Test*. Washington Square Press, 1971.

Mackinnon C. Working with Adult Survivors of Child Sexual Abuse: Theoretical Approaches, Long Term Effects and the Therapeutic Process. *European Journal of Clinical Hypnosis*, British Society of Medical & Clinical Hypnosis, 1995.

Mackinnon C. Legacy of Abuse: Long Term Effects and Symptoms. *European Journal of Clinical Hypnosis*, British Society of Medical & Clinical Hypnosis, 1996.

Mackinnon C. Beyond Sexual Abuse. *European Journal of Clinical Hypnosis*, British Society of Medical & Clinical Hypnosis, 1997.

Mackinnon C. Working with Adult Survivors of Child Sexual Abuse. *European Journal of Clinical Hypnosis*, British Society of Medical & Clinical Hypnosis, 1998.

McNally RJ. Research on Eye Movement Desensitisation and Reprocessing (EMDR) as a Treatment for PTSD. *PTSD Research Quarterly*, National Center for Post-Traumatic Stress Disorder, 1999.

Mahler MS, Pine F, Bergmann A. *The Psychological Birth of the Human Infant: Symbiosis and Individuation*. Basic Books, 2000.

Maslow A. *Toward a Psychology of Being*. John Wiley & Sons Inc, 1968.

Masson J. *The Assault on Truth: Freud and Child Sexual Abuse*. Fontana Press, 1992.

Masson J. *Against Therapy*. HarperCollins, 1993.

Matsakis A. *Post-Traumatic Stress Disorder: A Complete Treatment Guide*. New Harbinger Publications Inc, 1994.

Matsakis A. *I Can't Get Over It: A Handbook For Trauma Survivors*. New Harbinger Publications Inc, 1996.

Matthews A. *Being Happy*. Media Masters Pte Ltd, 1988.

Mearns D, Thorne B. *Person-Centred Counselling in Action*. Sage Publications, 1986.

Mayer A. *Sexual Abuse: Causes, Consequences and Treatment of Incestuous and Pedophilic Acts.* Learning Publications Inc, 1985.

Miller A. *Banished Knowledge: Facing Childhood Injuries.* Virago Press, 1997.

Miller GA. *Psychology: The Science of Mental Life.* Penguin Books, 1991.

Mitchell J. *The Selected Melanie Klein.* Penguin Books, 1991.

Morgan D. Memory. *The Journal*, National Council of Psychotherapists & National Council for Hypnotherapy, 1996.

Morgan D. The Defensive Persona. *The Journal*, National Council of Psychotherapists & National Council for Hypnotherapy, 1996.

Morgan D. *The Principles of Hypnotherapy.* Eildon Press, 1996.

Morison JA. Reported Recovered Memories of Child Sexual Abuse. *The Journal*, National Council of Psychotherapists & National Council for Hypnotherapy, Spring, 1998.

Morison JA. Reported Recovered Memories of Child Sexual Abuse: Implications for Clinical Practice. *The Journal*, National Council of Psychotherapists & National Council for Hypnotherapy, Summer/Autumn, 1998.

Morison JA. PTSD in Victims of Sexual Molestation: Its Incidence, Characteristics and Treatment Strategies. *Empathy*, Hypnotherapy Society, 2000.

Morton J, Andrews B, Bekerian D, Brewin C, Davies G, Mollon P. *Recovered Memories.* British Psychological Society, 1995.

Naish PLN. *What is Hypnosis? Current Theories and Research.* Open University Press, 1986.

Nelson-Jones R. *The Theory and Practice of Counselling.* Cassell, 1995.

Northcott I. Is Humanistic Psychology Too Simplistic to be a True "Third Force"? *Empathy*, Hypnotherapy Society, 2001.

Oates RK. *The Spectrum of Child Abuse: Assessment, Treatment and its After-Effects in Women.* Brunner/Mazel, 1996.

Ochberg FM, Wilson JP, Raphael B. *Posttraumatic Therapy*. International Handbook of Traumatic Stress Syndromes, Plenum Press, 1993.

O'Sullivan M. Post Traumatic Stress. *The Journal*, National Council of Psychotherapists & Hypnotherapy Register, 1995.

O'Sullivan M. Introducing PTSD. *Empathy*, Hypnotherapy Society, 2000.

O'Sullivan M. Categories of PTSD Sufferers. *Fidelity*, National Council of Psychotherapists, 2001.

Parkinson F. *Critical Incident Debriefing: Understanding and Dealing with Trauma*. Souvenir Press, 1997.

Parkinson F. *Post-Trauma Stress*. Sheldon Press, 1998.

Parks P. *Rescuing the Inner Child: Therapy for Adults Sexually Abused as Children*. Souvenir Press, 1990.

Parnell L. *Transforming Trauma: EMDR*. WW Norton & Co. Inc, 1997.

Parnell L. *EMDR in the Treatment of Adults Abused as Children*. WW Norton & Co. Inc, 1999.

Peck MS. *Further Along the Road Less Travelled: The Unending Journey Towards Spiritual Growth*. Simon & Schuster, 1997.

Peck MS. *The Road Less Travelled: The New Psychology of Love, Traditional Values and Spiritual Growth*. Simon & Schuster, 1997.

Peck MS. *The Road Less Travelled and Beyond: Spiritual Growth in an Age of Anxiety*. Simon & Schuster, 1999.

Peiffer V. *Positive Thinking*. Element Books, 1989.

Pendergast M. *Victims of Memory: Incest Accusations and Shattered Lives*. HarperCollins Publishers, 1996.

Philips G, Buncher L. *Gold Counselling: A Structured Psychotherapeutic Approach to the Mapping and Re-Aligning of Belief Systems*. Crown House Publishing Ltd, 2000.

Philips G, Watts T. *Rapid Cognitive Therapy: The Professional Therapist's Guide to Rapid Change Work*. Crown House Publishing Ltd, 1999.

Plowman J. Mind, Body and Regression: Using "Past Life Memories" to Solve Real Life Problems. *European Journal of Clinical Hypnosis*, British Society of Medical & Clinical Hypnosis, 1996.

Power M. Freud and the Unconscious. *The Psychologist*, British Psychological Society, 2000.

Reason J. The Freudian Slip Revised. *The Psychologist*, British Psychological Society, 2000.

Reber AS. *The Penguin Dictionary of Psychology*. Viking, 1985.

Reinhold M. *How to Survive in Spite of Your Parents: Coping with Hurtful Childhood Legacies*. Cedar, 1996.

Rogers M. False Memory Syndrome: Is There Such a Phenomenon? *The Journal*, National Council of Psychotherapists & National Council for Hypnotherapy, 1998.

Rosenhan DL, Seligman ME. *Abnormal Psychology*. WW Norton & Co. Ltd, 1995.

Roth S, Friedman MJ. *Childhood Trauma Remembered: A Report on the Current Scientific Knowledge Base and its Applications*. International Society for Traumatic Stress Studies, 1997.

Rothschild B. *Post-Traumatic Stress Disorder: Identification and Diagnosis*. Soziale Arbeit Schweiz, 1998.

Rothschild B. *The Body Remembers: The Psychophysiology of Trauma and Trauma Treatment*. WW Norton & Co. Inc, 2000.

Rothschild B. A Trauma Case History. *The Fulcrum*, Craniosacral Therapy Association of the United Kingdom, 2001.

Rowe R. *Beyond Fear*. HarperCollins Publishers, 1987.

Sayers J. *Mothers of Psychoanalysis: Helen Deutsch, Karen Horney, Anna Freud, and Melanie Klein*. WW Norton & Co. Inc, 1993.

Sayers J. *Kleinians: Psychoanalysis Inside Out*. Polarity Press, 2000.

Shapiro F, Forrest MS. *EMDR: The Breakthrough Therapy for Overcoming Anxiety, Stress and Trauma*. Basic Books, 1997.

Sills F, Degranges D. *Craniosacral Biodynamics: The Breath of Life, Biodynamics and Fundamental Skills Volume 1*. North Atlantic Books, 2001.

Silva J. *The Silva Mind Control Method*. HarperCollins Publishers, 1993.

Solms M. Freudian Dream Theory Today. *The Psychologist*, British Psychological Society, 2000.

Stettbacher JK. *Making Sense of Suffering: The Healing Confrontation with your Own Past*. Meridian, 1991.

Stewart I, Joines V. *TA Today: A New Introduction to Transactional Analysis*. Lifespace Publishing, 1987.

Stewart J. Notes on the Inferiority Complex, Anxiety/Panic Disorders and Depression. *The Journal*, National Council of Psychotherapists & Hypnotherapy Register, 1995.

Stewart J. ME (Myalgic Encephalomyelitis), PVFS (Post Viral Fatigue Syndrome), CFS (Chronic Fatigue Syndrome), Yuppie Flu, Malingerers Disease & English Sweat. *The Journal*, National Council of Psychotherapists & National Council for Hypnotherapy, 1996.

Stewart J. Memory. *The Journal*, National Council of Psychotherapists & National Council for Hypnotherapy, 1996.

Storr A. *Freud*. Oxford University Press, 1989.

Storr A. *Jung*. Fontana Press, 1995.

Storr A. *The Essential Jung*. Fontana Press, 1998.

Szasz T. *The Ethics of Psychoanalysis Psychotherapy: The Theory and Method of Autonomous Psychotherapy*. Syracuse University Press, 1988.

Van der Kolk BA. *The Body Keeps the Score: Memory and the Evolving Psychobiology of Post Traumatic Stress*. Harvard Medical School, 1994.

Van der Kolk BA, Van der Hart O, Burbridge H. *Approaches to the Treatment of PTSD*. Harvard Medical School, 1995.

Watkins JG. *The Practice of Clinical Hypnotherapy: Volume 1, Hypnotherapeutic Techniques*. Evington Publishing, 1987.

Watkins JG. *The Practice of Clinical Hypnotherapy: Volume 2, Hypnoanalytic Techniques.* Evington Publishing, 1987.

Watkins JG, Watkins HH. *Ego States: Theory and Therapy.* WW Norton & Co. Inc, 1997.

Webster R. *Freud's False Memories: Psychoananlysis and the Recovered Memory Movement.* The Orwell Press, 1996.

Whitfield CL. *Memory and Abuse: Remembering and Healing the Effects of Trauma.* Health Communications Inc, 1995.

Wickes FG. *The Inner World of Childhood: A Study in Analytical Psychology.* Appleton-Century-Crofts Inc, 1927.

Woolger R. Past Life Regression. *The Journal,* National Council of Psychotherapists & National Council for Hypnotherapy, 1996.

Yapko MD. *Suggestions of Abuse: True and False Memories of Childhood Sexual Trauma.* Simon & Schuster, 1994.

Yapko MD. *Essentials of Hypnosis.* Brunner/Mazel Inc, 1995.

Young BH, Ford JD, Ruzek JI, Friedman MJ, Gusman FD. *A Guidebook for Clinicians and Administrators.* The National Center for Post-Traumatic Stress Disorder, 1998.

Index

childhood development, 92,
331, 334, 336, 341–342, 348, 361
client-centred therapy, xiii, 48,
54, 71, 73–75, 77, 79, 81, 83, 85,
87, 89–91, 111, 136–137
coercive transference, 241
cognitions, 128, 133, 140–141
cognitive strategies, viii, 130
cognitive structure, 133–134
cognitive therapy, xiii–xiv,
127–133, 135, 137, 139, 141, 143,
326, 383, 393, 404
cognitive triad, 130
collective unconscious, 18, 24,
26–27, 232, 259, 267–269,
276–277, 299, 340
compensation, 39, 188–189, 200
complementary
countertransference, 256
complementary transaction,
310, 312
complex, 5, 23–24, 28, 39–40,
62–63, 65, 148, 150, 192, 217,
225, 229, 256, 266, 331–332,
335–339, 344, 367, 370, 384, 397,
406
composite memory, 163
compulsive disorders, 68
concordant countertransference,
255
conditions of self-worth, 86, 89
confluence, 118, 161
confusional states, 68
conscious awareness, xviii, xx,
6, 10, 12, 20, 23–24, 49, 111, 113,
151, 153–154, 161, 169, 185, 188,
190, 192–193, 261, 290, 318, 342
conscious mind, ix, 4, 9, 20–21,
24, 28, 52, 151, 156, 266, 373
contaminated ego-state, 308
control schemata, 134
control theory, 135–138
Controlling Parent ego-state,
307

coping-strategy, 49, 170, 304,
360
core ego-state, 47–49
countertransference, xix–xx, 12,
16, 28, 58, 174, 179, 229, 231,
233, 235, 237, 239, 241, 243,
245, 247, 249, 251–257, 263, 284,
375
countertransference proper, 255
crossed transaction, 312

death, 61, 63, 93, 95, 101, 103,
135, 137, 147, 155, 165, 170,
263, 269, 282, 290
defence-mechanisms, *See* defensive strategies
defensive strategies, xviii,
10–12, 14, 28, 47, 49, 52, 54, 65,
94, 99, 112, 123, 141, 157–158,
163, 170, 185–189, 191, 193, 195,
197, 199, 201, 203–209, 215–216,
223, 229, 259, 273, 290, 306, 377
deficiency needs, 80
deflection, 113–114
delusion, 309
delusional transference, 245
denial, 20, 87, 141, 169, 171, 173,
187–189, 192–193, 200, 273, 309,
339, 377
dependency states, 68, 344
depersonalisation, 106
depression, 64, 130, 139,
202–203, 317, 368, 370, 396–397,
401, 406
depressive disorders, 62, 384
depressive life-position, 321
depressive position, 63, 69, 320
desensitisation, 113, 395, 402
developmental phases, 342–343,
358
developmental psychology, 346
dichotomous thinking, 132
differentiation, 53, 63, 344

Analytical Hypnotherapy
Volume 2
Practical Applications
Jacquelyne Morison
with contributions from Georges Philips

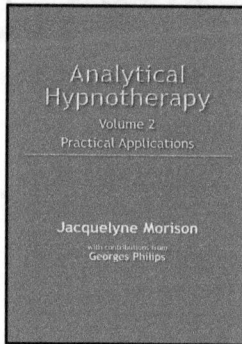

In this sequel to Volume 1 Jacquelyne Morison introduces the clinical practitioner to the practical applications of analytical hypnotherapy – the process of transforming theory into practice can now begin!

Providing a succinct and all-embracing overview of the topic the author not only removes the mystery enshrouding the practice, but also brings analytical hypnotherapy into the mainstream of clinical techniques. In-depth case studies and client profiles cover groundbreaking research areas, including: fear and anxiety disorders; sorrow and grief disorders; anger and rage disorders; and the nature of childhood abuse.

Analytical Hypnotherapy Volume 2 allows the hypnotherapist to accomplish an in-depth examination of the client's psyche. Psychotherapists and counsellors will equally benefit from this invaluable guide, which aptly demonstrates the importance of hypnotherapy in investigative methodology and practice.

PAPERBACK   400 PAGES   ISBN: 9781845904074

GOLD Counselling®
Second Edition
A Structured Psychotherapeutic Approach To The Mapping And Re-Aligning Of Belief Systems
Georges Philips & Lyn Buncher
with Brian Stevenson

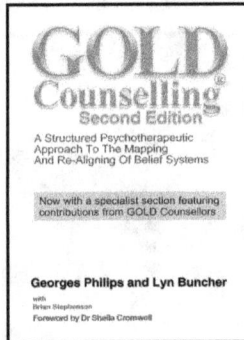

This highly acclaimed work has now been completely revised and expanded to reflect the latest advances made in this groundbreaking field. This second edition provides a wealth of additional material on beliefs, explaining in easily understandable terms what beliefs are, how they are formulated in our mind, the impact they have on our identity, and, most important of all, how they can be changed successfully. Also included are many worked examples that demonstrate each of the strategies.

PAPERBACK   296 PAGES   ISBN: 9781899836338

"Amazing, *GOLD Counselling* has become my most preferred method of helping clients help themselves. It's made me more efficient, effective and more confident."
– *Lyne Driscoll, counsellor and therapist.*

Rapid Cognitive Therapy
The Professional Therapist's Guide To Rapid Change Work

Georges Philips & Terence Watts

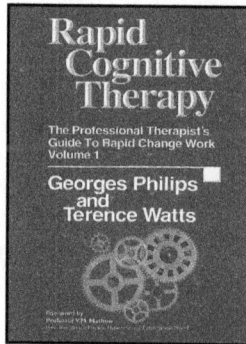

This book reaches way beyond a description of principles and outline of methods and techniques to provide an accessible technology for all. Nearly all the techniques here can be used as adjuncts to conventional behaviourist and analytical approaches to therapy including NLP and Gestalt work. As well as describing the art of RCT, the authors have provided the therapist with the means to get started quickly by outlining the structures for the first few sessions as well as giving full scripts for analytical and non-analytical work with the client.

HARDBACK   272 PAGES   9781899836376

"Written by two excellent and experienced therapists, [*Rapid Cognitive Therapy* joins] the ranks of modern publications in the domain of psychotherapeutic approaches."
– *Professor V. M. Mathew, President, British Medical Hypnotherapy Examination Board.*

Appointed EU Representative: Easy Access System Europe Oü, 16879218
Address:Mustamäe tee 50, 10621, Tallinn, Estonia
Contact Details: gpsr.requests@easproject.com,
+358 40 500 3575